Hello! 365 Food Processor Recipes

(Food Processor Recipes - Volume 1)

Best Food Processor Cookbook Ever For Beginners

Ms. Everyday

Copyright: Published in the United States by Ms. Everyday/ © MS. EVERYDAY

Published on January, 23 2020

All rights reserved. No part of this publication may be reproduced, stored in retrieval system, copied in any form or by any means, electronic, mechanical, photocopying, recording or otherwise transmitted without written permission from the publisher. Please do not participate in or encourage piracy of this material in any way. You must not circulate this book in any format. MS. EVERYDAY does not control or direct users' actions and is not responsible for the information or content shared, harm and/or actions of the book readers.

In accordance with the U.S. Copyright Act of 1976, the scanning, uploading and electronic sharing of any part of this book without the permission of the publisher constitute unlawful piracy and theft of the author's intellectual property. If you would like to use material from the book (other than just simply for reviewing the book), prior permission must be obtained by contacting the author at mseveryday@mrandmscooking.com

Thank you for your support of the author's rights.

Content

- CONTENT 3
- INTRODUCTION 9
- LIST OF ABBREVIATIONS 10
- **365 AMAZING FOOD PROCESSOR RECIPES** 11
    1. "close To Store-bought" Mayo 11
    2. Almond Ice Cream Terrine With Chocolate Truffles And Raspberry Sauce 11
    3. Almond Macaroons With Swiss Meringue Buttercream 12
    4. Almond Praline Semifreddo With Grappa-poached Apricots 13
    5. Almond-plum Buckle 14
    6. Amaretto Divine 15
    7. Amaretto-almond Streusel Pumpkin Pie ... 15
    8. Amarillo Ceviche Mixto 16
    9. Apple Pear Sauce 16
    10. Apple Upside-down Biscuit Cake 16
    11. Apple Walnut Torte 17
    12. Apple-almond Cheesecake 18
    13. Apple-clove Butter 19
    14. Apricot Galette 19
    15. Apricot-almond Gift Bread 20
    16. Apricot-pistachio Charoset 20
    17. Artichoke Jalapeno Hummus Dip 21
    18. Artichoke Ravioli With Tomatoes 21
    19. Arugula, Artichoke And Red Chile Hummus 23
    20. Asparagus 'guacamole' 23
    21. Autumn Apple-squash Crisp 24
    22. Avocado Aioli 24
    23. Avocado And Edamame Dip 25
    24. Avocado Compound Butter 25
    25. Avocado Hummus 26
    26. Avocado Peanut Butter Brownies (vegan) 26
    27. Balsamic-strawberry Pops 27
    28. Banana Basil Smoothie 27
    29. Banana Mud Ice Cream 27
    30. Banana Sorbet 28
    31. Banana-cinnamon French Toast 28
    32. Banana-fudge Sundaes 28
    33. Basil Aioli 29
    34. Basil And Garlic Mayonnaise 29
    35. Basil And Pesto Hummus 29
    36. Basil Garlic Mayonnaise 30
    37. Basil Pesto Risotto With Pan-roasted Scallops 30
    38. Beef Rendang 31
    39. Beef Sates With Southeast Asian Sauce 31
    40. Beefy Southwestern Corn Pudding Casserole 32
    41. Black And Green Olive Tapenade 33
    42. Black Bean And Chickpea Chili 33
    43. Black Bean And Roasted Tomato Soup 34
    44. Black Bean Hummus Without Tahini ... 34
    45. Black-bean Burgers 35
    46. Blender Hollandaise Sauce 35
    47. Blue Cheese And Chive Dressing 36
    48. Blueberry Crumble Pie 36
    49. Blueberry Granita 37
    50. Blueberry Shortbread Cheesecake 38
    51. Bourbon Walnut Pie 38
    52. Brazilian Banana And White Chocolate Ice Cream Torte 39
    53. Brazilian Peanut Fudge 40
    54. Broccoli Trees With Creamy White-bean Dip 40
    55. Bruschetta With Hummus 41
    56. Butter Pie Crust 41
    57. Buttercrust Pastry Dough 42
    58. Buttermilk Corn Bread 42
    59. Buttermilk Pie Crust Dough 43
    60. Butternut Squash Flan 43
    61. Butternut Squash Soup With Green Chili Coriander Chutney 44
    62. Cajun Ham Salad Sandwiches 44
    63. Cantaloupe Gelato 45
    64. Caramel Macadamia Nut Crunch 45
    65. Caramel-glazed Walnut Cake 46
    66. Caramel-orange Bûche De Noël 47
    67. Caramelized Nut Tart 48
    68. Caribbean-style Sofrito 49
    69. Cashew Butter 49
    70. Cashew Nut Fudge 50

71. Cauliflower Caraway Potato Soup 50
72. Cauliflower Fritters 51
73. Cauliflower Soup With Pecorino Romano And Truffle Oil 51
74. Cauliflower Soup With Seared Scallops, Lemon Oil, And American Caviar 52
75. Celery Apple Gazpacho 52
76. Celery Root Risotto And Pesto 53
77. Charentais Granita With Chantilly Cream 53
78. Chargrilled Sirloin With Mash And Salsa Verde 54
79. Charred Green Beans With Harissa And Almonds 55
80. Cheddar Cauliflower Soup 55
81. Cheesy Thumbprint Appetizers With Hot Pepper Jelly 56
82. Chef John's Chocolate Energy Bars 56
83. Cherry Linzertorte 57
84. Chicken And Hominy Soup 57
85. Chicken And Red Bell Pepper Salad Sandwiches 58
86. Chicken Artichoke Bacon Dip 58
87. Chicken Paillards With Radish-mint Chutney 59
88. Chicken Skewers With Tarragon-pistachio Pesto 59
89. Chicken Soup With Asparagus And Shiitakes, Served With Roasted Fennel Matzo Balls 60
90. Chicken Under A Brick With Fresh Herb And Garlic Sauce 61
91. Chicken With Olive Tapenade 61
92. Chickpea Slather 62
93. Chilled Honey-roasted Peach And Cardamom Soup With Vanilla Cream 62
94. Chilled Tomato Basil Soup 63
95. Chocolate Chip Apricot Bars 63
96. Chocolate Chunk And Apricot Cannoli 64
97. Chocolate Marble Cheesecake 64
98. Chocolate, Almond, And Coconut Vegan Fat Bombs 65
99. Chocolate, Caramel, And Walnut Tart . 65
100. Chocolate-almond Tofu Pie 66
101. Chocolate-filled Almond Macaroons 67
102. Cilantro Jalapeno Pesto With Lime 67
103. Cinnamon Energy Bites 68
104. Coffee-molasses Shoofly Pie 68
105. Colombian Aji 69
106. Cool-off-the-heat Avocado And Watermelon Salad 69
107. Crab-boil Spices 70
108. Cranberry And Blood Orange Relish 70
109. Cranberry And Raspberry Star Cookies 71
110. Cranberry Milk-chocolate Truffles 72
111. Cranberry Salsa 72
112. Cranberry-avocado Salsa 73
113. Cream Cheese Pie Topped With Peaches And Blackberries 73
114. Creamed Spinach With Croutons 74
115. Creamy Cashew Lime Bars (or Pie) 74
116. Creamy Jalapeno Ranch Dip 75
117. Creamy Mashed Plantains (pure De Platano) 75
118. Crostini With Sun-dried-tomato Tapenade 76
119. Crusty Potato Galette 76
120. Cuban Inspired Millet 77
121. Damson Tartlets 77
122. Dandelion Pesto 78
123. Deb's Red Pepper Pesto 78
124. Deb's Tapenade 79
125. Deliciosa Salsa Verde 79
126. Dessert Hummus 80
127. Detox Cilantro Pesto 80
128. Deviled Egg Appetizer Dip 81
129. Dilled Carrot Salad 81
130. Dilled Cheddar Cheese Batter Bread 82
131. Don't Knock It Until You Try It Zucchini Chocolate Banana Nut Milkshake 82
132. Dottie's Pate 82
133. Double Chocolate Pistachio Cookies ... 83
134. Double-crust Nectarine Raspberry Pies 84
135. Dried Fruit And Almond Haroseth 85
136. Dried-apple Tart With Crisp Crumble Topping 85
137. Dried-cranberry Spread 86
138. Dulce De Leche Cheesecake Bars 86
139. Easy Basil Pesto With Almonds 87
140. Easy Black Bean Hummus 87
141. Easy Kale Pesto 88
142. Edamame Burger 88

143.	Edamame Dip With Crudites	89
144.	Eggplant Pasta Bake	89
145.	Eser's Balsamic Salad Dressing	90
146.	Ez Restaurant-style Hummus	90
147.	Flank Steak Salad With Chimichurri Dressing	91
148.	Food Processor Pizza Dough	91
149.	Fresca Relish	92
150.	Frozen Boysenberry And White Chocolate Parfait	92
151.	Garlic Asparagus Soup	93
152.	Garlic Creme Fraiche	93
153.	Ginger Crunch Cake With Strawberry Sauce	94
154.	Gingered Carrot Soup	95
155.	Gluten-free Wacky Depression Era Chocolate Cake	95
156.	Grandma Bowen's 'girdle Buster' Cookie Pie	96
157.	Grandmother's Tart	96
158.	Greek-style Cheese Ball	97
159.	Green Chile Chimichurri	98
160.	Green Olive Pesto	98
161.	Green Olive Tapenade	98
162.	Greg's Hot Peach Pie	99
163.	Grilled Chicken Breast With Tomato-tarragon Sauce	99
164.	Grilled Chicken Salad With Radishes, Cucumbers, And Tarragon Pesto	100
165.	Grilled Halibut With Basil-shallot Butter	101
166.	Grilled Swordfish And Green Olive Relish	101
167.	Ham And Onion Spread	102
168.	Ham Glaze	102
169.	Ham Pate	102
170.	Hamersley's Bistro Tart Dough	103
171.	Hazelnut Breadsticks	103
172.	Hazelnut Linzer Cookies With Blackberry Jam	104
173.	Hazelnut Pesto	105
174.	Hazelnut Pesto Fish	105
175.	Hazelnut, Ricotta, And Lemon Pesto	106
176.	Homemade Peanut Butter	106
177.	Honey-glazed Peach Tart With Mascarpone Cream	106
178.	Hot Pepper Jelly	107
179.	Hurry-up Black Bean Dip	108
180.	Israeli Falafel	108
181.	Italian Rice Croquettes	109
182.	Italian Tuna Spread	110
183.	Japanese Salad Dressing	110
184.	Jerked Pork Chops	110
185.	Jerusalem Chickpea Sandwich Filling	111
186.	Kabocha Squash Pie (japanese Pumpkin Pie)	111
187.	Kahlúa-spiked Frozen Mocha Lattes	112
188.	Kanafa	113
189.	Key Lime Pie	113
190.	Kickin' Kale Pesto	114
191.	Kiwi Sorbet	114
192.	Lemon Cornmeal Cake With Raspberry Filling	114
193.	Lemon Custard Pies	115
194.	Lima-bean Crostini	116
195.	Linguine With Sun-dried Tomato Pesto	117
196.	Ma'amoul (nut-filled Cookies)	117
197.	Macadamia Nut Butter	118
198.	Maltaise Sauce For Asparagus	118
199.	Malted Milk Cookie Tart	119
200.	Mango Apricot Glaze	119
201.	Mango Guacamole	119
202.	Mango-lime Ice	120
203.	Mascarpone Cheesecake With Quince Compote	120
204.	Mashed Sweet Potatoes And Pears	121
205.	Master Hot Sauce Recipe	121
206.	Meatless Dairy-free Taco Dip	122
207.	Mediterranean Chickpea Latkes	122
208.	Mexican Pesto	123
209.	Mexican Pizza Webb	123
210.	Meyer Lemon Cranberry Scones	124
211.	Mini Mincemeat Pies	125
212.	Minted Pea Purée	126
213.	Mix-and-mash Root Vegetables	126
214.	Mojo Rojo	126
215.	Molasses Carob Chip Cookies	127
216.	Molasses Jumbos With Ginger Filling	127
217.	Mr. Lincoln And Cecile Brunner In A Jam	128
218.	Mushroom Caesar Salad	129
219.	Mussels On The Half Shell With Pesto	129

220. Neapolitan Sundae 130
221. Nectarine Almond Frangipane Tart 130
222. Nectarine And Almond Crisp 131
223. Nectarine And Plum Tartlets 132
224. Nectarine Daiquiri 132
225. North Carolina Coleslaw 133
226. Not Your Grandma's Chopped Chicken Liver 133
227. Nut Butter 134
228. Onion Pie 134
229. Onion, Cheese, And Bacon Tart 135
230. Paleo Chocolate Frosting 136
231. Parsley Pesto And Feta Phyllo Pizza .. 136
232. Pastry Dough 137
233. Peach Bellini 137
234. Peach Curd 138
235. Peanut Butter Tart With Caramel-peanut Glaze 138
236. Pear And Maple Crumble 139
237. Pear And Raisin Mince Pie With Lattice Crust 140
238. Pear-mango Salsa 141
239. Pecan Fig Bourbon Cake 141
240. Pecan, Caramel And Fudge Pie 142
241. Penne With Butternut-sage Sauce 142
242. Penne With Pea Pesto 143
243. Perfect Coconut Macaroons 143
244. Pimiento Mac And Cheese 144
245. Pistachio Brittle Cheesecake 144
246. Pistachio-crusted Rack Of Lamb 145
247. Pistou 146
248. Plantain Veggie Burgers 146
249. Plum Granita With Summer Fruit 146
250. Plum Streusel Coffeecake 147
251. Pork Chops With Mango Pineapple Sauce 148
252. Potato And Leek Purée 148
253. Potato Latkes 149
254. Potato, Carrot And Parsnip Soup 149
255. Potato, Corn, And Cherry Tomato Salad With Basil Dressing 150
256. Powdered Sugar 150
257. Provencal Vegetable And Goat Cheese Terrine 151
258. Pumpkin Clafouti 151
259. Quiche With Leeks, Mushrooms And Sweet Potatoes 152

260. Quick Puff Pastry 153
261. Quick Sun-dried Tomato And Basil Hummus 153
262. Quick Sweet Potato Bisque 154
263. Quince Apple Strudels With Quince Syrup 154
264. Quince Tarte Tatin 156
265. Raspberry And Lime Custard Tart 157
266. Raspberry Jam Tart With Almond Crumble 158
267. Raspberry Linzer Tart 159
268. Raw Cucumber Soup (gluten And Dairy-free) 159
269. Raw Pasta Sauce 160
270. Red Bean And Sausage Cakes With Poached Eggs And Cilantro Salsa 160
271. Red Chili And Honey-glazed Turkey With Ancho Pan Gravy 161
272. Red Lentil Dal 162
273. Red-fruit Puddings 163
274. Ricotta- And Walnut-stuffed Artichokes 163
275. Ripley's Bloody Mary Mix For Canning 164
276. Roasted Cornish Hens With Black-olive Butter 165
277. Roasted Garlic, Brie And Grape Crostini 165
278. Roasted Salsa 166
279. Roasted Vegetables With Pecan Gremolata 166
280. Roasted-almond Ricotta Pesto With Olives 167
281. Roasted-pepper And Almond Mayonnaise 168
282. Roman Garlic And Anchovy Salad Dressing 168
283. Rudy's Garlic Scape Pesto 168
284. Rum Balls 169
285. Rutabaga Purée 169
286. Salmon Rillettes 170
287. Salsa Quemada (roasted Tomato Salsa) 170
288. Sarson Ka Saag (indian Mustard Greens) 171
289. Sauerkraut Pierogi Filling 171
290. Sauteed Striped Bass With Mint Pesto

And Spiced Carrots 172
291. Scott's Holiday Cranberry Salad 173
292. Sea Bass With Red Pepper And Olive Tapenade 173
293. Sesame Balls With Drunken Fig Filling 174
294. Shrimp And Artichokes In Peppery Butter Sauce 175
295. Simple Basil-spinach Pesto 176
296. Simple Sweet Potato Soup 176
297. Simple Vegan Tzatziki Sauce 176
298. Small Pear And Almond Cakes 177
299. Smoked Salmon Rillettes On Tortilla Wafers 177
300. Smoked Trout Soufflé In A Phyllo Crust 178
301. Smoky Black Bean Dip 179
302. Sour Cream Chocolate-chip Cake 179
303. Southern Style Honey Butter 180
304. Spaghetti And Meatballs All'amatriciana 181
305. Spaghetti With Cauliflower, Green Olives, And Almonds 181
306. Spiced Carrot Spread 182
307. Spiced Streusel Apple Pie 183
308. Spicy Chipotle Grilled Chicken 183
309. Spicy Feta Dip..184
310. Spicy Roasted Red Pepper And Feta Hummus 184
311. Spicy Sweet Potato Spread 185
312. Spinach And Garlic Dip With Pita Triangles And Vegetables 185
313. Spinach And Garlic Scape Pesto 186
314. Spinach And Tofu Paneer 186
315. Standing Rib Roast With Winter-vegetable Crust 186
316. Steamed Vegetables With Basil Pecan Pesto 187
317. Strawberry Buttermilk Ice 188
318. Strawberry Cup 188
319. Strawberry Panachee 188
320. Strawberry Vinegar................................189
321. Strawberry-cheesecake Ice Cream 189
322. Strawberry-kiwi Sangria With Rosé Geranium 189
323. Strawberry-orange Sorbet 190
324. Summer Herb Pesto 190
325. Summer Peach Pie With Vanilla And Cardamom...191
326. Sun-dried Tomato Hummus 191
327. Sweet Potato Hummus.........................192
328. Sweet Potato Purée With Ginger And Cider 192
329. Sweet-pea Canapes 193
330. Tangy Rhubarb Salsa 193
331. Thai Shrimp Curry................................194
332. Three Basil Pesto 195
333. Toasted-hazelnut Cake 195
334. Tofu Dream Pudding And Pie Filling 196
335. Tomatillo-pepita Gazpacho 196
336. Tomato Chile Salsa................................197
337. Tomato, Dill And White Cheddar Soup 197
338. Torquato's Herb And Garlic Baked Tomatoes...198
339. Traditional Hummus.............................198
340. Truly Coconutty Cream Pie 199
341. Turkey Tonnato 200
342. Turtle Swirl Cheesecake 200
343. Tuscan Bean Soup With Prosciutto And Grated Parmigiano-reggiano 201
344. Tuscan Garlic-pepper Toasts 202
345. Two-potato Soup...................................202
346. Vanilla Chiffon Cake With Chocolate Sorbet 202
347. Vanilla Panna Cotta With Pear Jam ... 203
348. Vegan Broccoli-hazelnut Spread.........203
349. Vegan Gingerbread Scones..................204
350. Vegan Homemade Plain Cream Cheese 205
351. Vegan Keto Lemon Fat Bombs..........205
352. Viennese Linzertorte Cake 205
353. Vietnamese Chicken Sandwich (banh Mi) 206
354. Walnut Cheesecakes With Tokay Syrup 207
355. Walnut-herb Pesto.................................208
356. White Bean Dip With Pine Nuts 208
357. White Bean Purée 209
358. White Bean, Garlic, And Tomato Salsa 209
359. White Chocolate And Raspberry Cheesecake..209
360. White Clam Sauce Dip 210

361.	White Gazpacho	211
362.	Yam Soup With Coriander	211
363.	Zucchini Cucumber Gazpacho	212
364.	Zucchini Ginger Cupcakes	212
365.	Zucchini Poppers With Sour Cream Dip 213

INDEX 215

CONCLUSION 228

Introduction

***

Hi all,

Welcome to MrandMsCooking.com — a website created by a community of cooking enthusiasts with the goal of providing books for novice cooks featuring the best recipes, at the most affordable prices, and valuable gifts.

Thank you for choosing "Hello! 365 Food Processor Recipes" as your next destination!

All of us are yearning to be raised with so much love from family members and it's the happiest feeling to be with them always. We miss our family whenever we are away from home and always looking to that warm feeling that our home brings us. That is the reason why we always want to go home to our family after an exhausting day, either from work or school. Then we feel that happiness again once when all family members gather together to share and create sweet memories.

On the other hand, no matter how much you wanted to be always together, people will always become busy at work or school as this is the cycle of life. So make it a habit to eat your meals together whenever you have the chance to spend time with your whole beloved family.

I have written this series to you my dear friends, because I wanted to make your life easier and give you more time with your family in this busy life. Let's not miss a family meal if possible to give us time with our loved ones. I divided this series into different topics, so you have different options according to your daily cooking needs, they are:

- Budget Cooking Recipes
- Cooking For One Recipes
- Cooking For Two Recipes
- ...

It will now be more convenient and easier for you to plan your meals and spend more meaningful time with the family.

Go ahead, have some fun and cherish the memories together while enjoying your delicious meals!

I really appreciate that you have selected "Hello! 365 Food Processor Recipes" and for reading to the end. I anticipate that this book shall give you the source of strength during the times that you are really exhausted, as well as be your best friend in the comforts of your own home. Please also give me some love by sharing your own exciting cooking time in the comments segment below.

List of Abbreviations

_	_
C🧑‍🍳🧑‍🍳**King** LIST OF ABBREVIATIONS	
tbsp(s).	tablespoon(s)
tsp(s).	teaspoon(s)
c.	cup(s)
oz.	ounce(s)
lb(s).	pound(s)

365 Amazing Food Processor Recipes

***

1. "Close To Store-bought" Mayo

"This is a recipe for the perfect mayo."
Serving: 12 | Prep: 10m | Ready in: 10m

Ingredients

- 1 cup avocado oil
- 1/4 cup sesame oil
- 1/4 cup light olive oil
- 3 eggs
- 2 tbsps. lemon juice
- 1 1/2 tsps. mustard powder
- 1 tsp. brown mustard
- 3/4 tsp. salt

Direction

- In a glass bowl or measuring cup, combine olive oil, sesame oil, and avocado oil.
- In a food processor, place salt, brown mustard, mustard powder, lemon juice, and eggs. Turn the processor on and pour in the oil mixture slowly through the feeder tube until incorporated and the mayonnaise becomes thick and smooth, 2-3 minutes. Use a spatula to stir and incorporate any leftover oil drops on the top.

Nutrition Information

- Calories: 262 calories;
- Total Carbohydrate: 0.4 g
- Cholesterol: 46 mg
- Total Fat: 28.8 g
- Protein: 1.7 g
- Sodium: 168 mg

2. Almond Ice Cream Terrine With Chocolate Truffles And Raspberry Sauce

"An elegant dessert, bittersweet chocolate truffles."
Serving: Serves 12

Ingredients

- 1/2 cup whipping cream
- 2 tbsps. (1/4 stick) unsalted butter
- 4 oz. bittersweet (not unsweetened) or semisweet chocolate, chopped
- 1 1/2 tbsps. amaretto or other almond liqueur
- 2 1/2 cups whipping cream
- 1 1/4 cups whole milk
- 3/4 cup plus 2 tbsps. sugar
- 1 cup whole almonds, toasted, coarsely chopped
- 7 large egg yolks
- 1/2 tsp. almond extract
- 1 12-oz. package frozen unsweetened raspberries, thawed
- 6 tbsps. sugar
- 1/4 cup amaretto or other almond liqueur
- Fresh raspberries

Direction

- Prep truffles: in a small-size, heavy saucepan, boil butter and cream. Take off from heat. Put in chocolate; mix till smooth. Mix in amaretto. Transfer to a small-size bowl. Place in the freezer for 50 minutes, till firm enough to shape to balls.
- Line foil on a baking sheet. Spoon out level chocolate mixture teaspoonfuls with tsp.. Place on a baking sheet. Put in freezer for 20 minutes, till set. Form the chocolate to balls with hands; put back to the baking sheet and

- return in freezer. (May be done a week in advance. Keep in freezer with cover.)
- Prep ice cream: in big, heavy saucepan, mix milk, sugar and cream. Mix on moderate heat to dissolve the sugar. Boil. Put in chopped almonds. Let steep with cover for about 2 hours.
- Pass mixture of cream through fine strainer place above a bowl; get rid of the solids in strainer. Pour cream mixture back into the same saucepan. Let simmer. In a big bowl, mix the yolks to incorporate. Mix hot mixture of cream to yolks gradually. Pour mixture back into the saucepan. Mix on moderately-low heat for 3 minutes, till custard creates path on back of a spoon once finger is run across and thickens, (prevent it from boiling). Cool partially. Stir almond extract in. Pour into a bowl and refrigerate custard for no less than 3 hours or up to overnight, till cold.
- Line plastic wrap on a glass, 9x5x3-inch loaf dish, overlap the sides by 2-inch. Use ice cream maker to process the custard following directions of manufacturer. Remove the ice cream into prepped dish. Push truffles in ice cream, space them apart. Put cover on terrine and freeze for no less than 8 hours to overnight, till set.
- Prep sauce: use a processor to puree defrosted raspberries. Pass through a strainer placed above a bowl, forcing using back of spoon to release as much moisture as can be. Get rid of solids left in strainer. Mix amaretto and sugar in sauce. Refrigerate with cover. (Sauce and terrine may be prepped 2 days in advance. Store terrine in freezer and the sauce in refrigerator.)
- Transfer terrine on a platter. Remove plastic. Slice terrine making pieces measuring 3/4-inch thick. Serve along with fresh berries and sauce.

Nutrition Information

- Calories: 476
- Total Carbohydrate: 40 g
- Cholesterol: 182 mg
- Total Fat: 33 g
- Fiber: 4 g
- Protein: 7 g
- Sodium: 39 mg
- Saturated Fat: 16 g

3. Almond Macaroons With Swiss Meringue Buttercream

"A lovely recipe."
Serving: Makes 16 sandwich macaroons | Prep: 1.5h

Ingredients

- 3/4 cup whole almonds with skin (1/4 lb.), toasted and cooled completely
- 1 1/2 cups confectioners sugar
- 3 large egg whites, at room temperature for 30 minutes
- 1/4 tsp. salt
- 1/3 cup granulated sugar
- 1/4 tsp. pure vanilla extract
- 1/8 tsp. pure almond extract
- 2 large egg whites, at room temperature for 30 minutes
- 1/2 cup sugar
- 1/8 tsp. salt
- 2 sticks (1 cup) unsalted butter, softened
- 1/4 tsp. pure vanilla extract
- 1/8 tsp. pure almond extract
- parchment paper; a stand mixer fitted with whisk attachment; a pastry bag fitted with a 1/4-inch plain tip

Direction

- Macaroons: In lower and upper thirds of oven, put oven racks; preheat the oven to 300°F. Line parchment paper on 2 big baking sheets.
- Grind confectioners' sugar and almonds finely in a food processor.
- In mixer, beat salt and whites till they hold soft peaks at medium high speed.
- Lower speed to medium. Little at a time, add granulated sugar, beating; beat till whites hold

glossy, stiff peaks. In 2 batches, fold almond mixture into whites just till combined. Fold in almond and vanilla extracts. Put meringue in pastry bag; pipe 16 1 1/2-in. wide mounds on each lined baking sheet, 1-in. apart, 32 in total. Use a wet fingertip to smooth tops of mounds.
- Bake for 15-17 minutes till tops look dry and macaroons are puffed, switching sheets positions halfway through baking; macaroons should be chewy inside and crisp outside. Slide parchment with the macaroons on racks; cool for 10 minutes. Peel macaroons from parchment. Put on a rack; fully cool for 15 minutes.
- Buttercream: Vigorously whisk salt, sugar and whites till it is warm and sugar dissolves in cleaned mixer bowl above 4-qt. pot with barely simmering water. Put bowl in mixer; beat using cleaned whisk attachment on medium high speed till whites hold glossy, stiff peaks. Beat for 5 minutes till meringue is fully cool to touch, scraping bowl's sides down with rubber spatula.
- 1 piece at 1 time, add butter slowly with mixer on medium speed, beating well after each till incorporated. Meringue is too warm if buttercream appears soupy after adding some butter. Briefly chill bowl's bottom in a big bowl full of ice water for several seconds if so before beating in leftover butter. Beat till buttercream is smooth; it might look curdled before adding all butter, but it'll come back together when you finish beating. Add almond and vanilla extracts; beat for 1 minute.
- Assemble cookies: Put buttercream in cleaned pastry bag; pipe 1 tbsp. on flat sides of the 16 macaroons. Top using leftover 16 macaroons.
- Egg whites in buttercream aren't fully cooked, which could be a problem if salmonella is common in your area.
- You can make buttercream 1 week ahead, covered, chilled. Bring to room temperature; don't use a microwave, it'll take 3 hours normally. Before using, beat using electric mixer.
- Filled macaroons keep for 2 days in airtight container, chilled, layered between wax paper sheets. Before serving, bring to room temperature.

Nutrition Information

- Calories: 231
- Total Carbohydrate: 23 g
- Cholesterol: 31 mg
- Total Fat: 15 g
- Fiber: 1 g
- Protein: 3 g
- Sodium: 74 mg
- Saturated Fat: 8 g

4. Almond Praline Semifreddo With Grappa-poached Apricots

"So fun!"
Serving: Makes 4 servings | Prep: 1.25h

Ingredients

- 1/3 cup plus 1/4 cup sugar, divided
- 1/3 cup sliced almonds with skin (1 oz.), toasted and cooled
- 2 large eggs
- 1/8 tsp. pure almond extract
- 1 1/2 cups chilled heavy cream
- 1 cup water
- 2/3 cup sugar
- 1 (3-inch) strip lemon zest
- 1/2 cup grappa
- 8 firm-ripe apricots (1 1/2 to 1 3/4 lbs.), halved and pitted
- 1 tbsp. fresh lemon juice

Direction

- Semifreddo: line plastic wrap on 8 1/2 x 4 1/2-in. lightly oiled loaf pan; on all sides, leave 2-in. overhang. Oil baking sheet lightly.
- Cook 1/3 cup of sugar in a small dry heavy skillet on medium heat till it starts to melt, undisturbed. Cook till deep golden caramel, occasionally mixing with a fork.

- Mix in almonds to coat; scrape onto baking sheet and cool. Break to pieces. Pulse till praline is ground finely, not to a paste, in a food processor.
- Beat pinch salt, leftover 1/4 cup sugar and eggs in 2-qt. metal bowl above pot with simmering water with handheld electric mixer on high speed for 8 minutes till very thick and tripled in volume. Take off heat; beat for 5 minutes till it cools to room temperature. Mix in extract.
- Beat cream till it holds stiff peaks with cleaned beaters. Fold 1/3 whipped cream to lighten into egg mixture; fold in all but 1 tbsp. praline and leftover cream thoroughly yet gently. Keep 1 tbsp. praline as garnish. Put into loaf pan; freeze for minimum of 6 hours till firm, covered.
- Poach apricots: Simmer zest, sugar and water in 12-in. heavy skillet, mixing till sugar dissolves. Simmer for 5 minutes. Add grappa; simmer. Toss lemon juice and apricots; put in grappa syrup, cut sides down. Simmer for 5 minutes. Flip apricots; simmer for 1-3 minutes till just tender.
- Put apricots in 1 layer in a 13x9-in. dish with a slotted spoon. Boil syrup in skillet for 3 minutes till reduced to 1/2 cup; put on apricots and cool it to room temperature.
- Uncover semifreddo; invert onto chilled platter using the plastic wrap to pull it from the mold. Sprinkle top with reserved praline. Crosswise slice semifreddo; serve with syrup and apricots.
- You can make semifreddo 3 days ahead, kept, well wrapped, frozen.
- You can make apricots with syrup 2 days ahead, chilled.
- Eggs aren't fully cooked in this recipe.

Nutrition Information

- Calories: 778
- Total Carbohydrate: 86 g
- Cholesterol: 215 mg
- Total Fat: 40 g
- Fiber: 4 g
- Protein: 9 g
- Sodium: 75 mg
- Saturated Fat: 22 g

5. Almond-plum Buckle

"Don't skimp on garnish."
Serving: Makes 8 servings

Ingredients

- Nonstick vegetable oil spray
- 1/2 cup whole almonds (about 2 1/2 oz.)
- 1 1/2 cups all purpose flour
- 1 tsp. baking powder
- 1/4 tsp. fine sea salt
- 1 cup (2 sticks) unsalted butter, room temperature
- 1 cup plus 4 tsps. sugar
- 2 large eggs
- 1 tsp. vanilla extract
- 1/2 tsp. almond extract
- 1 1/4 lbs. plums (about 8 medium), halved, pitted, cut into 1/2-inch-thick slices
- 3/4 tsp. ground cinnamon

Direction

- In the middle of oven, put rack; preheat it to 350°F. Spray nonstick spray on 9-in. diameter cake pan that has 2-in. high sides. Line parchment paper round on bottom of the pan.
- Grind almonds finely in a processor; put in a medium bowl. Whisk in salt, baking powder and flour. Beat butter till fluffy with an electric mixer in big bowl. Add 1 cup of sugar; beat till blended well. One by one, add eggs; beat well after each addition. Beat in almond and vanilla extract then the flour mixture till incorporated.
- Put batter in a prepped pan; evenly spread and smooth top using spatula. Press plum slices gently into batter, flesh side down, in spoke pattern around middle of cake and outer rim, placing near each other. Mix 4 tsps. sugar and cinnamon in a small bowl; sprinkle on plums.

- Bake cake for 50 minutes till inserted tester in the middle exits clean; cool cake for 20 minutes in a pan on a rack. Run a small knife between pan and cake's sides to loosen. Onto platter, invert cake; remove parchment paper. Put another platter on top of the cake; firmly hold both platters together using both hands. Invert cake with plum side up; fully cool cake. Cut into wedges.

Nutrition Information

- Calories: 519
- Total Carbohydrate: 56 g
- Cholesterol: 108 mg
- Total Fat: 31 g
- Fiber: 3 g
- Protein: 7 g
- Sodium: 140 mg
- Saturated Fat: 16 g

6. Amaretto Divine

"A luscious dessert."
Serving: 10 | Prep: 30m | Ready in: 45m

Ingredients

- 1 (18.25 oz.) package yellow cake mix
- 1 cup non dairy amaretto flavored creamer
- 1 cup amaretto liqueur
- 3 eggs
- 1/3 cup vegetable oil
- 1 (3.5 oz.) package instant vanilla pudding mix
- 1 cup non dairy amaretto flavored creamer
- 1/4 cup amaretto liqueur
- 2 cups heavy cream, whipped
- 4 (1.4 oz.) bars chocolate covered toffee bars, chopped
- 1 (1.5 oz.) bar chocolate candy bar, melted
- 1/2 cup sliced almonds

Direction

- Preheat an oven to 165°C/325°F. Grease then flour 3 8-in. pans.
- Mix oil, eggs, 1 cup amaretto liqueur, 1 cup of amaretto flavored creamer and cake mix till blended. Evenly distribute cake batter to cake pans; in preheated oven, bake, being sure the cake layers don't overbake for 15 minutes. Before filling, fully cool.
- Amaretto whipped cream filling: mix 1 cup of amaretto flavored creamer, 1/4 cup amaretto liqueur and pudding mix; put aside till thick for 5 minutes. Fold whipped cream into amaretto mixture; mix in crushed chocolate covered toffee bars then use it to fill then frost cake's top, not sides. Drizzle with melted chocolate candy bar on cake; sprinkle with sliced almonds. Refrigerate till ready to serve.

Nutrition Information

- Calories: 888 calories;
- Total Carbohydrate: 93.6 g
- Cholesterol: 131 mg
- Total Fat: 48.1 g
- Protein: 7.4 g
- Sodium: 588 mg

7. Amaretto-almond Streusel Pumpkin Pie

Serving: Makes 8 to 10 servings

Ingredients

- 2 tbsps. amaretto liqueur
- Perfect Pumpkin Pie
- 20 Amaretti di Saronno cookies (about 4 1/4 oz.), crumbled into pieces that are 1/2 inch or smaller
- 1/4 cup sliced almonds

Direction

- In perfect pumpkin pie, use 2 tbsp. cream for amaretto liqueur.
- Mix almonds and cookie crumbs; before baking, sprinkle on filling. Bake then cool pie as mentioned.

- You can make it 8 hours ahead, standing in room temperature.

8. Amarillo Ceviche Mixto

"An amazing ceviche!"
Serving: 6 servings

Ingredients

- 1/3 cup freshly squeezed lime juice
- 1/3 cup freshly squeezed lemon juice
- 1 tbsp. aji amarillo paste (see Note)
- 1 tbsp. ground turmeric
- 1/4 cup clam juice
- 1 tbsp. grated fresh ginger
- Pinch of salt
- 1/2 lb. shrimp, peeled, deveined, and blanched
- 1/2 lb. octopus, cooked and sliced crosswise into 1/8-inch slices
- 1/2 lb. sautéed bay scallops
- 1 yellow tomato, seeded and diced
- 1 small yellow bell pepper, seeded and diced
- 1 tbsp. chopped fresh chives
- 2 tbsps. sliced green onions
- 1 tbsp. coarsely chopped fresh cilantro for garnish

Direction

- Puree all sauce ingredients till smooth in a food processor/blender. Mix green onions, chives, tomato, bell pepper, scallops, octopus, shrimp and sauce in nonreactive bowl; cover. Refrigerate for 1 hour. Garnish with chopped cilantro before serving.

Nutrition Information

- Calories: 111
- Total Carbohydrate: 8 g
- Cholesterol: 75 mg
- Total Fat: 1 g
- Fiber: 1 g
- Protein: 17 g
- Sodium: 522 mg

- Saturated Fat: 0 g

9. Apple Pear Sauce

"If desired, add sugar to taste after it cools."
Serving: 8 | Prep: 15m | Ready in: 35m

Ingredients

- 4 pears, cut into chunks
- 3 apples, cut into chunks
- 1/2 cup water
- 1 tsp. vanilla extract
- 1/4 tsp. ground cinnamon

Direction

- Heat skillet on medium heat. Add vanilla extract, water, apples and pears to hot skillet; cover. Simmer fruit mixture for about 10 minutes; uncover. Cook for 10-15 minutes till fruit is soft and most liquid evaporates.
- Take off heat; put fruit mixture and leftover liquid in food processor and process till smooth. Mix in cinnamon; refrigerate for maximum of 4 days or serve warm.

Nutrition Information

- Calories: 77 calories;
- Total Carbohydrate: 20.1 g
- Cholesterol: 0 mg
- Total Fat: 0.2 g
- Protein: 0.5 g
- Sodium: 2 mg

10. Apple Upside-down Biscuit Cake

Ingredients

- 3 tbsps. unsalted butter
- 1/2 cup packed light brown sugar

- 1 lb Granny Smith apples, peeled, cored, and cut into thin wedges
- 1 cup all-purpose flour
- 1/4 cup granulated sugar
- 1 tsp. baking powder
- 1/2 tsp. baking soda
- 1/2 tsp. salt
- 1/2 tsp. cinnamon
- 5 tbsps. cold unsalted butter, cut into pieces
- 1/2 cup well-shaken buttermilk
- Accompaniment: crème fraîche or sour cream (optional)

Direction

- Preheat an oven to 425°F.
- Topping: Heat butter till foam subsides in a 10-in. ovenproof, well-seasoned cast-iron is best, heavy skillet on medium heat. Mix in brown sugar; take off from the heat. Evenly spread mixture in skillet; put apples in 1 layer, overlapping.
- Cake: Blend cinnamon, salt, baking soda, baking powder, sugar and flour in food processor. Add butter; pulse till it looks like coarse meal. Put into a bowl; add buttermilk, mixing till it is moistened.
- Drop the batter over top of apples; spread gently, leaving 1-in. border around skillet's edge. Cake needs space to expand.
- Bake cake for 25-30 minutes till firm to the touch and golden brown in the center of the oven; cool cake for 3 minutes in a skillet on a rack. Invert onto a platter; replace any apples that stick to the skillet on cake.
- Serve while warm.

Nutrition Information

- Calories: 275
- Total Carbohydrate: 40 g
- Cholesterol: 31 mg
- Total Fat: 12 g
- Fiber: 2 g
- Protein: 3 g
- Sodium: 286 mg
- Saturated Fat: 7 g

11. Apple Walnut Torte

"Moist and delicious!"
Serving: Makes 8 servings | Prep: 45m

Ingredients

- 2 sticks unsalted butter, well softened, divided
- 1 1/2 cups sugar, divided
- 2 lbs. tart apples such as Granny Smith, Northern Spy, or Greening, peeled, halved lengthwise, and cored
- 3/4 tsp. salt, divided
- 1 1/2 cups all-purpose flour
- 1 1/2 tsps. baking powder
- 1/2 tsp. baking soda
- 3/4 tsp. ground allspice
- 1/2 tsp. cinnamon
- 1/4 tsp. grated nutmeg
- 1 1/2 cups walnuts (5 oz.), coarsely chopped, toasted, and cooled completely
- 2 large eggs
- 1 tsp. pure vanilla extract
- 1/4 tsp. pure almond extract
- 3 tbsps. apple jelly
- Equipment: a 9- by 3-inch round cake pan or a 9-inch springform pan wrapped in foil
- Accompaniment: Calvados vanilla cream

Direction

- Preheat an oven with rack in center to 350°F.
- Butter pan; on bottom, fit parchment paper round. Butter parchment; flour pan.
- Thickly spread 1/2 stick butter on bottom of 12-in. heavy skillet; evenly sprinkle 1/2 cup sugar on butter. Put apples on sugar, cut sides down; sprinkle 1/4 tsp. salt. Cook on medium heat for 15-20 minutes till apples are golden brown and tender and sugar is caramelized, occasionally flipping apples.
- Put apples in concentric circles on cake pan's bottom, cut sides down; put caramel from skillet over.

- Whisk leftover 1/2 tsp. salt, nutmeg, allspice, cinnamon, baking soda, baking powder and flour.
- Pulse leftover 1 cup sugar and walnuts till finely ground in a food processor.
- Use an electric mixer to beat leftover 1 1/2 sticks butter for 3 minutes till creamy in a bowl. Add walnut sugar; beat just till combined. One by one, add eggs; beat well after each. Beat in extracts; mix in flour mixture at low speed till just combined and batter is thick.
- Dollop batter on apples; evenly spread. Bake for 45-50 minutes till inserted wooden pick in middle exits clean and pulls away from pan's sides. Cool torte for 30 minutes in pan on rack. Put rack on torte; invert torte on rack.
- Melt apple jelly on low heat in small heavy saucepan, mixing. Generously brush jelly on apples; fully cool torte for 1-1 1/2 hours.

Nutrition Information

- Calories: 655
- Total Carbohydrate: 79 g
- Cholesterol: 107 mg
- Total Fat: 36 g
- Fiber: 5 g
- Protein: 7 g
- Sodium: 388 mg
- Saturated Fat: 16 g

12. Apple-almond Cheesecake

"This almond-flavored cheesecake is baked a day ahead and topped with apples sautéed in cinnamon and brown sugar."
Serving: Makes 12 servings

Ingredients

- 1 cup graham cracker crumbs
- 1 cup sliced almonds, toasted
- 6 tbsps. (3/4 stick) unsalted butter, melted
- 2 tbsps. golden brown sugar
- 1/4 tsp. salt
- 1 1/2 7-oz. packages almond paste, crumbled
- 3 8-oz. packages cream cheese, room temperature
- 6 tbsps. sugar
- 4 large eggs
- 4 large Jonagold apples (about 2 1/2 lbs.), peeled, cored, cut into 1/3-inch-thick slices
- 2 tbsps. fresh lemon juice
- 4 tbsps. unsalted butter
- 3/4 cup (packed) golden brown sugar
- 3/4 tsp. ground cinnamon

Direction

- To make crust: Set the oven to 350 degrees Fahrenheit. Butter a springform pan (10 inch diameter) Use 2 layers heavy-duty foil to wrap the bottom. In a medium bowl, mix all the ingredients to blend, slightly crumbling the almonds. Press the mixture 1 inch up the pan sides and onto the bottom. Bake until the crust sets, around 7 minutes. Keep the oven temperature.
- To make filling: In a processor, combine sugar, cream cheese, and almond paste, blend until it becomes smooth, scraping down the bowl sides sometimes, around 2 minutes. Mix in the eggs just until blended, then pour the filling in the crust. Bake for about 15 minutes. Turn the oven heat down to 325 degrees Fahrenheit and bake until the center sets and top looks dry, 45 more minutes. Cool, wrap with plastic, and keep in the refrigerator overnight. You can make this 2 days beforehand, keep refrigerated.
- For the apples: Toss the slices of apple with lemon juice in a big bowl. Use a big heavy skillet to melt 3 tbsps. of the butter over high heat. Add the apples and sauté until tender and golden, frequently stirring, 9 minutes. Sprinkle with cinnamon and brown sugar. Mix in the leftover 1 tbsp. of butter until glazed and coated, then slightly cool.
- Use a small sharp knife to run around the pan edge to loosen the cheesecake and release the pan sides. Place the apples that are room temperature or warm in concentric circles on top of the cheesecake, then brush them with

any of the juices left in the pan. Cut the cake into wedges and serve.

Nutrition Information

- Calories: 618
- Total Carbohydrate: 55 g
- Cholesterol: 150 mg
- Total Fat: 42 g
- Fiber: 5 g
- Protein: 10 g
- Sodium: 320 mg
- Saturated Fat: 19 g

13. Apple-clove Butter

Serving: Makes about 3 1/2 cups

Ingredients

- 4 lbs. Rome Beauty, Jonathan or McIntosh apples, peeled, cored, cut into 1-inch pieces
- 1 cup apple cider
- 1/4 cup orange juice
- 1 cinnamon stick, broken in half
- 3/4 cup (packed) golden brown sugar
- 2 tsps. grated orange peel
- 1/2 tsp. ground cloves

Direction

- Boil cinnamon stick, orange juice, cider and apples in big heavy saucepan. Lower heat to medium low and cover; simmer for 10 minutes till apples are very tender, occasionally mixing. Throw cinnamon stick.
- In processor, puree apple mixture; put in same saucepan. Mix in cloves, orange peel and brown sugar; simmer on medium low heat for 45 minutes till it mounds on spoon, is thick and dark in color, mixing frequently. Put in big bowl; fully cool. You can make it 1 week ahead, covered, refrigerated.

Nutrition Information

- Calories: 288

- Total Carbohydrate: 75 g
- Total Fat: 1 g
- Fiber: 8 g
- Protein: 1 g
- Sodium: 13 mg
- Saturated Fat: 0 g

14. Apricot Galette

"Serve with sweetened whipped cream."
Serving: Serves 6

Ingredients

- 1/4 cup sliced almonds
- 1/4 cup confectioners' sugar
- 6 fresh apricots (preferably underripe and very tart)
- half a 17 1/4-oz. package frozen puff pastry sheets (1 sheet)
- 1 tbsp. granulated sugar

Direction

- Preheat an oven to 425°F. Pulse confectioners' sugar and almonds till finely ground in food processor. Pit apricots; cut to 1/8-in. thick wedges. Unfold pastry sheet on lightly floured surface; cut 9-in. round out. Put round in buttered big shallow baking pan; use fork to prick pastry all over. Evenly put almond mixture on pastry; leave 1/4-in. border. Put apricot wedges decoratively over almond mixture, overlapping them. Sprinkle granulated sugar.
- Bake galette in center of oven for 30 minutes till edges are golden brown. Put galette on rack with a metal spatula; cool.

Nutrition Information

- Calories: 292
- Total Carbohydrate: 30 g
- Total Fat: 18 g
- Fiber: 2 g
- Protein: 4 g
- Sodium: 102 mg

- Saturated Fat: 4 g

15. Apricot-almond Gift Bread

"You can snip apricots using kitchen shears wiped with bit of oil or chop all nuts and fruits on a cutting board with a sharp knife if you don't want to use a food processor."
Serving: Makes 1 large loaf or 3 baby loaves

Ingredients

- 2 cups all-purpose flour
- 1 1/2 tsps. baking powder
- 1/2 tsp. baking soda
- 1/2 tsp. salt
- 1 cup granulated sugar
- 3 tbsps. wheat germ
- 1 cup dried apricots (moist-style)
- 1/2 cup (2 1/2 oz.) blanched almonds
- 1/3 cup canola or light olive oil
- 1 large egg, at room temperature
- 3/4 cup apricot nectar or buttermilk
- 1 tsp. almond extract
- 1 tsp. vanilla extract
- 2/3 cup sifted confectioners' sugar
- 2 to 3 tbsps. milk, water, or fruit juice (or as needed)
- Pan Preparation: Butter the pan(s) or spray with butter-flavor nonstick vegetable spray and dust with flour. Tap out the excess flour.
- 9- by 5- by 3-inch loaf pan or three 5 3/4- by 3 1/4- by 2-inch baby loaf pans; food processor and kitchen shears or cutting board and knife; wooden skewer or cake tester.

Direction

- Bread: In middle of oven, put rack. Preheat an oven to 350°F. Bake baby loaves for 40-45 minutes and big loaf for 60-65 minutes; prep pan/s as mentioned.
- Whisk wheat germ, sugar, salt, baking soda, baking powder and flour in a big bowl. Put generous 1 tbsp. flour mixture and apricots into food processor's bowl, if using; pulse till fruit is cut to small 1/4-in. bits. Alternately, cut up apricots with an oiled knife/oiled kitchen shears. Scrape apricot bits into bowl with flour. Chop nuts; add to dry ingredients.
- Whisk extracts, buttermilk/nectar, egg and oil in a medium bowl. Create a well in middle of dry ingredients; add oil-egg mixture. Mix/whisk to blend well, don't overmix it.
- Scrape batter into prepped pan/s, filling to 2/3 full. Bake for 40-45 minutes for smaller loaves, 60-65 minutes for a big loaf or as time mentioned for altitude in chart till inserted cake tester in middle exits clean and bread is golden brown. Cool in pan/s on wire rack.
- Icing: Optional Icing; Whisk liquid and sugar till smooth and thick in a small bowl. Drizzle icing over when bread is fully cooled; as it dries, it'll harden.

Nutrition Information

- Calories: 329
- Total Carbohydrate: 55 g
- Cholesterol: 16 mg
- Total Fat: 10 g
- Fiber: 3 g
- Protein: 6 g
- Sodium: 239 mg
- Saturated Fat: 1 g

16. Apricot-pistachio Charoset

"1 tbsp. at a time, add extra wine till you get preferred consistency if you want a moister version."
Serving: Makes about 2 cups

Ingredients

- 1 cup minced dried apricots, preferably Californian
- 1 cup unsalted shelled pistachio nuts (not dyed red), chopped and lightly toasted
- 1/3 cup sweet white wine, such as Bartenura Moscato d'Asti or Herzog Late Harvest Riesling
- 1 tbsp. plus one tsp. fresh lemon juice
- 1 tbsp. shredded fresh mint

- 10 threads saffron, crumbled

Direction

- Mix all the ingredients well in a big bowl; before serving, let apricots absorb the liquid for approximately 20 minutes.

Nutrition Information

- Calories: 180
- Total Carbohydrate: 20 g
- Total Fat: 9 g
- Fiber: 4 g
- Protein: 5 g
- Sodium: 3 mg
- Saturated Fat: 1 g

17. Artichoke Jalapeno Hummus Dip

""Refreshing hummus with a kick of spice.""
Serving: 8 | Prep: 10m | Ready in: 10m

Ingredients

- 1 (15 oz.) can chickpeas, drained
- 2 (6 oz.) jars artichoke hearts, drained
- 1/2 cup Greek yogurt
- 1/2 cup fresh basil
- 1/3 cup pickled jalapeno pepper slices
- 1/4 cup olive oil
- 1 lemon, juiced
- 2 tbsps. hemp seeds
- 2 cloves garlic
- 1 tsp. ground paprika
- 1 tsp. ground cayenne pepper
- 1/2 tsp. curry powder

Direction

- Mix curry powder, cayenne pepper, paprika, garlic, hemp seeds, lemon juice, olive oil, jalapeno pepper slices, Greek yogurt, basil, artichoke hearts, and chickpeas in a food processor. Blend it until it is smooth.

Nutrition Information

- Calories: 160 calories;
- Total Carbohydrate: 14.5 g
- Cholesterol: 3 mg
- Total Fat: 9.6 g
- Protein: 5.1 g
- Sodium: 411 mg

18. Artichoke Ravioli With Tomatoes

"Amazing!"
Serving: Makes 4 servings | Prep: 1.5h

Ingredients

- 1 1/2 cups all-purpose flour
- 2 large eggs
- 1/2 tsp. salt
- 2 tbsps. water
- 2 tbsps. unsalted butter, cut into pieces
- 1 small onion, chopped (1/2 cup)
- 1 (10-oz.) box frozen artichoke hearts, thawed and patted dry
- 1 oz. finely grated Parmigiano-Reggiano (1/2 cup)
- 1/3 cup chopped fresh flat-leaf parsley
- 1 large egg yolk
- 1/2 tsp. fresh lemon juice
- 1/4 tsp. salt
- 1/4 tsp. black pepper
- 3/4 tsp. freshly grated nutmeg
- 1 large egg white, lightly beaten with 2 tsps. water (for egg wash)
- 1 tbsp. unsalted butter, cut into pieces
- 3 medium plum tomatoes, trimmed and cut into 1/4-inch dice (3/4 cup)
- 1/4 cup water
- 1/3 cup heavy cream
- 1 oz. finely grated Parmigiano-Reggiano (1/2 cup)
- 1/4 tsp. salt
- 1/4 tsp. black pepper

- a pasta machine; a 3-inch round metal cookie cutter; a shallow oval 2-quart ceramic or glass baking dish (12 by 8 1/2 inches)

Direction

- Pasta dough in food processor: Blend water, salt, egg and flour till it starts to make a ball in processor; if dough is too dry, drop by drop, add more water. Dough should be firm yet not sticky. Process dough to knead it for 15 seconds. Put on floured surface; stand for 1 hour, covered with inverted bowl, to relax gluten and easily roll out.
- Dough by hand: On work surface (wooden is best), mound flour; create well in middle. Put water, salt and eggs in well; gently beat water and eggs with a fork till combined. Mix in enough flour slowly to make a paste, pulling in the flour nearest to egg mixture without making an opening in the well's outer wall. Knead leftover flour into mixture to make a dough using your hands; if dough is dry, drop by drop, add more water. Dough should be firm yet not sticky. Knead dough for 8-10 minutes till elastic and smooth. Cover using inverted bowl; stand to easily roll for 1 hour.
- Filling: Heat butter till foam subsides in 12-in. heavy skillet on medium high heat; sauté onion for 6 minutes till golden, occasionally mixing. Add artichoke hearts; sauté for 8-10 minutes till tender, mixing occasionally. Take off heat; slightly cool.
- In cleaned processor's bowl, put all except 3/4 cup artichoke mixture; keep leftover artichoke mixture in the skillet. Add nutmeg, pepper, salt, lemon juice, yolk, parsley and cheese; pulse till chopped coarsely.
- Roll pasta and create ravioli: Cut the pasta dough to 4 pieces; flatten every piece to rough rectangle. Use inverted big bowl to cover rectangles; put pasta machine's rollers on widest setting.
- Dust flour on 1 rectangle lightly; through rollers, feed. Keep leftover rectangles under the bowl. Fold rectangle in half; feed it through rollers, folded end first, 7-8 times, folding in half every time then feeding folded end through. If needed, dust flour to avoid sticking. Put dial on narrower/next setting. Without folding, feed dough through rolling; keep feeding dough through rollers one time at every setting till you hit narrowest setting. Dough will be 24-in. long 4-in. wide smooth sheet.
- Put dough sheet on floured work surface; drop 6 1 1/2-tsp. filling mounds in a row down middle of 1/2 of sheet, 1 1/2-in. apart. Brush egg wash around every mound; fold other 1/2 sheet on filling. Firmly press down around every mound, forcing air out. Air pockets can break your ravioli while cooking. Between mounds, cut pasta to 3-in. rounds with cutter. Line clean, not terry cloth, kitchen towel on big shallow baking pan; dust flour on towel. In it, put ravioli in 1 layer. 1 sheet at 1 time, create more ravioli with leftover pasta dough and leftover filling, putting ravioli on lined pan.
- In center position, put oven rack; preheat the oven to 350°F. Butter baking dish lightly.
- Boil 6-8-qt. pot of salted water. Add ravioli, mixing to separate carefully; cook for 6 minutes till pasta is tender, adjust heat to keep water on gently boil. Put in a colander using slotted spoon.
- Assemble then bake dish: Reheat reserved artichoke mixture in the skillet with butter on medium high heat as ravioli boils. Add water and tomatoes; cook for 5 minutes till tomatoes are soft, mixing.
- Put 1/2 ravioli on baking dish; put 1/2 cheese, 1/2 cream and 1/2 artichoke mixture over. Repeat using leftover cheese, cream, artichoke mixture and ravioli. Sprinkle pepper and salt.
- Bake for 15 minutes till cream is bubbly and ravioli heats through, uncovered.
- You can make dough 4 hours ahead, not rolled out, tightly wrapped with plastic wrap, chilled.
- You can make, not cook, ravioli 4 hours ahead, chilled, covered, in lined baking pan.

Nutrition Information

- Calories: 2495
- Total Carbohydrate: 282 g
- Cholesterol: 528 mg
- Total Fat: 142 g
- Fiber: 6 g
- Protein: 46 g
- Sodium: 1888 mg
- Saturated Fat: 73 g

19. Arugula, Artichoke And Red Chile Hummus

""*Hummus is an easy side dish to create and cheaper than buying from the store. You can also leave out some ingredients.*""
Serving: 10 | Prep: 15m | Ready in: 15m

Ingredients

- 1 (19 oz.) can chickpeas, drained and rinsed
- 1 banana pepper, seeded and chopped (optional)
- 1 cup artichoke hearts, drained and chopped
- 1 cup baby arugula, coarsely chopped
- 1/2 cup olive oil
- 1/2 cup apple cider vinegar
- 3 tbsps. tahini
- 2 tsps. ground cumin
- 1 tsp. bouquet garni
- 1/2 tsp. red pepper flakes
- salt to taste
- cracked black pepper to taste
- 2 tsps. water, or as needed

Direction

- Put pepper, salt, red pepper flakes, bouquet garni, cumin, tahini, apple cider vinegar, olive oil, baby arugula, artichoke hearts, banana pepper, and chickpeas in a food processor.
- Pule it 3-4 times at the beginning. After process it for around 1 minute. Scrape the sides of the bowl down. Keep on processing it until the big pieces become finely chopped and the hummus reaches your desired consistency, for around 1-2 minutes. Make it thinner if it's too thick by adding a few tsps. of water at a time.

Nutrition Information

- Calories: 195 calories;
- Total Carbohydrate: 14.3 g
- Cholesterol: 0 mg
- Total Fat: 14 g
- Protein: 3.8 g
- Sodium: 202 mg

20. Asparagus 'guacamole'

"*This spicy recipe with no avocados can be enjoyed with low-fat chips and vegetables, you can go easy in adding jalapeno peppers and or hot pepper sauce if you don't want more heat.*"
Serving: 10 | Prep: 20m | Ready in: 55m

Ingredients

- 1 1/2 lbs. asparagus, cut into small pieces
- 1 tbsp. fat-free Greek-style yogurt
- 1 tbsp. lime juice
- 1/4 cup chopped fresh cilantro
- 3 green onions, thinly sliced
- 1/2 jalapeno pepper, minced
- 1 tbsp. minced garlic
- 1 tomato, diced
- 1/2 tsp. Worcestershire sauce
- 1 dash hot pepper sauce
- salt and ground black pepper to taste

Direction

- Put asparagus in a steamer insert over a pot with an inch of water; boil. Cover then steam the asparagus for 5mins; move asparagus to a food processor bowl. Puree until smooth.
- In a big bowl, mix hot pepper sauce, asparagus puree, Worcestershire sauce, yogurt, tomato, lime juice, garlic, cilantro, jalapeno pepper, and green onions together. Gently stir to

combine. Sprinkle pepper and salt to season. Refrigerate to chill until completely cooled.

Nutrition Information

- Calories: 22 calories;
- Total Carbohydrate: 4.1 g
- Cholesterol: < 1 mg
- Total Fat: 0.3 g
- Protein: 1.9 g
- Sodium: 10 mg

21. Autumn Apple-squash Crisp

"A great dessert."
Serving: 12 | Prep: 30m | Ready in: 1h15m

Ingredients

- 4 1/2 cups butternut squash - peeled, seeded, and cut into 3/4-inch chunks
- 2/3 cup packed brown sugar
- 1/2 cup all-purpose flour
- 2 eggs
- 2 tsps. milk
- 2 tsps. vanilla extract
- 2 tsps. ground cinnamon
- 2 tsps. ground nutmeg
- 1/2 tsp. ground cloves
- 4 large Granny Smith apple - peeled, cored and chopped
- 2 large carrots, peeled and shredded
- 1 cup raisins
- Topping
- 2 cups rolled oats
- 1 cup wheat bran
- 1 cup packed brown sugar
- 1/2 cup whole wheat flour
- 1 tbsp. ground cinnamon
- 1/2 cup melted butter

Direction

- Preheat an oven to 175°C/350°F and grease 9x13-in. baking dish lightly.
- Put 1-in. water into bottom of pan. Put squash in a steamer basket fitted in pan; boil. Lower heat to medium and cover; steam squash for 15 minutes till pierced with a fork easily and tender. Cool.
- Pulse cloves, nutmeg, 2 tsp. cinnamon, vanilla, milk, eggs, 1/2 cup of all-purpose flour, 2/3 cup brown sugar and squash till smooth in a food processor's bowl. Put into a big mixing bowl; mix in raisins, carrots and apples till blended evenly. Spread mixture on bottom of prepped baking dish.
- Mix 1 tbsp. cinnamon, melted butter, 1/2 cup of whole wheat flour, 1 cup brown sugar, wheat bran and rolled oats till crumbly in a bowl; put topping on squash-apple mixture.
- In preheated oven, bake for 30-45 minutes till apples are tender and top is golden brown.

Nutrition Information

- Calories: 353 calories;
- Total Carbohydrate: 65.4 g
- Cholesterol: 51 mg
- Total Fat: 10.1 g
- Protein: 6.2 g
- Sodium: 86 mg

22. Avocado Aioli

""A creamy garlic sauce with avocado is simple and flexible used as dipping sauce, drizzle or as a dressing.""
Serving: 8

Ingredients

- 1 medium very ripe Avocado from Mexico
- 1/3 cup plain, fat-free Greek-style yogurt
- 1 tbsp. chopped basil
- 2 tsps. minced garlic
- 1 tsp. fresh lemon juice
- 1/2 tsp. salt
- 1/4 tsp. ground black pepper

Direction

- In a food processor, mix black pepper, salt, lemon juice, garlic, basil, yogurt and avocado and blend until just smooth. Use right away or keep in the refrigerator.

Nutrition Information

- Calories: 47 calories;
- Total Carbohydrate: 2.9 g
- Cholesterol: 0 mg
- Total Fat: 3.7 g
- Protein: 1.4 g
- Sodium: 151 mg

23. Avocado And Edamame Dip

"A recipe great as a spread for a sandwich or a dip for tortilla chips. Warm sauce can be minimized for a milder taste."
Serving: 6 | Prep: 15m | Ready in: 45m

Ingredients

- 6 oz. shelled edamame (green soybeans)
- 1/2 onion, chopped
- 1/2 cup tightly packed cilantro
- 2 tbsps. olive oil
- 1 large avocado, peeled, pitted and cubed
- 1 lemon, juiced
- 1 tbsp. chile-garlic sauce (such as Sriracha®)
- salt and pepper to taste

Direction

- In a food processor, put the olive oil, cilantro, onion and edamame. Blend until coarsely chopped. Stir in the chil-garlic sauce. Lemon juice and avocado; add pepper and salt for seasoning. Blend until becomes smooth. Place inside the refrigerator for 30 minutes until serving time.

Nutrition Information

- Calories: 171 calories;
- Total Carbohydrate: 11.3 g
- Cholesterol: 0 mg
- Total Fat: 13.5 g
- Protein: 5.1 g
- Sodium: 117 mg

24. Avocado Compound Butter

"This compound butter adds butter flavor to your meats and they are definitely much more delicious."
Serving: 8 | Prep: 15m | Ready in: 2h15m

Ingredients

- 2 Hass avocados - halved, pitted, and peeled
- 1/4 cup butter, at room temperature
- 2 jalapeno peppers, chopped
- 1 lime, zested and juiced
- 2 tsps. ground cumin
- 1 tsp. ground paprika
- salt and ground black pepper to taste

Direction

- In a food processor, add black pepper, salt, paprika, cumin, lime juice, lime zest, jalapeno peppers, butter and avocados; pulse for 1 to 2 minutes until the mixture gets smooth and well blended.
- Use large plastic wrap to cover your working surface. Place the avocado mixture in the middle of the plastic wrap. Fold the wrap's bottom edge over mixture and roll into a log, twist ends to seal. Let them chill in the fridge for 2 hours or in the freezer for 1 hour until the mixture is firm enough to the touch. Divide them into coins and serve.

Nutrition Information

- Calories: 138 calories;
- Total Carbohydrate: 5.8 g
- Cholesterol: 15 mg
- Total Fat: 13.3 g
- Protein: 1.3 g
- Sodium: 65 mg

25. Avocado Hummus

""This recipe is a blend if guacamole and hummus. This is far better than store bought guacamole and hummus. Chop ingredients and blend using a mixer for a chunky dip.""
Serving: 8 | Prep: 30m | Ready in: 30m

Ingredients

- 2 avocados - peeled, pitted, and chopped
- 1 (15 oz.) can chickpeas, drained
- 1 medium tomato, chopped (optional)
- 1 lime, juiced
- 1/2 cup freshly chopped cilantro
- 1/4 cup chopped red onion
- 2 tbsps. tahini (optional)
- 1 jalapeno pepper, seeded and chopped (optional)
- 1 tbsp. olive oil
- 3 cloves garlic, peeled and smashed
- 1 tsp. ground cumin
- 1/4 tsp. salt, or more to taste
- 2 tbsps. water, or as needed (optional)

Direction

- Using a large food processor, mix together until smooth the chickpeas, avocados, lime juice, tomato, cilantro, tahini, onion, jalapeño pepper, olive oil, garlic, salt and cumin. For a thinner consistency, add water until desired consistency is achieved.

Nutrition Information

- Calories: 170 calories;
- Total Carbohydrate: 15.7 g
- Cholesterol: 0 mg
- Total Fat: 11.6 g
- Protein: 3.8 g
- Sodium: 188 mg

26. Avocado Peanut Butter Brownies (vegan)

"These fudgy brownies are quick to make since you cook the peanut-butter and chocolate mixture beforehand. The use of avocado instead of butter makes it rich without the fat."
Serving: 20 | Prep: 15m | Ready in: 1h45m

Ingredients

- 1 cup natural creamy peanut butter
- 1 (12 oz.) bag chocolate chips
- 1 1/2 cups white sugar
- 1 avocado, peeled and pitted
- 1/2 cup soy milk
- 1/2 cup canola oil
- 1 cup whole-wheat flour
- 1 tsp. baking powder
- 1 tsp. salt

Direction

- Set oven to 350 degrees F or 175 degrees C and grease a baking pan (9 by 13 inches).
- In a saucepan, melt together sugar, chocolate chips, and peanut butter on low heat, continuously stirring, for about 5 minutes until the chocolate melts. Turn the heat up to medium and continue to stir for about 5 more minutes until the mixture starts to bubble then take away from the heat.
- In a food processor, blend together canola oil, soy milk, and avocado until smooth then stir into the chocolate mixture until blended well.
- In a big bowl, whisk together salt, baking powder, and flour until well combined. Add into the avocado and chocolate mixture, stirring until just incorporated, then, evenly pour onto the prepped baking pan.
- Bake in the oven for about 20 minutes until edges starts to turn crispy. Completely cool before you cut the brownies and serve.

Nutrition Information

- Calories: 304 calories;
- Total Carbohydrate: 33.8 g
- Cholesterol: 0 mg

- Total Fat: 18.8 g
- Protein: 5.2 g
- Sodium: 206 mg

27. Balsamic-strawberry Pops

"A fun recipe!"
Serving: Makes 6 to 8 pops

Ingredients

- 2 cups sliced, hulled strawberries (from about 1 lb. berries)
- 1/4 cup sugar
- 2 1/2 tbsps. good-quality balsamic vinegar
- Freshly ground black pepper

Direction

- Pulse sugar and strawberries till juicy and finely chopped yet still chunky, don't make it smooth, in a food processor. Put into a bowl; mix in few grinds of pepper and balsamic vinegar.
- Put mixture in ice pop molds; insert sticks. Freeze for a minimum of 6 hours – maximum of 1 week till firm.
- Unmold pops: On outsides of molds, run hot water for a few seconds; pull sticks gently.

Nutrition Information

- Calories: 48
- Total Carbohydrate: 12 g
- Total Fat: 0 g
- Fiber: 1 g
- Protein: 0 g
- Sodium: 2 mg
- Saturated Fat: 0 g

28. Banana Basil Smoothie

"You will love this creamy and rich smoothie if you're basil lover."
Serving: 2 | Prep: 5m | Ready in: 5m

Ingredients

- 2 bananas
- 1/4 cup heavy whipping cream
- 12 leaves fresh basil, or more to taste
- 1 tbsp. maple syrup
- 4 ice cubes

Direction

- In a blender or a food processor, mix ice cubes, maple syrup, basil, cream and bananas together, then blend until smooth.

Nutrition Information

- Calories: 234 calories;
- Total Carbohydrate: 34.6 g
- Cholesterol: 41 mg
- Total Fat: 11.4 g
- Protein: 2 g
- Sodium: 15 mg

29. Banana Mud Ice Cream

"A healthy treat! All ingredients are optional but banana."
Serving: 1 | Prep: 10m | Ready in: 6h10m

Ingredients

- 1 banana, sliced
- 2 tbsps. coconut milk (optional)
- 1/4 cup unsweetened cocoa powder (optional)
- 1 scoop protein powder
- 2 tbsps. peanut butter (optional)
- 2 tbsps. maple syrup (optional)
- 1 packet stevia powder (optional)

Direction

- Freeze the sliced banana for about 6 hours.

- Blend coconut milk and banana till smooth in a small blender/small food processor. Add stevia powder, maple syrup, peanut butter, protein powder and cocoa powder; blend till smooth.

Nutrition Information

- Calories: 681 calories;
- Total Carbohydrate: 77.9 g
- Cholesterol: 12 mg
- Total Fat: 27 g
- Protein: 51.3 g
- Sodium: 306 mg

30. Banana Sorbet

"This guilt-free food can be eaten by itself or enjoy with chocolate cookies! For a decadent treat, frozen cookies can be served alongside!"
Serving: 2 | Prep: 10m | Ready in: 10m

Ingredients

- 1 frozen banana
- 1 tsp. cold water
- 2 tsps. caramel sauce

Direction

- Use a food processor to pulse banana and water until chunky; blend in caramel sauce. Blend completely until smooth.

Nutrition Information

- Calories: 70 calories;
- Total Carbohydrate: 18 g
- Cholesterol: < 1 mg
- Total Fat: 0.2 g
- Protein: 0.7 g
- Sodium: 25 mg

31. Banana-cinnamon French Toast

"A simple recipe!"
Serving: Serves 2

Ingredients

- 1 large very ripe banana (about 8 oz.)
- 2 eggs
- 1/2 cup milk
- 1/2 tsp. ground cinnamon
- 4 slices whole wheat bread
- 3 tbsps. butter
- Maple syrup

Direction

- Blend initial 4 ingredients till smooth in processor; put in 13x9-in. pan. Put bread into milk mixture; soak for 20 minutes till all liquid is absorbed, occasionally turning bread.
- Melt butter on medium heat in big heavy skillet. Add bread; cook for 3 minutes per side till golden brown. Serve with syrup separately.

32. Banana-fudge Sundaes

Serving: Makes 6 servings | Prep: 15m

Ingredients

- 3 very ripe bananas, peeled, each cut crosswise into 4 pieces
- 1 14-oz. can sweetened condensed milk, divided
- 1 cup half and half
- 2 tbsps. light corn syrup
- 1 tbsp. fresh lemon juice
- 1/2 cup bittersweet chocolate chips
- 1 ripe banana, peeled, diced (for garnish)

Direction

- In a processor, puree lemon juice, corn syrup, half and half, 3/4 cup of condensed milk, and 3 bananas till smooth. Pour into ice cream

maker; process following directions of manufacturer. Remove to a container. Freeze for 4 hours, till firm.
- In a small-size saucepan, heat a tbsp. of water and half cup of sweetened condensed milk on moderate heat; put in chocolate. Mix till smooth and melted, putting additional teaspoonfuls of water in case sauce is too thick.
- Distribute ice cream between bowls. Sprinkle sauce on top; put diced banana over.

33. Basil Aioli

"Keeps for 1 week in the fridge."
Serving: 16 | Prep: 10m | Ready in: 1h10m

Ingredients

- 1 1/2 cups mayonnaise
- 2/3 cup chopped fresh basil
- 1 tbsp. chopped fresh garlic
- 1 tbsp. lemon juice
- 1 1/2 tsps. lemon zest

Direction

- Blend basil and mayonnaise till mayonnaise is slightly green and mixed in a food processor. Add garlic; process till blended well. Add zest and lemon juice; process for 30-45 seconds till well mixed.
- Put in a bowl; cover. Chill for 1 hour till flavors merge.

Nutrition Information

- Calories: 150 calories;
- Total Carbohydrate: 1 g
- Cholesterol: 8 mg
- Total Fat: 16.4 g
- Protein: 0.3 g
- Sodium: 117 mg

34. Basil And Garlic Mayonnaise

Serving: Makes about 1/2 cup

Ingredients

- 1/2 cup (packed) basil leaves, torn
- 1/2 garlic clove, peeled
- 1 1/2 tsps. red wine vinegar
- 1/2 cup light mayonnaise

Direction

- Blend red wine vinegar, garlic and basil till basil is chopped finely in a processor. Add mayonnaise; blend till smooth.

Nutrition Information

- Calories: 391
- Total Carbohydrate: 9 g
- Total Fat: 39 g
- Fiber: 0 g
- Protein: 2 g
- Sodium: 848 mg
- Saturated Fat: 5 g

35. Basil And Pesto Hummus

"A sweet, delicious hummus with basil and pesto taste, that can be eaten by itself or serve paired with crackers."
Serving: 5 | Prep: 10m | Ready in: 10m

Ingredients

- 1 (16 oz.) garbanzo beans (chickpeas), drained and rinsed
- 1/2 cup basil leaves
- 1 clove garlic
- 1 tbsp. olive oil
- 1/2 tsp. balsamic vinegar
- 1/2 tsp. soy sauce
- salt and ground black pepper to taste

Direction

- In a food processor, mix garlic, basil, and garbanzo beans, then pulse a few times. Scrape down the sides of the processor bowl using a spatula. Pulse again while drizzling in the olive oil. Stir in soy sauce and vinegar, and process until incorporated. Sprinkle pepper and salt to season.

Nutrition Information

- Calories: 134 calories;
- Total Carbohydrate: 21 g
- Cholesterol: 0 mg
- Total Fat: 3.8 g
- Protein: 4.7 g
- Sodium: 302 mg

36. Basil Garlic Mayonnaise

"A very versatile recipe."
Serving: Makes about 1 cup | Prep: 10m

Ingredients

- 1 cup coarsely chopped fresh basil
- 1 garlic clove, smashed
- 1/4 tsp. salt
- 1/8 tsp. cayenne
- 3/4 cup mayonnaise

Direction

- Pulse cayenne, salt, garlic and basil till finely chopped in a food processor. Add mayonnaise; blend till smooth. Chill to develop flavors for 1 hour, covered.

Nutrition Information

- Calories: 151
- Total Carbohydrate: 0 g
- Cholesterol: 8 mg
- Total Fat: 17 g
- Fiber: 0 g
- Protein: 0 g
- Sodium: 125 mg
- Saturated Fat: 2 g

37. Basil Pesto Risotto With Pan-roasted Scallops

"Creamy risotto."
Serving: 2 | Prep: 20m | Ready in: 1h

Ingredients

- Pesto:
- 1 cup fresh basil leaves
- 1 cup fresh spinach
- 1/4 cup pine nuts
- 2 tbsps. olive oil, or to taste
- 1 tbsp. grated fresh Parmesan cheese, or to taste
- ground black pepper to taste
- Risotto:
- 2 cups chicken stock
- 1 cup water
- 2 tbsps. butter
- 2 tbsps. chopped shallots
- 1 cup Arborio rice
- 1 pinch saffron (optional)
- 1/3 cup white wine
- 1/3 cup grated fresh Parmesan cheese
- Scallops:
- 4 sea scallops
- kosher salt and ground black pepper to taste
- 2 tbsps. butter
- 1 tbsp. olive oil

Direction

- In a food processor's bowl, put pine nuts, spinach and basil and pulse to chop. In a steady stream, add 2 tbsps. of olive oil till pesto turns creamy, pausing to scrape down the sides. Using a spoon, mix in black pepper and a tbsp. of Parmesan cheese.
- In individual saucepans over moderate heat, heat water and chicken stock for 5 minutes till simmering; lower the heat, put a cover on, and keep warm.
- In a big saucepan over moderate heat, melt 2 tbsps. of butter till frothy. Put in the shallots; cook and mix for 5 minutes till tender. Put in saffron and rice; mix till coated with butter.

- Add the wine and let simmer for 5 minutes till soaked in.
- Into the saucepan, put enough warm stock to barely cover the rice; cook and mix till soaked in. Keep putting in stock, then water, mixing continuously, for 20 minutes till every addition is soaked in, rice is soft but firm to the bite, and risotto is creamy and thick.
- Scoop the pesto into the risotto. Take saucepan off the heat; mix in 1/3 cup of Parmesan cheese.
- Using paper towels, blot scallops dry; add pepper and salt to season.
- In a skillet on moderate heat, melt 2 tbsps. butter along with a tbsp. of olive oil. In hot skillet, set the scallops and cook for 2 minutes, undisturbed, till deep golden brown on the bottom. Turn each scallop and sear on the other side for an additional 2 minutes till golden brown.
- Top risotto with scallops, serve.

Nutrition Information

- Calories: 1046 calories;
- Total Carbohydrate: 92.8 g
- Cholesterol: 110 mg
- Total Fat: 57.8 g
- Protein: 33.4 g
- Sodium: 1475 mg

38. Beef Rendang

"You can alter heat to suit your tastes."
Serving: 4 | Prep: 15m | Ready in: 48m

Ingredients

- 1/4 cup mild olive oil
- 4 shallots
- 1 mild red chile pepper, seeds removed, or to taste
- 3 large cloves garlic, minced
- 2 tsps. shrimp paste
- 1 2-inch piece fresh lemongrass
- 1 2-inch piece fresh ginger root
- 1 tsp. ground turmeric
- 3/4 cup coconut milk, or as needed
- 1/3 cup palm sugar
- 4 kaffir lime leaves
- 1 tsp. ground cinnamon
- 1/2 tsp. ground cloves
- 2 tsps. sea salt, or to taste
- 2 tsps. ground white pepper
- 2 1/4 lbs. beef sirloin, cubed

Direction

- Blend turmeric, gingerroot, lemongrass, shrimp paste, garlic, chile pepper, shallots and olive oil for 30-60 seconds till smooth paste forms in a food processor's bowl.
- Heat paste for 3 minutes till very fragrant in a big saucepan on medium heat. Add white pepper, sea salt, cloves, cinnamon, kaffir lime leaves, palm sugar and coconut milk; boil. Cook for 10 minutes till slightly thick. Mix in beef; lower the heat to gently simmer and cook for 20 minutes till sauce is thick and beef is tender, occasionally mixing. Remove kaffir lime leaves; serve.

Nutrition Information

- Calories: 653 calories;
- Total Carbohydrate: 32.6 g
- Cholesterol: 112 mg
- Total Fat: 37.5 g
- Protein: 47.6 g
- Sodium: 994 mg

39. Beef Sates With Southeast Asian Sauce

"Can be made in less than an hour."
Serving: Makes 12 satés

Ingredients

- 1/4 cup fresh lime juice
- 2 tbsps. water
- 4 tsps. soy sauce

- 2 garlic cloves
- 3 slices peeled fresh gingerroot, each the side of a quarter
- 1 tsp. sugar
- 1/4 tsp. dried hot red pepper flakes
- 3 tbsps. vegetable oil
- an 8-oz. filet mignon, cut into twenty-four 1-inch cubes
- 1/4 cup fresh coriander sprigs, washed well, spun dry, and chopped fine
- 1 tbsp. minced fresh mint leaves
- 1 scallion, minced
- twelve 8-inch bamboo skewers, soaked in water 30 minutes.

Direction

- Blend red pepper flakes, sugar, gingerroot, garlic, soy sauce, water and lime juice till smooth in blender or small food processor; add 2 tbsps. oil in stream as motor runs. Blend till sauce emulsifies.
- Toss leftover 1 tbsp. oil, 2 tbsps. sauce and filet in bowl; marinate for 15-30 minutes.
- Prep grill.
- On each skewer, thread 2 filet cubes; grill on oiled rack 5-6-inch above glowing coals for 3-4 minutes per side to get medium-rare.
- Serve dipping sauce with beef sates at room temperature.

Nutrition Information

- Calories: 82
- Total Carbohydrate: 1 g
- Cholesterol: 16 mg
- Total Fat: 7 g
- Fiber: 0 g
- Protein: 4 g
- Sodium: 107 mg
- Saturated Fat: 2 g

40. Beefy Southwestern Corn Pudding Casserole

"A delightfully different main dish meal."
Serving: 8 | Prep: 15m | Ready in: 1h10m

Ingredients

- cooking spray
- 8 corn tortillas, torn into 2-inch pieces
- 1 1/2 lbs. ground beef
- 1/2 cup salsa
- 1/2 tsp. garlic salt
- 1 sweet yellow onion, quartered
- 1 (10 oz.) package frozen corn
- 2 cups milk
- 1 cup shredded Cheddar cheese, divided
- 1 (4 oz.) can diced green chile peppers
- 1 (4 oz.) jar chopped pimento peppers
- 2 large eggs
- 1 tsp. hot sauce
- 1 tsp. smoked paprika
- 1/2 tsp. salt
- 1 (7.5 oz.) package corn bread mix (such as Jiffy®)
- 1 (6 oz.) can sliced black olives (optional)
- 2 green onions, thinly sliced, or to taste

Direction

- Heat an oven to 165°C or 325°F. Use cooking spray to coat a 9x13-inch baking dish.
- Place pieces of corn tortilla in prepped baking dish's bottom.
- Heat big skillet on moderately high heat. Cook beef in hot skillet while mixing for 5 to 7 minutes till crumbly and brown; strain and get rid of grease. Stir ground beef in bowl along with garlic salt and salsa; scoop mixture on top of tortillas.
- In food processor, put corn and onion; pulse to chop the onion coarsely. Put in salt, paprika, hot sauce, eggs, pimento peppers, green chile peppers, 1/2 cup of Cheddar cheese and milk; pulse to barely mix. Put in corn bread mix; pulse till just incorporated. Scoop mixture of corn bread on top of beef.

- Bake for 45 to 50 minutes in prepped oven till casserole sets in the center. Put olives, green onions and leftover half cup of Cheddar cheese on top of casserole. Allow Cheddar cheese to slightly melt for 5 minutes then serve.

Nutrition Information

- Calories: 499 calories;
- Total Carbohydrate: 46.8 g
- Cholesterol: 120 mg
- Total Fat: 23.5 g
- Protein: 27.3 g
- Sodium: 1334 mg

41. Black And Green Olive Tapenade

"A lovely tapenade."
Serving: Makes 1 heaping cup

Ingredients

- 1 cup Niçoise olives, pitted
- 1 cup small green French olives (Picholine), pitted
- 1/4 cup Oven-Dried Tomatoes, drained
- 1 tbsp. capers
- 1 garlic clove
- 1 anchovy fillet
- 1/2 tbsp. chopped fresh basil leaves
- 1/2 tbsp. chopped fresh thyme leaves
- 1/2 tbsp. chopped fresh flat-leaf parsley leaves
- 1/4 tbsp. chopped fresh oregano leaves
- 1/4 cup extra-virgin olive oil

Direction

- Use pulse button to process all ingredients but olive oil till well blended and coarsely chopped in food processor; process, adding olive oil slowly. Refrigerate in covered container; as needed, use.
- Prep ahead; tapenade keeps, in covered container, for maximum of 1 week, refrigerated.

Nutrition Information

- Calories: 779
- Total Carbohydrate: 19 g
- Cholesterol: 3 mg
- Total Fat: 80 g
- Fiber: 9 g
- Protein: 4 g
- Sodium: 2118 mg
- Saturated Fat: 11 g

42. Black Bean And Chickpea Chili

"A filling and easy to make recipe loaded with fresh vegetables and served on top of wild rice with shredded cheddar cheese or alongside tortilla chips."
Serving: 12 | Prep: 20m | Ready in: 1h

Ingredients

- 1 1/2 tbsps. olive oil
- 1 lb. ground turkey (optional)
- 1 onion, chopped
- 2 green bell peppers, seeded and chopped
- 5 carrots, peeled and sliced into rounds
- 1 tbsp. chili powder
- 1 1/2 tsps. ground cumin
- 1 tsp. ground black pepper
- 2 (14.5 oz.) cans canned diced tomatoes with their juice
- 1 cup frozen corn
- 1 (15 oz.) can black beans, drained and rinsed
- 1 (15 oz.) can garbanzo beans, drained and rinsed
- 1 1/2 cups chicken broth

Direction

- If you're using turkey: In a big saucepan, heat the oil on medium-high heat, then cook and stir the ground turkey for around 10 minutes, using a spoon to break it up while it cooks,

until the meat has no visible pink color. Take out the turkey meat and put aside; leave oil in the pan.
- In the saucepan, put the carrots, green peppers and onions and let it cook and stir for around 10 minutes, until the vegetables become tender and the onion turns translucent. Mix in the black pepper, cumin and chili powder, then pour in the chicken broth, garbanzo beans, black beans, frozen corn and diced tomatoes. Boil the mixture.
- In a food processor, put approximately 1 1/2 cups of the chili mixture and let it pure for around 1 minute, until it has a smooth consistency. Pour the puree back into the remaining chili to make it thick. Add the cooked turkey meat, then return the chili to a simmer on medium-low heat.

Nutrition Information

- Calories: 147 calories;
- Total Carbohydrate: 16.5 g
- Cholesterol: 28 mg
- Total Fat: 5.3 g
- Protein: 10.3 g
- Sodium: 214 mg

43. Black Bean And Roasted Tomato Soup

"A wonderful soup."
Serving: Serves 4

Ingredients

- 1 lb. plum tomatoes, halved lengthwise
- 1 large onion, halved lengthwise, cut into thin wedges
- 1 medium carrot, peeled, quartered
- 3 large garlic cloves, chopped
- 1 tbsp. olive oil
- 1/2 tsp. dried oregano
- 2 cups (or more) canned vegetable broth
- 3 1/4 cups cooked black beans or two 15-oz. cans black beans, rinsed, drained
- 1/2 cup plain nonfat yogurt

Direction

- Preheat an oven to 350°F. Mix carrot, onion and tomatoes in big roasting pan. Add oregano, oil and garlic; mix to coat veggies. Roast for 55 minutes till veggies are tender and brown, occasionally mixing. Cut carrot to small cubes; put aside. Put leftover veggies in processor. Put 2 cups broth in roasting pan; scrape browned bits up. Add 2 1/4 cups beans and broth in processor; puree veggie mixture till nearly smooth.
- Put soup in big heavy saucepan. Add leftover 1 cup beans; boil. Lower heat; simmer for 10 minutes till flavors blend; if soup is very thick, add more broth. Mix in carrot; season using pepper and salt. You can make it 1 day ahead then cover; chill. Before continuing, rewarm. Put soup in bowls; put dollop of yogurt on each.

44. Black Bean Hummus Without Tahini

"A low-fat, tahini-free hummus made with spicy black beans. You can store it up to 1 week in the fridge."
Serving: 8 | Prep: 10m | Ready in: 10m

Ingredients

- 1 (15 oz.) can no-salt-added black beans, drained and rinsed
- 1/4 cup fresh cilantro
- 1/4 cup lime juice
- 1 jalapeno pepper, trimmed and seeded
- 1 tbsp. sesame oil
- 4 cloves garlic
- 1 tsp. ground cumin
- 1/4 tsp. ground paprika
- 1/4 tsp. cayenne pepper

Direction

- In a blender or a food processor, process the cayenne pepper, paprika, cumin, garlic, sesame oil, jalapeño pepper, lime juice, cilantro and black beans until it becomes smooth.

Nutrition Information

- Calories: 62 calories;
- Total Carbohydrate: 8.8 g
- Cholesterol: 0 mg
- Total Fat: 1.8 g
- Protein: 3.1 g
- Sodium: 8 mg

45. Black-bean Burgers

"This is a pantry-friendly vegetarian burger recipe that has a Latin flair."
Serving: Makes 4 servings | Prep: 10m

Ingredients

- 2 (14-oz.) cans black beans, rinsed and drained, divided
- 3 tbsps. mayonnaise
- 1/3 cup plain dry bread crumbs
- 2 tsps. ground cumin
- 1 tsp. dried oregano, crumbled
- 1/4 tsp. cayenne
- 1/4 cup finely chopped cilantro
- 3 tbsps. vegetable oil
- 4 soft hamburger buns
- Accompaniments: sour cream; salsa; lettuce

Direction

- Use a food processor to pulse 1 can of beans along with cayenne, oregano, cumin, bread crumbs, and mayonnaise to form a coarse puree. Move to a bowl and stir in the leftover can of beans and cilantro, then form into 4 patties.
- Heat a heavy 12-inch skillet with oil over medium-high heat until it shimmers and cook the burgers until the outsides turn light brown and crisp, turning them over once, 5 minutes in total. Serve the burger on buns.

Nutrition Information

- Calories: 507
- Total Carbohydrate: 61 g
- Cholesterol: 4 mg
- Total Fat: 22 g
- Fiber: 15 g
- Protein: 18 g
- Sodium: 615 mg
- Saturated Fat: 3 g

46. Blender Hollandaise Sauce

"This Hollandaise sauce is delicious with asparagus and lemony flavor. You won't need a double boiler for this recipe and the sauce won't separate."
Serving: 6 | Prep: 5m | Ready in: 5m

Ingredients

- 3 egg yolks
- 1/4 tsp. Dijon mustard
- 1 tbsp. lemon juice
- 1 dash hot pepper sauce (e.g. Tabasco™)
- 1/2 cup butter

Direction

- Mix hot pepper sauce, lemon juice, mustard, and egg yolks together in the container of a blender. Put the lid on and process for 5 seconds.
- In a glass measuring cup, put butter. In the microwave, heat the butter until fully hot and melt, about 1 minute. Start the blender on high speed, and add butter to the egg yolk mixture in a thin flow. It should almost immediately get thickened. In the pan of hot tap water, put the container of the blender to keep warm until enjoying.

Nutrition Information

- Calories: 163 calories;
- Total Carbohydrate: 0.6 g
- Cholesterol: 143 mg
- Total Fat: 17.5 g

- Protein: 1.5 g
- Sodium: 119 mg

47. Blue Cheese And Chive Dressing

"A great dressing; omit buttermilk to make it a dip."
Serving: Makes about 1 1/4 cups

Ingredients

- 1/2 cup well-shaken buttermilk
- 1/2 cup mayonnaise
- 1 tbsp. fresh lemon juice
- 1/4 tsp. Worcestershire sauce
- 1 small garlic clove, minced
- 1/4 tsp. salt
- 1/4 cup fresh flat-leaf parsley leaves
- 2 oz. crumbled firm blue cheese (1/2 cup)
- 2 tbsps. finely chopped fresh chives
- 1/8 tsp. black pepper

Direction

- Blend salt, garlic, Worcestershire sauce, lemon juice, mayonnaise and buttermilk till smooth in a food processor.
- Add parsley; pulse till chopped. Add the blue cheese; pulse till dressing is slightly chunky and cheese is incorporated.
- Put in a bowl; mix in pepper and chives.
- Dressing keeps for 1 week, chilled, covered.

Nutrition Information

- Calories: 441
- Total Carbohydrate: 4 g
- Cholesterol: 40 mg
- Total Fat: 44 g
- Fiber: 0 g
- Protein: 8 g
- Sodium: 678 mg
- Saturated Fat: 11 g

48. Blueberry Crumble Pie

"Try topping of cinnamon-scented streusel with flowing berry juice. You will surely love it!"
Serving: 8 servings

Ingredients

- 1 1/4 cups unbleached all-purpose flour plus more for surface
- 1/2 cup (1 stick) chilled unsalted butter, cut into 1/2-inch cubes
- 1/2 tsp. kosher salt
- 2/3 cup plus 3 tbsps. sugar
- 2 1/2 tbsps. cornstarch
- 1 tsp. finely grated lemon zest plus 2 tbsps. fresh lemon juice
- 5 cups (1 lb. 10 oz.) fresh blueberries
- 3/4 cup unbleached all-purpose flour
- 3 tbsps. (packed) light brown sugar
- 1/2 tsps. cinnamon
- 1/4 tsp. salt
- 5 tbsps. unsalted butter, melted, cooled slightly
- A 9"-9 1/2"-diameter glass or metal pie dish, pie weights or dried beans to bake the crust.

Direction

- Prepare crust: Using a food processor, pulse salt, butter, and 1 1/4 cups of flour until the mixture looks like coarse meal with remaining few pea-sized pieces. Add 3 tbsp. of ice water into the mixture. Pulse until mixture forms moist clumps, pouring more water by teaspoonfuls if dry. On a lightly floured work surface, place the dough. Split into 4 portions. Work one piece at a time, smear each part of the dough twice in a forward motion to distribute the butter using your hand's heel. Gather all the 4 pieces of dough into a ball. Flatten the dough into a disk, use plastic to wrap and for at least 1 hour, chill until the dough becomes firm.
- On a lightly floured surface, roll the dough out into a 13-inch round. Put into a pie dish and slowly press the dough to the bottom and up to the sides of the dish. Fold the overhang

- under and crease edges decoratively. Using a fork, pierce the bottom of the crust on different portions. For about 30 minutes, chill until it becomes firm.
- Prepare a large baking sheet by lining with foil. Position rack at the center of the oven and set the oven to 375°F for preheating. Use a parchment paper or foil for lining the crust and add in pie weights to fill crust. Bake crust for about 20 minutes until set. Gently peel off the parchment and take out the pie weights. For about 12 minutes more, bake crust until pale golden. Place crust into a wire rack. Set aside to cool.
- Preparation of topping and filling: In a large bowl, beat lemon zest, cornstarch, and 2/3 cups of sugar. Stir in lemon juice and blueberries; coat by tossing gently and distribute evenly. For 20 to 30 minutes, set aside filling while occasionally tossing, until berries release its juices.
- In a medium bowl, beat the leftover 3 tbsps. of sugar, cinnamon, light brown sugar, flour, and salt. Stir in the melted butter. Combine topping with your fingertips to incorporate.
- Assembling: Set oven to 375°; preheat. Scoop the blueberry filling into the crust. Sprinkle over the topping. For about 1 hour and 15 minutes, bake until pie filling starts bubbling and the topping turns golden. If the browning is too quick, cover with foil after 30 minutes.
- Allow pie to cool in the wire rack.
- The dough can be done 2-days in advance. Keep it chilled.
- Pie can be baked 8 hours in advance. Set aside in room temperature.

Nutrition Information

- Calories: 394
- Total Carbohydrate: 53 g
- Cholesterol: 50 mg
- Total Fat: 19 g
- Fiber: 1 g
- Protein: 4 g
- Sodium: 195 mg
- Saturated Fat: 12 g

49. Blueberry Granita

"A cool and refreshing treat."
Serving: 4 | Prep: 15m | Ready in: 4h15m

Ingredients

- 2 1/2 cups blueberries
- 1/2 cup white sugar
- 3/4 cup water
- 1 tbsp. fresh lemon juice

Direction

- In food processor, process sugar and blueberries till smooth; drain using a fine-mesh strainer, forcing using wooden spoon to release blueberry puree from chunks of seeds or skin.
- In a glass, shallow baking dish or tray, mix the water, lemon juice and strained blueberry puree. Freeze dish; mix and scrape mixture of blueberry using fork one time per hour till equally icy and frozen, for 4 hours. Scrape to lighten and fluff ice crystals; scoop to cold glasses and serve.

Nutrition Information

- Calories: 149 calories;
- Total Carbohydrate: 38.5 g
- Cholesterol: 0 mg
- Total Fat: 0.3 g
- Protein: 0.7 g
- Sodium: 2 mg

50. Blueberry Shortbread Cheesecake

"This blueberry cheesecake has a different crust instead of one with graham crackers."
Serving: 12 | Prep: 30m | Ready in: 9h35m

Ingredients

- 3/4 cup unsalted butter
- 2 cups all-purpose flour
- 1/2 cup packed light brown sugar
- 1/2 tsp. salt
- 2 (8 oz.) packages cream cheese, softened
- 3 eggs
- 1 cup white sugar
- 1 pint sour cream
- 1 tsp. vanilla extract
- zest from 1 lemon
- 1 quart blueberries
- 1 cup white sugar
- 3 tbsps. cornstarch

Direction

- Set the oven to 175 degrees Celsius or 350 degrees Fahrenheit. In a food processor, combine salt, sugar, flour, and butter, process until it forms small lumps, then press it into the bottom of a baking dish (2 quarts).
- Bake until it turns golden brown, around 20 minutes, then take out of the oven. Turn down the oven heat to 165 degrees Celsius or 325 degrees Fahrenheit.
- In a bowl, beat together 1 cup sugar and cream cheese until creamy and soft. Stir in one egg at a time until it becomes smooth. Slowly stir in the lemon zest, vanilla, and sour cream, then pour the mixture onto the crust.
- Bake until it is firm to touch, about 45-55 minutes. At the same time, make the topping by blending cornstarch, sugar, and blueberries in a big saucepan over medium heat, cook until it thickens. Let the mixture cool.
- Pour the cool blueberry mixture atop the cream cheese layer. Chill the assembled cheesecake in the refrigerator overnight.

Nutrition Information

- Calories: 613 calories;
- Total Carbohydrate: 71.3 g
- Cholesterol: 135 mg
- Total Fat: 34.2 g
- Protein: 8.3 g
- Sodium: 331 mg

51. Bourbon Walnut Pie

"A very lovely dish."
Serving: Makes 8 to 10 servings

Ingredients

- 2 cups all purpose flour
- 1 tsp. sugar
- 1/4 tsp. salt
- 3/4 cup (1 1/2 sticks) chilled unsalted butter, cut into 1/2-inch pieces
- 1 large egg
- 1 tbsp. milk
- 1 cup dark corn syrup
- 1/2 cup sugar
- 3 large eggs
- 2 tbsps. (1/4 stick) unsalted butter, melted
- 2 tbsps. bourbon
- 1 1/2 tbsps. all purpose flour
- 1 tsp. vanilla extract
- 1/4 tsp. salt
- 3/4 cup chopped walnuts (about 3 oz.)
- 3/4 cup walnut halves (about 3 oz.)

Direction

- Crust: blend salt, sugar and flour in processor. Add butter; process till it looks like coarse meal with on/off turns. Whisk milk and egg to blend in small bowl; put in processor. Blend till you get moist clumps. Gather dough to a ball; flatten to a disk. Use plastic to wrap dough; refrigerate for 1 hour. You can prep dough 2 days ahead, kept refrigerated. Before rolling out, soften dough slightly.

- Filling: Preheat an oven to 350°F. Whisk salt, vanilla, flour, bourbon, butter, eggs, sugar and syrup to blend in a big bowl; mix in all the walnuts.
- Roll dough out to 14-in. round on floured surface; put in 9-in. diameter glass pie dish then fold edge under; decoratively crimp. Put filling in prepped crust; bake for 55 minutes till filling is set in middle when pie gets slightly shaken and crust is golden; fully cool pie in pan on rack.

Nutrition Information

- Calories: 631
- Total Carbohydrate: 75 g
- Cholesterol: 147 mg
- Total Fat: 32 g
- Fiber: 2 g
- Protein: 9 g
- Sodium: 253 mg
- Saturated Fat: 16 g

52. Brazilian Banana And White Chocolate Ice Cream Torte

"A perfect combination between rich ice cream with a nut crust and thick fudge sauce."
Serving: Serves 12

Ingredients

- 3 cups walnuts (about 12 oz.)
- 1 cup whole almonds
- 1/3 cup firmly packed dark brown sugar
- 1/4 cup (1/2 stick) unsalted butter, melted, cooled
- 3 cups whipping cream
- 1 cup half and half
- 3/4 cup sugar
- 4 large egg yolks
- 8 oz. imported white chocolate (such as Lindt), chopped
- 1 1/2 lbs. very ripe bananas
- 3 tbsps. fresh lemon juice
- 3/4 cup whipping cream
- 1/4 cup light corn syrup
- 8 oz. bittersweet (not unsweetened) or semisweet chocolate, chopped
- 3 large ripe bananas, peeled, cut on diagonal into 1/4-inch-wide slices
- 15 small strawberries with stems

Direction

- To make crust: Start preheating the oven to 350 deg F. In a processor, add sugar and all nuts, finely chop. Blend in butter until thoroughly combined. In the 9-inch-diameter springform pan, press mixture firmly 2 3/4-in.-high onto sides and the bottom. Let it freeze for 10 minutes. Bake for 20 minutes until light brown. Transfer to rack, cool.
- To make Ice Cream: In a heavy medium pot, simmer 1 cup cream, sugar, and half and half, stir occasionally. In a medium bowl, beat yolks. Add hot cream mixture into bowl, whisk. Put mixture back in pot, stirring over medium-low heat about 5 minutes, until custard is thick and a path remains on the back of a spoon whey a finger is drawn across, do not to let it boil. In a bowl, strain the mixture. Whisk in white chocolate until melted. Add remaining 2 cups cream into the bowl, combine. Let it cool down until cold.
- Peel and chop 1 1/2 lbs. of bananas. In processor, make a puree with lemon juice and bananas. Add puree into the custard, combine. Put in ice cream maker and process following the manufacturer's directions. In prepared crust, spoon ice cream; make top smooth. Cover and place in freezer overnight. You can make it 1 week ahead, keep it frozen.
- To make sauce: In medium pot, simmer syrup and cream. Lower heat to low. Whisk in chocolate until smooth. Let cool to lukewarm. (You can make 1 day ahead. Cover and cool. Before using, rewarm over low heat; remember not to boil.)
- Take pan sides off the torte. Top ice cream with strawberries and bananas in rows. Best served with sauce.

53. Brazilian Peanut Fudge

"Sweet treat that is like fudge with a hint of saltiness."
Serving: 12 | Prep: 10m | Ready in: 25m

Ingredients

- 1 (8 oz.) jar roasted peanuts, skins removed
- 1 (8 oz.) package tea biscuits (such as Marie Biscuits)
- 2 tbsps. white sugar
- 1 (14 oz.) can sweetened condensed milk

Direction

- Line a 9-inch square dish using waxed paper.
- In a food processor, blend the biscuits and peanuts together until the mixture forms coarse flour. Put in the sugar and blend until combined. Add the sweetened, condensed milk to the mixture and pulse until the mixture holds a ball that pulls away from the sides of the processor bowl.
- Remove the mixture to the lined dish and pat into an even layer with your hands. Let sit no less than 15 minutes, up to overnight. Take out of the dish and slice into squares to serve. Put in air-tight containers to store between uses.

Nutrition Information

- Calories: 306 calories;
- Total Carbohydrate: 37.9 g
- Cholesterol: 11 mg
- Total Fat: 14.7 g
- Protein: 8.3 g
- Sodium: 268 mg

54. Broccoli Trees With Creamy White-bean Dip

"A dairy-free dip."
Serving: Makes 8 (side dish or hors d'oeuvre) servings | Prep: 25m

Ingredients

- 2 lb. broccoli, cut into 1 1/2-inch-wide spears
- 1 garlic clove
- 1 (19-oz.) can white beans such as cannellini, drained and rinsed
- 3/4 cup silken tofu (6 1/2 oz.), drained and gently rinsed
- 2 1/2 tbsps. fresh lemon juice
- 1 tbsp. extra-virgin olive oil
- 1/4 tsp. ground cumin
- Pinch of cayenne

Direction

- Blanch broccoli for 2 minutes in a pot with boiling salted water, 6-qt. water to 1 tbsp. salt, uncovered. In a colander, drain. Plunge colander with broccoli immediately into ice bath to cease cooking; drain. Spread out broccoli on a kitchen towel; dry. Broccoli will stay crisp.
- Through feed tube, drop garlic as food processor's motor runs; process till chopped finely. Add 1/2 tsp. salt and leftover ingredients but broccoli; puree till smooth. Through fine-mesh sieve, force dip into bowl; discard solids. Serve dip with broccoli.
- You can cook broccoli 1 day ahead, chilled in sealed bag. You can make dip 2 days ahead, covered, chilled. Before serving, bring to room temperature.

Nutrition Information

- Calories: 148
- Total Carbohydrate: 23 g
- Total Fat: 3 g
- Fiber: 6 g
- Protein: 10 g
- Sodium: 44 mg

- Saturated Fat: 1 g

55. Bruschetta With Hummus

"Bruschetta with hummus, topped with tomatoes and feta cheese."

Serving: 6 | Prep: 20m | Ready in: 8h23m

Ingredients

- 1 (14 oz.) can garbanzo beans, drained
- 3 tbsps. fresh lemon juice
- 1/4 tsp. chopped fresh garlic
- 1/4 tsp. ground cumin
- 2 tsps. olive oil
- 1/4 cup butter, softened
- 12 slices ciabatta bread
- 1/4 cup grated Parmesan cheese
- 1 tsp. paprika
- 24 slices roma (plum) tomatoes
- 1/2 cup crumbled feta cheese
- 1 tsp. dried oregano
- 1 tsp. garlic powder

Direction

- In a food processor, add olive oil, cumin, garlic, lemon juice, and drained garbanzos. Process for 1 minute until blended. Transfer hummus to the refrigerator and chill overnight. Before making bruschetta, bring the hummus to room temperature.
- Layer 1 tsp. of butter on each ciabatta slice and sprinkle 1 tsp. of Parmesan cheese. Broil for 3 minutes until ciabatta slices are golden. Take out from the oven and layer a tablespoonful of hummus. Dust paprika over.
- Top each slice with feta cheese and slices of tomatoes, and dust with garlic powder and oregano. Serve.

Nutrition Information

- Calories: 534 calories;
- Total Carbohydrate: 76.4 g
- Cholesterol: 34 mg
- Total Fat: 17.8 g
- Protein: 17.2 g
- Sodium: 1112 mg

56. Butter Pie Crust

Serving: Makes 2 nine-inch deep-dish crusts

Ingredients

- 2 1/2 cups all purpose flour
- 1 tbsp. sugar
- 3/4 tsp. salt
- 1 cup (2 sticks) chilled unsalted butter, cut into 1/2-inch cubes
- 6 tbsps. (about) ice water

Direction

- In processor, mix salt, sugar and flour. Add butter; pulse till coarse meal forms. Blend in enough of ice water slowly to make moist clumps. Bring dough to ball; halve. Shape dough to 2 balls and flatten to disks. In plastic, wrap each; chill for 2 hours – overnight.

Nutrition Information

- Calories: 1407
- Total Carbohydrate: 126 g
- Cholesterol: 244 mg
- Total Fat: 94 g
- Fiber: 4 g
- Protein: 17 g
- Sodium: 745 mg
- Saturated Fat: 59 g

57. Buttercrust Pastry Dough

"Be sure to use ice cold water and frozen butter. For a savory recipe, cut down sugar a bit."

Serving: 6 | Prep: 15m | Ready in: 1h15m

Ingredients

- 2 cups all-purpose flour, divided
- 1/2 cup butter, cut into 12 cubes, frozen
- 1 tbsp. sugar
- 1 tsp. salt
- 6 tbsps. ice water

Direction

- Into food processor's bowl, put blade insert. Add 1 cup flour; sprinkle flour with frozen butter cubes. Add salt, sugar and leftover 1 cup flour; cover. In short on and off bursts, pulse for 1 minute till butter looks crumbly and breaks to small pieces. Drizzle in ice water; with longer on and off pulses, pulse for 10-12 seconds till it looks like crumbs and is pale yellow. Use spatula to scrape down sides; pulse 1-2 times.
- Put mixture on work surface. Bring together pieces to make tight round dough ball; slightly flatten. In plastic wrap, wrap; refrigerate for minimum of 1 hour – overnight prior to rolling out.

Nutrition Information

- Calories: 295 calories;
- Total Carbohydrate: 33.9 g
- Cholesterol: 41 mg
- Total Fat: 15.8 g
- Protein: 4.5 g
- Sodium: 498 mg

58. Buttermilk Corn Bread

Serving: Makes 12 servings

Ingredients

- 1 1/3 cups all purpose flour
- 1 1/3 cups yellow cornmeal
- 2 tsps. baking powder
- 1 tsp. salt
- 3/4 tsp. baking soda
- 1 1/3 cups buttermilk
- 1/2 cup (1 stick) unsalted butter, melted
- 2 large eggs

Direction

- Preheat an oven to 375 °F. Butter square 9 inches baking pan. Into medium bowl, sift baking soda, salt, baking powder, cornmeal and flour. In big bowl, beat eggs, butter and buttermilk to incorporate. Put the dry ingredients and mix barely till combined. Into prepped pan, put the batter.
- Bake for half an hour till surrounding edges are golden brown and an inserted tester into middle gets out clean. Cool in the pan on a rack. May be done in advance. Place cover and allow to sit at room temperature for up to 2 days or 2 weeks in freezer.

Nutrition Information

- Calories: 206
- Total Carbohydrate: 26 g
- Cholesterol: 52 mg
- Total Fat: 9 g
- Fiber: 1 g
- Protein: 5 g
- Sodium: 205 mg
- Saturated Fat: 5 g

59. Buttermilk Pie Crust Dough

Serving: Makes enough for 2 crusts

Ingredients

- 2 1/2 cups unbleached all purpose flour
- 2 tbsps. sugar
- 1 tsp. salt
- 1/2 cup (1 stick) chilled unsalted butter, diced
- 1/2 cup chilled solid vegetable shortening
- 1/4 cup plus 2 tbsps. buttermilk

Direction

- In a big bowl, combine salt, sugar, and flour, then add the shortening and butter. Use a pastry blender or your hands to cut them in until the mixture looks like a coarse meal. Pour in the buttermilk and use a fork to stir to form moist clumps. You can make the dough in the processor. Use on/off turns to cut the shortening and butter into the dry ingredients to form a coarse meal. Pour in the buttermilk and process to form moist clumps. Press the mixture together to form the dough and divide in half. Gather them into balls and flatten into disks. Separately wrap and chill for 1 hour. You can make this ahead, keep refrigerated for 1 week or freeze for 1 month. Allow the dough to sit at room temperature to slightly soften before you use it.

Nutrition Information

- Calories: 1496
- Total Carbohydrate: 134 g
- Cholesterol: 124 mg
- Total Fat: 99 g
- Fiber: 4 g
- Protein: 18 g
- Sodium: 751 mg
- Saturated Fat: 42 g

60. Butternut Squash Flan

"Healthy and yummy."
Serving: Makes 18 spa servings or 9 standard servings

Ingredients

- 1 small butternut squash (about 1 1/2 lbs.), halved length-wise and seeded
- 1 1/2 cups whole milk
- 4 large egg whites
- 2 large eggs
- 1/4 cup maple syrup
- 3 tbsps. pure vanilla extract
- 1 1/2 tsps. ground ginger
- 1 tsp. ground cinnamon
- 1/2 tsp. ground nutmeg
- 1/4 tsp. ground cloves
- Garnish: fresh berries, kiwi or orange slices, and mint sprigs (optional)

Direction

- Preheat an oven to 350°F. Line nonstick liner/parchment paper on big rimmed baking sheet.
- Put squash on baking sheet, cut side down; roast for 40-50 minutes till fully tender when knife pierces it. Scoop out flesh when cool enough to handle; discard skin. Put 1 1/2 cups in a food processor. Keep leftover for another time.
- From skin, scrape squash flesh; put 1 1/2 cups into food processor. Put aside.
- Heat warm milk in double boiler/metal bowl above pan with simmering water till steaming. Put into squash in processor; puree for 1-3 minutes till very smooth. Add cloves, nutmeg, cinnamon, ginger, vanilla, maple syrup, eggs and egg whites; process for 30-60 seconds till smooth.
- Evenly divide batter to 9 5-oz. or 18 3-oz. custard cups/ramekins. Put ramekins into big roasting pan; add hot water into pan to reach halfway up ramekin's sides. Use foil to cover whole pan; bake for 32-35 for 5-oz. ramekins or 22-25 minutes for 3-oz. ramekins till flans set in center.

- Put roasting pan on cooling rack; rest flans in water till room temperature, uncovered. Take ramekins from water; refrigerate for 3 hours till thoroughly chilled.
- Serve flans in ramekins. Alternately, slide around each ramekin's side with flexible knife, slightly pulling from bottom to break the seal. Cover using dessert plate; to unmold, invert. Garnish with mint sprigs and fruit; serve.
- Refrigerate ramekins uncovered to prevent condensation or cover once chilled for longer storage because they're creamier if chilled before serving.

61. Butternut Squash Soup With Green Chili Coriander Chutney

Serving: Makes about 10 cups, serving 8

Ingredients

- 1/4 cup sliced blanched almonds
- 1/4 cup sweetened flaked coconut
- 2 jalapeño chilies, (wear rubber gloves)
- 2 cups loosely packed coriander
- 2 cups chopped onion
- 2 tbsps. butter
- 2 tbsps. vegetable oil
- a 3- to 3 1/2-lb. butternut squash, peeled, halved, the seeds and strings discarded, and the flesh cut into 1/2-inch pieces
- 6 cups chicken broth
- two 4-inch strips of orange zest
- 1 1/2 cups freshly squeezed orange juice
- 8 coriander sprigs for garnish

Direction

- Prep chutney: process 1/3 cup of water, a pinch of salt, jalapeño, coconut and almonds in food processor or blender till mixture is finely ground. Put in coriander; process mixture till finely ground. (This recipe makes dry chutney, which has a bit grainy texture.) You can make chutney 8 hours ahead; keep in refrigerator with cover. Yields approximately a cup.
- Prep soup: cook onion in oil and butter in kettle on medium low heat while mixing, till soften, put in half cup of water and squash; let mixture cook with cover, on medium low heat for 20 minutes to half an hour, or till squash softens. Put in zest, juice and broth, and let mixture simmer about 15 minutes, with no cover. Purée mixture in a food processor or blender doing it in batches then filter using a sieve right in a big bowl. Soup can be done one day ahead; keep in refrigerator with cover.
- Scoop soup to eight bowls and jazz every serving up with a coriander sprig and approximately 1 tbsp. chutney, to mix in soup.

Nutrition Information

- Calories: 331
- Total Carbohydrate: 47 g
- Cholesterol: 13 mg
- Total Fat: 16 g
- Fiber: 13 g
- Protein: 11 g
- Sodium: 283 mg
- Saturated Fat: 4 g

62. Cajun Ham Salad Sandwiches

"This deviled ham is not too spicy and made with leftover spiral ham."
Serving: 4 | Prep: 20m | Ready in: 20m

Ingredients

- 6 sweet bread and butter pickles
- 1/4 red onion, cut into large chunks
- 2 stalks celery, cut into large chunks
- 10 oz. baked ham, trimmed and cut into 1-inch chunks
- 2 tbsps. mayonnaise
- 1 tbsp. whole-grain Dijon mustard
- 1/2 tsp. Cajun seasoning (optional)
- 8 slices rye bread
- 8 lettuce leaves

Direction

- In a food processor, combine celery, onion, and pickles, then pulse to make it medium-fine. Add the ham and pulse to make 1/4 inch-diameter pieces.
- In a bowl, stir Cajun seasoning, Dijon mustard, mayonnaise, and the ham mixture.
- Divide the ham salad mixture into 4 rye bread slices and lay 2 lettuce leaves onto each one. Cover with the remaining slices of bread.

Nutrition Information

- Calories: 466 calories;
- Total Carbohydrate: 50.3 g
- Cholesterol: 42 mg
- Total Fat: 20.7 g
- Protein: 19 g
- Sodium: 1806 mg

63. Cantaloupe Gelato

Serving: Makes about 1 quart

Ingredients

- 1 cup minus 1 tbsp. superfine granulated sugar
- 1/2 cup plus 1 tbsp. bottled or filtered still water (not distilled)
- 1 cantaloupe (about 3 lbs.)
- 2 tbsps. fresh lemon juice
- 1 tbsp. lightly beaten egg white*
- If egg safety is a problem in your area, substitute powdered egg whites reconstituted by following package instructions.

Direction

- Heat water and sugar in a heavy, small saucepan, mixing till sugar dissolves. Let syrup cool down. Trim rind from melon and get rid of the seeds. Slice melon making chunks and purée in food processor sufficient to get 2 cups. Pour the purée into bowl and mix in lemon juice and syrup. Refrigerate mixture of melon till cold for maximum of 24 hours.
- Mix egg white in; transfer ice-cream maker to freeze. Serve gelato right or put into an airtight container freeze to solidify for maximum of 3 hours.

64. Caramel Macadamia Nut Crunch

"This recipe calls just for 1/4 of Ming Tsai's butter shortbread cookie dough."
Serving: Makes 20 cookies

Ingredients

- 1 cup sugar
- 1 cup heavy cream
- 1 lb. macadamia pieces, or whole nuts, roughly chopped
- 1 chilled log of butter shortbread cookie dough

Direction

- Heat an oven to 325 degrees F. Oil one baking sheet, desirably with rim.
- Mix half cup water and sugar in a medium-size saucepan. Heat on moderate heat for 3 minutes, till mixture starts to come to a simmer. Put on pan cover and keep on simmering, letting steam from the cooking mixture to wash down the pan sides. Uncover and keep simmering for 7 to 8 minutes till mixture becomes golden. Take off from stove immediately, and, add cream cautiously in a steady, slow stream in pan to prevent mixture from bubbling over; avid mixing. Set pot back to stove, turn the heat to low, and slowly mix mixture with wooden spoon, till cream incorporates fully.
- Turn the caramel into a heat-proof, medium-size bowl, put in nuts, and mix to cover nuts equally. Pour the mixture into baking sheet, scattering it smoothly, and bake 12 to 15 minutes, till dark brown. Let brittle cool down

to room temperature and, in food processor, by hand or a cleaver, coarsely chop mixture.
- Slice log making 20 rounds measuring half-inch, force 1 cut side of every round to brittle, and place rounds on a parchment-covered or nonstick cookie sheet(s), spacing 2-inch apart on every side.
- Bake for 15 to 20 minutes till golden brown in color. Take cookies using spatula and transfer onto a wire rack to cool.

65. Caramel-glazed Walnut Cake

Serving: Serves 8

Ingredients

- 8 1-inch-thick slices French bread, crust trimmed, bread cut into cubes
- 1 1/2 cups walnuts, lightly toasted
- 1 cup sugar
- 4 large egg yolks
- 2 tbsps. dark rum
- 4 tsps. instant espresso coffee powder dissolved in 1 tsp. water
- 1 tsp. grated lemon peel
- 6 large egg whites
- Pinch of salt
- 1/2 cup sugar
- 2 tbsps. water
- 8 walnut halves

Direction

- To make the cake: Set the oven to 350 degrees Fahrenheit. Butter a 9 inch spingform pan and line the bottom using parchment paper, then butter it. Use flour to dust the pan. Grind the bread finely in a processor and spread onto a baking sheet. Bake until it turns golden, occasionally stirring, around 10 minutes. Grind the breadcrumbs finely using a processor, measure out 3/4 cup of crumbs and reserve the leftovers for another recipe. Grind the nuts finely in a processor.
- Use an electric mixer to beat the yolks with 3/4 cup of sugar in a big bowl until it thickens, around 3 minutes. Beat in peel, coffee powder mixture, and rum. Mix in the ground nuts and 3/4 cup of crumbs. In another big bowl, beat together salt and whites to form soft peaks. Slowly add the leftover 1/4 cup of sugar, beating until it is stiff. Fold 1/3 of the whites into the batter and fold in the remainder in 2 batches.
- Spoon the batter in the pan and bake until a tester comes out clean once inserted in the center, roughly 45 minutes. Cool the cake in the pan on a rack for 10 minutes and turn the cake out. Peel off the parchment and turn the cake over, then cool on the rack for 15 minutes.
- Use foil to line a baking sheet and grease lightly with oil. Place the cake on it.
- To make the caramel: In a medium heavy pan, combine water and sugar and stir over medium-low heat until the sugar has dissolved. Turn up the heat to medium-high and boil without mixing until it is amber, using a wet pastry brush to brush the pan sides down and occasionally swirling the pan, around 6 minutes.
- Pour the caramel over the cake top. Oil the knife tip and cut through the caramel layer only right away to mark out 8 servings. Garnish with the walnut halves and completely cool.

Nutrition Information

- Calories: 268
- Total Carbohydrate: 44 g
- Cholesterol: 92 mg
- Total Fat: 7 g
- Fiber: 1 g
- Protein: 6 g
- Sodium: 143 mg
- Saturated Fat: 1 g

66. Caramel-orange Bûche De Noël

"Decorate this version of Christmas log with fresh currants or Candied Cranberries."
Serving: Serves 8

Ingredients

- 6 large egg yolks
- 1/3 cup firmly packed dark brown sugar
- 2 tbsps. all purpose flour
- 1 1/2 cups half and half
- 8 oz. imported white chocolate (such as Lindt), chopped
- 1 1/2 tsps. grated orange peel
- 1 1/2 cups toasted sliced almonds
- 2 tbsps. unbleached all purpose flour
- 6 large eggs, separated
- 10 tbsps. firmly packed dark brown sugar
- 1 tsp. grated orange peel
- 1/2 tsp. vanilla extract
- 1/2 tsp. cream of tartar
- 1/8 tsp. salt
- Powdered sugar
- 1 cup (2 sticks) unsalted butter, room temperature
- 1 tbsp. Grand Marnier or other orange liqueur
- Pine twigs
- 1 cup sugar
- 2 tbsps. water
- 1/2 cup cranberries

Direction

- To make buttercream: In a medium bowl, whisk flour, sugar and egg yolks till well blended. In a heavy medium saucepan, simmer half-and-half then gradually whisk the hot half-and-half into the egg mixture. Bring the egg mixture back to the same saucepan then cook while constantly stirring till boil and thick. Place the mixture into a medium bowl. Stir orange peel and chocolate into the mixture till smooth. Press onto the pastry cream surface with plastic wrap to prevent the skin forming. Let cool completely. You can prepare pastry cream 1 day ahead and store in the fridge. Before continuing, bring to room temperature.
- To make cake: Preheat the oven to 300°F. Spread butter and line parchment on an 11x17-in. jelly roll pan. Spread butter and flour on the parchment. In a processor, coarsely grind flour with toasted almonds. In a medium bowl, use an electric mixer to beat 5 tbsp. of brown sugar with yolks till it forms slowly dissolving ribbons when you lift off the beaters. Stir in vanilla extract and orange peel. In a large bowl, beat salt and cream of tartar with whites using a clean dry beaters till it forms soft peaks. Slowly add in the leftover 5 tbsp. of brown sugar and beat till stiff but not dry. Fold whites into the yolk mixture and fold in almond mixture gently.
- Evenly spread batter in the prepped pan. Bake for 30 minutes till a toothpick comes out clean after being inserted into the middle. Let a small sharp knife run around sides of the pan if needed to loosen the cake. Let the cake on parchment slide onto rack and cool.
- Let the cake on parchment slide onto a work surface. Use knife as aid to loosen cake from the parchment. Sift over the cake with powdered sugar then invert the cake onto a cookie sheet. Sprinkle powdered sugar over then invert onto a separate parchment sheet.
- In a large bowl, use an electric mixer to beat butter till fluffy and light. Add in Grand Marnier and beat. Add 1/4 cup of pastry cream at a time, beat to blend after each addition.
- Spread over the cake with 1/2 of the buttercream, leave 1/2-in. on the border. Roll up the cake jelly roll fashion, begin at 1 long side then place on parchment, seam side facing down. Put aside 1/2 cup of buttercream then spread over cake with the leftover buttercream. At each end of the cake, cut 2 inches off on diagonal. Move the cake onto a platter. Form branches by attach ends of the cake to top. Spread over the seams and the cake ends with the reserved 1/2 cup of buttercream. Cover and store in the fridge till the buttercream is firm, for at least 1 hour. You

can prepare the cake for 1 day ahead. Store in the fridge, covered. Before serving, allow the cake to stand for 20 minutes at room temperature.
- Place pine twigs on platter and on the cake. Add cranberries for garnish.
- To prepare cranberries: In a heavy small saucepan, cook 2 tbsp. of water and 1/2 cup of sugar over low heat, stir to dissolve the sugar. Place on top of a double boiler then place in cranberries. Cover the berry mixture and set over simmering water to cook and stir occasionally for 45 minutes. Take away from over the water and allow the cranberry mixture to stand overnight at room temperature.
- Spread the leftover 1/2 cup of sugar on a plate. Drain well the cranberries then place on the sugar and turn till coated. Allow to dry for at least 30 minutes. You can prepare this 3 days in advance. Cover and store in the fridge.

Nutrition Information

- Calories: 900
- Total Carbohydrate: 84 g
- Cholesterol: 362 mg
- Total Fat: 58 g
- Fiber: 4 g
- Protein: 16 g
- Sodium: 152 mg
- Saturated Fat: 27 g

67. Caramelized Nut Tart

"Winter tart that works nicely with any combination of nuts."
Serving: Serves 10

Ingredients

- 1 1/2 cups all purpose flour
- 2 tbsps. sugar
- 1/2 tsp. ground cinnamon
- 1/4 tsp. ground nutmeg
- 1/4 tsp. salt
- 1/2 cup (1 stick) chilled unsalted butter, cut into 1/2-inch pieces
- 1 tsp. vanilla extract
- 3 tbsps. (about) ice water
- 1 1/4 cups sugar
- 1/4 cup water
- 2/3 cup whipping cream
- 2 tbsps. (1/4 stick) unsalted butter, cut into small pieces
- 1 tbsp. honey
- 1 tsp. vanilla extract
- 1 cup walnuts, coarsely chopped
- 1/2 cup pecans, coarsely chopped
- 1/2 cup slivered blanched almonds
- 1 oz. good-quality white chocolate (such as Lindt or Baker's), chopped
- Whipped cream (optional)

Direction

- Prep crust: use processor to combine salt, nutmeg, cinnamon, sugar and flour. Put in butter. Pulse with on/off turns till mixture looks much like a coarse meal. Combine in vanilla and sufficient ice water by tablespoonfuls till moist clumps form. Collect the dough forming to a ball; flatten pat to a disk. Use plastic to wrap and chill for 2 hours till set.
- Heat an oven to 375 degrees F. Unroll dough on floured counter to make round that measures 12-inch. Remove dough into a 9 1/2-inch across tart pan with detachable base. Fold in the overhang and pinch to form double-thick, high-standing sides. Prick the entire dough using a fork. Place in freeze for about 15 minutes.
- Let crust bake for 20 minutes, till firm yet still light in color, pricking using fork in case crust bubbles. Turn onto rack; cool down. Raise the oven heat to 400 degrees F.
- Prep filling: in a medium, heavy saucepan, mix quarter cup water and sugar. Mix on moderately-low heat to dissolve the sugar. Raise the heat. Let boil without mixing for 9 minutes till caramel turn into a deep amber color, brushing down pan sides from time to

time using wet pastry brush and tilting the pan. Lowe the heat to moderate. Mix in cream slowly, (mixture will become bubbly). Mix till caramel becomes smooth. Put in honey, vanilla and butter. Mix till thoroughly incorporated. Stir in the entire nuts.
- Transfer mixture of caramel to crust. Bake for 20 minutes, till filling is entirely bubbling. Cool fully onto a rack.
- In double boiler top place above hot water, mix white chocolate barely till smooth and melted. Take off from above water. Sprinkle chocolate on top of tart in a decorative manner with fork. Rest till chocolate is firm, approximately half an hour. (May be done eight hours in advance. Rest at room temperature.)
- Serve along with cream, if wished.

Nutrition Information

- Calories: 505
- Total Carbohydrate: 50 g
- Cholesterol: 49 mg
- Total Fat: 33 g
- Fiber: 3 g
- Protein: 6 g
- Sodium: 71 mg
- Saturated Fat: 12 g

68. Caribbean-style Sofrito

"Sofrito is a vegetable and herb mixture popular in Cuba, Puerto Rico and the Dominican Republic and is used to season meat, bean, and rice dishes in Afro-Latin/Caribbean cuisine. Its salt-less flavor and genuine taste entices those not familiar with Caribbean cooking. It may be modified for vegans due to its vegetarian-friendly ingredients. Quantities of the ingredients may be revised to your personal liking."
Serving: 96 | Prep: 45m | Ready in: 45m

Ingredients

- 2 green bell peppers, cut into 1/4 inch cubes
- 2 red bell peppers, cut into 1/4 inch cubes
- 1 orange bell pepper, cut into 1/4 inch cubes
- 1 yellow bell pepper, cut into 1/4 inch cubes
- 10 tomatoes, cored and coarsely chopped
- 1 bunch green onions, chopped
- 1 1/2 bunches fresh cilantro leaves, chopped
- 6 fresh tomatillos, husks removed
- 1 cup chopped garlic

Direction

- In a blender or food processor bowl, add red, orange, yellow, and green bell peppers. Mix in tomatillos, tomatoes, green onions, garlic, and cilantro. Make a chunky or smooth mixture by blending or pulsing based on your choice. Place in a container and cover, it can last up to 5 days when refrigerated or 45 days when frozen.

Nutrition Information

- Calories: 8 calories;
- Total Carbohydrate: 1.7 g
- Cholesterol: 0 mg
- Total Fat: 0.1 g
- Protein: 0.4 g
- Sodium: 2 mg

69. Cashew Butter

"To avoid separating oil, keep refrigerated in a sealable container."
Serving: 34 | Prep: 15m | Ready in: 15m

Ingredients

- 3 cups unsalted cashews (such as Stock & Barrel®), divided
- 1/3 cup vegetable oil, or more as needed
- 1 tsp. sea salt

Direction

- While drizzling vegetable oil in mixture to make it move, process 1 cup cashews in bowl of food processor. Alternating with oil, put cashews in food processor; process. Add sea salt when all cashews are added; process for 10-15 minutes till you get preferred texture.

Nutrition Information

- Calories: 88 calories;
- Total Carbohydrate: 4 g
- Cholesterol: 0 mg
- Total Fat: 7.7 g
- Protein: 1.9 g
- Sodium: 129 mg

70. Cashew Nut Fudge

"This fudge is made using cashews soaked in water, drained, and cooked with sugar. You can also use walnuts, pistachios, or almonds."
Serving: Makes about 3 dozen pieces

Ingredients

- 2 cups raw cashew nuts (1/2 lb.)
- 3/4 cup sugar
- 1 tbsp. butter
- 2 tsps. rose water
- 3 three-inch-square pieces of silver foil (vark, optional)

Direction

- Place cashew nuts in a bowl and pour in boiling water to cover, then soak them for 1 hour. Drain and place in a food processor or electric blender container, reduce them to a fine paste, adding a bit of water or milk if it starts to clog.
- Grease a baking pan that's a 9-inch-square or mark out a 9-inch square on a cookie sheet and grease it.
- Heat up a nonstick frying pan (minimum of 9-inch diameter) over medium heat for about 2 minutes. Add the nut paste with the sugar. Turn the heat down to medium-low and cook while constantly stirring and scraping the bottom and sides of the pan using a flat spatula for about 20 minutes, or until the fudge is sticky and thick. Stir in butter.
- On the oiled square of cookie sheet or in the oiled pan, place the fudge. Use spatula to pat it gradually to spread evenly. Allow to cool well.
- Once cool, use rose water to brush the top and allow to briefly dry. Press silver foil on top of the fudge and cut 1 1/2-inch diamond or square pieces with a knife dipped in cold water.
- You can keep this at room temperature, sealed tightly, up to 3 weeks, or store inside the refrigerator for several months.
- The fudge is regularly garnished with edible silver leaf (as called varq or vark), real silver that is hammerced into sheets so tissue-thin that they are harmless to ingest. Silver leaf is sandwiched between two paper pieces because of its extreme fragility. To use it, peel off one paper piece and place the vark on top of the food with the metal side facing down. Pat the vark onto the food lightly and peel off the remaining paper piece.
- Add rose water to have a flowery essence.

71. Cauliflower Caraway Potato Soup

"You can make this in under 1 hour."
Serving: Makes about 3 1/2 cups, serving 2

Ingredients

- 1/2 lb. boiling potatoes
- 1/2 cup chopped cauliflower leaves
- 1/4 cup chopped white part of scallion
- 1/4 tsp. caraway seeds
- 2 cups 1-inch cauliflower flowerets
- 1/3 cup thinly sliced scallion greens
- freshly grated Parmesan to taste

Direction

- Simmer 3 1/2 cups water, caraway seeds, white part of scallion, cauliflower leaves and potatoes, peeled then cut to 1/2-in. pieces in a saucepan till potatoes are very tender for 15 minutes. Puree mixture coarse in a food processor/blender. Mix flowerets and puree in the pan; simmer soup till flowerets are tender for 5 minutes. Mix in pepper and salt to taste and scallion greens; serve soup with parmesan sprinkled over.

72. Cauliflower Fritters

"A nice way to enjoy cauliflower is having a battered and fried cauliflower. It's a good snack! They are lovely dunked in yogurt."
Serving: 12 | Prep: 30m | Ready in: 1h

Ingredients

- 1 head cauliflower, broken into small florets
- 1 onion
- 7 sprigs fresh parsley
- 5 cloves garlic
- 1 1/2 cups all-purpose flour
- 1 tsp. salt
- 1/4 tsp. ground black pepper
- 1 tsp. ground cumin
- 1 tsp. ground allspice
- 1/2 tsp. ground cinnamon
- 1/4 tsp. ground cloves
- 1/4 tsp. ground nutmeg
- 1 tsp. active dry yeast
- 1 cup warm water
- 1/4 cup vegetable oil
- 1/4 cup olive oil
- 4 eggs

Direction

- Parboil cauliflower for no more than ten minutes. It should remain firm. Put aside to cool.
- Finely slice together the parsley and onion in a food processor and then drain thoroughly. Use a pestle and mortar to crush the garlic or crush with bottom of a drinking glass.
- As the onion mixture is draining, in a large mixing bowl, mix nutmeg, cloves, cinnamon, allspice, cumin, pepper, salt and flour. Drizzle dry yeast atop flour. Mix crushed garlic together with warm water and place mixture atop flour. Combine thoroughly, then cover and put aside the dough for ten minutes to let it rise.
- Mix olive oil with vegetable oil and start heating in large saucepan (the oil should be half inch deep). Heat to a temperature of 180 degrees C (365 degrees F).
- Beat eggs until they're light and frothy. Then quickly fold them into dough. Add parsley, onions and cauliflower. Add flour in case the consistency of batter becomes too runny. Add water if too thick. Consistency should be just like a thick pancake batter that is not too thick and not too runny.
- Gently slide a spoonful of batter in the oil and then flatten by spreading it out. Cook 3 to 4 patties at a time on a medium-high heat while flipping until golden brown. Use a slotted spoon to remove the patties and place on paper towels to drain.

Nutrition Information

- Calories: 184 calories;
- Total Carbohydrate: 16.4 g
- Cholesterol: 62 mg
- Total Fat: 11.3 g
- Protein: 5.3 g
- Sodium: 326 mg

73. Cauliflower Soup With Pecorino Romano And Truffle Oil

"Truffle oil makes this soup special."
Serving: Makes 6 servings

Ingredients

- 2 oz. applewood-smoked bacon (about 2 1/2 slices), chopped
- 1 cup chopped onion
- 3/4 cup chopped celery
- 2 garlic cloves, chopped

- 6 cups 1-inch pieces cauliflower (cut from 1 large head)
- 3 1/2 cups (or more) low-salt chicken broth
- 1 3/4-inch cube Pecorino Romano cheese plus additional cheese shavings for serving
- 1/2 cup heavy whipping cream
- White or black truffle oil (for drizzling)

Direction

- In a big, heavy saucepan, sauté bacon on moderate heat till some fat releases and golden brown in color. Put in celery, garlic and onion. Cook with cover for 7 minutes, till vegetables are tender, mixing from time to time. Put in 3 1/2 cups broth, cauliflower and cheese cube. Boil. Lower the heat to moderately-low, and let simmer with cover for 20 minutes, till cauliflower soften.
- Use processor to puree soup in batches. Transfer back to same pan. Put in cream; let soup simmer. Add extra broth by quarter cupfuls to thin it if wished. Add pepper and salt to season. May be done a day in advance. Cool a bit; refrigerate with cover. Reheat then continue.
- Scoop soup in bowls. Scatter cheese shavings over; sprinkle with truffle oil.

74. Cauliflower Soup With Seared Scallops, Lemon Oil, And American Caviar

"An amazing recipe."
Serving: Makes 6 servings

Ingredients

- 3 tbsps. vegetable oil, divided
- 1 cup chopped white onion
- 1 garlic clove, sliced
- 3 3/4 cups (1/2- to 3/4-inch pieces cauliflower (from 1 large head)
- 1 1/2 cups low-salt chicken broth
- 1 1/2 cups whipping cream
- Coarse kosher salt
- Freshly ground white pepper
- 1 leek (white and pale green parts only), cut into 1/8-inch-thick rounds
- 6 sea scallops, patted dry
- 1 (30-gm) jar American white sturgeon caviar (about 1 oz.)
- 6 tsps. purchased lemon-infused grapeseed oil
- Finely chopped fresh chives

Direction

- Heat 2 tbsp. oil on medium heat in a big heavy saucepan. Add garlic and onion; sauté for 5 minutes till onion is soft. Add cream, broth and cauliflower; boil. Lower heat to low; cover partially. Gently simmer for 18 minutes till cauliflower is tender. In small batches, puree soup till smooth in blender. Put in same saucepan; season soup using white pepper and kosher salt. You can make it 1 day ahead; slightly cool. Cover; chill. Before serving, rewarm.
- Blanch leek for 1 minute in small saucepan with boiling salted water; drain. Put some leek in middle of every bowl. Heat leftover 1 tbsp. oil on high heat in medium skillet. Sprinkle pepper and salt on scallops; sear for 1 1/2 minutes per side till opaque in middle and brown. In every bowl, put 1 scallop on leek; put caviar on scallop. Put soup around scallop; drizzle 1 tsp. lemon oil. Sprinkle chives.

75. Celery Apple Gazpacho

Serving: Makes about 4 cups | Prep: 15m

Ingredients

- 8 to 9 celery ribs, chopped (3 cups)
- 1 Granny Smith apple, peeled and cored
- 1 1/2 cups cold water
- 1 tbsp. fresh lemon juice
- 1 tsp. salt
- 1 (3-inch) piece baguette, crust discarded
- 1/4 cup blanched almonds, chopped
- 2 tbsps. extra-virgin olive oil

- Garnish: thin celery matchstick curls

Direction

- Puree salt, lemon juice, water, apple and celery till smooth in a blender; chill mixture for 1 hour in a blender, covered. Reblend. Through a fine-mesh sieve, strain. Soak bread for 3 minutes in strained soup. Rinse blender; pulse almonds till ground finely. Add soup with bread; blend. In a slow stream, add oil as motor runs, blend till emulsified.

76. Celery Root Risotto And Pesto

"A fun pesto."
Serving: Makes 2 main-course servings

Ingredients

- 2 medium celery roots (celeriac) with leafy tops
- 1/4 cup olive oil
- 3 tbsps. butter
- 1 1/2 cups chopped leek (white and pale green parts only)
- 3/4 cup arborio or medium-grain white rice
- 3 cups (about) low-salt chicken broth
- 1 cup grated Parmesan cheese, divided

Direction

- Blend oil and 1 1/2 cups of packed celery root leaves till leaves are minced in mini-processor; season pesto with pepper and salt to taste.
- Peel celery roots and cut to 1/3-in. thick slices. Cut slices to 1/3-in. cubes to get 2 cups. Melt butter in big heavy saucepan on medium low heat. Mix in leek and celery root cubes; cover. Cook for 10 minutes till celery root is tender yet not brown, mixing often. Stir in rice; mix for 1 minute. Add broth and raise heat; boil. Lower heat; simmer for 20 minutes till risotto is creamy and rice is tender, occasionally mixing. Stir in 3/4 cup of cheese; season risotto with pepper and salt to taste.
- Divide risotto between bowls; swirl some pesto on top. Serve with remaining cheese and pesto.

Nutrition Information

- Calories: 1040
- Total Carbohydrate: 88 g
- Cholesterol: 84 mg
- Total Fat: 62 g
- Fiber: 4 g
- Protein: 36 g
- Sodium: 1058 mg
- Saturated Fat: 25 g

77. Charentais Granita With Chantilly Cream

"A contrast of both temperature and texture. Shredded orange peel adds to the melon's flavor and layering icy granita with whipped cream."
Serving: Makes 6 servings

Ingredients

- 1/2 cup sugar
- 1/2 cup water
- 1 1/2 tbsps. finely grated orange peel
- 3 cups chilled 1-inch cubes peeled seeded Charentais or other melon
- 1 cup chilled whipping cream
- 2 tbsps. powdered sugar
- Fresh mint sprigs (optional)

Direction

- How to prepare: mix half cup water, orange peel and sugar in small pot. Simmer on high heat, dissolve sugar by stirring. Lower heat to medium and simmer for a minute. Put into a pan, 8x8x2-in. and let cool.
- Make a puree with melon in a processor until smooth but make sure some texture remains. Put a scant two cups of melon puree and syrup in the pan. Blend completely by whisking. Freeze until completely frozen, for

about 4 hours; stir with fork every 1 and a half hours. Put cover on and keep frozen.
- Beat sugar and cream in moderate-sized bowl until peaks form with an electric mixer. Use fork to scrape granita in icy flakes. Scoop 2 rounded tbsp. granita in six glasses. Top with 1 rounded tbsp. whipped cream. Repeat layers again and top with mint sprigs, if wanted. Serve right away.

Nutrition Information

- Calories: 223
- Total Carbohydrate: 28 g
- Cholesterol: 44 mg
- Total Fat: 12 g
- Fiber: 1 g
- Protein: 2 g
- Sodium: 29 mg
- Saturated Fat: 8 g

78. Chargrilled Sirloin With Mash And Salsa Verde

"Get thick sirloin steaks, and grain-fed are best. Bring to room temperature first."
Serving: makes 4-6 servings

Ingredients

- 6 potatoes, peeled
- salt
- 1 1/2 oz. butter
- 1/2 tsp. freshly ground black pepper
- 1/2 cup light cream, hot
- 4 8 oz. thick sirloin steaks
- olive oil
- 4 tbsps. demi-glace, heated
- 1/2 bunch flat-leaf parsley
- 3 eggs, hard-boiled
- 10 anchovies
- 4 cloves garlic
- 2 slices bread, crusts removed, soaked in milk and gently squeezed dry
- 2 tbsps. capers
- 1 1/2 oz. parmesan cheese
- 5 tbsps. olive oil
- juice of 5 lemons
- salt and freshly ground black pepper

Direction

- Mashed potato: Cover potato in cold water in a saucepan. If desired, add salt. Boil; cover. Simmer till tender for 20-25 minutes. Drain; put potato in saucepan. Put saucepan on low heat; let potato and pan dry for 1 minute. Take off heat; mash potatoes using potato masher. Add pepper and butter; put on low heat. Vigorously mix with a wooden spoon. Add hot cream, or as much as needed, slowly till mixture is fluffy and light.
- Make salsa verde as potatoes cook. Blend all ingredients to a paste in a food processor.
- Chargrill sirloins. Turn on gas barbecue to be sure fire burns down to very hot embers. Rub pepper and olive oil on steaks. Put a grill above fire; cook for 8-10 minutes on both sides to get rare steak. Put into a warm place; rest for 15 minutes.
- Serve: Put steaks onto warm plates; put hot mashed potato alongside. Put heated demi-glace on steak; put salsa verde over.

Nutrition Information

- Calories: 1579
- Total Carbohydrate: 75 g
- Cholesterol: 457 mg
- Total Fat: 103 g
- Fiber: 11 g
- Protein: 89 g
- Sodium: 2098 mg
- Saturated Fat: 38 g

79. Charred Green Beans With Harissa And Almonds

"Easy and vibrant."
Serving: Makes 4 to 6 servings | Prep: 30m

Ingredients

- 1 small red bell pepper (about 7 oz.) or 1 roasted red pepper from jar
- 3 red jalapeños or Fresno chiles
- 3 garlic cloves, minced
- 1 tsp. kosher salt plus more for seasoning
- 3 tbsps. olive oil, divided
- 2 tbsps. fresh lemon juice
- 1/4 tsp. ground coriander
- 1/4 tsp. ground cumin
- Freshly ground black pepper
- 2 lbs. green beans, ends trimmed
- 1/4 cup roasted unsalted almonds, coarsely chopped

Direction

- Char jalapenos and bell peppers, if using fresh, till charred all over and soft for 12-15 minutes under broiler or directly above gas flame. Put in medium bowl; use plastic wrap to cover. Steam for 15 minutes.
- Peel, seed then mince jalapeno and bell peppers. Pulse 1 tsp. salt, garlic, chiles and peppers, scraping bowl's sides down, to make coarse paste in a food processor. Pulse in cumin, coriander, lemon juice and 1 tbsp. oil; season harissa with black pepper and salt.
- In medium bowl, put beans; drizzle leftover 2 tbsp. oil. Season with black pepper and salt; toss till coated. Heat big cast-iron skillet/other big heavy skillet on high heat. Cook beans in batches for 6-8 minutes till crisp tender yet charred and blistered in places, occasionally turning. Or, cook in grill basket on grill. Put in a big bowl; toss with almonds and harissa. Serve in room temperature/warm.

80. Cheddar Cauliflower Soup

""This soup is perfect for sneaking vegetables into your family's diet. Disguised vegetables benefit your family's diet. The carrots will give this dish the same color as adding the cheddar cheese. This blended dish is always a hit at our table and freezes very well.""
Serving: 6 | Prep: 20m | Ready in: 40m

Ingredients

- 1 tbsp. olive oil
- 1 onion, roughly chopped
- 3 cloves garlic, smashed
- 4 cups chicken broth
- 2 cups peeled and cubed potatoes
- 2 cups peeled and chopped carrot
- 1 large head cauliflower, stemmed and chopped
- 1/4 tsp. dried dill weed
- 1 pinch mustard powder
- 6 oz. grated Cheddar cheese
- salt and ground black pepper to taste

Direction

- Put olive oil in a large pot and heat it over medium heat. Stir in garlic and onion and cook for 5-7 minutes until the onion is transparent.
- Mix the carrots, chicken broth, and potatoes into the onion mixture. Boil the mixture before reducing the heat to medium-low. Simmer for 10-15 minutes until the potatoes and carrots are tender.
- Use a slotted spoon to strain the vegetables from the chicken broth. Working in batches, blend the vegetables in a food processor.
- Pour the pureed vegetables back into the broth. Simmer the mixture.
- Stir in dill, mustard powder, and cauliflower.
- In small batches, mix Cheddar cheese into the broth mixture for 5-10 minutes until the cheese is completely melted. Season the mixture with black pepper and salt.

Nutrition Information

- Calories: 238 calories;
- Total Carbohydrate: 23.4 g
- Cholesterol: 30 mg
- Total Fat: 12 g
- Protein: 11.6 g
- Sodium: 253 mg

81. Cheesy Thumbprint Appetizers With Hot Pepper Jelly

"Sweet and savory cookies filled with pepper jelly."
Serving: 20 | Prep: 15m | Ready in: 55m

Ingredients

- 2 cups shredded Cheddar cheese
- 1 cup all-purpose flour
- 6 tbsps. chilled butter, chopped
- 1/2 cup hot pepper jelly

Direction

- In a food processor, add butter, flour, and Cheddar cheese and blend until the dough forms into a ball and has a coarse-meal texture. Use plastic wrap to wrap the dough and transfer to the refrigerator to chill for 30 minutes.
- Preheat oven to 200°C/400°F.
- Divide the dough into 1 1/2-inch balls. Arrange on a baking sheet, 1 inch apart.
- Bake for 5 minutes. Remove from the oven and make an indentation on each ball by pressing your thumb down the top. Fill the indentation with 1 tsp. of pepper jelly. Bake for 5 minutes, or until the edges turn golden brown.

Nutrition Information

- Calories: 119 calories;
- Total Carbohydrate: 10.2 g
- Cholesterol: 21 mg
- Total Fat: 7.3 g
- Protein: 3.5 g
- Sodium: 97 mg

82. Chef John's Chocolate Energy Bars

"Healthy and cheap energy bar recipes."
Serving: 12 | Prep: 15m | Ready in: 3h

Ingredients

- 2 cups pitted Medjool dates, roughly chopped
- 2 cups raw cashews
- 1 cup raw or roasted unsalted almonds
- 3/4 cup high-quality unsweetened cocoa powder (such as Guittard® Cocoa Rouge)
- 2 tbsps. coconut oil, melted
- 1/2 cup unsweetened shredded coconut
- 2 tsps. vanilla extract
- 1 tbsp. cold espresso, or more as needed (or water)
- 1/2 tsp. kosher salt
- 1/2 pinch cayenne pepper

Direction

- In food processor bowl, put salt, cayenne, cold coffee, vanilla, coconut oil, cocoa, dates, coconut, almonds and cashews. Start by pulsing on and off; process for 1 minute. Check if mixture is moist enough and sticky to stick together. If needed, add more coffee. Process till it is a chunky mass.
- Line plastic wrap on baking pan. Put mixture into pan. Use spatula to press down till mixture is even. Put plastic wrap layer on surface; use your hands to smooth again.
- Refrigerate for 2-3 hours till firm and cold.
- Remove from pan; unwrap. Slice to bars of preferred size. Store in fridge in a zip top back.

Nutrition Information

- Calories: 343 calories;
- Total Carbohydrate: 36 g
- Cholesterol: 0 mg
- Total Fat: 22.2 g
- Protein: 8.1 g
- Sodium: 230 mg

83. Cherry Linzertorte

"Make cookies with leftover dough: Roll dough out to 1/4-in. thick then cut decorative shapes out; bake on parchment-lined sheet for 10 minutes till golden at 350°F."
Serving: Makes 8 to 10 servings

Ingredients

- 1 1/4 cups hazelnuts (about 5 oz.), toasted, husked, cooled
- 2 1/3 cups all purpose flour
- 3/4 cup sugar
- 2 tsps. ground cinnamon
- 1/2 tsp. baking powder
- 1/2 tsp. salt
- 1/4 tsp. ground nutmeg
- 1 cup (2 sticks) chilled unsalted butter, cut into 1/2-inch pieces
- 3 large egg yolks
- 1 tbsp. vanilla extract
- 1 1/2 cups cherry preserves (preferably imported; about 18 oz.)
- Powdered sugar (optional)

Direction

- Preheat an oven to 350°F. Butter the 9-in. diameter tart pan that has removable bottom. Finely chop 1/3 cup flour and nuts in processor; put into big bowl. Add leftover 2 cups flour and following 5 ingredients in bowl; whisk to blend then add butter. Blend ingredients till coarse meal forms for a few minutes using electric mixer on low speed. Add vanilla and egg yolks; beat till moist clumps form. Bring dough to ball; up sides and bottom of prepped pan, press 1 1/2 cups of packed dough. Spread preserved in dough. Roll leftover dough to 13x10-in. rectangle on parchment paper sheet. Freeze rectangle to firm for 5 minutes. Cut 12 lengthwise 1/2-in. wide strips from rectangle. Put 6 strips across torte, evenly spacing. Put 6 extra strips across torte in opposing direction, making lattice. Seal strip's ends to dough edge; trim extra. Keep all dough scraps to create cookies (optional).
- Bake torte for 40 minutes till preserves thickly bubble and crust is golden brown; fully cool torte on rack. You can make it 2 days ahead. Use foil to cover; keep in room temperature.
- Free torte from pan by pushing up bottom of pan. Sift powdered sugar on torte's edge (optional); serve.

Nutrition Information

- Calories: 714
- Total Carbohydrate: 92 g
- Cholesterol: 130 mg
- Total Fat: 36 g
- Fiber: 4 g
- Protein: 8 g
- Sodium: 195 mg
- Saturated Fat: 16 g

84. Chicken And Hominy Soup

"This is a simple main-course soup that is perfect alone or together with toppings like sour cream, tortilla chips, and avocado."
Serving: Makes 8 main-course servings | Prep: 20m

Ingredients

- 3 tbsps. olive oil
- 3 bunches green onions, sliced
- 4 tsps. ground cumin
- 2 1/2 tsps. smoked paprika
- 10 cups low-salt chicken broth
- 1 (14 1/2-oz.) can petite tomatoes in juice
- 1 purchased roast chicken, meat shredded, skin and bones discarded
- 4 tsps. hot pepper sauce
- 3 (15-oz.) cans golden or white hominy in juice
- 1 cup chopped fresh cilantro

Direction

- Over medium-high heat, heat oil in a heavy large pot then add paprika, green onions, and cumin. Sauté for five minutes. Add hot pepper sauce, broth, chicken and tomatoes along with juice. In a blender or processor, puree hominy together with juice. Stir into the soup. Boil. Decrease the heat and let to simmer for 15 minutes. Mix in cilantro. Spoon the soup into bowls.

85. Chicken And Red Bell Pepper Salad Sandwiches

"This Chilean sandwich features cooked bell pepper and creamy chicken. For an appetizer, you can prepare this recipe using cocktail bread. You can also add more mayo if you want it creamier."
Serving: 2 | Prep: 10m | Ready in: 1h

Ingredients

- 2 skinless, boneless chicken breast halves
- 1/2 red bell pepper, seeded
- 1/4 cup mayonnaise
- 1 tbsp. heavy cream
- salt and pepper to taste
- 4 slices white bread

Direction

- Boil a big pot of water; add in chicken. Cook for 20 mins until the juices are clear and the chicken is not pink in the middle. An inserted thermometer in the middle of the chicken should register 74°C or 165°F; drain. Let the chicken cool for a bit then chop.
- Cook bell pepper in a small pot of boiling water for 10 mins until soft.
- In a food processor, blend mayonnaise, bell pepper, cream, and chicken together until it is mostly smooth; sprinkle pepper and salt to season. Slather 1/2 of the mixture over the 2 bread slices, top with remaining bread to sandwich.

Nutrition Information

- Calories: 505 calories;
- Total Carbohydrate: 28.2 g
- Cholesterol: 78 mg

- Total Fat: 32 g
- Protein: 25.3 g
- Sodium: 548 mg

86. Chicken Artichoke Bacon Dip

""This dip recipe started out as a trial but was successfully delicious the first time. Just mix as many ingredients in a blender as you want.""
Serving: 8 | Prep: 20m | Ready in: 50m

Ingredients

- 1 (14 oz.) can artichoke hearts, rinsed and drained
- 1 (3 oz.) package cooked chicken breast, cut into 1/2-inch pieces
- 1 1/2 cups fresh spinach, chopped
- 4 strips cooked bacon, coarsely chopped
- 1/2 cup mayonnaise
- 1/2 cup shredded mozzarella cheese
- 2 oz. Neufchatel cheese, cut into cubes
- 2 tbsps. milk, or more to taste
- 1 clove garlic, minced
- 2 slices Swiss cheese, cut into strips
- ground black pepper to taste
- 1 pinch cayenne pepper, or to taste (optional)

Direction

- Prepare the oven and set to 350°F or 175°C to preheat it.
- Use a food processor or blender and combine chicken breast, bacon, spinach, artichoke hearts, mozzarella cheese, mayonnaise, milk, Swiss cheese, garlic, Neufchatel cheese, cayenne pepper and black pepper. Transfer the mixture into a baking dish, spread
- Let it bake between 30 to 40 minutes or until top starts to bubble and until browned.

Nutrition Information

- Calories: 179 calories;
- Total Carbohydrate: 8.2 g
- Cholesterol: 31 mg

- Total Fat: 12.2 g
- Protein: 9.5 g
- Sodium: 490 mg

87. Chicken Paillards With Radish-mint Chutney

"Yummy!"
Serving: Serves 2; can be doubled

Ingredients

- 1 garlic clove
- 1/2 small jalepeño chili
- 1/4 cup (packed) fresh mint leaves
- 1/4 cup olive oil
- 5 medium radishes, trimmed
- 2 tbsps. walnut pieces
- 2 skinless boneless chicken breast halves

Direction

- Preheat a broiler. Drop chili and garlic through feed tube with processor running; process till chopped finely. Scrape down work bowl's sides. Add oil and mint; blend well, occasionally scraping bowl side's down. Place 2 tbsp. of mixture in a small bowl; put aside. Add walnuts and radishes to processor mixture; process till nuts are chopped finely with on/off turns. Put chutney in the bowl; season with pepper and salt.
- Pound lightly each chicken piece between waxed paper sheets with rolling pin to even 1/2-in. thickness; sprinkle chicken with pepper and salt. Spread the leftover 2 tbsp. mint mixture on both chicken piece's sides; broil chicken for 3 minutes per side till cooked through and brown.
- Put chicken on plates. Put chutney on top; serve.

Nutrition Information

- Calories: 402
- Total Carbohydrate: 4 g
- Cholesterol: 64 mg
- Total Fat: 34 g
- Fiber: 2 g
- Protein: 21 g
- Sodium: 49 mg
- Saturated Fat: 5 g

88. Chicken Skewers With Tarragon-pistachio Pesto

"While you're at the grill, have someone prepare pita chips and hummus so that guests have something to snack on. The skewers are best served with rice and ideally a bottle of rose."
Serving: Makes 4 servings | Prep: 40m

Ingredients

- 1/2 cup chopped fresh Italian parsley
- 2 tbsps. chopped fresh tarragon
- 2 tbsps. unsalted natural pistachios
- 1 tbsp. fresh lemon juice
- 1 medium garlic clove, peeled
- 1/4 cup olive oil
- 16 1-inch pieces red onion (1/3 inch thick)
- 16 1-inch squares red bell pepper
- 8 lemon slices, halved
- 1 lb. chicken tenders (about 8 large)
- 8 metal skewers

Direction

- Blend the first five ingredients in a processor. Add in 1/4 cup of olive oil and blend until a slightly coarse paste starts to form. Add in 2 tbsps. of water and season with pepper and salt. Keep 3 tbsps. of pesto in a bowl for brushing the vegetables and chicken, then reserve the rest of the pesto.
- Set barbecue to medium high heat. Apply oil to grill with a brush. Thread an onion, a bell pepper square, half a lemon slice, chicken tender lengthwise, an onion, a bell pepper square and half a lemon slice on each skewer alternately, should make 8 skewers. Apply olive oil to chicken and vegetables on skewers

with a brush and the 3 tbsps. of pesto from bowl. Drizzle skewers with pepper and salt. Grill skewers for 6-8 minutes a side until vegetables are softened and chicken is heated through. Serve with left pesto.

89. Chicken Soup With Asparagus And Shiitakes, Served With Roasted Fennel Matzo Balls

"A delicious soup!"
Serving: Makes 8 servings

Ingredients

- 2 small-medium fennel bulbs (about 1 lb., weighed with 2 inches of top stalks)
- 2 tbsps. olive oil
- 1/2 cup chicken broth, preferably homemade or good-quality, low-sodium purchased
- 1 tbsp. coarsely chopped garlic
- Salt and freshly ground black pepper
- 3/4 tsp. chopped fresh thyme
- 1/4 tsp. fennel seeds, ground in a spice grinder or with a mortar and pestle (optional)
- 2 large eggs
- About 1/2 cup plus 2 tbsps. matzo meal
- 7 cups homemade chicken broth
- 1/4 lb. fresh shiitake mushrooms, stems removed and reserved for another use or discarded, caps wiped clean with a damp paper towel and thinly sliced
- 12 to 15 thin asparagus spears, trimmed and cut into 1-inch pieces

Direction

- Matzo balls: Preheat an oven to 400°F. Cut fennel stalks off; keep for another time as this are good for fish broths and stews. Put aside 2 tbsp. if there are nice feathery fronds to garnish soup. Quarter the bulbs; trim away any tough parts, bottom hard core and stems. Get a shallow baking pan big enough to fit the fennel in a single layer; add 1 tbsp. oil. Add fennel; toss till coated well. Roast for 20 minutes till fennel is pale gold. Flip the fennel; roast for 10 minutes more. Mix in 1/2 tsp. thyme, pepper and salt to taste, garlic and broth; cover the pan with foil. Cook till fennel is very soft for 35-45 minutes more. Remove the foil; mix. Roast to evaporate most of the liquid for a few more minutes. Put garlic and fennel in a food processor; coarsely chop. Add fennel seeds (optional), pepper to taste, 1 tsp. salt and 1/4 tsp. of thyme; through the feed tube, add leftover 1 tbsp. oil with the machine on.
- Scrape the mixture into a big bowl. Get any extra; you need 1 cup puree. One by one, whisk in eggs. Add matzo meal; mix well. Don't add more matzo meal if you can make a lump into a very soft walnut-sized ball; when you chill it, batter will be firmer. Add enough matzo meal to do so if needed. Refrigerate so matzo meal can absorb seasoning and liquid for at least 2-4 hours.
- Rapidly boil 1 tbsp. salt and 4-qt. water in a lidded, wide big pot when ready to cook. If needed, dip hands into cold water; roll batter into a walnut-sized balls. Lower the heat to a gentle boil when water is furiously boiling, and all balls are rolled. One by one, slide in balls carefully; tightly cover the pot.
- Lower the heat to a simmer; cover on low heat, without uncovering, for 30 minutes. They'll cook by steam and direct heat, which makes them swell and puff; lift lid to let some steam escape. Take a dumpling out; halve. It should be fully cooked through, fluffy and light. Cook for several minutes if not. Gently remove balls with a big slotted spoon/skimmer; they're too fragile to get poured into colander.
- Begin the soup when matzo balls are nearly ready. Simmer broth in a big pot. Add asparagus, mushrooms and matzo balls; simmer till veggies are tender for 5 minutes.
- Put matzo balls in a shallow soup bowls using a slotted spoon; put veggies and hot soup on them. Garnish using reserved chopped fennel fronds.

- You can cook the matzo balls 2-3 hours ahead; drain. Cover with some broth to retain moist then put aside till it's time to reheat.
- You can puree matzo balls with other veggies like shallots, mushrooms, leeks, carrots and beets. Roasted veggies absorb less moisture compared to steamed/boiled ones, which means you need less matzo meal so they're lighter. They are also more flavorful.

Nutrition Information

- Calories: 173
- Total Carbohydrate: 18 g
- Cholesterol: 53 mg
- Total Fat: 8 g
- Fiber: 3 g
- Protein: 9 g
- Sodium: 751 mg
- Saturated Fat: 2 g

90. Chicken Under A Brick With Fresh Herb And Garlic Sauce

Serving: Makes 8 servings

Ingredients

- 12 garlic cloves, peeled, divided
- 1 1/2 cups (packed) fresh Italian parsley sprig tops
- 1/3 cup white balsamic vinegar
- 1/4 cup (packed) fresh mint leaves
- 1/4 cup (packed) fresh basil leaves
- 1 tsp. dried oregano
- 1/4 tsp. dried crushed red pepper
- 1 cup olive oil
- 8 large boneless chicken breast halves with skin
- Nonstick vegetable oil spray
- 8 bricks, each wrapped in foil

Direction

- Cook eight garlic cloves about 2 minutes cloves in boiling water. Stain garlic. Put in processor; cool down. Put in the leftover four garlic cloves along with the following 6 ingredients. Pour in oil gradually while motor is running, processing to form thick sauce. Add salt to season. May be done 2 days in advance. Turn into bowl; refrigerate with cover.
- In a resealable, big plastic bag, put the chicken. Put in half cup of sauce and flip to evenly cover. Refrigerate for no less than half an hour to 4 hours, flipping bag from time to time.
- Use a nonstick spray to coat grill rack and prep barbecue for moderately-high heat. Put the chicken on grill with skin side facing down. Place a brick wrapped in foil on top of every piece. Grill for 5 minutes, till skin crisp and turn golden brown. Take bricks out. Flip the chicken over; grill for 5 minutes, till cooked fully. Place the chicken onto a platter. Scoop some sauce on top. Serve, separately pass the rest of the sauce.

Nutrition Information

- Calories: 468
- Total Carbohydrate: 4 g
- Cholesterol: 70 mg
- Total Fat: 39 g
- Fiber: 1 g
- Protein: 23 g
- Sodium: 79 mg
- Saturated Fat: 7 g

91. Chicken With Olive Tapenade

"Healthy and yummy."
Serving: Makes 4 servings

Ingredients

- Vegetable oil cooking spray
- 1/2 cup pitted Spanish black olives
- 1/2 cup pitted Spanish green olives
- 1 bottle (12 oz.) marinated artichokes, drained, and liquid reserved
- 4 boneless, skinless chicken cutlets (4 oz. each)

- 1 lb. potatoes, peeled and cut into 2-inch-by-1/4-inch wedges
- 1 lb. sweet potatoes, peeled and cut into 2-inch-by-1/4-inch wedges
- 1 tsp. finely chopped fresh rosemary
- 1 tsp. salt, divided
- 1 lb. zucchini, cut into 1/2-inch slices
- 1/4 cup chopped red onion
- 1/4 cup white wine
- 1/4 cup low-sodium chicken broth

Direction

- Heat a grill. Fold 4 18-in. long foil pieces in half then unfold; coat inside using cooking spray. Blend 1 tbsp. leftover artichoke liquid and olives till paste forms in a food processor. Put 1 cutlet in the middle of 1 half of every foil piece; put 1/4 olive paste on each top. Toss 1/2 tsp. salt, rosemary, 1/4 cup reserved artichoke liquid and all potatoes; evenly divide potatoes to packets, putting them next to the chicken. Combine artichokes, zucchini, onion and remaining 1/2 tsp. salt; divide evenly among packets, placing them to other side of chicken. Mix broth and wine in a bowl. To close, fold foil; crimp 2 sides of every packet and leave 1 side open. Put 2 tbsp. wine-broth mixture in every packet. To seal, crimp third packet's side; put on grill. Close the lid; cook for 12 minutes till packets are fully puffed. Cut foil to open carefully; serve.

92. Chickpea Slather

"Strain and wash chickpeas well before using."

Ingredients

- 1 can (15 oz.) chickpeas (garbanzos), rinsed and drained
- 1/4 cup tahini (sesame-seed paste)
- 3 tbsps. warm water
- 3 tbsps. extra-virgin olive oil
- Zest of 1 lemon
- Juice of 1 1/2 lemons
- 2 tsps. finely minced garlic
- 1 tsp. ground cumin
- Salt and pepper, to taste

Direction

- Use a food processor to blend all of ingredients till smooth. Keep in refrigerator, with a cover, for maximum of 7 days.

93. Chilled Honey-roasted Peach And Cardamom Soup With Vanilla Cream

"An amazing recipe!"
Serving: Makes 4 servings

Ingredients

- 3 large peaches (1 1/4 to 1 1/2 lbs.), peeled, halved, pitted
- 2 tbsps. (packed) golden brown sugar
- 1 1/2 tbsps. honey
- 1 1/2 cups fresh orange juice
- 1/2 tsp. ground cardamom
- 1/4 tsp. fleur de sel* or fine sea salt
- 1 to 2 tsps. fresh lemon juice
- 1/4 cup crème fraîche or sour cream
- 1 4-inch piece vanilla bean, split lengthwise
- Fresh peach slices (optional)

Direction

- Preheat an oven to 350°F. Line parchment paper on rimmed baking sheet. Toss honey, sugar and peaches in a big bowl. Put peaches on prepped baking sheet, cut side down. Roast peaches for 15 minutes; flip. Bake for 10 minutes till juices start to caramelize and tender. Scrape pan juices and peaches into food processor. Cool; blend till smooth. Add salt, cardamom and orange juice; blend till smooth. Put soup in medium bowl; season with lemon juice to taste. Cover; refrigerate for minimum of 2- maximum of 8 hours till cold.

- In small bowl, put crème fraiche. From vanilla bean halves, scrape in seeds; stir well. Put soup in 4 bowls; put dollop of vanilla cream on top. If desired, garnish using fresh peach slices.

Nutrition Information

- Calories: 182
- Total Carbohydrate: 38 g
- Cholesterol: 7 mg
- Total Fat: 3 g
- Fiber: 3 g
- Protein: 2 g
- Sodium: 155 mg
- Saturated Fat: 2 g

94. Chilled Tomato Basil Soup

Serving: Makes about 6 cups, serving 6

Ingredients

- 2 1/2 lbs. (about 6) tomatoes, cored and cut into chunks
- 1 tbsp. cornstarch
- 1/2 cup beef broth
- 1 tbsp. fresh lemon juice
- 1/2 tsp. sugar
- 10 whole fresh basil leaves plus 1/3 cup chopped fresh basil leaves for garnish
- sour cream for garnish
- extra-virgin olive oil for drizzling the soup
- as an accompaniment
- 1 large garlic clove, minced or forced through a garlic press
- 1/4 cup olive oil
- a French baguette, cut lengthwise into 6 long wedges
- coarse salt to taste

Direction

- Soup: puree tomatoes in a food processor. Through a fine-sieve, force puree into saucepan, pressing on solids hard. Mix broth and cornstarch in a small bowl; mix mixture into tomato puree. Boil, mixing; take off heat. Mix in pepper and salt to taste, whole basil leaves, sugar and lemon juice. Cool soup then chill for minimum of 8 hours, covered. You can make soup 2 days ahead, kept chilled, covered.
- Discard whole basil leaves. Put soup in six bowls; garnish each serving using some chopped basil and dollop of sour cream. Drizzle oil on soup; serve with toasts.
- Garlic baguette toasts: Cook garlic in oil in a small skillet on medium heat till it starts to be golden, mixing. Brush oil on bread wedges; bake them on a baking sheet for 10 minutes till golden in center of preheated 375°F oven. Sprinkle salt on roasts; break in half. Creates 12 toasts.

95. Chocolate Chip Apricot Bars

Serving: Makes 16 bars

Ingredients

- 6 oz. dried apricots (about 1 cup firmly packed), chopped fine
- 1/4 cup granulated sugar
- 3/4 cup water
- 1 tsp. vanilla extract
- 1 1/3 cups pecans (about 4 oz.)
- 1 cup all-purpose flour
- 2/3 cup firmly packed light brown sugar
- 1/2 tsp. salt
- 2/3 cup semisweet chocolate chips
- 1 stick (1/2 cup) cold unsalted butter, cut into bits
- confectioners' sugar for sprinkling bars

Direction

- Prep apricot filling: mix granulated sugar, water and apricots in a heavy, 1 1/2-quart saucepan; let simmer for 15 minutes with cover. Uncover and allow mixture to simmer, mixing and crushing apricots, till extra

moisture evaporates and filling thickens. Mix in vanilla.
- Heat an oven to 350 degrees F. and oil a square, 8-inch baking pan then dust with flour, knock out extra flour.
- Prep chocolate chip mixture: toast pecans for 8 to 10 minutes in the center of the oven in one shallow baking pan till golden brown in color; cool down. Process salt, brown sugar, flour and pecans in food processor to chop pecans coarsely. Put in butter and chocolate chips and process till mixture of pecan looks much like coarse crumbs.
- Force approximately 1/2 mixture of chocolate chip on prepped baking pan's bottom and smear apricot filling evenly over. Crumble top of apricot filling evenly with the rest of chocolate chip mixture, press it down a bit, and let confection bake in the center of oven till golden, or for 60 minutes. Allow confection to cool fully in pan on rack. Dust confectioners' sugar on confection and slice making 16 bars.

Nutrition Information

- Calories: 239
- Total Carbohydrate: 31 g
- Cholesterol: 15 mg
- Total Fat: 13 g
- Fiber: 2 g
- Protein: 2 g
- Sodium: 79 mg
- Saturated Fat: 5 g

96. Chocolate Chunk And Apricot Cannoli

"Delectable and easy."
Serving: Makes 6

Ingredients

- 1 cup ricotta cheese (preferably whole-milk)
- 1/4 cup mascarpone cheese
- 1/2 cup apricot preserves
- 3 oz. bittersweet (not unsweetened) or semisweet chocolate, finely chopped
- 6 purchased cannoli shells
- Ground coffee
- Powdered sugar

Direction

- In processor, puree ricotta; blend in mascarpone. Add the preserves; process till incorporated yet some small chunks are left. Add chocolate; combine with on/off turns till just blended, don't puree.
- Put mixture in pastry bag without tip then pipe into shells; sprinkle coffee on cheese filling ends. Chill till cold. You can make it 6 hours ahead, kept refrigerated. Sift the powdered sugar on cannoli.

97. Chocolate Marble Cheesecake

"Light and creamy."

Ingredients

- 2 tbsp. slivered blanched almonds
- Vegetable oil cooking spray
- 6 chocolate wafers
- 15 oz. (1 3/4 cups) part-skim ricotta
- 8 oz. lowfat cream cheese, room temperature
- 1 cup sugar
- 1/2 cup lowfat sour cream
- 1 large whole egg
- 2 egg whites
- 1/4 tsp. almond extract (or to taste)
- 2 tbsp. all-purpose flour
- 1/4 tsp. salt
- 2 tbsp. amaretto (if desired)
- 3 tbsp. unsweetened cocoa powder
- 1/2 tsp. instant-espresso powder
- 3 tbsp. bittersweet chocolate chips

Direction

- Heat an oven to 350°. On small baking sheet, toast almonds for 10 minutes, occasionally mixing. Remove from oven; lower heat to 325°. Use cooking spray to coat 8-in. springform pan. Use foil to wrap outside of pan to avoid seepage. Process almonds and chocolate wafers to fine crumbs in a food processor. Sprinkle 2-3 tbsp. crumbs on bottom of pan, enough to lightly coat bottom. Shake pan to evenly distribute; keep leftover crumbs.

- Filling: Puree ricotta for 1 minute till smooth in a food processor. Add salt, flour, almond extract, egg whites, egg, sour cream, sugar and cream cheese; puree till smooth. Whisk espresso powder, cocoa powder, 2 tbsp. hot water and amaretto (optional, or same hot water amount) till well combined in a bowl; mix in chocolate chips. Mix 1 cup plain filling in the chocolate mixture; put aside. Put leftover plain filling in prepped pan. In circular pattern, drizzle chocolate filling on plain filing. Create circular strokes to make swirls in plain filling using a knife. Put 1-in. hot water in shallow baking pan; put springform pan into baking pan. Bake for 45-55 minutes till slightly soft in middle and cheesecake is firm around edge. Around pan's inside, run knife. Remove foil; cool on rack. Chill before removing pan's sides for 6 hours – overnight. Press reserved crumbs on cheesecake's sides.

98. Chocolate, Almond, And Coconut Vegan Fat Bombs

"I you want an energy boost, experiment with these keto and vegan coconut almond fat bombs. They're rich in flavor and have no carbs! Ideal when stored in the freezer."
Serving: 20 | Prep: 10m | Ready in: 25m

Ingredients

- 1 cup shredded unsweetened coconut, divided
- 1/2 cup melted coconut oil
- 1/2 cup almonds, finely chopped
- 1/2 cup coconut milk
- 1/2 cup chopped Medjool dates
- 1 tbsp. low-calorie natural sweetener (such as Swerve®)

Direction

- In the bowl of a food processor, blend sweetener, half cup of shredded coconut, coconut milk, coconut oil, dates, and almonds for about 2 minutes until the resulting mixture is creamy. Place in a freezer for about 15 minutes until set.
- Form the mixture into one-inch balls and then roll into the remaining half cup of shredded coconut.

Nutrition Information

- Calories: 122 calories;
- Total Carbohydrate: 5.8 g
- Cholesterol: 0 mg
- Total Fat: 11.5 g
- Protein: 1.3 g
- Sodium: 3 mg

99. Chocolate, Caramel, And Walnut Tart

"A wonderful dessert!"
Serving: Makes 10 to 12 servings

Ingredients

- 1 1/2 cups all purpose flour
- 1/4 tsp. salt
- 1/2 cup (1 stick) chilled unsalted butter, cut into 1/2-inch cubes
- 4 tbsps. (or more) ice water
- 1 cup sugar (preferably baker's sugar or other superfine sugar)
- 1/4 cup water
- 1 cup heavy whipping cream
- 1/4 cup (1/2 stick) unsalted butter, room temperature
- 2 tbsps. honey
- 2 tsps. vanilla extract

- 2 oz. bittersweet (not unsweetened) or semisweet chocolate, chopped
- 2 oz. semisweet chocolate, chopped
- 2 1/4 cups (about 9 oz.) walnuts, toasted, cut into 1/4-inch pieces
- Vanilla ice cream

Direction

- Crust: Blend salt and flour for 5 seconds in a processor. Put butter in the processor; blend till coarse meal forms with on/off turns. Add 4 tbsp. ice water; blend till dough just starts to come together. If dry, add extra ice water by teaspoonfuls. Gather the dough and flatten into disk. Wrap; chill for at least an hour.
- Roll the dough out to a 14-in. round on a lightly floured surface. Put dough on 11-in. diameter tart pan that has a removable bottom; cut all off but 1/2-in. overhang. Fold overhang in; press, making double-thick sides. Use a fork to pierce crust all over; chill for 30 minutes.
- Preheat an oven to 400°F. Line foil on crust; fill with pie weights/dried beans. Bake for 20 minutes. Remove beans and foil; bake for 20 minutes more till golden. If crust bubbles, press with fork's back. Fully cool.
- Filling: Mix 1/4 cup water and 1 cup sugar in a big heavy saucepan on low heat till sugar melts. Increase the heat; boil, brushing pan sides down using wet pastry brush. Boil for 8 minutes till deep amber color, occasionally swirling pan, without mixing. Take off from the heat. Add cream; it'll bubble up. Put pan back on low heat; whisk caramel till smooth. Add vanilla, honey and butter; whisk for 3 minutes till sauce slightly thickens. Take off from the heat. Add all the chocolate; whisk till smooth. Mix in nuts; in crust, spread the filling. Chill tart for at least 3 hours – overnight till firm; serve with ice cream.

100. Chocolate-almond Tofu Pie

"There are a lot of variations that can be done to this versatile recipe."
Serving: 8 | Prep: 15m | Ready in: 4h40m

Ingredients

- 1/2 cup butter, melted
- 1 1/2 (4.8 oz.) packages graham crackers, broken into small pieces
- 1/2 cup almonds
- 3 cups semisweet chocolate chips
- 2 (12 oz.) packages silken tofu, drained
- 2 tbsps. vanilla extract

Direction

- Heat the oven to 200°C or 400°F.
- Put graham crackers, almonds and butter in a food processor. Process with cover till mixture looks much like coarse crumb. Remove crumbs into a pie plate measuring 9-inches, and force on plate's bottom making a crust. Rinse and dry the food processor's bowl; put aside.
- Bake for 15 minutes in prepped oven till pale golden. Take out of the oven; cool down, about 15 minutes.
- Meantime, in double boiler top above just-barely simmering water, liquify the chocolate, use a rubber spatula to mix often and scrape down sides to prevent burning. Put tofu, vanilla extract and chocolate in clean food processor. Process till smooth, scrape down sides a few times. Transfer the mixture of chocolate in prepped crust. Refrigerate for 4 hours then serve.

Nutrition Information

- Calories: 636 calories;
- Total Carbohydrate: 63.1 g
- Cholesterol: 31 mg
- Total Fat: 41.5 g
- Protein: 13.2 g
- Sodium: 249 mg

101. Chocolate-filled Almond Macaroons

Serving: Makes about 20 sandwich cookies

Ingredients

- 7 oz. almond paste
- 1 cup sugar
- 2 large egg whites
- 40 whole almonds (about)
- 1/4 cup whipping cream
- 2 tbsps. (1/4 stick) unsalted butter
- 1/2 tsp. grated orange peel
- 6 oz. bittersweet (not unsweetened) or semisweet chocolate, finely chopped

Direction

- Set the oven to 375 degrees Fahrenheit. Butter big nonstick heavy cookie sheets generously. In a processor, blend egg whites, sugar, and almond paste until smooth. Drop slightly round teaspoonfuls of the dough onto the sheets, evenly spacing them. Press an almond on each mound and bake until they are golden brown, roughly 10 minutes. Allow the cookies to rest on the sheets just until cool enough to touch, around 5 minutes. Use a spatula to move the cookies to a rack to completely cool. You can make this a day ahead, store them at room temperature in an airtight container.
- Bring orange peel, butter, and cream in a small heavy pan to a simmer. Turn the heat down to low and add the chocolate, stirring until smooth. Take away from the heat and let sit until thick yet spreadable, roughly 20 minutes.
- Spread some ganache on the flat side of a cookie and sandwich with another cookie's flat side. Repeat with leftover ganache and cookies. You can make these 2 days beforehand, refrigerate while covered in an airtight container. Bring the cookies to room temperature before you serve.

Nutrition Information

- Calories: 160
- Total Carbohydrate: 21 g
- Cholesterol: 6 mg
- Total Fat: 9 g
- Fiber: 1 g
- Protein: 2 g
- Sodium: 9 mg
- Saturated Fat: 3 g

102. Cilantro Jalapeno Pesto With Lime

"Lessen spiciness by lessening jalapeno and removing seeds and white membrane. Or add all if you like spice."
Serving: 6 | Prep: 10m | Ready in: 10m

Ingredients

- 1 bunch fresh cilantro
- 2 1/2 tbsps. toasted pine nuts
- 1/4 cup extra virgin olive oil
- 5 cloves garlic
- 1 tbsp. fresh lime juice
- 1/2 fresh jalapeno pepper, seeded
- 1/4 cup grated Parmesan cheese

Direction

- In a blender, pulse parmesan cheese, jalapeno pepper, lime juice, garlic, olive oil, pine nuts and cilantro until it has a paste-like, soft consistency.

Nutrition Information

- Calories: 129 calories;
- Total Carbohydrate: 1.9 g
- Cholesterol: 4 mg
- Total Fat: 12.4 g
- Protein: 2.8 g
- Sodium: 69 mg

103. Cinnamon Energy Bites

"Date-and-cashew-based cinnamon bites"
Serving: 20 | Prep: 15m | Ready in: 45m

Ingredients

- 6 dates, pitted
- 1 cup raw cashews
- 1 tbsp. flax seed meal
- 1/8 tsp. ground cinnamon
- 1 pinch salt
- 1 tbsp. coconut oil

Direction

- In a blender or food processor, mix salt, cinnamon, flax meal, cashews and dates; process till extremely well combined. While motor is running, put coconut oil and process till mixture gathers together.
- Roll the mixture making 20 rounds, approximately the size of big gum ball and set on baking sheet or plate. Put in freezer for a minimum of half an hour. Retain energy rounds stored in refrigerator or freezer.

Nutrition Information

- Calories: 54 calories;
- Total Carbohydrate: 4.2 g
- Cholesterol: 0 mg
- Total Fat: 4 g
- Protein: 1.2 g
- Sodium: 52 mg

104. Coffee-molasses Shoofly Pie

"An amazing pie."
Serving: Makes 8 to 10 servings

Ingredients

- 1 1/3 cups all purpose flour
- 1 1/2 tsps. sugar
- 1/2 tsp. salt
- 1/3 cup solid vegetable shortening, frozen, diced
- 1/4 cup (1/2 stick) chilled unsalted butter, cut into 1/2-inch cubes
- 4 tbsps. (about) ice water
- 1 egg white, beaten to blend
- 1 cup all purpose flour
- 1/2 cup (packed) golden brown sugar
- 1/2 cup (1 stick) chilled unsalted butter, cut into 1/2-inch cubes
- 1 cup hot water
- 1/2 tsp. instant espresso powder
- 1 tsp. baking soda
- 3/4 cup light corn syrup
- 1/4 cup mild-flavored (light) molasses
- 1 tsp. vanilla extract
- 1/4 tsp. salt
- 1/8 tsp. ground cinnamon
- Powdered sugar
- Vanilla ice cream

Direction

- Crust: Blend salt, sugar and flour for 5 seconds in processor. Add butter and shortening; blend till coarse meal forms with on/off turns. Add 3 tbsp. ice water; briefly blend. 1 tsp. at a time, add more ice water; blend till moist clumps form with on/off turns. Gather dough together and flatten to disk. In plastic, wrap; chill for minimum of 1 hour – maximum of 1 day.
- Preheat an oven to 400°F. Roll dough out to 13-in. round on lightly floured surface. Put dough in 9-in. diameter glass pie dish; to 3/4-in., trim overhang. Fold overhang under; decoratively crimp edge. Use a fork to pierce crust all over; freeze for 10 minutes. Line foil on crust; fill with pie weights/dried beans. Bake crust for 25 minutes till sides are set. Remove beans and foil; bake crust for 10 minutes till starting to color; if crust bubbles, press with fork's back. Remove from oven; to seal, brush some egg white on crust. Lower oven temperature down to 350°F.
- Meanwhile, prep filling: Mix brown sugar and flour in a medium bowl. Add butter; use back

of fork to cut in till even-size crumbs form and blended. Mix espresso powder and 1 cup hot water in separate medium bowl then add baking soda. Whisk in cinnamon, salt, vanilla, molasses and corn syrup.
- Sprinkle hot crust with crumb mixture; add molasses mixture. Bake pie for 35 minutes till filling is set in middle. Put pie on rack; fully cool.
- Sift powdered sugar on pie. Cut to wedges; serve with ice cream.

Nutrition Information

- Calories: 548
- Total Carbohydrate: 77 g
- Cholesterol: 46 mg
- Total Fat: 26 g
- Fiber: 1 g
- Protein: 4 g
- Sodium: 389 mg
- Saturated Fat: 13 g

105. Colombian Aji

"This Colombian recipe is for aji."
Serving: 16 | Prep: 10m | Ready in: 10m

Ingredients

- 10 jalapeno peppers, seeded
- 1/4 cup water
- 1/4 cup white vinegar
- 1/4 cup fresh lemon juice
- 1 1/2 cups chopped green onions
- 1 cup chopped cilantro
- 2 tsps. salt

Direction

- Combine salt, cilantro, green onions, lemon juice, vinegar, water, and jalapenos in a blender and blend until smooth, then refrigerate until ready to serve.

Nutrition Information

- Calories: 7 calories;
- Total Carbohydrate: 1.7 g
- Cholesterol: 0 mg
- Total Fat: 0.1 g
- Protein: 0.4 g
- Sodium: 294 mg

106. Cool-off-the-heat Avocado And Watermelon Salad

"So wonderful!"
Serving: 6 | Prep: 30m | Ready in: 30m

Ingredients

- 2 cups chopped green leaf lettuce
- 1/4 cup sunflower sprouts
- 1 avocado, cut into 1/2-inch cubes
- 1/4 cup cubed seeded watermelon
- 1 tbsp. chopped fresh cilantro, or to taste
- Dressing:
- 6 tbsps. orange juice
- 2 tbsps. red wine vinegar
- 1 tbsp. honey
- 1 tbsp. heavy cream
- 1 tsp. Dijon mustard
- 3/4 cup olive oil
- 2 tbsps. olive oil
- 1 tsp. finely chopped fresh mint leaves
- salt and ground black pepper to taste

Direction

- In a bowl, mix sprouts and lettuce; put watermelon cubes and avocado over. Sprinkle cilantro.
- Blend mustard, cream, honey, vinegar and orange juice in a food processor/blender. Drizzle in 3/4 cup and 2 tbsp. oil slowly as blender runs; blend in pepper, salt and mint.

Nutrition Information

- Calories: 366 calories;
- Total Carbohydrate: 9.2 g

- Cholesterol: 3 mg
- Total Fat: 37.4 g
- Protein: 1.2 g
- Sodium: 53 mg

107. Crab-boil Spices

"A very simple recipe."
Serving: Makes about 1 cup

Ingredients

- 1/4 cup pickling spices
- 2 tbsps. mustard seeds
- 2 tbsps. whole black peppercorns
- 1 tbsp. celery seeds
- 2 tbsps. dried hot red pepper flakes
- 2 tsps. ground ginger
- 5 bay leaves
- 2 tsps. dried oregano
- 1 tbsp. minced dried chives
- 1/4 cup sea salt

Direction

- Pulse all ingredients to a coarse powder in a food processor; crab-boil spices keep for a few months in well-sealed container in dark, cool place.

Nutrition Information

- Calories: 93
- Total Carbohydrate: 14 g
- Total Fat: 5 g
- Fiber: 5 g
- Protein: 4 g
- Sodium: 64 mg
- Saturated Fat: 1 g

108. Cranberry And Blood Orange Relish

"Only 3 ingredients for a fresh and bright uncooked relish."
Serving: Makes about 2 1/2 cups

Ingredients

- 4 blood oranges
- 1 12-oz. bag fresh cranberries
- 2/3 cup sugar

Direction

- Remove peel from three blood oranges including white pith. Slice between membranes with sharp and small knife to loosen segments right in a small-size bowl. Put aside the bowl containing segments of blood orange. Slice the rest of unpeeled blood orange making eight portions and put into a food processor. Put in 2/3 cup of sugar and fresh cranberries; process with on/off turns to chop the mixture finely. Remove the relish into a medium-size bowl; mix in segments of blood orange. Chill relish with cover overnight. DO AHEAD: Cranberry relish may be done 2 days in advance. Keep in refrigerator. Let com to room temperature then serve.

Nutrition Information

- Calories: 230
- Total Carbohydrate: 59 g
- Total Fat: 0 g
- Fiber: 7 g
- Protein: 2 g
- Sodium: 2 mg
- Saturated Fat: 0 g

109. Cranberry And Raspberry Star Cookies

"Great for the holidays."
Serving: Makes about 36 sandwich cookies

Ingredients

- 3/4 cup (1 1/2 sticks) unsalted butter, room temperature
- 1 tsp. vanilla extract
- 1/4 tsp. grated lemon peel
- 1 cup sugar
- 1 large egg
- 1 egg yolk
- 2 1/4 cups all purpose flour
- 1/4 cup cornstarch
- 1/4 tsp. (generous) ground cloves
- 1 cup fresh cranberries
- 1/4 cup sugar
- 3/4 cup raspberry preserves
- Powdered sugar

Direction

- Cookies: Cream lemon, vanilla and butter using electric mixer till light in bowl. Add sugar slowly; beat till blended. Beat in yolk and egg. Mix cloves, cornstarch and flour. Beat 1/2 dry ingredients into the butter mixture; mix in leftover dry ingredients. Bring dough to ball; it'll be soft. Divide the dough to 4 pieces; flatten each to disk. In plastic, wrap each; chill for 1 hour.
- Preheat an oven to 350°F. Butter big heavy nonstick cookie sheets. Roll out 1 dough piece to 1/8-in. thick on floured surface; keep leftover refrigerated. Using floured 3-in. star cutter, cut star-shaped cookies out; put on prepped cookie sheets, 1/2-in. apart. Use 2nd dough piece to repeat rolling then cutting. Bring scraps together and reroll. If it is soft, chill briefly. Cut extra 3-in. star cookies out. Chill cookies for 10 minutes. Bake for 10 minutes till edges are golden; on rack, cool.
- Roll 3rd dough piece to 1/8-in. thick on lightly floured surface. Using floured 3-in. star cutter, cut star-shaped cookies out. Using 1 3/4-2-in. star cutter, cut out smaller star of middle of every 3-in. star. Put star outlines on prepped cookie sheets with floured metal spatula for aid. Using 4th dough piece, repeat rolling then cutting star outlines. Gather star centers and scraps; reroll, briefly chilling dough if soft. Cut 3-in. stars out. Cut out smaller stars of every 3-in. star. Put centers and star outlines on prepped cookie sheets; chill cookies for 10 minutes. Bake for 9 minutes till edges are golden brown. Put cookies on rack; cool.
- Filling: Chop sugar and cranberries finely in processor; put mixture in medium heavy saucepan. Stir in preserves; cook on medium high heat for 8 minutes till reduces to scant 1 cup, occasionally mixing. Put into bowl; cool.
- Spread 1 tsp. jam filling on middle of every 3-in. cookie using metal icing spatula, spread towards points of star slightly. Sift powdered sugar on star outlines lightly. Put star outlines on jam-topped cookies, sugar side up. You can make it ahead; keep in airtight containers in single layers. Freeze for maximum of 2 weeks/refrigerate for maximum of 4 days. Stand in room temperature for 10 minutes before serving.

Nutrition Information

- Calories: 118
- Total Carbohydrate: 19 g
- Cholesterol: 19 mg
- Total Fat: 4 g
- Fiber: 0 g
- Protein: 1 g
- Sodium: 5 mg
- Saturated Fat: 3 g

110. Cranberry Milk-chocolate Truffles

"These truffles call for Valrhona 40% cacao milk chocolate."
Serving: Makes about 60 cranberry milk-chocolate truffles

Ingredients

- 9 oz. fine-quality milk chocolate* such as Valrhona "40% cacao"
- 1/2 cup heavy cream
- 1/2 stick (1/4 cup) unsalted butter
- 1/8 tsp. salt
- 1 1/2 cups (8 oz.) unsweetened dried cranberries
- parchment paper
- 9 oz. fine-quality milk chocolate* such as Valrhona "40% cacao"
- 1/2 cup unsweetened dried cranberries(about 2 1/2 oz.)
- *available at some specialty foods shops

Direction

- Prep truffle mixture: chop the chocolate. Let butter, salt and cream in small saucepan come barely to a boil; mix cranberries in. Take pan off heat and rest mixture for about 10 minutes. Process cranberry mixture and chocolate in food processor till smooth then pour into one small-size bowl. Refrigerate mixture of truffle with cover, till extremely firm, for no less than half a day to three days.
- Line wax paper on a tray.
- Scoop out mixture of truffle using a melon-ball cutter, an-inch in size and form to smooth balls between your hand palms, transfer truffles onto the tray. Refrigerate truffles for 3 hours, till firm. Let truffles come to a room temperature prior to continuing, for about 20 minutes.
- Coat and garnish truffles: grease and line one baking sheet using parchment paper.
- Temper the chocolate. (Or, chop the chocolate and liquify chocolate in a small-size, metal bowl or in double boiler placed above saucepan with just simmering water, mixing till smooth.)
- On a fork, balance a truffle, (avoid spearing) and keep fork on top of chocolate. Scoop chocolate on ball, allow the excess to drip off. Place truffle back onto tray and place 1 small dried cranberry piece on top. Coat and jazz up the rest of truffles in same process. Refrigerate truffles for 3 hours, with no cover, till firm. You may keep truffles in airtight container, placed between wax paper sheets and refrigerate for 2 weeks. Let truffles come to room temperature then serve.

111. Cranberry Salsa

"This quick and easy recipe is the perfect substitute for the cranberry sauce from stores."
Serving: 8 | Prep: 15m | Ready in: 15m

Ingredients

- 1 (12 oz.) bag fresh cranberries
- 6 tbsps. white sugar
- 2 tbsps. brandy-based orange liqueur (such as Grand Marnier®)
- 1/2 cucumber - peeled, seeded, and diced
- 2 stalks celery, chopped
- 4 slices pickled jalapeno pepper, finely chopped

Direction

- In a food processor, pulse cranberries until they are finely chopped. The cranberries should have a bit of texture left; move to a serving bowl. Mix in jalapeno, sugar, celery, cucumber, and orange liqueur. Let it stand for 15mins at room temperature for the flavors to blend in with each other. Serve.

Nutrition Information

- Calories: 72 calories;
- Total Carbohydrate: 16.9 g
- Cholesterol: 0 mg
- Total Fat: 0.1 g

- Protein: 0.3 g
- Sodium: 43 mg

112. Cranberry-avocado Salsa

"Try to make salsa 1 hour – 1 day ahead before serving to blend flavors."
Serving: Makes about 3 1/2 cups

Ingredients

- 1 yellow bell pepper
- 1 12-oz. bag fresh or frozen cranberries (3 cups)
- 1/2 cup sugar
- 1/4 cup orange juice
- 1 medium jalapeño chili, seeded, chopped
- 1 tbsp. grated orange peel
- 2 ripe avocados, halved, pitted, peeled, diced
- 1/4 cup chopped fresh cilantro

Direction

- Char bell pepper till blackened on all sides in broiler/above gas flame. In paper bag, enclose for 10 minutes. Peel, seed then chop bell pepper.
- Coarsely chop cranberries with orange juice and sugar in processor with on/off turns; put in medium bowl. Add orange peel, jalapeno and bell pepper. You can make it 1 day ahead, refrigerated, covered. Mix cilantro and avocados into salsa; season with pepper and salt to taste.

Nutrition Information

- Calories: 181
- Total Carbohydrate: 28 g
- Total Fat: 9 g
- Fiber: 6 g
- Protein: 2 g
- Sodium: 6 mg
- Saturated Fat: 1 g

113. Cream Cheese Pie Topped With Peaches And Blackberries

"So easy!"
Serving: Serves 8

Ingredients

- 1/2 cup unsalted butter, melted
- 1/2 tsp. almond extract
- 2 1/2 cups shortbread cookie crumbs (about 10 oz.)
- 8 oz. Philadelphia-brand cream cheese, room temperature
- 3/4 cup powdered sugar
- 1/2 cup whipping cream
- 1 tsp. vanilla extract
- 1/2 tsp. almond extract
- 3 large peaches, peeled, pitted, sliced
- 2 1/2-pint baskets fresh blackberries
- 1/4 cup peach jam, melted

Direction

- Crust: Preheat an oven to 325°F and butter 10-in. diameter glass pie dish. Blend extract and butter in medium bowl; stir in crumbs. Up sides and on bottom of prepped dish, press crumb mixture. Bake crust for 8 minutes till golden; fully cool crust.
- Filling and topping: In processor, blend cream cheese till smooth. Add almond extract, vanilla extract, cream and sugar; blend till very smooth, scraping bowl's sides down occasionally. In prepped crust, spread filling; refrigerate for 2 hours till filling is firm. You can make it 1 day ahead, kept refrigerated, covered.
- Put peach slices around pie's edge. In middle, put blackberries. Lightly brush warm jam on fruit to glaze; refrigerate the pie for maximum of 3 hours.

Nutrition Information

- Calories: 563
- Total Carbohydrate: 57 g
- Cholesterol: 78 mg

- Total Fat: 36 g
- Fiber: 6 g
- Protein: 6 g
- Sodium: 240 mg
- Saturated Fat: 19 g

114. Creamed Spinach With Croutons

Serving: Makes 4 to 6 servings

Ingredients

- 2 slices of homemade-type white bread, cut into 1/4-inch cubes
- 1 1/2 tbsps. unsalted butter, melted
- 2 lbs. spinach (about 3 bunches), coarse stems discarded and the leaves washed well and drained
- 1/4 cup minced shallot or onion
- 1 1/2 tbsps. unsalted butter
- 1 1/2 tbsps. all-purpose flour
- 1 cup milk
- 3 tbsps. sour cream
- 1/2 tsp. freshly grated nutmeg
- 1 to 2 tsps. fresh lemon juice

Direction

- Croutons: Preheat an oven to 350°F. Toss salt to taste, butter and bread cubes in a small bowl; spread on baking sheet. Bake for 8-10 minutes till golden in center of oven.
- Creamed spinach: Cook spinach in water clinging to leaves in a kettle on medium heat for 5-6 minutes till wilted, mixing 1-2 times, covered. Refresh under cold water; drain in a colander well. By handfuls, squeeze out extra water; puree spinach in a food processor.
- Cook shallot in butter in a heavy saucepan on medium low heat till soft, mixing. Add flour; cook roux for 3 minutes, mixing. Add milk, whisking; boil, whisking. Simmer for 3 minutes, whisking. Add pepper and salt to taste, lemon juice, nutmeg, sour cream and spinach puree; heat creamed spinach on medium low heat till heated through, mixing. Serve croutons with creamed spinach underneath.

Nutrition Information

- Calories: 248
- Total Carbohydrate: 24 g
- Cholesterol: 34 mg
- Total Fat: 14 g
- Fiber: 7 g
- Protein: 12 g
- Sodium: 308 mg
- Saturated Fat: 8 g

115. Creamy Cashew Lime Bars (or Pie)

"A thick, creamy and full of goodness dairy-free recipe that can be made as a pie or bars."
Serving: 8 | Prep: 15m | Ready in: 35m

Ingredients

- Crust:
- 1 cup walnuts
- 1 cup coconut sugar
- 2 tbsps. coconut oil
- 1 tbsp. honey
- Filling:
- 1 1/4 cups cashews
- 10 tbsps. lime juice
- 1/2 cup honey
- 5 tbsps. coconut oil
- 1 tbsp. grated lime zest
- 2 pinches salt, or more to taste
- 1/2 tsp. grated lime zest

Direction

- In the bowl of a food processor, mix together the 1 tbsp. of honey, 2 tbsp. of coconut oil, coconut sugar and walnuts; pulse for about 3 minutes, until forming fine, moist crumbs. Press the crust mixture into the bottom of a 9-inch square baking dish.

- In a blender, put the salt, 1 tbsp. lime zest, 5 tbsp. coconut oil, 1/2 cup honey, lime juice and cashews. Blend together for about 4 minutes until it becomes very smooth. Pour the filling mixture on top of the prepped crust.
- Chill in the fridge for a minimum of 20 minutes until it sets, then put 1/2 tsp. of lime zest on top prior to serving.

Nutrition Information

- Calories: 470 calories;
- Total Carbohydrate: 48.2 g
- Cholesterol: 0 mg
- Total Fat: 31.6 g
- Protein: 5.7 g
- Sodium: 183 mg

116. Creamy Jalapeno Ranch Dip

"A lovely creamy dip."
Serving: 10 | Prep: 15m | Ready in: 15m

Ingredients

- 1 cup buttermilk
- 1 (4 oz.) can chopped green chilies
- 1/2 cup reduced-fat mayonnaise
- 1/3 cup seeded and chopped jalapeno pepper
- 1/3 cup chopped fresh cilantro
- 1 tbsp. minced garlic
- 1 (1 oz.) package ranch dressing mix
- lime, juiced

Direction

- Blend lime juice, ranch dressing mix, garlic, cilantro, jalapeno pepper, mayonnaise, green chilies and buttermilk till mostly smooth in a blender/food processor.

Nutrition Information

- Calories: 43 calories;
- Total Carbohydrate: 7.2 g
- Cholesterol: < 1 mg
- Total Fat: 1.1 g
- Protein: 1.1 g
- Sodium: 466 mg

117. Creamy Mashed Plantains (pure De Platano)

"A traditional Venezuelan recipe for a side."
Serving: 2 | Prep: 20m | Ready in: 35m

Ingredients

- 2 very ripe (black) plantains, peeled
- 4 cups water
- 1 tsp. salt
- 1 1/2 tbsps. butter
- 1 tbsp. milk
- 1 pinch ground nutmeg
- 1 pinch ground white pepper
- 1 oz. cheese, crumbled

Direction

- Cover plantains with water and salt in a big pot; boil. Cook for 10-15 minutes till plantains are pierced easily with a fork. Drain plantains. To remove veins, lengthwise cut; cut to smaller pieces.
- Pulse white pepper, nutmeg, milk, butter and plantains till creamy in a food processor; sprinkle cheese.

Nutrition Information

- Calories: 323 calories;
- Total Carbohydrate: 58.8 g
- Cholesterol: 28 mg
- Total Fat: 10.8 g
- Protein: 4.4 g
- Sodium: 1267 mg

118. Crostini With Sun-dried-tomato Tapenade

Serving: Makes about 36

Ingredients

- 1 cup pitted Kalamata olives or other brine-cured black olives
- 3/4 cup drained oil-packed sun-dried tomatoes
- 2/3 cup olive oil
- 1/4 cup drained capers
- 3/4 tsp. dried oregano
- 1 French-bread baguette, cut into 1/2-inch-thick slices
- Additional olive oil

Direction

- Use processor to chop tomatoes and olives finely with on/off turns. Put in capers, oregano and 2/3 cup of oil; process to puree coarsely. Pour into a bowl. (Tapenade may be done 3 days in advance. Chill with cover. Let come to room temperature the use.)
- Heat an oven to 350 degrees F. Put slices of bread onto baking sheet. Brush with more oil slightly. Bake for 10 minutes, till golden. Smear toasts with tomato tapenade to serve.

Nutrition Information

- Calories: 69
- Total Carbohydrate: 5 g
- Total Fat: 5 g
- Fiber: 0 g
- Protein: 1 g
- Sodium: 99 mg
- Saturated Fat: 1 g

119. Crusty Potato Galette

"You can make this in under 1 hour."
Serving: Serves 2

Ingredients

- 1 tbsp. unsalted butter, melted
- 1 tbsp. vegetable oil
- 3/4 lb. boiling or baking potatoes, scrubbed but not peeled
- 1/4 tsp. crumbled dried rosemary

Direction

- Mix oil and butter in a small bowl. Slice potatoes thin with a mandolin/other hand-held slicing device or food processor with 1-milimeter slicing bade. Brush some butter mixture on bottom of 9-in. cast-iron skillet quickly to avoid discoloring potatoes. Cover it using potato slices, in one layer, overlapping them. Brush some leftover butter mixture on potatoes. Sprinkle some rosemary over. Season with pepper and salt. Layer the leftover potatoes with leftover butter mixture and rosemary the same way.
- Heat mixture till it starts to sizzle on medium high heat. Put skillet in center of preheated 450°F oven; bake galette till potatoes are tender and it is golden for 25 minutes. Cut galette to wedges.

Nutrition Information

- Calories: 248
- Total Carbohydrate: 31 g
- Cholesterol: 15 mg
- Total Fat: 13 g
- Fiber: 2 g
- Protein: 4 g
- Sodium: 9 mg
- Saturated Fat: 4 g

120. Cuban Inspired Millet

"I learned how to make a sofrito from u Cuban suegra. I followed this exact process (without tomatoes and plus a carrot) to enhance the millet. You can serve warm or cold."
Serving: 8 | Prep: 20m | Ready in: 55m

Ingredients

- 1 carrot, chopped
- 2 cloves garlic, crushed
- 1 tbsp. olive oil
- 1 onion, chopped
- 1 green bell pepper, chopped
- 1 cup millet
- 2 cups vegetable broth
- salt and ground black pepper to taste
- 1/4 cup chopped fresh cilantro, or more to taste

Direction

- In a food processor, blend garlic and carrot until they are finely chopped.
- Over medium heat, heat olive oil in a pot and then cook while stirring the carrot mixture, green bell pepper and onion for about 10 minutes until softened. Stir in millet for about 3 minutes until toasted and fragrant.
- Add the vegetable broth into the millet mixture and then season with black pepper and salt. Decrease the heat and let to simmer for about 20 minutes until the millet is tender and all the broth is absorbed. Mix in cilantro.

Nutrition Information

- Calories: 130 calories;
- Total Carbohydrate: 22.5 g
- Cholesterol: 0 mg
- Total Fat: 2.9 g
- Protein: 3.4 g
- Sodium: 123 mg

121. Damson Tartlets

"Beautiful recipe!"
Serving: Makes 6 servings | Prep: 45m

Ingredients

- 2 1/2 cups all-purpose flour
- 2 sticks (1/2 lb.) cold unsalted butter, cut into 1/2-inch cubes
- 1 cup confectioners sugar
- 3 large egg yolks
- 1 lb. damson plums or prune plums
- 1 3/4 cups sugar
- 2 tbsps. white wine
- 1 Turkish or 1/2 California bay leaf
- 1 cup heavy cream
- 1/2 vanilla bean, split lengthwise
- 1 tbsp. sugar
- 1/2 tsp. grated lemon zest
- Equipment: 6 (4-inch) fluted tartlet pans

Direction

- Pastry dough: Pulse confectioners' sugar, butter and flour till it looks like coarse meal in food processor. Add egg yolks; pulse till dough forms.
- Put dough on lightly floured surface; halve. Shape each half to 4-in. 1-in. thick square; in plastic wrap, wrap. Freeze for minimum of 2 hours till solid.
- As pastry freezes, make compote: Simmer bay leaf, wine, sugar and whole plums in medium heavy saucepan on medium low heat till sugar dissolves, occasionally mixing, covered; don't boil over juices. Lower heat to low; simmer for 30 minutes till plums fall apart, occasionally mixing, covered. Put in a bowl; chill till cold, uncovered. Cover. Discard bay leaf and pits. If desired, add bit of confectioners' sugar to taste.
- Bake pastry: From 1 frozen square, grate coarsely pastry into tartlet pans, evenly dividing. Keep leftover dough for another time. Press dough flakes in tartlet pans to line sides and bottoms evenly. Use a fork to prick

- bottoms all over; freeze tartlets for minimum of 1 hour till firm.
- Preheat an oven with rack in center to 425°F.
- In shallow baking pan, put tartlets; put in oven. Lower oven temperature to 400°F; bake for 15-18 minutes till shells get golden all over.
- Put tartlet pans on rack; fully cool. Remove shells from pans.
- Cream filling: In a big bowl, put cream. From vanilla bean, scrape seeds into cream; beat in zest and sugar using an electric mixer till cream holds stiff peaks then fold in 2 tbsp. plum compote; divide cream to tartlet shells. Put some leftover compote on top; serve. You'll have lots of compote remaining.
- Use black/slightly sweeter red plums for prune/damson plums and 2 tbsp. lemon juice for wine, greater acidity, if needed.
- You can freeze pastry for maximum of 1 month.
- Compote keeps for 2 weeks, chilled, covered.

Nutrition Information

- Calories: 1124
- Total Carbohydrate: 170 g
- Cholesterol: 228 mg
- Total Fat: 48 g
- Fiber: 7 g
- Protein: 10 g
- Sodium: 27 mg
- Saturated Fat: 30 g

122. Dandelion Pesto

"Only harvest from untreated lawns or organic gardens for fresh produce like dandelion."
Serving: 16 | Prep: 10m | Ready in: 10m

Ingredients

- 2 cups dandelion greens
- 1/2 cup olive oil
- 1/2 cup grated Parmesan cheese
- 2 tsps. crushed garlic
- salt to taste (optional)
- 1 pinch red pepper flakes, or to taste (optional)

Direction

- In a food processor, blend garlic, parmesan cheese, olive oil and dandelion greens until smooth. Season with red pepper flakes and salt.

Nutrition Information

- Calories: 74 calories;
- Total Carbohydrate: 0.9 g
- Cholesterol: 2 mg
- Total Fat: 7.5 g
- Protein: 1.2 g
- Sodium: 44 mg

123. Deb's Red Pepper Pesto

"A quick summer recipe."
Serving: 10 | Prep: 10m | Ready in: 20m

Ingredients

- 2 bunches fresh basil, stems removed
- 1 tsp. extra-virgin olive oil, or as needed
- 2 cloves garlic, minced, or more to taste
- 2 oz. pine nuts
- 3 roasted red bell peppers, seeded and peeled, or more to taste
- 1 lemon, juiced
- 1 tbsp. balsamic vinegar, or more to taste
- 1 tbsp. grated Parmesan cheese, or to taste
- salt and ground black pepper to taste
- 3 tbsps. extra-virgin olive oil, or more as desired
- 2 tbsps. cooked corn kernels, or as desired (optional)

Direction

- In food processor, put basil.
- Use 1 tsp. olive oil to coat bottom of a skillet; heat on medium. Mix and cook garlic for 2-3 minutes till lightly browned. Put cooked garlic in basil.

- Heat another skillet on medium high heat then add pine nuts; cook for 3-5 minutes till fragrant and toasted. Put roasted red bell pepper and toasted pine nuts in basil mixture.
- Process basil mixture till chunky and evenly combined.
- Mix pepper, salt, parmesan cheese, balsamic vinegar and lemon juice into red bell pepper mixture and process till you get desired consistency, adding 3 tbsp. olive little by little. Add corn; process till mixed.

Nutrition Information

- Calories: 86 calories;
- Total Carbohydrate: 2.9 g
- Cholesterol: < 1 mg
- Total Fat: 7.7 g
- Protein: 2.3 g
- Sodium: 255 mg

124. Deb's Tapenade

"This olive dip can be used to top meat or as an appetizer along with veggies, peppers, crackers, bread sticks, or baguettes to dip."
Serving: 12 | Prep: 20m | Ready in: 20m

Ingredients

- 2 (6 oz.) cans sliced black olives, drained
- 3 tbsps. capers
- 1/2 cup minced onion
- 1 clove garlic, minced
- 2 tbsps. chopped fresh parsley
- 1/4 cup grated Parmesan cheese
- 2 tbsps. olive oil
- 2 tbsps. balsamic vinegar
- 1/2 tsp. salt
- 1/2 tsp. ground black pepper
- 1/4 cup chopped red bell pepper

Direction

- Place olives in a blender or food processor and pulse until chopped slightly, then move to a bowl and put aside.
- In a food processor or blender, combine half the red bell peppers, black pepper, salt, balsamic vinegar, olive oil, Parmesan cheese, parsley, garlic, onion, and capers, then blend until chopped finely. Add to the olives and mix, then sprinkle with the leftover red pepper.

Nutrition Information

- Calories: 66 calories;
- Total Carbohydrate: 3.3 g
- Cholesterol: 1 mg
- Total Fat: 5.8 g
- Protein: 1.1 g
- Sodium: 435 mg

125. Deliciosa Salsa Verde

"Take the seeds out of the peppers if you aren't a fan of spicy food."
Serving: 8 | Prep: 20m | Ready in: 25m

Ingredients

- 1 1/2 lbs. fresh tomatillos - husked, peeled, and halved
- 1/2 cup cilantro leaves
- 1/4 cup chopped white onion
- 1 jalapeno pepper, diced
- 1 serrano pepper, diced
- 1 lime, juiced
- 1/8 tsp. white sugar

Direction

- Preheat oven broiler. Set oven rack about 6-in. away from heat source. Put tomatillos on a baking sheet, cut side down.
- Broil in the preheated oven for about 5 minutes until slightly charred.
- Put tomatillos in a food processor. Add sugar, lime juice, serrano pepper, jalapeno pepper, onion and cilantro. Pulse until it's well mixed.

Nutrition Information

- Calories: 32 calories;
- Total Carbohydrate: 6.2 g
- Cholesterol: 0 mg
- Total Fat: 0.9 g
- Protein: 1 g
- Sodium: 3 mg

126. Dessert Hummus

"This is a sweet variation of the hummus with poppy seeds."
Serving: 10 | Prep: 35m | Ready in: 40m

Ingredients

- Poppy Seed Paste:
- 2 1/2 cups white poppy seeds
- 2 1/2 cups black poppy seeds
- 1 1/2 cups coconut water
- 2 tbsps. butter, softened, or to taste
- 2 tbsps. honey, or to taste
- Dessert Hummus:
- 2 1/2 cups macadamia nuts
- 1/4 cup coconut water
- 2 tbsps. lemon juice
- 2 tbsps. orange juice
- 1 1/2 tbsps. grated fresh ginger
- 1 tbsp. lime juice
- 1 tbsp. olive oil
- 1 tbsp. raw sugar, or to taste
- 1 sprig mint, leaves removed and stem discarded, or to taste
- 2 tsps. poppyseed oil
- 1 tsp. grated orange zest, or to taste
- 1 pinch sea salt (optional)
- Spice Topping:
- 2 tbsps. ground cinnamon
- 2 tbsps. ground cloves
- 2 pinches ground cardamom
- 2 pinches ground nutmeg

Direction

- Set an oven to preheat at 175°C (350°F). On a rimmed baking tray, spread the black and white poppy seeds.
- Bake in the preheated oven for 5-8 minutes until aromatic and lightly roasted.
- In a blender or mortar and pestle, put in the poppy seeds and grind it into a fine flour. Stir in butter and 1 1/2 cup of coconut water then blend the paste until it reaches a pourable consistency and creamy. To make it fairly sweet, put in enough honey.
- In a blender or a food processor, stir in salt, orange zest, poppyseed oil, mint, sugar, olive oil, lime juice, ginger, orange juice, lemon juice, 1/4 cup of coconut water and macadamia nuts. Mix in 1 1/2 cup of poppy seed paste and process until the hummus becomes smooth, then move to a serving bowl.
- To make the spice topping, mix together in a small bowl the nutmeg, cardamom, cloves and cinnamon. Sprinkle on top of hummus.

Nutrition Information

- Calories: 678 calories;
- Total Carbohydrate: 29.8 g
- Cholesterol: 6 mg
- Total Fat: 60.5 g
- Protein: 15.3 g
- Sodium: 113 mg

127. Detox Cilantro Pesto

"I like eating this on crackers or bread."
Serving: 12 | Prep: 15m | Ready in: 15m

Ingredients

- 1/4 cup Brazil nuts
- 1/4 cup soy nuts
- 1/2 cup grated Parmesan cheese
- 2 tbsps. ground flax seeds
- 1 tbsp. lemon juice
- 4 cloves garlic, crushed

- 1 tsp. lime juice
- 1 tsp. chile powder
- 1 bunch chopped fresh cilantro
- 1/4 cup olive oil, or as desired

Direction

- In a food processor, chop soy nuts and Brazil nuts. Pulse in chile powder, lime juice, garlic, lemon juice, ground flax seeds and parmesan cheese until combined. Pulse in cilantro until chopped finely. Put olive oil. Process to form a thick sauce on low speed.

Nutrition Information

- Calories: 101 calories;
- Total Carbohydrate: 2.7 g
- Cholesterol: 3 mg
- Total Fat: 8.8 g
- Protein: 3.5 g
- Sodium: 54 mg

128. Deviled Egg Appetizer Dip

"This is a twist to deviled eggs and is served with crackers."
Serving: 24 | Prep: 20m | Ready in: 35m

Ingredients

- 12 eggs
- 1 cup mayonnaise
- 1 tbsp. Dijon mustard
- 2 tbsps. white wine vinegar
- 1 tsp. red hot sauce

Direction

- Put the eggs in a pan and cover them with water, then boil. Take away from the heat and allow the eggs to cook in the hot water without the heat for 12 minutes. Pour out the hot water and place the eggs in a bowl with ice water for them to cool.
- Peel the eggs and cut in half. Cut 1/2 of the egg whites and place in a bowl.
- Place the yolks and leftover egg whites in a food processor with hot sauce, white wine vinegar, Dijon mustard, and mayonnaise, process until smooth and move to a bowl. Fold in the chopped egg whites and serve.

Nutrition Information

- Calories: 98 calories;
- Total Carbohydrate: 0.6 g
- Cholesterol: 85 mg
- Total Fat: 9.5 g
- Protein: 2.9 g
- Sodium: 104 mg

129. Dilled Carrot Salad

"A simple recipe."
Serving: Serves 2

Ingredients

- 1 tbsp. vegetable oil
- 1 tbsp. white-wine vinegar
- 2 tsps. Dijon mustard
- 1 tbsp. chopped fresh dill sprigs
- 1 tsp. sugar
- 1 bunch carrots (about 3/4 lb.)

Direction

- Whisk all ingredients but carrots in a bowl; season with pepper and salt. Grate carrots using big holes of hand grater/food processor with fine-shredding disk. Mix into vinaigrette.

Nutrition Information

- Calories: 145
- Total Carbohydrate: 19 g
- Total Fat: 8 g
- Fiber: 5 g
- Protein: 2 g
- Sodium: 174 mg
- Saturated Fat: 1 g

130. Dilled Cheddar Cheese Batter Bread

Serving: Makes 1 loaf

Ingredients

- 3/4 cup milk
- 1 1/2 tbsps. dill seeds, coarsely chopped
- 1 tbsp. honey
- 1/4 cup canola oil
- 3 eggs, room temperature, beaten to blend
- 2 1/2 cups whole wheat flour
- 1 package dry yeast
- 1 1/2 tsps. salt
- 3 1/2 cups packed grated sharp cheddar cheese
- 3 tbsps. chopped fresh dill

Direction

- Simmer initial 3 ingredients in small saucepan; cool it to 120°F. Whisk in eggs and oil. Mix 2 cups cheese, yeast, salt and 1 1/2 cups flour in an electric mixer's big bowl. Add fresh dill and warm liquid mixture; beat for 3 minutes. Add leftover 1 1/4 cups flour; beat for 2 minutes. Scrape down bowl's sides. Use plastic wrap to cover bowl; rise dough for 1 hour 15 minutes till doubled in a draft-free warm area.
- Preheat an oven to 350°F and butter 9x5x3-in. loaf pan; don't mix batter down. Put 1/2 batter in pan; sprinkle leftover 1 1/2 cups cheese. Cover using leftover batter; smooth top. Cover; rise for 30 minutes till batter reaches pan's top in a draft-free warm area.
- Bake for 45 minutes till bread sounds hollow when tapped and golden brown. Turn onto rack; cool.

Nutrition Information

- Calories: 258
- Total Carbohydrate: 19 g
- Cholesterol: 64 mg
- Total Fat: 16 g
- Fiber: 3 g
- Protein: 12 g
- Sodium: 203 mg
- Saturated Fat: 6 g

131. Don't Knock It Until You Try It Zucchini Chocolate Banana Nut Milkshake

""I tried making these 2 giant zucchini that I found in my garden into a whole new meal. I finally came up to this delicious dessert, and my kids can't stop talking about it.""
Serving: 4 | Prep: 10m | Ready in: 10m

Ingredients

- 1 cup grated zucchini, frozen
- 2 large ripe bananas, peeled and frozen
- 2 tbsps. cocoa powder
- 1/4 cup chopped peanuts
- 1/2 cup sugar
- 1 cup half and half

Direction

- Process cocoa powder, sugar, half-and-half, peanuts, zucchini, and bananas in a food processor until creamy, smooth, and thick.

Nutrition Information

- Calories: 300 calories;
- Total Carbohydrate: 47.6 g
- Cholesterol: 22 mg
- Total Fat: 12.1 g
- Protein: 5.6 g
- Sodium: 30 mg

132. Dottie's Pate

"This recipe is for cocktail parties that can be pair with other firm crackers or bagel!"
Serving: 20 | Prep: 15m | Ready in: 2h30m

Ingredients

- 1 lb. chicken livers, rinsed and trimmed

- 2/3 cup thinly sliced onion
- 1 clove garlic, chopped
- 2 bay leaves
- 1/4 tsp. dried thyme
- 1 cup water
- 1 tsp. salt
- 3/4 cup butter, softened
- 2 dashes hot pepper sauce (such as Tabasco®)
- 1 tsp. salt
- ground black pepper to taste
- 2 tbsps. cognac

Direction

- Combine the bay leaves, thyme, water, 1 tsp. of salt, garlic, onion and chicken livers together in the saucepan and make it boil. Minimize the heat, and cook for 7 to 8 minutes until the livers are well done. Get the saucepan from the heat, and cool down for 5 minutes. Take the bay leaves out from the saucepan.
- Prepare a blender and put the liver mixture then blend; mix in the butter, about 1 tbsp. at a time. Add in the black pepper, cognac, 1 more tsp. of salt, and hot pepper sauce.
- Blend well until it becomes smooth; Transfer into a serving bowl and place inside the refrigerator until firm enough.

Nutrition Information

- Calories: 95 calories;
- Total Carbohydrate: 0.5 g
- Cholesterol: 97 mg
- Total Fat: 8 g
- Protein: 4 g
- Sodium: 301 mg

133. Double Chocolate Pistachio Cookies

"This raw food dish has no refined sugar, dairy, soy, or wheat. You can also leave out the coffee beans if you want."
Serving: 2 | Prep: 20m | Ready in: 1h20m

Ingredients

- 1/4 cup ground pistachios
- 2 tbsps. ground flax seed
- 1 tbsp. unsweetened cocoa powder
- 2 tsps. finely ground coffee beans (optional)
- 3 dried figs, stems removed, cut in quarters
- 3 dates, pitted and chopped
- 2 tsps. ground cinnamon
- 1 tbsp. agave nectar
- 1 fresh strawberry

Direction

- In a bowl, stir together the coffee beans, cocoa powder, flax seed, and pistachios.
- In a food processor, blend the strawberry, agave nectar, cinnamon, dates, and figs until combined thoroughly.
- Stir the fruit mix into the pistachio mixture and mix to form into a workable dough.
- Divide the dough in half and pat each one into a flat cookie shape. Place them on a plate and refrigerate for around 1 hour, flipping them after 30 minutes.

Nutrition Information

- Calories: 277 calories;
- Total Carbohydrate: 46.1 g
- Cholesterol: 0 mg
- Total Fat: 10.8 g
- Protein: 6.4 g
- Sodium: 73 mg

134. Double-crust Nectarine Raspberry Pies

"Fragrant and amazing pies."
Serving: Makes 2 (9-inch) pies | Prep: 1.5h

Ingredients

- 5 cups all-purpose flour
- 3 sticks (1 1/2 cups) cold unsalted butter, cut into 1/2-inch cubes but left in sticks
- 1/2 cup cold vegetable shortening (preferably trans-fat-free)
- 1 tsp. salt
- About 3/4 cup ice water
- 1 tbsp. milk
- 2 tbsps. sugar
- 6 lb nectarines
- 3 cups raspberries (3/4 lb.)
- 3 tbsps. fresh lemon juice
- 1/4 cup quick-cooking tapioca
- 1/4 cup cornstarch
- 1/4 tsp. salt
- 1 1/2 cups sugar
- a pastry or bench scraper; an electric coffee/spice grinder; 2 (9-inch) glass or metal pie plates (5-cup capacity)

Direction

- Pastry: Blend 1/2 tsp. salt, 1/4 cup shortening, 1 1/2 sticks butter and 2 1/2 cups flour till it looks like coarse meal with few roughly pea-sized butter lumps with pastry blender/fingertips/pulse in food processor. Evenly drizzle 5 tbsp. ice water; pulse/mix gently with a fork till incorporated.
- Squeeze small handful; put more ice water in dough, 1 tbsp. at a time, pulsing/mixing just till combined if it doesn't hold together. Don't overwork mixture; it'll be tough.
- Turn dough out on work surface; divide to 6 portions. Smear each portion 1-2 times with heel of hand to distribute fat in a forward motion. Use scraper to gather all dough together; press to 2 balls. Flatten each to 5-in. disk. In same manner, make 2 more disk with leftover 1/2 tsp. salt, 1/4 cup shortening, 1 1/2 sticks butter and 2 1/2 cups flour. Chill dough for minimum of 1 hour till firm, each disk tightly wrapped in plastic wrap.
- As dough chills, prep filling: Cut nectarines to 1/2-in. wide wedges; toss with lemon juice and raspberries in a big bowl.
- Grind tapioca in grinder to powder; whisk with sugar, salt and cornstarch in small bowl. Don't toss with fruit till dough gets rolled out.
- Roll pastry and prep pies: In oven's lower third, put oven rack. On rack, put big foil sheet; preheat the oven to 425°F.
- One by one, roll 2 dough disks out, keep leftover disks chilled, with lightly floured rolling pin to 13-in. rounds on lightly floured surface. Fit in pie plates; don't trim. Chill till needed.
- For top crusts, roll leftover 2 disks out in same manner; put aside and keep flat.
- Toss fruit and sugar mixture gently; divide to pie shells.
- Use pastry rounds to cover pies; use kitchen shears to trim edges, leaving 1/2-in. overhang. Press the edges together; decoratively crimp. Brush milk on pastry tops; sprinkle 2 tbsp. sugar total all over. Cut few steam vents on top of every pie using small sharp knife.
- Bake pie for 20 minutes on foil. Lower oven temperature to 375°F; bake for 40 minutes till filling is bubbly and crusts are golden brown, frequently checking, covering each pie's edge with foil strip/pie shield if the crusts brown too quickly.
- Cool pies for minimum of 2 hours on racks to room temperature.
- You can chill dough in disks for maximum 1 day.
- You can make pie shells 1 day ahead, loosely covered, chilled. You can roll out then chill pastry rounds, layered between plastic wrap sheets, for top crust. Bring the pastry rounds, before assembling pies, to cool room temperature.

Nutrition Information

- Calories: 4395
- Total Carbohydrate: 609 g
- Cholesterol: 367 mg
- Total Fat: 207 g
- Fiber: 43 g
- Protein: 52 g
- Sodium: 1551 mg
- Saturated Fat: 104 g

135. Dried Fruit And Almond Haroseth

"An amazing recipe!"
Serving: Makes about 1 3/4 cups

Ingredients

- 3/4 cup pitted dates (about 4 oz.)
- 1/3 cup raisins
- 6 small Calimyrna figs, stemmed
- 1 small orange, seeded, cubed
- 1/3 cup coarsely chopped almonds
- 1/2 tsp. ground cinnamon
- 1/8 tsp. cayenne pepper
- 1/4 cup dry red wine

Direction

- Chop initial 7 ingredients coarsely in a processor. Add the wine; blend till orange is chopped finely yet it is still chunky with on/off turns. Put in a bowl. You can make it 4 hours ahead, chilled, covered.

Nutrition Information

- Calories: 174
- Total Carbohydrate: 34 g
- Total Fat: 4 g
- Fiber: 5 g
- Protein: 3 g
- Sodium: 2 mg
- Saturated Fat: 0 g

136. Dried-apple Tart With Crisp Crumble Topping

Serving: Serves 8 to 10

Ingredients

- 12 oz. dried apples (preferably Granny Smith)
- 1/2 cup packed light brown sugar
- 4 cups water
- 2 cups apple cider
- 1 tbsp. fresh lemon juice
- four 3-inch cinnamon sticks
- 3/4 stick (6 tbsps.) cold unsalted butter
- 3/4 cup all-purpose flour
- 1/2 cup granulated sugar
- 1 1/4 sticks (10 tbsps.) cold unsalted butter
- 1 1/2 cups all-purpose flour
- 1/2 cup confectioners' sugar
- Accompaniment: whipped cream or vanilla ice cream

Direction

- Filling: Simmer pinch salt and filling ingredients in 5-qt. heavy kettle for 15 minutes till apples are fully plumped, covered. Uncover mixture; simmer for 1 hour till extra liquid is absorbed/evaporated and thick, occasionally mixing. As liquid is absorbed/evaporated, lower heat and frequently stir mixture to avoid scorching toward end of cooking. Throw cinnamon sticks. You can make filling 2 days ahead, cooled then covered, chilled.
- Topping: Cut butter to 1/2-in. pieces. Pulse granulated sugar, flour and butter till crumbly in a food processor. Put topping in a bowl; chill till ready to use, covered.
- When topping and filling are done, make pastry dough: Preheat an oven to 375°F.
- Cut butter to 1/2-in. pieces. Pulse pinch salt and pastry dough ingredients till mixture starts to gather together in cleaned food processor.
- Evenly press dough up the side and bottom of 11-in. tart pan that has removable fluted rim.

Use foil to line shell; bake in center of oven for 12 minutes till shell is set. Remove foil gently; leave foil on then bake for 2 minutes if foil sticks to the shell. Bake shell for 5 minutes till edge is golden; tart shell won't be fully cooked.
- Put filling into shell immediately; evenly crumble topping on filling. Bake tart in center of oven till topping is golden for 30 minutes. Cool tart in the pan on the rack. You can make tart 1 day ahead, kept in pan, chilled, covered. Reheat tart if desired, uncovered. Or, before serving, bring to room temperature. Take off pan's side.
- Serve with ice cream or whipped cream.

Nutrition Information

- Calories: 597
- Total Carbohydrate: 97 g
- Cholesterol: 61 mg
- Total Fat: 24 g
- Fiber: 5 g
- Protein: 4 g
- Sodium: 52 mg
- Saturated Fat: 15 g

137. Dried-cranberry Spread

"A great recipe."
Serving: Makes about 1 cup

Ingredients

- Nonstick vegetable oil spray
- 1/4 cup dried cranberries
- 1 8-oz. container nonfat cream cheese, room temperature
- 1/4 cup soft fresh goat cheese (such as Montrachet; about 1 3/4 oz.)
- 2 tbsps. plain nonfat yogurt
- 2 to 3 tsps. honey

Direction

- Spray nonstick spray on metal blade of processor. Put dried cranberries in a processor; chop coarsely. Add 2 tsp. honey, nonfat yogurt, goat cheese and nonfat cream cheese; process till blended well. Taste; if desired, add 1 tsp. honey. Put spread in bowl. You can make it 3 days ahead, refrigerated, covered.

138. Dulce De Leche Cheesecake Bars

"So wonderful!"
Serving: Makes 24

Ingredients

- Nonstick vegetable oil spray
- 2 1/4 cups finely ground graham crackers (from about 17 whole graham crackers)
- 2 tbsps. sugar
- 1/4 tsp. ground cinnamon
- 10 tbsps. (1 1/4 sticks) unsalted butter, melted
- 3 8-oz. packages Philadelphia-brand cream cheese, room temperature
- 1 cup sugar
- 3 large eggs
- 1/2 cup purchased dulce de leche*
- 2 tsps. vanilla extract
- 2/3 cup purchased dulce de leche
- 3 tbsps. (or more) heavy whipping cream
- Fleur de sel**

Direction

- Crust: Preheat an oven to 350°F. Use nonstick spray to coat a 13x9x2-in. metal baking pan. Mix sugar, cinnamon and graham cracker crumbs in medium bowl then add melted butter; mix till coated. Put crumb mixture in pan; evenly press on pan's bottom. Bake for 10 minutes till crust is light golden; fully cool on rack.
- Filling: Blend sugar and cream cheese for 1 minute till creamy and smooth in processor, occasionally stopping to scrape bowl's sides down. One by one, add eggs; process to blend between additions for 3-5 seconds. Add vanilla and dulce de leche; process for 10 seconds till

blended. Evenly spread batter on cooled curst; bake for 38 minutes till edges are slightly cracked and puffed and set in middle. Put on rack; fully cool.
- Glaze: Heat 3 tbsp. cream and dulce de leche in 10-sec intervals till melted in microwave-safe bowl. Mix to blend; if too thick to pour, add extra cream by teaspoonfuls. Cream amount varies on dulce de leche brand. Put glaze on cooled cheesecake; evenly spread. Refrigerate for 1 hour till chilled; glaze won't be firm. You can make it 2 days ahead, covered, chilled.
- Lengthwise cut cheesecake to 4 strips and crosswise to 6 strips, making 24 bars. Sprinkle fleur de sel on bars.

Nutrition Information

- Calories: 282
- Total Carbohydrate: 25 g
- Cholesterol: 74 mg
- Total Fat: 19 g
- Fiber: 0 g
- Protein: 4 g
- Sodium: 176 mg
- Saturated Fat: 10 g

139. Easy Basil Pesto With Almonds

"I use almonds as a cheaper substitute for pine nuts. Keep leftovers in a small jar with olive oil drizzled on top in the fridge."
Serving: 4 | Prep: 5m | Ready in: 5m

Ingredients

- 2 cups fresh basil leaves
- 1/2 cup Parmesan cheese
- 1/4 cup whole raw almonds
- 1/4 cup extra-virgin olive oil, or more as needed
- 1 clove garlic, peeled

Direction

- In a food processor, pulse garlic, olive oil, almonds, Parmesan cheese and basil until blended. Pour more olive oil in as processor runs until pesto is smooth and thick.

Nutrition Information

- Calories: 226 calories;
- Total Carbohydrate: 3 g
- Cholesterol: 9 mg
- Total Fat: 21.5 g
- Protein: 6.4 g
- Sodium: 154 mg

140. Easy Black Bean Hummus

"An easy to make flavorful hummus that can be a replacement to your meat in sandwiches. You can put less lemon juice or add more spices according to your preference."
Serving: 12 | Prep: 10m | Ready in: 10m

Ingredients

- 1 (15 oz.) can black beans, rinsed and drained
- 2 tsps. lemon juice
- 1 tbsp. dried basil
- 1 tsp. garlic powder

Direction

- In a food processor, blend together the garlic powder, basil, lemon juice and black beans until it becomes thick.

Nutrition Information

- Calories: 34 calories;
- Total Carbohydrate: 6.2 g
- Cholesterol: 0 mg
- Total Fat: 0.1 g
- Protein: 2.2 g
- Sodium: 136 mg

141. Easy Kale Pesto

"Keep pesto in plastic containers/glass jars and keep in the fridge for 1 week, refrigerated."
Serving: 12 | Prep: 15m | Ready in: 15m

Ingredients

- 1 cup extra-virgin olive oil
- 3 cloves garlic, peeled
- 12 cups firmly packed chopped kale leaves
- 1 cup pine nuts
- 1 cup grated Parmesan cheese
- salt to taste

Direction

- In a food processor, put garlic and olive oil. Pulse for about 10 seconds until garlic is chopped. In batches if needed, add kale in. Pulse for 20 seconds until blended evenly. Scrape sides of bowl down.
- Mix in parmesan cheese and pine nuts to kale mixture. Pulse until it's smooth. Season using salt.

Nutrition Information

- Calories: 295 calories;
- Total Carbohydrate: 8.8 g
- Cholesterol: 6 mg
- Total Fat: 26.8 g
- Protein: 7.5 g
- Sodium: 144 mg

142. Edamame Burger

"Wheat Free green burgers."
Serving: 16 Burgers

Ingredients

- 2 cups (340 g) shelled and frozen edamame
- 1 can (15 oz., or 420 g) chickpeas, with liquid
- 8 oz. (227 g) sliced mushrooms
- 1/2 cup (65 g) finely ground raw cashews
- 1/2 cup (60 g) nutritional yeast
- 4 cloves garlic
- 1/2 tsp. ground cumin
- 1/4 tsp. liquid smoke (optional)
- 1 tsp. Bragg's Liquid Aminos or soy sauce
- Salt and pepper, to taste
- 3 1/2 cups (420 g) chickpea flour
- Oil, for frying

Direction

- In a saucepot, put whole can of chickpeas as well as the liquid and frozen edamame, and warm completely. This is to thaw edamame; skip this step if using fresh or precooked edamame.
- In a food processor, mix salt and pepper, liquid aminos, liquid smoke, cumin, garlic, yeast, cashews, mushrooms, chickpeas and liquid and edamame and blend till smooth. Put into a big bowl.
- Gradually add flour till a thicker consistency is created. You may have to add just a small amount of flour or a lot, based on moisture content of the mixture.
- In refrigerator, put the entire bowl for 20 minutes to half an hour to toughen up and make it uncomplicated to handle once shaping the patties. Shape into 16 patties.
- In a sauté pan, heat the oil and fry patties for 4 to 5 minutes, or till golden brown on every side.

Nutrition Information

- Calories: 268
- Total Carbohydrate: 22 g
- Total Fat: 16 g
- Fiber: 5 g
- Protein: 11 g
- Sodium: 194 mg
- Saturated Fat: 1 g

143. Edamame Dip With Crudites

"A light starter and a smart alternative to fussy holiday hors d'oeuvres."
| Prep: 30m

Ingredients

- 4 large carrots
- 3 celery ribs, strings removed with a vegetable peeler
- 1 seedless cucumber (usually plastic-wrapped), halved lengthwise and cored
- 1 bunch radishes
- 1 lb fresh or frozen shelled edamame (soybeans; 3 cups)
- 2 1/2 tsps. salt
- 1 tbsp. chopped garlic
- 5 tbsps. extra-virgin olive oil
- 1 tbsp. fresh lime juice
- 1 tsp. sugar
- 1/2 tsp. black pepper
- 1/4 cup chopped fresh cilantro

Direction

- Slice cucumber, celery and carrots making half-inch-wide and 2 1/2-inch long sticks. Slice the radishes lengthwise making quarter-inch-thick pieces. With cold water and ice, fill a big bowl and soak slice vegetables in ice water to retain crisp while preparing dip.
- In a 3-quart heavy saucepan, cook edamame in 1 1/2-quart boiling water along with 1 1/2 tsps. salt for 3 minutes, then set 3/4 cup cooking liquid aside and let edamame drain in a colander. Wash under cold water till cool.
- Dry the saucepan and put 3 tbsps. oil and the garlic, then allow to cook over low heat for 3 to 5 minutes, mixing from time to time, till garlic is light golden.
- In a food processor, purée garlic-oil mixture and 2 cups edamame till smooth. In a stream, put half-cup of the reserved edamame-cooking water while the motor is running. Put the leftover tsp. salt, remaining 2 tbsps. oil, pepper, sugar, lime juice and the leftover cup of edamame and pulse till slightly lumpy. To thin, put the leftover quarter cup of cooking liquid if wished, then mix in the cilantro.
- Turn dip onto serving dish and serve together with drained and patted dry vegetables for dipping.
- Notes: Vegetables can be sliced a day in advance and refrigerate in an enclosed moistened-paper-towels-lined-plastic-bag. In case slicing vegetables in advance, ice bath is not needed.
- Dip, not added with cilantro, can be prepared a day in advance and refrigerate with cover. Come to room temperature and mix in the cilantro prior to serving.

144. Eggplant Pasta Bake

"Creamy and filling."
Serving: 8 | Prep: 45m | Ready in: 1h20m

Ingredients

- 1 large eggplant, peeled and thinly sliced
- 1/2 lb. dry penne pasta
- 1 large onion, chopped
- 1 red bell pepper, chopped
- 2 cloves garlic
- 1 ancho chile pepper, chopped (optional)
- 2 tbsps. olive oil
- 6 tbsps. butter
- 6 tbsps. all-purpose flour
- 2 cups milk
- 1 (12 oz.) package vegetarian burger crumbles
- 1 1/2 cups shredded mozzarella cheese

Direction

- Preheat an oven to 190°C/375°F. Oil a big, deep casserole dish lightly. Boil a big pot with lightly salted water. Add pasta; cook till al dente for 8-10 minutes. Drain.
- Put sliced eggplant on the greased cookie sheet; bake for 20 minutes in preheated oven.
- Puree ancho chile pepper (optional), garlic, bell pepper and onion in a food processor. Add 1 tbsp. water if too thick. Heat oil on

medium heat in a big skillet. Put onion mixture in pan; cook about 10 minutes, till liquid evaporates and is thick, occasionally mixing. Take off heat; put aside.
- Melt butter on low heat in medium saucepan; mix in flour till smooth. Add milk, mixing till smooth. Take off heat.
- Put 1/2 baked eggplant in greased casserole dish; put 1/2 white sauce in, covering eggplant. Spread veggie crumbs on white sauce, pasta then bell pepper puree layer. Cover pepper and onion mixture with leftover eggplant; put leftover white sauce on eggplant. Sprinkle mozzarella cheese on casserole.
- In preheated oven, bake for 35 minutes, uncovered. Before serving, stand for 10 minutes.

Nutrition Information

- Calories: 420 calories;
- Total Carbohydrate: 40.9 g
- Cholesterol: 41 mg
- Total Fat: 19.5 g
- Protein: 21 g
- Sodium: 383 mg

145. Eser's Balsamic Salad Dressing

"Keep leftover dressing in shakable sealed container for 2 weeks in the fridge."
Serving: 8 | Prep: 10m | Ready in: 10m

Ingredients

- 3 tbsps. balsamic vinegar
- 1 tbsp. honey, or more to taste
- 1 tbsp. Dijon mustard
- 1 clove garlic, crushed
- 1/2 tsp. dried oregano
- salt and ground black pepper to taste
- 1/3 cup olive oil, or more as needed

Direction

- In food processor, mix black pepper, salt, oregano, garlic, mustard, honey and balsamic vinegar. Turn on food processor; in steady stream, put olive oil into balsamic vinegar mixture till salad dressing is creamy and thick.

Nutrition Information

- Calories: 94 calories;
- Total Carbohydrate: 3.6 g
- Cholesterol: 0 mg
- Total Fat: 9 g
- Protein: 0.1 g
- Sodium: 68 mg

146. Ez Restaurant-style Hummus

"This perfect hummus recipe is best when the lemon juice and beans sit first but is also good when blended altogether. Upon serving, make a well in the middle then drizzle with olive oil and put ground paprika. You may top it with Greek olives, tomatoes or dice cucumbers for decoration. Serve alongside pita bread."
Serving: 24 | Prep: 10m | Ready in: 25m

Ingredients

- 1 1/2 (15.5 oz.) cans garbanzo beans, drained with liquid (aquafaba) reserved
- 1/3 cup fresh lemon juice
- 1/4 cup well-stirred tahini (Middle Eastern sesame paste)
- 1 tbsp. olive oil
- 3 cloves garlic, minced
- 1/8 tsp. ground cayenne
- 1/8 tsp. white sugar
- 1 pinch salt and ground black pepper

Direction

- In a food processor, soak the lemon juice, 1 1/2 tbsp. of reserved aquafaba and garbanzo beans for about 15 minutes until flavors blend.
- Process the soaked garbanzo beans until it becomes roughly chopped. Stir in black

pepper, salt, sugar, cayenne, garlic, olive oil and tahini, then process, putting in reserved aquafaba to thin out until the desired consistency was achieved and is smooth.

Nutrition Information

- Calories: 54 calories;
- Total Carbohydrate: 7.2 g
- Cholesterol: 0 mg
- Total Fat: 2.2 g
- Protein: 1.8 g
- Sodium: 92 mg

147. Flank Steak Salad With Chimichurri Dressing

"A quick recipe."
Serving: Makes 6 servings | Prep: 15m

Ingredients

- 1 large bunch fresh Italian parsley
- 2 tbsps. fresh oregano leaves
- 3 garlic cloves, peeled
- 1/2 cup olive oil
- 1/4 cup red wine vinegar
- 1 tsp. chipotle hot pepper sauce
- 1 1 1/2-lb. flank steak
- 8 oz. mixed baby greens
- 1 12-oz. container marinated small fresh mozzarella balls,* drained

Direction

- Prepare barbecue to medium high heat. Blend garlic, oregano and parsley with stems for 10 seconds in a processor. Add hot pepper sauce, vinegar and 1/2 cup oil; blend till nearly smooth. Season the dressing with pepper and salt to taste.
- Brush oil on grill rack; sprinkle pepper and salt on both sides of steak. Grill steaks, 5 minutes on each side for medium-rare, to desired doneness. Put steak on a work surface; rest for 5 minutes.
- Meanwhile, toss some dressing and greens in a big bowl; put on a big platter. Sprinkle mozzarella over.
- On slight diagonal, slice steak across grain thinly; put the steak on top of greens. Drizzle with leftover dressing.

Nutrition Information

- Calories: 536
- Total Carbohydrate: 5 g
- Cholesterol: 122 mg
- Total Fat: 40 g
- Fiber: 2 g
- Protein: 38 g
- Sodium: 457 mg
- Saturated Fat: 14 g

148. Food Processor Pizza Dough

"A quick recipe."
Serving: Makes about 1 lb. of dough | Prep: 10m

Ingredients

- 3/4 tsp. active dry yeast
- 1/2 tsp. fine sea salt
- 1 2/3 cups bread flour, plus more for surface

Direction

- Pulse 1 2/3 cups flour, salt and yeast till combined in a food processor. Add 3/4 cup of 100-110°F water as motor runs; process for 30 seconds till ball forms.
- Turn out dough on lightly floured work surface; should appear slightly shaggy and stick to counter. By teaspoonful, add more warm water till tacky if dough is too dry. Knead for 5 minutes till dough is elastic and smooth. Divide to 2 balls, each makes 12-14-in. pizza.
- Put balls in separate big resealable bags/containers; chill for minimum of overnight – maximum of 2 days.
- You can make dough 3 months ahead. Wrap balls in plastic tightly; freeze.

Nutrition Information

- Calories: 209
- Total Carbohydrate: 42 g
- Total Fat: 1 g
- Fiber: 2 g
- Protein: 7 g
- Sodium: 134 mg
- Saturated Fat: 0 g

149. Fresca Relish

"For an alternative to classic salsa, you can simply create this relish into a dip. This is one of the simple ways to make you eat veggies. This healthy relish is great as a side dish or on fish tacos. If you want some additional taste, you can add herbs like cilantro or parsley. Enjoy!"
Serving: 6 | Prep: 15m | Ready in: 1h15m

Ingredients

- 1 large sweet onion, coarsely chopped
- 8 baby carrots
- 1 large green bell pepper, stemmed and seeded
- 1 cucumber, coarsely chopped
- 6 small radishes
- 4 broccoli florets
- 5 cherry tomatoes
- 3 cloves garlic
- 2 tbsps. vinaigrette
- 1 tbsp. juice from jarred pepperoncini peppers (optional)
- 1 tsp. kosher salt
- 1 tsp. ground black pepper

Direction

- In a food processor, combine the cherry tomatoes, cucumber, green bell pepper, carrots, garlic, onion, broccoli, radishes, vinaigrette, pepper, salt, and pepperoncini juice. Pulse the ingredients until chopped evenly. Refrigerate the relish for at least 1 hour until the flavors are well-blended.

Nutrition Information

- Calories: 85 calories;
- Total Carbohydrate: 18.6 g
- Cholesterol: 0 mg
- Total Fat: 0.6 g
- Protein: 4.3 g
- Sodium: 496 mg

150. Frozen Boysenberry And White Chocolate Parfait

"This delicious dessert needed to be prepared 1 day ahead."
Serving: Serves 6

Ingredients

- 1 16-oz. bag frozen boysenberries or blackberries, thawed
- 1/4 cup sugar
- 1 tbsp. crème de
- 1/2 tsp. fresh lemon juice
- 3/4 cup sugar
- 1/4 cup water
- 6 large egg yolks
- 3 oz. imported white chocolate (such as Lindt), chopped, melted
- 2 tsps. vanilla extract
- 1 2/3 cups chilled whipping cream
- 1 16-oz. bag frozen boysenberries or blackberries, thawed
- 1/4 cup sugar
- 2 tbsps. crème de
- Fresh boysenberries, blackberries or strawberries
- Fresh mint sprigs

Direction

- To prepare Parfait: Line plastic wrap on a 9x5-inch loaf pan. In a blender, puree 1/4 cup of sugar and berries till just smooth then strain. Measure 1 1/3 cups puree then put in a heavy small saucepan. Set aside any leftover puree for sauce. Over medium heat, simmer while occasionally stirring 1 1/3 cups puree for 8

minutes till reduced to scant 1 cup. Move to a bowl and let chill for 30 minutes. Add in lemon juice and cassis; stir. Store reduced puree in the fridge till ready to use.
- In a medium metal bowl, combine yolks, water and 3/4 cup sugar. Place bowl over a saucepan of simmering water. Beat yolk mixture by a hand-held electric mixer while occasionally scraping down the bowl's sides for 5 minutes till a candy thermometer reads 140°F. Keep cooking and beating constantly for 3 minutes. Take away from over water. Beat in vanilla extract and melted chocolate till cool. In a separate bowl, beat whipping cream till stiff peaks form. In chocolate mixture, gently mix 1/4 whipped cream then fold in the leftover whipped cream.
- In a medium bowl, place 1 1/3 cups chocolate mixture. Fold in the berry puree that has been reduced. Fill 1/3 of the leftover chocolate mixture in the prepped loaf pan. Add berry-chocolate mixture to cover. Place the leftover chocolate mixture on top. Smooth the top then store the parfait in the freezer overnight. You can prepare this 2 days ahead.
- To prepare sauce: In a processor or a blender, puree crème de cassis, sugar and frozen boysenberries till smooth. Strain. Add in any puree that was set aside from parfait.
- Remove the frozen parfait from the mold. Remove the plastic wrap. Cut into slices with 1/2-in. thick. Sprinkle with sauce. Add fresh mint sprigs and berries to garnish.

151. Garlic Asparagus Soup

"A refreshing and light soup that can be served as a side dish or a main course."
Serving: 4 | Prep: 15m | Ready in: 30m

Ingredients

- 1 tbsp. olive oil
- 5 cloves garlic, thinly sliced
- 4 green onions, coarsely chopped
- 1 1/2 lbs. asparagus, trimmed and coarsely chopped
- 2 (14 oz.) cans vegetable broth
- salt and ground black pepper to taste

Direction

- In a saucepan, heat the olive oil on medium heat.
- In a saucepan, cook and stir the green onions and garlic for about 3 minutes, until the garlic turns just golden in color.
- Cook and stir green onions and garlic with asparagus for around 2 minutes more until it turns a bit soft.
- Pour in vegetable broth, then boil. Lower the heat and let it simmer for about 10 minutes, until the asparagus becomes soft. Turn off the heat and let it cool a bit.
- In the blender, pour the soup then fill not more than halfway full. Put lid to cover. Start the blender carefully and use several quick pulses to get the soup moving prior to leaving it on to puree. Puree in batches until it has a smooth consistency.
- Put the soup back into the saucepan and reheat, then sprinkle ground black pepper and salt to season.

Nutrition Information

- Calories: 101 calories;
- Total Carbohydrate: 13.3 g
- Cholesterol: 0 mg
- Total Fat: 4.1 g
- Protein: 5.1 g
- Sodium: 409 mg

152. Garlic Crème Fraiche

"Keeps for 1 week, refrigerated."
Serving: 8 | Prep: 15m | Ready in: 12h15m

Ingredients

- 1 cup heavy whipping cream
- 2 tbsps. buttermilk

- 2 large cloves garlic
- 1/2 tbsp. kosher salt
- 1 tbsp. lemon juice, or as needed

Direction

- In a bowl, mix buttermilk and heavy cream; cover. Put aside for 12-16 hours till thick yet pourable in a warm place. Mix; refrigerate for maximum of 1 week.
- Cut garlic; sprinkle salt over. Pulverize with knife's blade. Mix garlic juice into the cream mixture.
- Put cream mixture into food processor; slowly add lemon juice, blending on low speed, stopping once sauce gets fluffy consistency.

Nutrition Information

- Calories: 106 calories;
- Total Carbohydrate: 1.6 g
- Cholesterol: 41 mg
- Total Fat: 11 g
- Protein: 0.8 g
- Sodium: 376 mg

153. Ginger Crunch Cake With Strawberry Sauce

Serving: Makes 1 Cake

Ingredients

- 1 cup pecans, toasted and chopped fine
- 1/2 cup gingersnap cookie crumbs (from about eight 2-inch gingersnaps)
- 1/2 cup firmly packed light brown sugar
- 1/2 stick (1/4 cup) unsalted butter, melted
- 1 3/4 cups all-purpose flour
- 3/4 tsp. baking soda
- 3/4 tsp. ground ginger
- 3/4 tsp. cinnamon
- 3/4 tsp. salt
- 3/4 cup unsulfured molasses
- 2/3 cup buttermilk
- 1/3 cup granulated sugar
- 3/4 stick (6 tbsps.) unsalted butter, softened
- 1 large egg, beaten lightly
- 3 cups well-chilled heavy cream
- 1 tsp. vanilla extract
- 4 tbsps. granulated sugar
- 1 pint strawberries
- 1 tbsp. fresh lemon juice
- Garnish: strawberries, with leaves and blossoms if desired (not recommended for eating)

Direction

- Heat an oven to 350 degrees F. Oil 3 cake pans measuring 8- by 2-inch.
- Crunch topping: mix crunch ingredients for topping in small bowl, mixing till blended. Distribute topping between pans and evenly force on bottom.
- Ginger cake: mix salt, cinnamon, ginger, baking soda and flour in a big bowl. Put in the rest of ingredients for ginger cake and whip for 2 minutes at high speed of an electric mixer. Scatter batter on crunch topping in pans gently; bake in top third and bottom third of the oven for 20 minutes, changing pans position in oven midway through, or till an inserted tester in the middle of every layer exits clean.
- Flip cake layers to wax paper-lined-racks right away and cool fully. You can make cake layers 2 weeks in advance, use plastic wrap to wrap individually and place in freezer. Defrost layers in fridge then proceed with recipe.
- Whip vanilla, 2 tbsps. of granulated sugar and 2 cups of cream using cold electric mixer's beaters in a cold bowl just till it holds firm peaks.
- Cake Assembly: place a layer of cake onto cake plate with crunch side facing up and smear with heaping 1 cup whipped cream. Redo with one more layer of cake and one more heaping cup of whipped cream put the third layer of cake, crunch side facing up, on top. Keep the top bare, smear the rest of whipped cream on cake side to cover (the finishing coating will be added on the latter part). Cover

cake in plastic wrap loosely and refrigerate for no less than 4 hours (to facilitate cutting) to a day.
- Hull the strawberries and cut 1/2 of them. Crush slices of berries along with leftover 2 tbsps. of granulated sugar and lemon juice using potato masher in bowl. Purée the rest of the berries in food processor and filter using fine sieve right in a bowl containing mixture of mashed berry. Sauce can be prep a day in advance; cover and chill.
- Whip the leftover cup cream using cold electric mixer's beaters in a cold bowl till it barely holds firm peaks and smear on cake side in a decorative manner. Place several whole strawberries over cake, jazz plate up using more whole strawberries.
- Serve strawberry sauce and cake together.

Nutrition Information

- Calories: 7378
- Total Carbohydrate: 733 g
- Cholesterol: 1476 mg
- Total Fat: 485 g
- Fiber: 27 g
- Protein: 67 g
- Sodium: 4087 mg
- Saturated Fat: 251 g

154. Gingered Carrot Soup

"A perfect beginning for an autumn lunch or dinner."
Serving: 4

Ingredients

- 2 tbsps. olive oil
- 1/2 cup minced onion
- 1/4 cup grated fresh ginger
- 2 cloves garlic, minced
- 4 cups Kitchen Basics® Original or Unsalted Chicken Stock
- 4 cups sliced peeled carrots
- 1/2 cup evaporated milk (or for an alternative with less fat, use half and half)
- 1/4 tsp. ground cumin

Direction

- Over medium-high heat, heat oil in a heavy large saucepan. Add 1/4 cup minced ginger, garlic, and onion; sauté for about 8 minutes, until the onion is transparent. Add 4 cups sliced carrots and 4 cups chicken stock. Cover and simmer about 30 minutes, until the carrots are softened.
- In a blender or processor, puree the mixture in batches. Put it back to the saucepan over low heat. Mix half-and-half and cumin. Season to taste with pepper and salt.

Nutrition Information

- Calories: 187 calories;
- Total Carbohydrate: 19.3 g
- Cholesterol: 9 mg
- Total Fat: 9.5 g
- Protein: 8.7 g
- Sodium: 550 mg

155. Gluten-free Wacky Depression Era Chocolate Cake

"Gluten-free and vegan chocolate cake."
Serving: 12 | Prep: 10m | Ready in: 1h55m

Ingredients

- cooking spray
- 1 1/2 cups rice flour
- 2 cups dark brown sugar
- 1/2 tsp. salt
- 1 tbsp. baking soda
- 2/3 cup unsweetened cocoa powder
- 2/3 cup olive oil
- 1 (15 oz.) can garbanzo beans, with liquid
- 1 3/4 cups water
- 2 tbsps. white vinegar

Direction

- Heat an oven to 175°C or 35° F. Use cooking spray to coat a baking pan measuring 9x12-inch and sprinkle with rice flour.
- Use a food processor to mix cocoa powder, baking soda, salt, brown sugar and rice flour; pulse till combined thoroughly. Stir in olive oil. Add in garbanzo beans including the liquid; puree till smooth. Gradually mix in water. Blend in vinegar; batter will become thin. Transfer the batter to prepped baking pan.
- Bake for 45 to 50 minutes in prepped oven till edges detach from pan. Cool down about an hour then serve, or it will be crumbly.

Nutrition Information

- Calories: 357 calories;
- Total Carbohydrate: 59.7 g
- Cholesterol: 0 mg
- Total Fat: 13.2 g
- Protein: 3.3 g
- Sodium: 473 mg

156. Grandma Bowen's 'girdle Buster' Cookie Pie

"Layer pudding and cream cheese mixture on cookie crust."
Serving: 10 | Prep: 20m | Ready in: 32m

Ingredients

- 18 chocolate sandwich cookies with extra creme filling (such as Double Stuf Oreos®), or more to taste
- 4 tbsps. butter, melted
- 2 cups cold milk
- 1 (3.4 oz.) package instant chocolate pudding mix (such as Jell-O®)
- 2 (8 oz.) packages cream cheese, softened
- 1 (12 oz.) container frozen whipped topping, thawed
- 1/3 cup confectioners' sugar

Direction

- Heat an oven to 150 ° C or 300 ° F.
- Use food processor to process cookies till crushed finely. Stir in liquified butter. Force the crust mixture to 9x9-inch baking dish's bottom and quarter inch up edges.
- Bake for 7 minutes in prepped oven. Put aside and cool down.
- Mix pudding mix and milk about two minutes. Rest for 5 minutes, till thicken.
- Wipe clean the food processor and process a cup of whipped topping, confectioners' sugar and cream cheese together. Layer top of baked crust with cream cheese mixture. Scatter pudding over. Finish with the rest of the whipped topping.

Nutrition Information

- Calories: 497 calories;
- Total Carbohydrate: 39.8 g
- Cholesterol: 65 mg
- Total Fat: 35.6 g
- Protein: 6.7 g
- Sodium: 413 mg

157. Grandmother's Tart

"An old pastry recipe."
Serving: Serves 8 to 10

Ingredients

- 2 cups all purpose flour
- 1/2 cup sugar
- 1 tsp. packed grated lemon peel
- 1/2 tsp. (scant) salt
- 1/2 cup plus 2 tbsps. (1/4 sticks) chilled unsalted butter, diced
- 2 large egg yolks
- 1 large egg
- 1 cup cherry or apricot-pineapple preserves
- Powdered sugar

Direction

- Preheat an oven to 350°F. Blend salt, lemon peel, sugar and flour for 10 seconds in processor. Add butter; process till coarse meal forms. Add egg and yolks; process till moist clumps form. Put dough on work surface. Gather the dough to ball; knead for 1 minute.
- Halve dough to 2 pieces, one slightly bigger than other. Press bigger dough piece on halfway up sides and bottom evenly on 9-in. diameter tart pan that has a removable bottom. In crust, spread 1 cup preserves. Cut leftover dough to 12 even pieces. Between work surface and hands, roll pieces to pencil-thin ropes. Put 6 ropes on preserves, evenly spacing; to seal, press ends at crust edge then trim excess dough. Put leftover 6 ropes in opposing direction, evenly spacing, making lattice pattern. To seal, press ends in crust edge; trim excess dough.
- Bake tart for 50 minutes till crust is golden brown; if bottom crust bubbles, pierce with toothpick. Cool tart in the pan on the rack. You can make it 8 hours ahead, standing in room temperature. Remove the pan sides. Sift powdered sugar on tart lightly. Cut to wedges; serve.

Nutrition Information

- Calories: 428
- Total Carbohydrate: 65 g
- Cholesterol: 107 mg
- Total Fat: 16 g
- Fiber: 1 g
- Protein: 5 g
- Sodium: 172 mg
- Saturated Fat: 10 g

158. Greek-style Cheese Ball

"A satisfying recipe!"
Serving: 10 | Prep: 25m | Ready in: 25m

Ingredients

- 1 (8 oz.) package cream cheese, softened
- 1/4 cup mayonnaise
- 2 tbsps. balsamic vinegar
- 10 oz. shredded Cheddar cheese
- 1 (8 oz.) package crumbled feta cheese
- 1/4 cup grated Parmesan cheese
- 1 tbsp. dried oregano
- 2 tsps. onion powder
- 1 tsp. garlic powder
- 1/4 cup pecan halves
- 3/4 cup pine nuts, divided

Direction

- Mix balsamic vinegar, mayonnaise and cream cheese till smooth in a bowl.
- Mix garlic powder, onion powder, oregano, parmesan cheese, cheddar cheese and feta cheese in another bowl. Mix cheddar cheese mixture into the cream cheese mixture.
- Pulse 1/4 cup pine nuts and pecans till crumbly in a blender/food processor. Mix leftover 1/2 cup pine nuts into the pecan mixture; spread 1/4 pecan mixture on plate.
- Shape cheese mixture to 2 5-in. balls. In pecan mixture, roll each ball till coated fully; as needed, add more pecan mixture.

Nutrition Information

- Calories: 383 calories;
- Total Carbohydrate: 5.3 g
- Cholesterol: 78 mg
- Total Fat: 34.1 g
- Protein: 15.6 g
- Sodium: 559 mg

159. Green Chile Chimichurri

"Green sauce served over grilled chicken, pork or whatever else you like."
Serving: 8 | Prep: 10m | Ready in: 10m

Ingredients

- 1 (4 oz.) can chopped green chiles
- 1 bunch cilantro leaves, stems removed
- 5 cloves garlic, or more to taste
- 1 lime, juiced
- 1/4 cup olive oil, separated, or to taste
- salt and ground black pepper to taste

Direction

- In a food processor's bowl, combine 2 tbsps. olive oil, lime juice, garlic, cilantro and green chiles. Add leftover olive oil in thinnish stream along feed tube till mixture attains consistency of a sauce. Add pepper and salt to season; process to incorporate.

Nutrition Information

- Calories: 68 calories;
- Total Carbohydrate: 2 g
- Cholesterol: 0 mg
- Total Fat: 6.8 g
- Protein: 0.4 g
- Sodium: 187 mg

160. Green Olive Pesto

"You can make this within 1 hour."
Serving: Makes about 1 1/2 cups

Ingredients

- 1 cup firmly packed drained pimiento-stuffed green olives, rinsed well and patted dry
- 1/3 cup pine nuts
- 1 garlic clove, minced and mashed to a paste with 1/4 tsp. salt
- 1 cup finely chopped fresh parsley leaves
- 1/4 cup extra-virgin olive oil
- 2 tbsps. freshly grated Parmesan

Direction

- Puree parsley, garlic paste, pine nuts and olives in a food processor; add oil in stream as motor runs. Add parmesan; blend the mixture well. Serve with pesto with 1-lb. cooked and drained pasta; keep 3/4 cup paste liquid to thin the pesto. Or serve the pesto as a cracker spread.

Nutrition Information

- Calories: 364
- Total Carbohydrate: 5 g
- Cholesterol: 6 mg
- Total Fat: 37 g
- Fiber: 3 g
- Protein: 7 g
- Sodium: 765 mg
- Saturated Fat: 6 g

161. Green Olive Tapenade

"A great recipe to make drink from olive."
Serving: Makes about 3 cups

Ingredients

- 10 oil-packed anchovy fillets, finely chopped
- 1 cup Castelvetrano olives, pitted, crushed
- 1 cup Cerignola olives, pitted, crushed
- 1 cup coarsely chopped parsley
- 1 cup olive oil
- 1/4 cup coarsely chopped, drained capers
- 2 tbsps. finely grated lemon zest
- 1/4 cup fresh lemon juice
- Kosher salt, freshly ground pepper

Direction

- In a medium bowl or big jar, combine together lemon juice, lemon zest, capers, oil, parsley, both olives and anchovies, then season with pepper and salt.

- You can make tapenade 1 week in advance. Cover and chill.

Nutrition Information

- Calories: 386
- Total Carbohydrate: 4 g
- Cholesterol: 6 mg
- Total Fat: 41 g
- Fiber: 2 g
- Protein: 3 g
- Sodium: 656 mg
- Saturated Fat: 6 g

162. Greg's Hot Peach Pie

"Spicy and sweet."
Serving: 8 | Prep: 20m | Ready in: 1h40m

Ingredients

- 1 1/2 cups all-purpose flour
- 1/2 tsp. salt
- 9 tbsps. cold unsalted butter, cut into 1/4-inch cubes
- 3 tbsps. ice-cold peach nectar, or as needed
- 4 large fresh peaches - peeled, pitted and chopped
- 6 large fresh peaches - peeled, pitted, and sliced
- 3 habanero peppers, seeded and minced (wear gloves), or to taste
- 1/3 cup all-purpose flour
- 1 cup white sugar
- 1/4 cup unsalted butter, softened

Direction

- Briefly pulse salt and 1 1/2 cups flour 1-2 times to mix in a food processor's work bowl. Add 9 tbsp. chilled unsalted butter; pulse 4-5 times, several seconds each time, till it looks like coarse crumbs. 1 tbsp. at a time, drizzle peach nectar into dough till dough gathers itself to crumbly mass as machine runs. Put dough into bowl; shape to ball. Wrap in plastic wrap and refrigerate for 30 minutes to hydrate dough.
- Preheat an oven to 175°C/350°F.
- Pulse 4 chopped peaches to puree for 1 minute in the food processor. 1 tsp. at a time, add minced habanero peppers; puree till smooth. Put leftover 6 sliced peaches in bowl; lightly toss with habanero puree.
- Mix 1/4 cup softened unsalted butter, white sugar and 1/3 cup flour till it makes a crumbly mixture in a bowl; put aside streusel.
- Halve dough; roll every half to 10-in. diameter circle. Fit 1 dough circle in 9-in. pie dish. Put peach-habanero filing on bottom pie crust; sprinkle crumble sugar streusel. Onto pie, fit top crust; to seal edges, crimp with a fork. Cut few slices on top crust to vent steam.
- In preheated oven, bake for 50 minutes till filling is thick and bubbly and crust is golden brown.

Nutrition Information

- Calories: 412 calories;
- Total Carbohydrate: 57.9 g
- Cholesterol: 50 mg
- Total Fat: 19 g
- Protein: 3.3 g
- Sodium: 156 mg

163. Grilled Chicken Breast With Tomato-tarragon Sauce

"A great dinner recipe for summer."
Serving: 2 servings; can be doubled

Ingredients

- 3 tbsps. chopped fresh tarragon
- 2 1/2 tbsps. olive oil (preferably extra-virgin)
- 1 1/4 tsps. minced garlic
- 2 boneless chicken breast halves with skin
- 1 3/4 cups chopped tomato with seeds (about 1 large tomato)
- 2 tsps. balsamic vinegar
- Fresh tarragon sprigs (optional)

Direction

- Prepare barbecue to medium high heat. Whisk 1 tsp. garlic, 1 1/2 tbsp. oil and 2 tbsp. tarragon to blend in a shallow dish. Pound the chicken lightly with a rolling pin to uniform 1/2-in. thickness between waxed paper sheets. Sprinkle pepper and salt on chicken. Put chicken in tarragon mixture; flip to coat. Stand for 10 minutes.
- Meanwhile, blend leftover 1 tbsp. oil and tomato till smooth in a processor. Add leftover 1/4 tsp. garlic, leftover 1 tbsp. tarragon and vinegar; use on/off turns to just mix in. Season sauce with pepper and salt to taste.
- Grill the chicken for 4 minutes per side till cooked through and brown; put chicken on plates. Put sauce around the chicken; if desired, garnish with tarragon sprigs. Serve.

Nutrition Information

- Calories: 338
- Total Carbohydrate: 8 g
- Cholesterol: 56 mg
- Total Fat: 25 g
- Fiber: 2 g
- Protein: 20 g
- Sodium: 65 mg
- Saturated Fat: 5 g

---

164. Grilled Chicken Salad With Radishes, Cucumbers, And Tarragon Pesto

"Great spring flavors."
Serving: Makes 4 servings | Prep: 45m

Ingredients

- 1/4 cup (packed) fresh tarragon leaves plus 2 tsps. chopped
- 1/4 cup (packed) fresh Italian parsley leaves
- 4 tbsps. pine nuts, divided
- 5 tsps. fresh lemon juice, divided
- 2 tsps. chopped shallot
- 6 tbsps. (or more) olive oil, divided, plus additional for brushing
- 4 boneless chicken breast halves
- 4 1/2-inch-thick slices country-style French or sourdough bread
- 1 5-oz. package mixed baby greens
- 1 cup thinly sliced radishes (from 1 large bunch)
- 1 cup thinly sliced Japanese cucumbers (about 1 1/2)

Direction

- Coarsely chop shallot, 1 tsp. lemon juice, 2 tbsp. pine nuts, parsley and 1/4 cup tarragon leaves in a mini processor; add 3 tbsp. olive oil gradually as machine is running. Season pesto with pepper and salt to taste; by teaspoonfuls, add more olive oil to thin if needed.
- Whisk 3 tbsp. oil, the leftover 4 tsp. lemon juice and 2 tsp. chopped tarragon in a small bowl; season the dressing with pepper and salt.
- Prep barbecue to medium high heat; brush oil on both sides of chicken breasts. Sprinkle pepper and salt; grill for 7-8 minutes per side till chicken is cooked through, skin is crisp and grill marks form. Put on work surface; rest for 5 minutes. Brush oil on both sides of bread with clean brush; sprinkle pepper and salt. Grill for 2-3 minutes per side till dark-brown grill marks show on both sides.
- Put cucumbers, radishes and greens in a big bowl; toss with dressing. Season with pepper and salt to taste; divide salad into 4 plates.
- Crosswise cut grilled chicken breasts into 1/3-in. thick slices; put 1 sliced chicken breast over salad on each plate. Scoop tarragon pesto on chicken; sprinkle the leftover 2 tbsp. pine nuts on salads. Serve it with grilled bread slices.

165. Grilled Halibut With Basil-shallot Butter

"A versatile recipe."
Serving: Makes 6 servings

Ingredients

- 1 1/2 cups (loosely packed) fresh basil leaves
- 1 large shallot, coarsely chopped
- 8 tbsps. (1/2 cup) unsalted butter, room temperature
- 1 tsp. grated lemon peel
- 6 6-oz. halibut fillets
- Extra-virgin olive oil

Direction

- In mini food processor, chop shallot and basil finely. 2 tbsp. at a time, add butter; process till blended, occasionally stopping to scrape down sides. Put in small bowl; mix in lemon peel. Season shallot-basil butter using salt.
- Prep barbecue to medium heat. Rub olive oil on both sides of fish fillets; grill for 4 minutes per side till fillets just opaque in middle. Put fish on plates; spread some shallot-basil butter on fish immediately. Serve with extra shallot-basil butter alongside.

Nutrition Information

- Calories: 327
- Total Carbohydrate: 2 g
- Cholesterol: 124 mg
- Total Fat: 21 g
- Fiber: 1 g
- Protein: 32 g
- Sodium: 120 mg
- Saturated Fat: 11 g

166. Grilled Swordfish And Green Olive Relish

Serving: Serves 2

Ingredients

- 1/4 cup drained bottled pimiento-stuffed green olives
- 1 small garlic clove, minced and mashed to a paste with a pinch of salt
- 2 tbsps. finely chopped fresh parsley leaves
- 2 tbsps. extra-virgin olive oil
- 2 tsps. fresh lemon juice
- two 6-oz. swordfish steaks (each about 1 inch thick)
- olive oil for brushing swordfish

Direction

- Prep grill.
- Prepare relish: blend olives in food processor till finely chopped. Put in the rest of relish ingredients and pulse to mince the olives.
- Brush oil on each sides of swordfish and add pepper and salt to season. Let fish grill for 4 minutes per side over rack place 5- to 6-inch above glowing coals, or till barely cooked fully. (Or, you may grill the fish on medium heat in a well-seasoned and hot ridged grill pan.)
- Top swordfish with relish and serve.

Nutrition Information

- Calories: 415
- Total Carbohydrate: 2 g
- Cholesterol: 112 mg
- Total Fat: 30 g
- Fiber: 1 g
- Protein: 34 g
- Sodium: 374 mg
- Saturated Fat: 5 g

167. Ham And Onion Spread

Serving: Makes about 1 3/4 cups

Ingredients

- 6 oz. ham (about 1 1/3 cups chopped)
- 1/4 cup chopped celery
- 1/4 cup chopped onion
- 1/4 cup mayonnaise or reduced-calorie mayonnaise
- 3 tbsps. sweet pickle relish

Direction

- Use processor to chop ham finely. Put in relish, mayonnaise, onion and celery, and blend to barely form coarse paste. Pour the spread into a medium-size bowl. Add pepper and salt to season. (May be prepped a day in advance. Refrigerate with cover.)

Nutrition Information

- Calories: 189
- Total Carbohydrate: 7 g
- Cholesterol: 30 mg
- Total Fat: 15 g
- Fiber: 1 g
- Protein: 7 g
- Sodium: 666 mg
- Saturated Fat: 3 g

168. Ham Glaze

"This is a delish ham glaze made of orange juice and mango chutney that brings an interesting flavor for your ham."
Serving: 10 | Prep: 10m | Ready in: 10m

Ingredients

- 1/2 cup brown sugar
- 3 cloves garlic
- 1/2 cup mango chutney
- 2 tsps. orange zest
- 1/8 cup orange juice
- 1/4 cup Dijon mustard

Direction

- In the work bowl of a food processor, mix together mustard, orange juice, orange zest, mango chutney, garlic and brown sugar, then process until smooth.

Nutrition Information

- Calories: 85 calories;
- Total Carbohydrate: 18.8 g
- Cholesterol: 0 mg
- Total Fat: 1.3 g
- Protein: 0.1 g
- Sodium: 282 mg

169. Ham Pate

"Perfect for finger sandwiches or crackers."
Serving: 4 | Prep: 15m | Ready in: 15m

Ingredients

- 4 oz. cubed cooked ham
- 2 tbsps. ranch salad dressing (such as Hidden Valley® Original Ranch®)
- 1 tbsp. capers with juice
- 2 tsps. prepared mustard
- 2 tsps. finely chopped onion
- 1 pinch minced garlic

Direction

- Get a food processor and put in the garlic, onion, mustard, capers, ranch dressing and ham; blend well until you reach the consistency you want.

Nutrition Information

- Calories: 109 calories;
- Total Carbohydrate: 0.8 g
- Cholesterol: 18 mg
- Total Fat: 9.2 g
- Protein: 5.5 g
- Sodium: 524 mg

170. Hamersley's Bistro Tart Dough

"This is a light and flaky pastry dough that works for sweet and savory tarts."
Serving: Makes 12-Ounces, Enough for One 10-inch Tart or 6 Individual Tarts

Ingredients

- 1 1/2 cups all-purpose flour
- 1/2 tsp. kosher salt
- 10 tbsps. unsalted butter, cut into small cubes and well chilled
- 4 to 5 tbsps. ice water

Direction

- Mix the salt and the flour in a mixing bowl. Quickly cut butter into flour with your fingers or a pastry blender until the pieces of butter are the size of large peas. (Or, cut butter into flour by pulsing it about 8 to 10 times in a food processor, do not to overmix and overheat the butter.)
- Turn out the mixture on a clean surface and create a well in the middle of flour. Add ice water into the well. Mix the water and the flour mixture with just your fingertips, working quickly. Work just until the water has been absorbed. Dough will be ragged and should stick together once you squeeze it. In case it looks dry, drizzle some more drops of water.
- Shape dough into a log of approximately eight inches long and should be parallel to the edge of the work surface. Press down and away from you all along line of dough using the heel of your hand. Gather up the dough using a pastry scraper, then form it back into a log and repeat the smearing action. This method, which is called fraisage, helps form sheets of butter in the dough and creates a light crust that resembles puff pastry.
- Shape up the dough using pastry scraper into a ball; the dough may not completely pull together at this time. Cover dough well with plastic wrap, then flatten a little and leave to sit in the fridge for at least 30 minutes before you roll it. You can keep the dough in the fridge for 2 days maximum. Or, freeze the dough while wrapped well and defrost for 1 day in the fridge before using.
- Roll and form the dough as directed in the recipe.
- To blind-bake tart crust: Heat an oven to 375°F. Line aluminum foil onto the mold and fill the foil with rice, dried beans, or baking weights. Then, bake for 12 minutes. Take out the foil and beans and continue baking until crust is browned well. Transfer from the oven and allow crust to cool a little before you assemble your tart.

171. Hazelnut Breadsticks

"You have to make the starter 1 day ahead. You can shape breadsticks however you want before baking."
Serving: Makes 21

Ingredients

- 1/2 cup plus 1 tbsp. warm water (105°F to 115°F.)
- 2 1/2 cups unbleached all purpose flour
- 1 1/2 tsps. dry yeast
- 1/4 cup olive oil
- 1/4 cup fresh sage leaves
- 1/2 cup toasted hazelnuts, ground
- 1/4 cup warm whole milk (105°F to 115°F.)
- 1 tsp. salt

Direction

- Mix 1 tsp. yeast, 1/2 cup flour and 1/2 cup warm water to blend well in big bowl; cover. Stand starter overnight in room temperature.
- Heat oil on medium low heat in small heavy saucepan. Add sage; sauté for 7 minutes till crisp. Cool.
- Mix 1/2 tsp. yeast and leftover 1 tbsp. water to blend in small bowl; stand to dissolve yeast for 10 minutes. Put into a processor.

- In processor, add salt, milk, hazelnuts and leftover 2 cups flour in yeast mixture. Process with on/off turns till it forms small moist clumps. Add starter and sage-oil mixture; process till just big moist clumps form. Put dough on clean work surface and bring dough to a ball; knead for 4 minutes till dough is elastic and smooth. Shape dough to a ball.
- Oil another big bowl lightly. Add dough; turn till coated. Use plastic wrap to cover bowl then towel; rise in draft-free warm area for 1 hour till doubled in volume. Punch dough down; cover. Rest for 15 minutes.
- Preheat an oven to 400°F. Oil 3 big baking sheets lightly. Turn out dough onto floured work surface; briefly knead till smooth then divide dough to thirds.
- Divide 1 dough third to 7 even pieces; roll a dough piece between work surface and palms to 13-in. long rope. Put rope on baking sheet; repeat using leftover 6 dough pieces, evenly spacing ropes apart. Shape 1 end of every rope decoratively if desired; rise for 10 minutes. Bake the breadsticks for 20 minutes till very crisp and golden. Put on racks; cool.
- Meanwhile, form 2nd dough third to 7 breadsticks; rise for 10 minutes. Bake like earlier. Repeat using final dough third. You can make it ahead; tightly wrap. Keep for 1 day in room temperature/freeze for maximum of 2 weeks.

Nutrition Information

- Calories: 105
- Total Carbohydrate: 13 g
- Cholesterol: 0 mg
- Total Fat: 5 g
- Fiber: 1 g
- Protein: 2 g
- Sodium: 74 mg
- Saturated Fat: 1 g

172. Hazelnut Linzer Cookies With Blackberry Jam

Serving: Makes about 36 sandwiches

Ingredients

- 1 1/4 cups all purpose flour
- 2 tsps. ground cinnamon
- 1 tsp. baking powder
- 1/2 tsp. freshly grated nutmeg
- 1/2 tsp. salt
- 3/4 cup (1 1/2 sticks) unsalted butter, room temperature
- 1 cup powdered sugar plus more for decorating
- 5 tsps. (packed) finely grated orange peel
- 2 tsps. grated lemon peel
- 3 large egg yolks
- 1 1/4 cups hazelnuts, finely ground in processor (about 1 1/2 cups ground)
- Blackberry jam

Direction

- In a medium bowl, whisk together the first 5 ingredients to blend. In a big bowl, beat citrus peels, 1 cup of powdered sugar, and the butter until fluffy, then beat in the egg yolks. Beat in the dry ingredients in 4 batches, then beat in the nuts. Gather the dough to form a ball and flatten into a disk. Chill the dough, wrapped, for a minimum of 1 hour up to a day.
- Set the oven to 325 degrees Fahrenheit and line parchment paper onto 2 rimmed big baking sheets. Roll half the dough out on a lightly floured surface until 1/8 inch thickness. Use a round 2 inch cutter to cut out rounds. Use a round 3/4 inch cutter to cut out the middle of half the rounds, making rings. Move them to the prepared sheets. Gather up the scraps of dough and chill.
- Bake the cookies, reversing after the sheets 10 minutes, until turning golden, roughly 22 minutes in total. Completely cool on the sheets and repeat until all the dough is baked. You

can store them airtight at room temperature up to 2 days or in the freezer up to 2 weeks.
- Place the cookie rings on a work area and sift powdered sugar over top. Spread 1 tsp. of jam onto each of the cookie rounds and press the rings onto them. You can assemble the cookies a day ahead, store between wax paper sheets in an airtight container at room temperature.

Nutrition Information

- Calories: 84
- Total Carbohydrate: 7 g
- Cholesterol: 26 mg
- Total Fat: 6 g
- Fiber: 0 g
- Protein: 1 g
- Sodium: 40 mg
- Saturated Fat: 3 g

173. Hazelnut Pesto

"A simple pesto."
Serving: Makes about 1 1/2 cups

Ingredients

- 1 cup hazelnuts (about 4 1/2 oz.), toasted lightly and skinned
- 2 cups packed fresh flat-leafed parsley leaves (about 1 large bunch), washed and dried
- 2 large garlic cloves
- 3/4 cup olive oil
- 2 tbsps. hazelnut oil if desired
- freshly ground black pepper

Direction

- Blend salt and pepper to taste and pesto ingredients till smooth in a food processor; pesto keeps, surface covered in plastic wrap, frozen for 1 month or chilled for 1 week.

Nutrition Information

- Calories: 210
- Total Carbohydrate: 3 g

- Total Fat: 22 g
- Fiber: 1 g
- Protein: 2 g
- Sodium: 4 mg
- Saturated Fat: 3 g

174. Hazelnut Pesto Fish

Serving: Makes 4 servings | Prep: 20m

Ingredients

- 1 large garlic clove
- 1 cup fresh cilantro sprigs
- 1/2 cup hazelnuts, toasted
- 1/4 tsp. cayenne
- 1/2 tsp. salt
- 1/3 cup olive oil
- 1 1/2 lb arctic char fillets with skin
- Accompaniment: lime wedges

Direction

- In center position, put oven rack; preheat the oven to 375°F.
- Drop garlic into food processor to chop finely as motor runs; shut off motor. Add 1/4 tsp. salt, cayenne, nuts and cilantro; blend till chopped coarsely. Add oil as motor runs; blend till incorporated and coarse.
- Put fillets in lightly oiled baking dish, skin sides down; sprinkle leftover 1/4 tsp. salt. Put pesto on fish; bake for 12-17 minutes, varies on fillet's thickness, till just cooked through and fish is opaque.

Nutrition Information

- Calories: 622
- Total Carbohydrate: 3 g
- Cholesterol: 94 mg
- Total Fat: 51 g
- Fiber: 2 g
- Protein: 37 g
- Sodium: 393 mg
- Saturated Fat: 8 g

175. Hazelnut, Ricotta, And Lemon Pesto

"Tasty!"
Serving: Makes about 2 1/3 cups

Ingredients

- 1 garlic clove, peeled
- 1/2 cup hazelnuts, toasted, husked (about 2 oz.)
- 1/2 cup coarsely chopped fresh basil
- 5 tbsps. extra-virgin olive oil, divided
- 1 1/2 cups whole-milk ricotta cheese (from one 15-oz. container)
- 3 tbsps. fresh lemon juice
- 1 1/2 tsps. (packed) finely grated lemon peel
- 3 tbsps. freshly grated Pecorino Romano cheese
- Fine sea salt

Direction

- Drop garlic clove in machine as processor runs; blend till chopped finely. Add 2 tbsp. olive oil, basil and hazelnuts; process till basil and hazelnuts are chopped finely. Add leftover 3 tbsp. olive oil, lemon peel, lemon juice and ricotta cheese; process till blended well. Put mixture in small bowl; mix in Pecorino Romano cheese then season with freshly ground black pepper and sea salt to taste. You can make it 2 days ahead, refrigerated, covered.

Nutrition Information

- Calories: 367
- Total Carbohydrate: 6 g
- Cholesterol: 46 mg
- Total Fat: 34 g
- Fiber: 1 g
- Protein: 13 g
- Sodium: 289 mg
- Saturated Fat: 10 g

176. Homemade Peanut Butter

"This peanut butter recipe is absolutely one of the best you've ever seen."
Serving: 25 | Prep: 5m | Ready in: 5m

Ingredients

- 2 tbsps. peanut oil
- 2 lbs. honey roasted peanuts

Direction

- In the bowl of a food processor, add the peanut oil, then turn on the processor. Gradually add in the peanuts while the motor is running and process until smooth, about 2 minutes. If necessary, scrape down the sides of the bowl while processing. Keep in an airtight container in the fridge for storage.

Nutrition Information

- Calories: 191 calories;
- Total Carbohydrate: 12.7 g
- Cholesterol: 0 mg
- Total Fat: 10.1 g
- Protein: 12.7 g
- Sodium: 181 mg

177. Honey-glazed Peach Tart With Mascarpone Cream

Serving: Makes 6 servings

Ingredients

- 1 1/2 cups all purpose flour
- 3 tbsps. powdered sugar
- 1/4 tsp. salt
- 1/2 cup (1 stick) chilled unsalted butter, cut into 1/2-inch cubes
- 3 1/2 tbsps. (about) ice water
- 1/4 cup sugar
- 3 tbsps. all purpose flour

- 2 tsps. grated lemon peel
- 6 ripe medium peaches, peeled, halved, pitted, cut into 1/2-inch-thick slices (about 4 cups)
- 2 tbsps. honey
- 2 tbsps. chilled unsalted butter, cut into small pieces
- 2 tbsps. sliced almonds
- 2 tbsps. peach preserves, melted
- 1 cup chilled whipping cream
- 6 tbsps. mascarpone cheese*
- 2 tbsps. sugar
- 1/4 tsp. vanilla extract

Direction

- Crust: In a processor, blend salt, sugar and flour. Cut in butter till pea-sized pieces form with on/off turns. By tablespoonfuls, add enough ice water to make moist clumps as machine runs. Gather the dough into a ball; flatten into a disk. In plastic, wrap; refrigerate for 1 hour.
- Roll the dough out to 12-in. round on a lightly floured surface. Put in 9-in. diameter tart pan that has removable bottom. To 1-in., trim overhang. Fold overhang in; press to make double-thick sides. Press crust's inside edge to push it 1/8-1/4-in. above pan's top edge. Use fork to pierce bottom of the crust; refrigerate for 1 hour.
- Preheat an oven to 400°F. Bake the tart for 25 minutes till golden; if bubbles form, pierce with fork. You can make it 1 day ahead then cool; wrap using plastic and keep in room temperature.
- Filling: Mix lemon peel, flour and sugar to blend in a big bowl. Add peaches; toss to coat. Put in baked crust; drizzle peach mixture with honey. Dot with butter; sprinkle with almonds. Bake for 35 minutes till almonds are toasted and peaches are tender. Brush peach preserves on almonds and fruit; before serving, cool for 15 minutes. You can make it 6 hours ahead; keep tart in room temperature.
- Mascarpone cream: Beat vanilla, sugar, mascarpone and cream with an electric mixer till peaks form in big bowl. Cut tart into 6 wedges. Put dollops of mascarpone cream over; serve.

Nutrition Information

- Calories: 638
- Total Carbohydrate: 71 g
- Cholesterol: 111 mg
- Total Fat: 38 g
- Fiber: 4 g
- Protein: 7 g
- Sodium: 169 mg
- Saturated Fat: 23 g

178. Hot Pepper Jelly

"So lovely."
Serving: 48 | Prep: 30m | Ready in: 1h45m

Ingredients

- 2 1/2 cups finely chopped red bell peppers
- 1 1/4 cups finely chopped green bell peppers
- 1/4 cup finely chopped jalapeno peppers
- 1 cup apple cider vinegar
- 1 (1.75 oz.) package powdered pectin
- 5 cups white sugar

Direction

- Follow manufacturer's instructions to sterilize 6 lids and 8-oz. canning jars; in the hot water canner, heat water.
- Put jalapeno peppers, green and red bell peppers in a big saucepan on high heat; mix in fruit pectin and vinegar. Put mixture on a full rolling boil, constantly mixing. Mix in sugar quickly. Put back on a full rolling boil for exactly 1 minute, constantly mixing. Take off from the heat; skim off any foam.
- Put jelly in sterile jars quickly; fill each to within 1/4-in. of tops. Use flat lids to cover; tightly screw on bands.
- Put jars in a rack; lower the jars into the canner slowly. Water should fully cover the jars; should be hot yet not boiling. Boil water; process for 5 minutes.

Nutrition Information

- Calories: 88 calories;
- Total Carbohydrate: 22.5 g
- Cholesterol: 0 mg
- Total Fat: 0 g
- Protein: 0.1 g
- Sodium: 3 mg

179. Hurry-up Black Bean Dip

"You can bring this simple pureed dip on the next potluck!"
Serving: Makes 6 to 8 servings

Ingredients

- 1 medium red onion, chopped
- 2 (16-oz.) cans black beans, drained and rinsed
- 2 tbsps. balsamic vinegar
- 1 tbsp. fresh orange or lime juice
- 1 tbsp. chopped fresh cilantro
- 1 tbsp. olive oil
- 1 garlic clove, peeled
- 1 tsp. ground cumin
- Salt and freshly ground pepper, to taste
- Tortilla chips and, if you're with that sort of crowd, assorted cut-up raw vegetables

Direction

- Set aside a tbsp. of red onion in a cup for garnish.
- Puree cumin, garlic, oil, cilantro, orange juice, vinegar, remaining red onion and beans in a food processor or blender.
- Move the dip in a bowl; sprinkle pepper and salt. Add the reserved red onion on top then serve with vegetables and tortilla chips.

Nutrition Information

- Calories: 174
- Total Carbohydrate: 29 g
- Total Fat: 3 g
- Fiber: 11 g
- Protein: 10 g

- Sodium: 422 mg
- Saturated Fat: 0 g

180. Israeli Falafel

"So amazing!"
Serving: Makes about 20 balls or disks

Ingredients

- 1/2 cup tahini (sesame seed paste)
- 4 1/2 tsps. fresh lemon juice
- 1/2 small onion, chopped (about 1/4 cup)
- 1/2 tsp. kosher salt
- 1/2 tsp. ground black pepper
- 1 cup dried chickpeas, refrigerated overnight in water to cover by 2 inches, then drained, or 1 cup canned chickpeas, drained
- 1 small onion, diced (about 1/2 cup)
- 2 cloves garlic, peeled and smashed
- 2 tbsps. fresh parsley, finely chopped
- 1 tsp. ground cumin
- 1 tsp. ground coriander
- 1 tsp. salt
- 1/2 tsp. dried red pepper flakes
- 1/2 tsp. baking soda
- About 6 cups vegetable oil for frying
- 5 to 6 pita breads, top 1/3 cut off each
- 2 plum tomatoes, seeded and diced
- 1 small onion, diced
- 1 green bell pepper, seeded and diced
- 1 cucumber, peeled, seeded, and diced
- Pickled turnip*
- Mango amba (pickle)*
- Harissa hot sauce
- *Available from ethnicgrocer.com

Direction

- Tahini sauce: Process 1/4 cup water and all ingredients to smooth paste in a blender/food processor. You can make sauce ahead, refrigerated for maximum of 1 day, covered.
- Falafel: Pulse baking soda, red pepper flakes, salt, coriander, cumin, parsley, garlic, onion and chickpeas till crumbly and finely chopped

- (it'll look like wet breadcrumbs, don't over process to paste, the balls will be heavy) in a food processor. You can make it ahead, refrigerated for maximum of 1 day, covered.
- Heat 3-in. oil till thermometer reads 350°F in a big shallow skillet on medium high heat.
- Shape mixture, using 2 tsp./falafel scoop, to 1-in. diameter balls/disks. Carefully lower into hot oil, 5 per batch; fry for 1-2 minutes till deep golden brown, occasionally turning. On paper towels, drain. Repeat to fry leftover falafel, putting oil back between each batch to 350°F.
- Serve: Divide the falafel balls to pita pockets; tuck in mango amba, pickled turnip, cucumber, pepper, onion and diced tomatoes. Drizzle in harissa sauce and tahini sauce; immediately serve.

181. Italian Rice Croquettes

"A great recipe to try out on your next party event."
Serving: 40 | Prep: 50m | Ready in: 1h40m

Ingredients

- 2 lbs. chicken giblets
- 1 cup water
- 1/2 tsp. salt
- 4 cups salted water
- 2 cups long grain white rice, uncooked
- 2 cups grated Parmesan cheese
- 1/2 cup marinara sauce
- 1/4 cup dry bread crumbs
- 2 large eggs
- 2 tbsps. chopped fresh parsley
- salt and freshly ground black pepper to taste
- 1 cup dry bread crumbs for coating
- vegetable oil for frying

Direction

- In a pressure cooker, mix 1 cup water, chicken giblets and 1/2 tsp. salt and cook for about 20 minutes.
- Drain giblets. Allow it to cool for about 10 minutes then cut giblets, either by hand or using a food processor; put aside.
- Combine rice and water in a pot over high heat and cook until it starts to boil. Turn heat down to medium-low and simmer, covered, for 20-25 minutes until all the liquid has been absorbed and rice is soft.
- Cool the cooked rice by spreading it onto a baking tray for about 5 minutes. Scoop up rice when cooled onto a large bowl.
- Combine marinara sauce, grated Parmesan cheese, eggs, 1/4 cup bread crumbs, ground pepper, salt, parsley and the giblets. Place plastic wrap to cover and store in the fridge for 1 hour.
- Take rice and giblet mixture from the fridge and form 2-inch football-shaped croquettes.
- Dredge croquettes in bread crumbs and arrange them on a baking tray.
- Heat oil in a big skillet over medium-high temperature. Fry breaded croquettes for about 10 minutes until browned on all sides. Line a plate with paper towels to help absorb excess oil and place fried croquettes onto the plate.

Nutrition Information

- Calories: 99 calories;
- Total Carbohydrate: 10.4 g
- Cholesterol: 60 mg
- Total Fat: 3.2 g
- Protein: 6.9 g
- Sodium: 140 mg

182. Italian Tuna Spread

""A recipe that is part of antipasti spread. Present with Melba toast, crostini, or crackers at room temperature. Keep inside the refrigerator with a cover. Place it back at room temperature to reuse. Avoid reheating in a microwave or else it become goop. This is the best recipe you will ever have. Use a thin slice of tomato, toasted bread and iceberg lettuce. Delicious!""
Serving: 8 | Prep: 15m | Ready in: 15m

Ingredients

- 3 (4.5 oz.) cans tuna packed in olive oil, drained
- 1/2 cup unsalted butter at room temperature
- 3 tbsps. capers, drained
- 1 tbsp. chopped Italian flat-leaf parsley
- 1 tsp. lemon juice (optional)
- salt and ground black pepper to taste

Direction

- In a food processor, mix the pepper, salt, lemon juice, parsley, capers, butter and tuna until turns smooth.

Nutrition Information

- Calories: 158 calories;
- Total Carbohydrate: 0.3 g
- Cholesterol: 45 mg
- Total Fat: 11.9 g
- Protein: 12.4 g
- Sodium: 121 mg

183. Japanese Salad Dressing

"You can refrigerate for 5 days in airtight container if not serving at once; mix well/shake before serving."
Serving: 5 | Prep: 15m | Ready in: 15m

Ingredients

- 2 tbsps. minced fresh ginger root
- 1/3 cup minced onion
- 1/4 cup minced celery
- 1/4 cup low-sodium soy sauce
- 1/2 lime, juiced
- 1 tbsp. white sugar
- 1 tbsp. ketchup
- 1/4 tsp. ground black pepper
- 1/2 cup vegetable oil

Direction

- Pulse celery, onion and ginger till thoroughly combined in a food processor; use a spatula to scrape down food processor's sides. Add pepper, ketchup, sugar, lime juice and soy sauce for 10-20 seconds till combined. In a thin stream, stream oil into the mixture as processor runs; process till blended well.

Nutrition Information

- Calories: 220 calories;
- Total Carbohydrate: 6.3 g
- Cholesterol: 0 mg
- Total Fat: 21.9 g
- Protein: 0.9 g
- Sodium: 464 mg

184. Jerked Pork Chops

"A popular recipe!"
Serving: Makes 6 servings

Ingredients

- 1/4 cup allspice berries
- 1-inch cinnamon stick
- 1 tsp. freshly grated nutmeg
- 1 Scotch bonnet chile, stemmed, halved, and seeded
- 1/2 medium red onion, diced
- 1/2 cup finely chopped scallions (white and green parts)
- 3 cloves garlic, roughly chopped
- 3 tbsps. peeled and minced ginger
- 1 tbsp. chopped fresh thyme
- 1 tbsp. sugar
- 1 tbsp. soy sauce

- 2 tbsps. Worcestershire sauce
- 3 tbsps. fresh lime juice
- 1/4 cup dark rum
- 6 loin pork chops, about 1 1/2 inches thick
- Kosher salt and freshly ground black pepper to taste
- 1 1/2 cups Golden Pineapple Chutney

Direction

- Marinate: Toast allspice berries till fragrant in a dry skillet on medium heat; grind with cinnamon stick finely in a spice mill. Put into food processor.
- Add all leftover marinade ingredients in processor; blend till smooth.
- Season pork chops with pepper and salt; rub all over with marinade. Put on plate; cover. Refrigerate for minimum of 4 hours – better overnight.
- Prep medium-hot fire in grill.
- Take pork from marinade; put on grill. Grill for 7 minutes per side, flipping once; internal temperature of chop should read 150° for well done, 140° for medium. Cooking time is less for thinner chops.
- Serve with chutney.

Nutrition Information

- Calories: 603
- Total Carbohydrate: 64 g
- Cholesterol: 137 mg
- Total Fat: 19 g
- Fiber: 3 g
- Protein: 43 g
- Sodium: 797 mg
- Saturated Fat: 6 g

185. Jerusalem Chickpea Sandwich Filling

"Tasty recipe!"
Serving: makes about 2 cups (enough for 4 sandwiches)

Ingredients

- 1 small rib celery, quartered, or 1 broccoli stalk, trimmed, peeled, and quartered
- 1 3/4 cups cooked chickpeas or 1 (15-oz.) can chickpeas, drained (rinsed if nonorganic)
- 5 to 6 tbsps. Lemon-Tahini Sauce
- 2 to 3 tbsps. freshly squeezed lemon juice
- 1/2 tsp. salt, or to taste

Direction

- Pulse celery till coarsely chopped in a food processor. Add salt, 2 tbsp. lemon juice, 5 tbsp. sauce and chickpeas; pulse to make coarse puree. Taste; add more salt, lemon juice/or and sauce as needed.

186. Kabocha Squash Pie (Japanese Pumpkin Pie)

"So tasty!"
Serving: 8 | Prep: 20m | Ready in: 1h15m

Ingredients

- Crust
- 3/4 cup graham crackers, crushed
- 1/2 cup all-purpose flour
- 1/8 cup light soy butter
- 1 tbsp. soy milk
- 1/4 tsp. ground cinnamon
- Filling
- 2 1/3 cups kabocha squash - halved, peeled, seeded and cut into 1 1/2 inch cubes
- 2/3 cup silken tofu
- 1 tsp. vanilla extract
- 1/4 cup white sugar
- 1/2 tsp. ground cinnamon
- 1/4 tsp. ground nutmeg

Direction

- Preheat an oven to 175°C/350°F.
- In a mixing bowl, mix flour and graham cracker crumbs; mix in soy butter till it is crumbly. Create well in center of flour mixture. Add soymilk; mix to make soft dough. Turn out dough on lightly floured surface; briefly knead. In plastic wrap, wrap; refrigerate for 20 minutes.
- Roll dough out to 1/4-in. thick on lightly floured surface. Fit pie crust in 7-in. diameter pie plate; poke holes on bottom with a fork.
- In preheated oven, bake crust for 15 minutes till pale golden; on rack, cool.
- Put 1-in. water on bottom of pan. Put kabocha in steamer basket fitted into pan; boil. Lower heat to medium and cover; steam squash for 15 minutes till easily pierced with fork and tender. Cool.
- Blend kabocha till smooth in a food processor's bowl/blender. Mix nutmeg, cinnamon, sugar, vanilla and tofu into kabocha mixture; blend till very smooth. Put into prepped crust.
- In preheated oven, bake for 20 minutes till middle is set; don't overbake, filling will crack.

Nutrition Information

- Calories: 137 calories;
- Total Carbohydrate: 23.1 g
- Cholesterol: < 1 mg
- Total Fat: 3.3 g
- Protein: 4.2 g
- Sodium: 65 mg

187. Kahlúa-spiked Frozen Mocha Lattes

"A lovely treat."
Serving: Makes 6 lattes | Prep: 30m

Ingredients

- 3/4 cup sugar
- 5 1/2 tsps. instant espresso powder
- 4 tsps. natural unsweetened cocoa powder
- 2 pinches of salt
- 2 1/2 cups water, divided
- 2 cups half and half
- 3/4 cup chilled heavy whipping cream
- 1 1/2 tbsps. (packed) golden brown sugar
- 1/2 tsp. (scant) vanilla extract
- 3/4 cup Kahlúa or other coffee-flavored liqueur
- Even easier: Instead of making whipped cream, try and organic all-natural aerosol whipped cream, like Clover Farms.
- Ice cube trays (enough to make about forty-five 1 3/4 x 1 3/4 x 1 1/4-inch ice cubes)

Direction

- Whisk pinch salt and initial 3 ingredients in medium saucepan; whisk in 1 cup of water slowly, whisking till smooth. Cook on medium high heat for 3 minutes till it just starts to boil and sugar is dissolved, whisking often; take off heat. Add half and half and 1 1/2 cups water; whisk to blend. Put in pitchers. Put espresso mixture in ice cube trays; fill cubes nearly to top. Creates around 45 ice cubes. In trays, freeze espresso mixture. You can make it 1 month ahead; keep espresso ice cubes, frozen, in resealable plastic bags.
- Beat pinch salt, vanilla, brown sugar and cream using electric mixer till peaks form in medium bowl; cover. Chill.
- Put 6 glasses/glass coffee mugs into freezer for 15 minutes. Put 1/4 cup kahlua and 14 espresso ice cubes in processor in 3 batches; blend for 30 seconds till smooth and thick. Divide to 2 chilled mugs; put in freezer. Repeat twice using chilled mugs, kahlua and espresso ice cubes. You can make it 1 hour ahead, kept frozen.
- Put sweetened whipped cream on frozen mocha lattes; serve.

188. Kanafa

"You can use ricotta-mozzarella mix for Nabulsi cheese and other lower-fat products."
Serving: 8 | Prep: 25m | Ready in: 1h

Ingredients

- 1 (16 oz.) box shredded phyllo dough (kataifi)
- 1 (15 oz.) container ricotta cheese
- 1 cup shredded mozzarella cheese
- 1/3 cup white sugar
- 12 oz. unsalted butter
- For the syrup:
- 1 cup white sugar
- 1/2 cup water
- 1 tsp. lemon juice
- 1/8 tsp. rose water (optional)

Direction

- Preheat the oven to 200°C/400°F.
- Finely chop the frozen, shredded phyllo dough till strands are the size of a rice grain in a food processor. Put dough into a big mixing bowl. Mix 1/3 cup sugar, mozzarella and ricotta together in another bowl.
- Heat butter in a big liquid measuring cup/bowl with a spout in a microwave till fully melted; sit for a few minutes till thick white foam forms on top. Use a spoon to skim foam off to clarify butter.
- Put butter into bowl of phyllo dough carefully; don't add white milk solids on bottom of the clarified butter. Mix butter and dough together with your hands; take handfuls of dough then rub between your palms to be sure the butter got absorbed.
- Spread the buttered phyllo dough evenly into a 9x13-in. pan; press it into edges and bottom firmly. Spread the cheese mixture onto the dough; avoid pan's edges.
- In the preheated oven, bake for 30-35 minutes till dough edges are bubbly and brown and cheese is slightly golden.
- Prepare syrup as kanafa bakes. Boil 1/2 cup sugar and water in a small saucepan on medium high heat; lower the heat to medium. Mix in lemon juice; simmer for 5-7 minutes till thick and sugar melts; stir constantly, don't let the mixture caramelize and turn golden. Take off from the heat. Add rose water; put aside.
- Take kanafa from the oven. Put a big platter/baking sheet on the baking dish. Invert the baking dish onto the platter carefully so phyllo is on top using oven mitts. Put the syrup on kanafa. Cut into pieces; serve while hot.

Nutrition Information

- Calories: 663 calories;
- Total Carbohydrate: 59.2 g
- Cholesterol: 116 mg
- Total Fat: 42.1 g
- Protein: 12.9 g
- Sodium: 278 mg

189. Key Lime Pie

"This drink tastes like pie"
Serving: 2 | Prep: 5m | Ready in: 5m

Ingredients

- 1/2 lime, cut into wedges
- 4 fluid oz. vodka
- 1 1/2 fluid oz. frozen limeade concentrate, thawed
- 1 tsp. vanilla extract
- 2 twists lime zest, garnish

Direction

- In a mixing glass, place lime wedges in the bottom and muddle properly. Add ice to cover, pour in vanilla, lime juice and vodka. Shake properly, then stain mixture into stemmed cocktail glasses. Decorate with a twist of lime.

190. Kickin' Kale Pesto

"A vibrant recipe."
Serving: 10 | Prep: 10m | Ready in: 10m

Ingredients

- 1 bunch lacinato (dinosaur) kale, stems removed
- 1/2 cup grated Parmesan cheese
- 1/3 cup pine nuts
- 1/4 cup habanero-infused extra-virgin olive oil
- 3 cloves garlic, minced
- 2 tbsps. Meyer lemon juice
- 2 pinches freshly ground black pepper
- 1 pinch kosher salt

Direction

- Blend kosher salt, black pepper, lemon juice, garlic, olive oil, pine nuts, parmesan cheese and kale for 30-60 seconds till it has a pesto consistency in a food processor.

Nutrition Information

- Calories: 115 calories;
- Total Carbohydrate: 5.2 g
- Cholesterol: 4 mg
- Total Fat: 9.3 g
- Protein: 4 g
- Sodium: 133 mg

191. Kiwi Sorbet

"A fun kiwifruit sorbet."
Serving: Serves 4 to 6 (makes about 3 1/2 cups) servings | Prep: 15m

Ingredients

- 2 lbs. tender ripe green kiwifruit
- 3/4 cup superfine granulated sugar
- Equipment: an ice cream maker

Direction

- Peel then chop kiwis; pulse with sugar till smooth in food processor. Chill for 1 hour till cold.
- In ice cream maker, freeze; put in airtight container. Put in freeze for 1 hour minimum to firm up.
- You can ripen kiwi by keeping in sealed paper bag with banana.

Nutrition Information

- Calories: 283
- Total Carbohydrate: 71 g
- Total Fat: 1 g
- Fiber: 7 g
- Protein: 3 g
- Sodium: 7 mg
- Saturated Fat: 0 g

192. Lemon Cornmeal Cake With Raspberry Filling

"A fun cake recipe."
Serving: Serves 12

Ingredients

- 2 cups frozen unsweetened raspberries, thawed
- 2 tbsps. sugar
- 1 tbsp. cornstarch
- 3/4 cup (1 1/2 sticks) unsalted butter, room temperature
- 3/4 cup sugar
- 3 large eggs
- 1 1/4 cups cake flour
- 2 tsps. baking powder
- 1/4 tsp. salt
- 1/2 cup yellow cornmeal
- 6 tsps. grated lemon peel
- 2 tsps. lemon extract
- 2 cups chilled whipping cream
- 2 tbsps. sugar
- 1 tsp. lemon extract

- 3 tsps. grated lemon peel
- 3/4 cup sliced almonds, toasted

Direction

- Filling: In processor, puree berries; strain into medium heavy saucepan. Add cornstarch and sugar; mix on medium heat for 3 minutes till it thickens and boils. Cool and cover; chill for 2 hours till cold.
- Cake: Preheat an oven to 350°F. Butter 9-in. diameter cake pan that has 2-in. high sides lightly. Line parchment paper on bottom; butter parchment. Use flour to dust pan; shake excess out. Beat butter using electric mixer till fluffy in a big bowl. One by one, add eggs; beat well after each. Sift salt, baking powder and flour into medium bowl; mix in cornmeal. Put in butter mixture; beat till just blended. Mix in extract and lemon peel.
- Put batter in prepped pan; bake for 35 minutes till inserted toothpick in middle exits with several moist crumbs attached and cake is golden. Put cake on rack; cool. To loosen cake, cut around pan sides using knife; turn out cake and peel off parchment.
- Frosting: Beat extract, sugar and cream till soft peaks form in big bowl; beat in 1 1/2 tsp. lemon peel. Put 2/3 cup frosting aside for decoration.
- Horizontally cut cake to 3 layers using serrated knife. Put 1 layer on platter using 9-in. diameter tart pan's bottom as aid. Spread 1/2 filling over then spread 1 cup frosting on filling. Put 2nd cake layer over; spread leftover filling. Spread 1 cup frosting on filling; put 3rd cake layer over. Spread leftover frosting on top and sides of cake. Press nuts onto cake's sides. Put reserved 2/3 cup frosting in pastry bag with medium star tip; around cake's top edge, pipe. Scatter 1 1/2 tsp. lemon peel on cake's top. You can make it 4 hours ahead. Use cake dome to cover; refrigerate. Before serving, stand for 1 hour in room temperature.

Nutrition Information

- Calories: 424
- Total Carbohydrate: 39 g
- Cholesterol: 121 mg
- Total Fat: 28 g
- Fiber: 3 g
- Protein: 6 g
- Sodium: 143 mg
- Saturated Fat: 16 g

193. Lemon Custard Pies

"An old dessert."
Serving: Makes 2 pies or 16 servings

Ingredients

- 6 large eggs
- 1 cup sugar
- 1 cup fresh lemon juice
- 4 large egg yolks
- 2 tbsps. grated lemon peel
- 1 cup (2 sticks) unsalted butter, cut into pieces
- 1/2 cup half and half
- 1 tbsp. vanilla extract
- 2 cups all purpose flour
- 3 tbsps. powdered sugar
- 1/4 tsp. salt
- 1/2 cup (1 stick) chilled unsalted butter, cut into pieces
- 3 tbsps. chilled vegetable shortening, cut into pieces
- 6 tbsps. (about) ice water
- Whipped cream (optional)
- Lemon slices (optional)
- Fresh mint (optional)

Direction

- Filling: whisk initial 5 ingredients to blend in a big heavy saucepan. Add butter; whisk on medium heat for 13 minutes till filling leaves path on spoon's back when you draw a finger across and thickens, don't boil. Mix in vanilla and half and half; whisk for 6 minutes till filling starts to bubble, smooth and very thick. Put in a bowl. Cool for 15 minutes, occasionally mixing. Cover; chill for 4 hours

- till very cold. You can make it 3 days ahead, kept chilled.
- Crusts: In processor, mix salt, powdered sugar and flour. Add shortening and butter; process till it looks like coarse meal with on/off turns. Add 5 tbsp. water; process till moist clumps form. If dough is dry, add extra water by teaspoonfuls. Gather dough to ball; divide to 2 even pieces. Flatten it to disks. In plastic, wrap; chill for 1 hour till firm. You can make it 1 day ahead, kept chilled.
- Preheat an oven to 375°F. Roll 1 dough disk out to 12-13-in. round on lightly floured surface. Put dough in 9-in. glass pie plate; to 1/2-in., trim overhang. Keep dough scraps. Fold dough edge under; decoratively crimp. Repeat rolling using 2nd dough disk; place in separate 9-in. glass pie plate and freeze for 10 minutes till firm.
- Line foil on crusts; fill with pie weights/dried beans. Bake crusts for 20 minutes till sides are set. Remove beans and foil; bake for 12 minutes till crusts are pale golden. If crusts bubble, pierce with toothpick. Fully cool crusts on racks; maintain the oven temperature.
- Roll dough scraps out to 1/8-in. thick on floured surface; put on baking sheet. Bake for 10 minutes till golden; cool. Maintain the oven temperature. Crumble the pastry to small pieces and wrap; keep in room temperature.
- In each crust, put 1/2 filling; bake for 18 minutes till filling is set in middle. Cool pies. Chill for 2 hours till cold. You can make it 1 day ahead; cover. Keep chilled. Sprinkle the crumbled pastry on pies; use mint, lemon slices and whipped cream to garnish pies, if desired.

Nutrition Information

- Calories: 341
- Total Carbohydrate: 28 g
- Cholesterol: 164 mg
- Total Fat: 24 g
- Fiber: 1 g
- Protein: 5 g
- Sodium: 71 mg

- Saturated Fat: 13 g

194. Lima-bean Crostini

Serving: Makes 8 servings

Ingredients

- 1 (1-lb.) box frozen lima beans
- 2 cups extra-virgin olive oil
- 2 whole dried red peppers
- 1 6-inch stalk rosemary
- 2 garlic cloves, thinly sliced
- Juice of 1 lemon
- Salt and black pepper to taste
- 1 baguette

Direction

- In simmering water, soften beans for 2 minutes. Heat garlic, rosemary, red peppers and oil in another pan over medium low heat till rosemary begins to sizzle. Turn heat off. Drain beans well; add to pan. Soak for 30 minutes in oil. Remove rosemary leaves from stalk; discard 1 red pepper and stalk. Puree leftover red pepper, lemon juice, rosemary leaves, garlic, oil and beans in blender or food processor. Add black pepper and salt. Drizzle extra-virgin olive oil. Serve with crostini.
- Slice baguette to 1-in. slice. Drizzle black pepper, salt and olive oil to taste. Bake till just browned and crisp in a 375° oven.

Nutrition Information

- Calories: 658
- Total Carbohydrate: 34 g
- Total Fat: 56 g
- Fiber: 5 g
- Protein: 8 g
- Sodium: 435 mg
- Saturated Fat: 8 g

195. Linguine With Sun-dried Tomato Pesto

"This is a pesto you can keep refrigerated up to 2 weeks. You can add 3 cups cooked diced chicken to pasta to make a main course for 4."
Serving: 4 first-course servings

Ingredients

- 1 cup drained oil-packed sun-dried tomatoes (about 6 oz.)
- 1/2 cup grated Romano cheese or Parmesan cheese
- 1/4 cup chopped fresh basil or 1 tbsp. dried
- 2 tbsps. pine nuts, toasted
- 3 garlic cloves
- 3/4 cup olive oil
- 3/4 lb. linguine pasta

Direction

- In a food processor, combine garlic, pine nuts, basil, Romano cheese, and sun-dried tomatoes. As the machine runs, slowly pour in the olive oil and process to form a smooth past. You can make this 2 weeks beforehand, cover and refrigerate.
- Cook the linguine in a big pot with boiling salted water just until tender yet firm to bite. Drain and put aside 1/2 cup of the cooking liquid. Combine 3/4 cup of tomato pesto with the reserved cooking liquid in the same pot. Add the linguine and toss over medium-high heat till coated, adding more pesto if you want. Season to taste with pepper and salt, then serve.

Nutrition Information

- Calories: 860
- Total Carbohydrate: 75 g
- Cholesterol: 17 mg
- Total Fat: 55 g
- Fiber: 5 g
- Protein: 19 g
- Sodium: 356 mg
- Saturated Fat: 10 g

196. Ma'amoul (nut-filled Cookies)

"These cookies are wonderful."
Serving: Makes 35 - 40 cookies

Ingredients

- 2 1/2 cups unbleached all-purpose flour
- 1/2 cup semolina flour
- 10 oz. (2 1/2 sticks) pareve margarine or 1 lb. (2 sticks) butter
- 2 tsps. vegetable oil
- 1/4-1/2 cup water
- Confectioners' sugar
- 1 1/2 cups roughly ground walnuts
- 1 tsp. cinnamon
- 1/2 cup sugar

Direction

- In food processor fitted with steel blade, put oil, margarine, semolina and flour for dough. Gradually pour in water, pulse to form a soft dough. Put aside in refrigerator with cover about 10 to 15 minutes.
- Mix cinnamon, sugar and walnuts for filling.
- Heat an oven to 350 °.
- Use ma'amoul mold or tear off a dough piece approximately walnut-size. Form to ball and empty the middle. Stuff with heaping 1 tsp. walnut filling. Mold dough to enclose using your hands.
- Proceed with the remaining dough.
- Arrange cookies on ungreased cookie sheet. Create designs on each cookie top using tweezers with serrated edge or fork tines, make sure not to pierce thorough crust.
- Bake for approximately half an hour in oven. Prevent from browning; cookies need to look white. Cool down. Roll into confectioners' sugar once firm.

197. Macadamia Nut Butter

""An excellent macadamia nut butter on Hawaiian or other muffins or breads.""
Serving: 4 | Prep: 5m | Ready in: 15m

Ingredients

- 1/4 cup unsalted macadamia nuts
- 1/4 cup unsalted butter, at room temperature
- 2 tsps. cognac

Direction

- Prepare the oven by preheating to 350°F (175°C). Place macadamia nuts on a baking sheet then scatter.
- Place the nuts in preheated oven and bake for 7-10 minutes until toasted lightly. Allow it to cool.
- In a food processor or a blender, put the nuts; pulse until grounded finely. Add cognac and butter. Pulse until just mixed. Avoid over mixing, or the butter will get hot and separate.
- Turn macadamia nut butter to a log or pack in a crock. Keep in the refrigerator, covered, until serving time.

Nutrition Information

- Calories: 170 calories;
- Total Carbohydrate: 1.1 g
- Cholesterol: 31 mg
- Total Fat: 17.8 g
- Protein: 0.8 g
- Sodium: 2 mg

198. Maltaise Sauce For Asparagus

"This won't take you more than 45 minutes to prepare."
Serving: Makes about 1 cup

Ingredients

- 2 large egg yolks
- 1 tbsp. fresh lemon juice
- a pinch of freshly ground white pepper
- 1 stick (1/2 cup) unsalted butter, melted and cooled
- 1 tsp. grated orange zest (preferably from a blood orange ,available seasonally at specialty product markets)
- 1 tbsp. plus 1 tsp. fresh orange juice (preferably from a blood orange)

Direction

- Put the white pepper, a pinch of salt, lemon juice and egg yolks in a food processor or blender; then with the motor running add the butter in a stream. Add orange juice and zest; blend well. Force the mixture through a fine sieve set over a small bowl; keep it warm, cover its surface with a buttered round of wax paper, put in a pan of warm water. Pour the sauce over asparagus; then serve.

Nutrition Information

- Calories: 117
- Total Carbohydrate: 1 g
- Cholesterol: 77 mg
- Total Fat: 13 g
- Fiber: 0 g
- Protein: 1 g
- Sodium: 4 mg
- Saturated Fat: 8 g

199. Malted Milk Cookie Tart

"You can use 9-in. buttered glass pie dish for 9-in. diameter tart pan; cool tart in dish. Cut."
Serving: Makes 16 wedges | Prep: 30m

Ingredients

- 1 1/2 cups all purpose flour
- 1 cup malted milk powder
- 1/2 cup sugar
- 1 tsp. (scant) coarse kosher salt
- 1 cup (2 sticks) unsalted butter, cut into 1-inch pieces, room temperature
- 1/2 cup bittersweet chocolate chips (about 3 oz.; do not exceed 61% cacao)
- 1/2 cup malted milk balls, coarsely chopped

Direction

- Preheat an oven to 325°F. Pulse coarse salt, sugar, malted milk powder and flour in processor. Add butter; pulse till moist clumps form. Put dough on work surface; bring to ball. Evenly press on bottom of 9-in. diameter tart pan that has removable bottom.
- Bake crust for 45 minutes till evenly golden brown. Scatter with chocolate chips; stand to soften for 5 minutes. Spread melted chocolate on hot crust in the well that appears as middle sinks. Sprinkle with malted milk balls; fully cool. Take tart from pan then cut to wedges.

200. Mango Apricot Glaze

"This glaze is great for fish, chicken, or pork."
Serving: 48 | Prep: 15m | Ready in: 35m

Ingredients

- 1 1/2 cups rice wine vinegar
- 1/2 cup raw sugar
- 2 ripe mangoes, peeled and chopped
- 4 fresh apricots, pitted and chopped
- 1 tbsp. chopped fresh ginger root
- 1 tbsp. honey
- 1 tbsp. fresh lime juice

Direction

- Boil sugar and rice vinegar in a saucepan until the sugar has dissolved. Cook over medium heat, constantly stirring, for 10 minutes. Stir in the ginger, apricots, and mangoes, and cook while occasionally stirring until the fruit is tender and starts to break apart, 10 more minutes. Move to a food processor or blender and add lime juice and honey, then process until it is smooth.

Nutrition Information

- Calories: 15 calories;
- Total Carbohydrate: 3.8 g
- Cholesterol: 0 mg
- Total Fat: 0 g
- Protein: 0.1 g
- Sodium: < 1 mg

201. Mango Guacamole

"This recipe used to be made by my mother every summer and mangoes are everywhere. Tangy, sweet and spicy recipe."
Serving: 8 | Prep: 20m | Ready in: 20m

Ingredients

- 2 tbsps. minced white onion
- 2 limes, juiced
- 2 serrano chile peppers, or to taste
- 2 limes, juiced
- sea salt to taste
- 4 ripe avocados, peeled and pitted
- 1/4 cup chopped fresh cilantro
- 1 large mango - peeled, seeded, and chopped

Direction

- Get a small bowl and mix together the juice of 2 limes and onion; let the onion soak for an hour in the lime juice. Drain and remove excess juice. Set aside the onion.
- Put the salt, the juice of 2 limes, and serrano chile peppers together in a food processor then

grind until there's no more big portion of pepper left. Stir in 1 avocado and blend until becomes smooth; do it again with the left avocados. Place the mixture in serving bowl; add in the mango, cilantro and onion, then fold into the avocado mixture. Present at a room temperature.

Nutrition Information

- Calories: 198 calories;
- Total Carbohydrate: 19 g
- Cholesterol: 0 mg
- Total Fat: 14.9 g
- Protein: 2.5 g
- Sodium: 49 mg

202. Mango-lime Ice

""Try this Mexican dessert with different sweet fruits. Raspberries work best with this recipe.""
Serving: Makes 8 servings

Ingredients

- 4 large mangoes (about 3 1/2 lbs. total), peeled and coarsely chopped
- Zest of 1 orange
- 1 1/4 cups sugar
- 1/3 cup freshly squeezed lime juice

Direction

- Combine 1 cup of water, lime juice, sugar, orange zest, and mangoes in the bowl of a food processor. Process until smooth. In a large bowl, pour the syrup through a fine-mesh sieve set and gently press mixture through. Discard any solids. There should be about 3 cups of syrup. Store in a freezer-safe dish and cover with plastic. Freeze the mixture for about 2 hours until it is firm 2 inches from the sides. Scrape the frozen mixture into a food processor and process until the mixture is slushy. Repeat freezing and processing twice. Before serving, freeze for at least 1 hour. The ice can be made and stored in the freezer ahead of time. Wrap it well and it should last up to 2 weeks.

Nutrition Information

- Calories: 257
- Total Carbohydrate: 65 g
- Total Fat: 1 g
- Fiber: 4 g
- Protein: 2 g
- Sodium: 3 mg
- Saturated Fat: 0 g

203. Mascarpone Cheesecake With Quince Compote

"A no-bake cheesecake."
Serving: Makes 12 servings

Ingredients

- 1 1/3 cups pecans, toasted
- 1/2 cup walnuts, toasted
- 1/2 cup (packed) golden brown sugar
- 1/2 cup (1 stick) unsalted butter, melted
- 3 1/2 cups whipping cream
- 1/4 cup water
- 3 1/2 tsps. unflavored gelatin (from 2 envelopes)
- 3 1/2 cups plus 2 tbsps. mascarpone cheese* (about 28 1/2 oz.; from four 8-oz. containers)
- 1 1/4 cups powdered sugar, sifted
- Quince Compote

Direction

- Crust: Preheat an oven to 375°F. Grind brown sugar and nuts coarsely in processor then blend in melted butter. On bottom, not sides, of the 9-in. diameter springform pan that has 2 1/2-in. high sides, press mixture; bake for 12 minutes till crust is set. Fully cool crust.
- Filling: In medium bowl, put 3 cups cream. Into small heatproof bowl, put 1/4 cup water; sprinkle gelatin. Stand for 15 minutes. Put bowl with gelatin into small skillet with barely

simmering water; mix for 2 minutes till gelatin is dissolved. Take bowl from water. Put leftover 1/2 cup cream in gelatin. Put gelatin into the cream in bowl; gently whisk till blended well.
- Beat powdered sugar and mascarpone using electric mixer till smooth in big bowl; beat in gelatin-cream mixture till smooth. Put filling on cooled crust; cover. Chill overnight. You can prep it 2 days ahead, kept chilled.
- To loosen cheesecake, cut around pan side using small sharp knife; remove pan sides. Put cake on platter and cut cake to wedges; serve with compote.

Nutrition Information

- Calories: 659
- Total Carbohydrate: 26 g
- Cholesterol: 170 mg
- Total Fat: 61 g
- Fiber: 1 g
- Protein: 7 g
- Sodium: 270 mg
- Saturated Fat: 32 g

204. Mashed Sweet Potatoes And Pears

"So amazing!"
Serving: 6 | Prep: 20m | Ready in: 50m

Ingredients

- 2 pears, peeled and sliced
- 1/2 cup dry white wine
- 1/4 cup water
- 3 sweet potatoes, peeled and cubed
- 1 cup evaporated milk
- 1/4 tsp. vanilla extract
- 1/4 cup brown sugar
- 2 tbsps. butter
- 1/2 tsp. ground cinnamon
- 1/2 tsp. ground nutmeg

Direction

- Boil water, wine and pears in a small saucepan on high heat. Lower heat to medium-low; simmer for 5-10 minutes till pears are soft. Discard pears from wine; put aside.
- In a big pot, put sweet potatoes and add water to cover; boil on high heat. Lower heat to medium-low and cover; simmer for 20 minutes till tender. Drain; let steam dry potatoes for 1-2 minutes.
- Stir nutmeg, cinnamon, butter, brown sugar, vanilla, evaporated milk and reserved pears into sweet potatoes; mash till smooth. Put in a serving dish; serve hot.

Nutrition Information

- Calories: 232 calories;
- Total Carbohydrate: 35.7 g
- Cholesterol: 22 mg
- Total Fat: 7.2 g
- Protein: 4.2 g
- Sodium: 112 mg

205. Master Hot Sauce Recipe

Serving: Makes about 2 1/2 cups

Ingredients

- 1 lb. stemmed fresh chiles (such as jalapeño, serrano, Fresno, or habanero; use one variety or mix and match)
- 2 tbsps. kosher salt
- 1 1/2 cups distilled white vinegar

Direction

- Pulse kosher salt and chiles till coarse puree forms in food processor. Put in 1-qt. glass jar; screw on lid loosely. Stand for 12 hours to slightly ferment in room temperature.
- Mix in vinegar; screw on lid loosely. Stand chile mixture for minimum of 1- maximum of 7 days in room temperature. Taste everyday; the flavor gets deeper the longer it sits.

- Puree mixture for 1 minute till smooth in a blender/food processor. Inside a funnel, put a fine-mesh sieve. Through sieve, strain mixture into clean glass bottle. The hot sauce gets thinner and might separate after straining; vigorously shake before every use. You can make it maximum of 4 months ahead, kept refrigerated.

Nutrition Information

- Calories: 49
- Total Carbohydrate: 8 g
- Total Fat: 0 g
- Fiber: 1 g
- Protein: 2 g
- Sodium: 377 mg
- Saturated Fat: 0 g

206. Meatless Dairy-free Taco Dip

"A lactose free dip that's healthy and a little spicy."
Serving: 4 | Prep: 10m | Ready in: 27m

Ingredients

- 1 (15 oz.) can garbanzo beans, drained
- 1/2 cup canned diced tomatoes with green chile peppers and onions
- 1 canned roasted red pepper, diced
- 1 small jalapeno pepper, diced
- 1 tsp. sriracha sauce
- 1 tsp. garlic powder
- 1 tsp. chili powder
- 1/2 (1 oz.) packet taco seasoning mix

Direction

- Mix and cook chili powder, garlic powder, sriracha sauce, jalapeno pepper, roasted red pepper, diced tomatoes and garbanzo beans in a saucepan on medium heat for 15 minutes till beans are heated through and soft. Drain all liquid from the mixture except 1 tbsp..
- Mix taco seasoning into the bean mixture; cook for 2 minutes till flavors merge.

- Put bean mixture in a food processor; puree to the preferred consistency. Put dip in a serving bowl.

Nutrition Information

- Calories: 113 calories;
- Total Carbohydrate: 21.7 g
- Cholesterol: 0 mg
- Total Fat: 1.1 g
- Protein: 4.2 g
- Sodium: 734 mg

207. Mediterranean Chickpea Latkes

"Drizzle the latkes with pomegranate molasses."
Serving: Makes about 24

Ingredients

- 1 15-oz. can garbanzo beans (chickpeas), rinsed, drained
- 2 garlic cloves
- 1 tbsp. fresh rosemary
- 3 large eggs
- 6 tbsps. water
- 2 tbsps. extra-virgin olive oil
- 3 tbsps. all purpose flour
- 1 1/2 tsps. ground cumin
- 1 tsp. salt
- 1/2 tsp. ground black pepper
- 1/2 tsp. baking powder
- 6 tbsps. (or more) olive oil
- Pomegranate seeds (optional)

Direction

- Use processor to process garlic, rosemary and garbanzo beans to a rough paste. Put in 6 tbsps. water, extra-virgin olive oil and eggs; process till smooth. Put in baking powder, pepper, salt, cumin and flour, and process. Transfer the batter to a bowl.
- In a big, heavy skillet, heat 6 tbsps. of oil on moderately-high heat till hot yet do not let it

smoke. Drop heaping tablespoonfuls of batter in hot oil; do it in batches. Cook for a minute on each side, till golden. Turn latkes onto paper towels with slotted spatula and let drain. Put additional oil into skillet as need be and heat till hot then put in additional batter. Remove latkes to plates. If wished, scatter pomegranate seeds over to serve.

Nutrition Information

- Calories: 78
- Total Carbohydrate: 5 g
- Cholesterol: 23 mg
- Total Fat: 6 g
- Fiber: 1 g
- Protein: 2 g
- Sodium: 78 mg
- Saturated Fat: 1 g

208. Mexican Pesto

"A classic pesto."
Serving: 6 | Prep: 10m | Ready in: 10m

Ingredients

- 1/4 cup hulled pumpkin seeds (pepitas)
- 1 bunch cilantro
- 1/4 cup grated cotija cheese
- 4 cloves garlic
- 1 serrano chile pepper, seeded
- 1/2 tsp. salt
- 6 tbsps. olive oil

Direction

- Pulse pumpkin seeds till coarsely chopped in a blender/food processor. Add olive oil, salt, chile pepper, garlic, cheese and cilantro; cover. Process till smooth, scraping bowl's sides with spatula as needed.

Nutrition Information

- Calories: 176 calories;
- Total Carbohydrate: 2.4 g
- Cholesterol: 6 mg
- Total Fat: 17.8 g
- Protein: 2.9 g
- Sodium: 262 mg

209. Mexican Pizza Webb

Serving: Serves 4

Ingredients

- 1 cup plus 2 tbsps. warm water
- a 1/4-oz. package active dry yeast (2 1/2 tsps.)
- 1/2 tsp. sugar
- 3 tbsps. peanut oil
- 2 1/3 cups all-purpose flour
- 2/3 cup cornmeal plus additional for sprinkling pizza pan
- 1 tsp. salt
- 1/2 tsp. ground cumin
- 1 1/2 lbs. fresh tomatillos*, husks discarded
- 1 small onion, sliced thin
- 2 garlic cloves, sliced thin
- 2 tbsps. peanut oil
- 1/4 cup packed fresh coriander sprigs, washed well, spun dry, and chopped
- 1 tbsp. fresh lime juice
- 1 lb. fresh chorizo* or other spicy fresh pork sausage, casings discarded
- 3/4 lb. Colby, Cheddar, Monterey jack, or a mixture grated coarse (about 1 1/2 cups)
- 2 fresh poblano chilies*, roasted (procedure follows) and cut into thin strips (wear rubber gloves)
- 2 scallions, sliced thin
- 1/4 cup thinly sliced drained pimento-stuffed green olives
- 1/4 cup cooked black beans, rinsed if canned
- *available at Mexican markets, some specialty foods shops, and some supermarkets

Direction

- Dough: Heat 1/2 cup water to about 110°F in a small saucepan; put in a big bowl. Mix in sugar and yeast; stand till foamy for 5 minutes.

- Mix in dough ingredients and leftover water to make a dough; knead for 10 minutes till elastic and smooth on lightly floured surface.
- In lightly oiled deep bowl, put dough; turn to coat. Rise for 1 hour till doubled in bulk in a warm place, loosely covered. Or, rise dough in the fridge overnight till doubled in bulk, loosely covered.
- Sauce: Blanch tomatillos for 1 minute in 4-qt. saucepan with boiling water; in colander, drain. Cut every tomatillo to 8 wedges. Cook garlic and onion in oil in a big heavy skillet on medium heat till onion is pale golden, occasionally mixing. Add tomatillos; cook on medium heat till reduced to 1 1/4 cups and tomatillos are soft, occasionally mixing. Slightly cool; puree till smooth in a food processor. Put sauce in a bowl; mix in salt to taste, lime juice and coriander.
- Cook sausage till brown and cooked through in a big heavy skillet on medium high heat, breaking up lumps, mixing. Put sausage on paper towels with a slotted spoon; drain.
- Preheat an oven to 525°F. On top shelf, adjust oven rack. Sprinkle extra cornmeal on 16-in. perforated pizza pan.
- Punch dough down; roll out to 17-in. circle with floured rolling pin on lightly floured work surface. Fit dough in pan, making an edge; bake for 5 minutes.
- Spread sauce on partially cooked dough; leave 1/2-in. border around edge. Sprinkle beans, olives, chilies, scallions, cheese and sausage.
- Bake pizza till crust is pale golden and cheese is melted for 10 minutes.
- Roast peppers: Char peppers above an open flame using long-handled fork for 2-3 minutes till skins blacken, turning them. Or, broil peppers on broiler pan's rack under preheated broiler 2-in. from heat for 15-25 minutes total, turning every 5 minutes, till skins are charred and blistered. Put peppers in a bowl; steam till cool to handle, covered. Starting at blossom end, peel, keeping peppers whole; cut off tops. Discard ribs and seeds. When handling chilies, wear rubber gloves.

Nutrition Information

- Calories: 1233
- Total Carbohydrate: 97 g
- Cholesterol: 134 mg
- Total Fat: 73 g
- Fiber: 9 g
- Protein: 49 g
- Sodium: 1600 mg
- Saturated Fat: 25 g

210. Meyer Lemon Cranberry Scones

"A lovely recipe."
Serving: Makes 16

Ingredients

- 2 tbsps. freshly grated lemon zest (from about 3 lemons; preferably Meyer)
- 2 1/2 cups all-purpose flour
- 1/2 cup sugar plus 3 tbsps. additional if using fresh cranberries
- 1 tbsp. baking powder
- 1/2 tsp. salt
- 3/4 stick (6 tbsps.) cold unsalted butter, cut into bits
- 1 1/4 cups fresh cranberries, chopped coarse, or 1 1/4 cups dried cranberries or dried cherries
- 1 large egg
- 1 large egg yolk
- 1 cup heavy cream
- Accompaniment: crème fraîche or whipped cream

Direction

- Preheat an oven to 400°F. Line parchment paper on a big baking sheet.
- Remove zest from lemons with a vegetable peeler. Chop fine; keep lemons for another time.

- Pulse zest, butter, salt, baking powder, 1/2 cup sugar and flour till it looks like coarse meal in a food processor; put into a big bowl.
- Toss 3 tbsp. sugar and fresh cranberries in a small bowl; mix into flour mixture. Add to flour mixture if using dried fruit.
- Beat yolk and egg lightly in another small bowl; mix in cream. Put egg mixture in flour mixture; mix just till combined.
- Pat dough with floured hands to 1-in. thick 8-in. diameter round on well-floured surface; cut as many rounds out as possible with 2-in. round cutter/rim of glass dipped into flour; reroll scraps as needed. Put rounds on baking sheet, 1-in. apart; bake in center of oven till pale golden for 15-20 minutes.
- Serve scones warm with whipped cream/crème fraiche. Scones keep for 1 day, chilled, wrapped in plastic wrap then foil separately, or frozen for 1 week.

Nutrition Information

- Calories: 211
- Total Carbohydrate: 26 g
- Cholesterol: 55 mg
- Total Fat: 11 g
- Fiber: 1 g
- Protein: 3 g
- Sodium: 135 mg
- Saturated Fat: 6 g

211. Mini Mincemeat Pies

"This recipe is for mincemeat tartlets you can top with some hard sauce made with brandy, powdered sugar, and softened butter."
Serving: Makes 18

Ingredients

- 1 3/4 cups all purpose flour
- 10 tbsps. powdered sugar
- 3 1/4 tsps. grated orange peel
- 1/4 tsp. salt
- 1/2 cup (1 stick) chilled unsalted butter, cut into 1/2-inch pieces
- 1 large egg yolk
- 2 tbsps. (or more) orange juice
- 3/4 cup purchased mincemeat from jar
- 3 tbsps. minced crystallized ginger
- 1/4 tsp. ground cinnamon
- 1 egg, beaten to blend (for glaze)

Direction

- In a processor, mix salt, 2 1/2 tsps. of orange peel, 6 tbsps. of powdered sugar, and flour. Add the butter and process until it looks like coarse meal. In a small bowl, whisk together 2 tbsps. of orange juice and egg yolk, then add into the processor. Blend to form moist clumps, adding in more teaspoonfuls of juice if it is dry. Gather the dough into a ball and flatten into a disk, then chill for about 30 minutes.
- Butter 18 mini muffin cups (1 3/4 inch diameter). In a small bowl, mix together 3/4 tsp. of peel, the leftover 4 tbsps. of powdered sugar, cinnamon, crystallized ginger, and mincemeat. Roll the dough to a 17 inch round on a floured surface. Use a 2 1/2 inch diameter cookie cutter to cut out 18 rounds of dough. Press a round in the bottom and up the sides of each of the muffin cups. Use a 1 3/4 - 2 inch diameter cookie cutter to cut 18 more rounds of dough, re-rolling the dough if needed. Fill the crust in each of the muffin cups with 1 heaping tsp. of filling. Brush edges of the smaller dough rounds with egg glaze and place 1 round on top of each filled cup with the glazed-side down, pressing the edges to seal. Cut a small X in the middle of each pie. You can make this 4 hours beforehand, cover the pies and leftover glaze individually then chill.
- Set the oven to 375 degrees Fahrenheit. Use the leftover egg glaze to brush the pies and bake until the crusts become golden, around 20 minutes. Use a small knife to cut around the pies to loosen and turn them out onto a rack. Serve the pies at room temperature or warm.

Nutrition Information

- Calories: 122
- Total Carbohydrate: 16 g
- Cholesterol: 33 mg
- Total Fat: 6 g
- Fiber: 0 g
- Protein: 2 g
- Sodium: 40 mg
- Saturated Fat: 3 g

212. Minted Pea Purée

"You can make this in under 1 hour."
Serving: Serves 8

Ingredients

- three 10-oz. packages frozen peas, thawed
- 1/3 cup fresh mint leaves plus fresh mint sprigs for garnish if desired
- 3 tbsps. half-and-half, or to taste
- 3 tbsps. unsalted butter, cut into bits

Direction

- Boil mint leaves, 1/4 cup water and peas in a big saucepan till peas are tender for 4 minutes, covered. Drain the mixture well; puree with pepper and salt to taste, butter and half and half in a food processor. You can make the puree 1 day ahead, kept chilled, covered, then reheated. Put puree in a serving dish; garnish with mint sprigs.

Nutrition Information

- Calories: 127
- Total Carbohydrate: 15 g
- Cholesterol: 14 mg
- Total Fat: 5 g
- Fiber: 5 g
- Protein: 6 g
- Sodium: 118 mg
- Saturated Fat: 3 g

213. Mix-and-mash Root Vegetables

"Satisfying and simple side dish."
Serving: Serves 6

Ingredients

- 1 lb. turnips, peeled
- 1 lb. large carrots, peeled
- 1 lb. parsnips, peeled
- 1/4 cup (1/2 stick) butter
- Ground nutmeg

Direction

- Cut vegetables to 1/2-inch pieces; put in a heavy medium saucepan. Put enough water in to cover; boil. Cook for 12 minutes till vegetables are tender; drain. Put in the processor; add butter. Process to coarse puree. Otherwise, put vegetables in same pan; add butter. Mash to a coarse puree. Season with pepper, salt and nutmeg; serve.

214. Mojo Rojo

"This is a chile-based sauce you can add for heat and color to blanched broccoli, green beans, or cauliflower."
Serving: Makes 1 1/4 cups

Ingredients

- 8 garlic cloves
- 2 dried guindilla or New Mexico chiles
- 2 tsps. smoked paprika
- 1 tsp. ground cumin
- 1 tsp. kosher salt
- 1 cup extra-virgin olive oil
- 1 tsp. Sherry vinegar

Direction

- In a food processor, process 1 tsp. of kosher salt, 1 tsp. of ground cumin, 2 tsps. of smoked paprika, 2 dried New Mexico chiles or guindilla, and 8 cloves of garlic, scraping down the bowl's sides occasionally, until it forms a smooth paste. As the machine runs, drizzle in 1 cup of extra-virgin olive oil and process until blended well. Add 1 tsp. of water and 1 tsp. of Sherry vinegar, processing to blend, then season with some salt.

215. Molasses Carob Chip Cookies

"You can use peanuts or cashews for almonds."
Serving: 30 | Prep: 20m | Ready in: 27m

Ingredients

- 1 cup regular rolled oats
- 2/3 cup almonds
- 1/4 cup vegetable oil
- 1/2 cup butter, room temperature
- 1/4 cup molasses
- 1/4 cup turbinado sugar
- 1 egg
- 1 tsp. baking soda
- 1 1/4 cups whole wheat flour
- 1/4 cup unsweetened dried coconut
- 1 cup unsweetened carob chips

Direction

- Preheat an oven to 175°C/350°F. Grease 2 baking sheets lightly.
- Process oats till finely chopped in food processor's bowl. Put ground oats into measuring cups; add extra oats to create full cup. Put aside.
- Process vegetable oil and almonds till paste-like and smooth in a food processor's bowl. Scrape almond mixture into mixing bowl. Add egg, turbinado sugar, molasses and butter to mixing bowl with nut mixtures; beat together ingredients till blended well. Mix in carob chips, coconut, whole wheat flour, oats and baking soda; thoroughly blend. By teaspoonfuls, drop on prepped baking sheets, 2-in. apart.
- In preheated oven, bake for 7 minutes till tops look dry and set. Remove from oven. Put on racks; cool.

Nutrition Information

- Calories: 130 calories;
- Total Carbohydrate: 12.7 g
- Cholesterol: 14 mg
- Total Fat: 8 g
- Protein: 2.5 g
- Sodium: 93 mg

216. Molasses Jumbos With Ginger Filling

Serving: Makes about 2 dozen cookies

Ingredients

- 2/3 cup firmly packed light brown sugar
- 1/2 cup light molasses
- 1/2 cup (1 stick) unsalted butter
- 1 extra-large egg
- 1 tbsp. cider vinegar
- 2 tsps. vanilla
- 3 cups sifted all purpose flour
- 3/4 tsp. ground ginger
- 3/4 tsp. baking soda
- 3/4 tsp. cinnamon
- 1/2 tsp. salt
- 1/2 tsp. ground cloves
- 1/4 tsp. ground cardamom
- Melted butter
- All purpose flour
- 2 1/2 cups powdered sugar
- 7 tbsps. chopped crystallized ginger (3 oz.)
- 4 tbsps. ginger marmalade
- 4 tbsps. well-chilled unsalted butter, cut into 4 pieces

Direction

- To prepare cookies: In a 2-3 quart heavy pan, stir butter, molasses, and sugar together over

low heat until the butter has melted, then cool to lukewarm.
- Stir in the vanilla, vinegar, and egg. Combine the next 6 of the ingredients with 3 cups of flour and slowly stir into the molasses mixture. Chill while covered for 1 1/2 hours till firm. You can make this 3 days beforehand.
- Invert the baking sheets and cover the undersides with foil. Brush them with some melted butter and dust each with flour, shaking off the excess. Form the dough into 1-inch balls and place them on the foil 3 inches apart. Flatten each of the cookies into a 3 inch round (you can use the bottom of a saucepan wrapped in plastic to do this). Chill the cookies for 1 1/2 hours.
- Set the oven to 325 degrees Fahrenheit and bake the cookies until they have the color of honey, roughly 14 minutes. Slide the foil onto a work area and press each of the cookies gently to flatten using a spatula, then cool. You can make this 2 days beforehand, store them in an airtight container.
- To prepare filling: In a processor, blend 3 1/2 tbsps. of ginger and 1 1/4 cups of sugar, stopping occasionally to scrape down the sides of the bowl, until the ginger is minced, around 2 minutes. Add 2 tbsps. each of butter and marmalade, then process until blended well and thick, 1 1/2 minutes. Move to a small bowl. Repeat the process with the remaining butter, marmalade, ginger, and sugar, then add to the bowl. You can make this a day beforehand, keep them refrigerated. Bring to room temperature before you continue.
- Spread 1 tbsp. of the filling onto the bottom of the cookie, smoothing out to the edges. Press another cookie bottom firmly onto the filling. Repeat with leftover cookies. You can make cookies 6 hours beforehand, store them uncovered to keep them crispy.

Nutrition Information

- Calories: 232
- Total Carbohydrate: 41 g
- Cholesterol: 26 mg
- Total Fat: 7 g
- Fiber: 1 g
- Protein: 2 g
- Sodium: 102 mg
- Saturated Fat: 4 g

217. Mr. Lincoln And Cecile Brunner In A Jam

"A lovely rose petal jam."
Serving: 80 | Prep: 20m | Ready in: 25m

Ingredients

- 1 cup fresh, fragrant rose petals
- 2 tbsps. fresh lemon juice
- 2 1/2 cups white sugar
- 1 (1.75 oz.) package dry pectin
- 1 1/2 cups water

Direction

- Process 3/4 cup water, lemon juice and rose petals in a blender/food processor. Add sugar slowly till blended thoroughly. Put mixture in a big bowl; a big mixing bowl with a pouring spout is the best. Put aside.
- Mix 3/4 cup water and pectin to combine in a small saucepan; Stir to dissolve. Boil. Boil the pectin hard for a minute.
- Put pectin on rose petal mixture; mix. It'll very quickly start to set. Pour/spoon mixture in clean containers; refrigerate. It will continue to set as it cools.

Nutrition Information

- Calories: 24 calories;
- Total Carbohydrate: 6.3 g
- Cholesterol: 0 mg
- Total Fat: 0 g
- Protein: 0 g
- Sodium: < 1 mg

218. Mushroom Caesar Salad

Serving: Serves 4

Ingredients

- 1/4 cup fresh lemon juice
- 4 anchovy fillets
- 2 large garlic cloves
- 2 tsps. drained capers
- 2 tsps. Dijon mustard
- 2 tsps. prepared white horseradish
- 1 tsp. Worcestershire sauce
- 2 dashes of hot pepper sauce (such as Tabasco)
- 3/4 cup olive oil
- 1/2 lb. mushrooms, thinly sliced
- 1 large head romaine lettuce, torn into bite-size pieces
- 2 cups purchased garlic-flavored croutons
- 1/2 cup grated Parmesan cheese

Direction

- In a processor, process the initial eight ingredients till nearly smooth. Pour in oil slowly; blend to form thick dressing. Add pepper and salt to season. May be prepped a day in advance. Refrigerate with cover.
- Toss a third cup of dressing and mushrooms in a medium-size bowl. Marinate, about 15 minutes. Put the lettuce in a big bowl. Put in croutons, cheese and mushrooms. Toss along with sufficient dressing to liberally coat. Add pepper and salt to season.

Nutrition Information

- Calories: 572
- Total Carbohydrate: 24 g
- Cholesterol: 14 mg
- Total Fat: 49 g
- Fiber: 6 g
- Protein: 13 g
- Sodium: 675 mg
- Saturated Fat: 9 g

219. Mussels On The Half Shell With Pesto

Serving: Makes 40

Ingredients

- 1 cup dry white wine
- 1 cup water
- 1/4 cup chopped shallots
- 2 tbsps. white wine vinegar
- 4 garlic cloves, crushed with side of knife
- 40 fresh mussels, scrubbed, debearded
- 4 cups fresh basil leaves
- 4 garlic cloves, chopped
- 3 tbsps. olive oil
- 6 tbsps. freshly grated Parmesan cheese
- 2 tbsps. low-fat mayonnaise

Direction

- Boil initial 5 ingredients in a big pot. Put mussels in pot in batches; cover. Cook for 4 minutes till mussels open. Put mussels in big bowl using slotted spoon; discard unopened ones. Cool mussels and strain cooking liquid; keep 1 cup.
- From shells, remove mussels; keep half of every shell. Put mussels in medium bowl; refrigerate.
- In processor, finely chop garlic and basil. Add oil and reserved 1 cup of cooking liquid slowly as processor runs; process till blended well. Blend in mayonnaise and cheese. Put pesto in big bowl; season with pepper and salt. Add mussels; toss to coat. Chill for minimum of 1 hour. You can make it 1 day ahead and refrigerate kept shells.
- Put pesto and mussels in reserved shells; put on platter.

220. Neapolitan Sundae

Serving: Serves 4

Ingredients

- 1/2 cup frozen strawberries in syrup, thawed
- 1/2 cup sliced fresh strawberries
- 4 tbsps. amaretto liqueur or brandy
- 3 oz. bittersweet (not unsweetened) or semisweet chocolate, chopped
- 1/4 cup plus 2 tbsps. whipping cream
- 1 pint strawberry ice cream
- 1 pint vanilla ice cream
- 1 pint chocolate chocolate chip ice cream
- 1 basket strawberries, sliced
- Whipped cream
- 1/2 cup sliced almonds, toasted
- Chocolate sprinkles
- 4 maraschino cherries with stems, drained

Direction

- Use a processor to puree 1/2 cup of fresh strawberries along with the frozen strawberries, then move to a small bowl and stir in 1 tbsp. of amaretto.
- In a small heavy saucepan, melt the chocolate and whipping cream over low heat, stirring until it becomes smooth. Mix in the leftover 3 tbsps. of amaretto and cool the mixture to lukewarm.
- Spoon 1/4 cup of the chocolate sauce into each of the 4 sundae dishes and scoop some of each ice cream into each dish. Spoon a bit of the strawberry sauce over top. Top with a dollop of whipped cream and sliced strawberries. Sprinkle with chocolate sprinkles and sliced almonds and top each with maraschino cherries to serve.

221. Nectarine Almond Frangipane Tart

"A gorgeous dessert."
Serving: Makes 8 servings | Prep: 1h

Ingredients

- 1 cup all-purpose flour
- 3 tbsps. sugar
- 1/2 tsp. salt
- 3/4 stick (6 tbsps.) cold unsalted butter, cut into 1/2-inch pieces
- 1/2 tsp. finely grated fresh lemon zest
- 2 large egg yolks
- 1/2 tsp. vanilla
- 1 1/2 tsps. water
- 7 to 8 oz almond paste (not marzipan or almond filling)
- 1/2 stick (1/4 cup) unsalted butter, softened
- 3 tbsps. sugar
- 1/8 tsp. almond extract
- 2 large eggs
- 3 tbsps. all-purpose flour
- 1/2 tsp. salt
- 1 1/4 lb firm-ripe nectarines
- 1/3 cup peach preserves
- 2 tbsps. water
- 1 tbsp. Disaronno Amaretto (optional)
- a pastry or bench scraper; an 11- by 8- by 1-inch rectangular or 11-inch round fluted tart pan with a removable bottom; pie weights or raw rice

Direction

- Dough: In center position, put oven rack; preheat it to 375°F.
- Pulse salt, sugar and flour till combined in a food processor. Add zest and butter; pulse till it looks like coarse meal with some roughly pea-sized small butter lumps. Add water, vanilla and yolks; pulse till dough starts to make big clumps and just incorporated.
- Turn out dough onto work surface; divide to 4 portions. With heel of hand, smear each

- portion once to distribute fat in a forward motion. Using scraper, gather dough together; shape to ball. Flatten to rectangle.
- In tart pan, put dough; pat out to an even layer up sides and on bottom so it extends 1/4-in. above rim with well-floured fingers. Chill for 30 minutes.
- Use a fork to prick tart shell lightly all over; line with foil. Fill using pie weights. Bake shell for 15 minutes till golden around edge. Remove weights and foil carefully; bake for 15 minutes till shell gets golden all over. Fully cool shell in pan on rack and leave oven on.
- Filling: Use an electric mixer on medium high speed to beat almond extract, sugar, butter and almond paste for 3 minutes till creamy in a bowl. Lower speed to low; one by one, add eggs, beating well after each. Mix in salt and flour.
- Halve nectarines; discard pits. Cut to 1/4-in. wide wedges.
- Evenly spread frangipane filling in tart shells. Skin sides down, decoratively stand nectarine in filling, without pushing too fat into the filling.
- Bake tart for 1 1/4 hours till nectarine's edges are golden brown and frangipane is golden and puffed.
- Glaze: Heat water and preserves in 1-qt. saucepan on medium high heat till preserves melt, mixing. Take off heat; force through fine-mesh sieve into small bowl. Discard solids. If using, mix in amaretto.
- Generously brush glaze on top of hot tart; cool for 15 minutes in pan on rack. Remove pan's sides; fully cool tart for 2 hours.
- Pears can be roasted, without almond crunch, 1 day ahead. Fully cool then covered, chilled; pears may slightly discolor. Reheat for 10 minutes, basting once using pan juices, in preheated 350°F oven.
- You can make almond crunch 4 days ahead, kept in room temperature in an airtight container.

Nutrition Information

- Calories: 486
- Total Carbohydrate: 56 g
- Cholesterol: 131 mg
- Total Fat: 27 g
- Fiber: 3 g
- Protein: 8 g
- Sodium: 334 mg
- Saturated Fat: 11 g

222. Nectarine And Almond Crisp

"Best served with créme fraîche that's lightly sweetened, or whipped cream with ice cream on top."
Serving: Makes 8 servings

Ingredients

- 3/4 cup plus 1 tbsp. all purpose flour
- 1/2 cup (packed) golden brown sugar, divided
- 1 1/4 tsps. ground cardamom, divided
- 1 tsp. ground ginger, divided
- 1/4 tsp. salt
- 2 oz. almond paste (about 1/3 cup), crumbled
- 6 tbsps. (3/4 stick) chilled unsalted butter, cut into 1/2-inch cubes
- 1 1/2 cups sliced almonds
- 2 1/2 to 2 3/4 lbs. nectarines (about 8 cups), each cut into 8 wedges
- 1/2 cup apricot preserves

Direction

- Set the oven for preheating to 400°F. Prepare and grease an 11 x 7 x 2 inches glass baking dish with butter. Combine a quarter cup of brown sugar, 3/4 cup flour, salt, half a tsp. of ginger and 3/4 tsp. cardamom in a processor. Drop in almond paste and process again until fine crumbs have formed. Drop the butter and pulse until mixture begins to clump together. Pour the mixture to a bowl and mix in almonds.
- Combine apricot preserves, a quarter cup sugar, nectarine wedges, the rest of a tbsp. of

flour, half a tsp. of ginger and 1/2 tsp. of cardamom in big bowl; toss to coat. Pour to the prepared baking dish and sprinkle topping on top. Put in the preheated oven and bake for about 40 minutes until the nectarines have softened, topping turns golden, and the juices are bubbling all over the edges. Let it cool for at least 20 minutes before serving.

223. Nectarine And Plum Tartlets

"You can make these tartlets a day in advance, placing them in one layer onto a plastic shallow container."
Serving: Makes 6 servings

Ingredients

- 2 cups all purpose flour
- 1/4 cup sugar
- Pinch of salt
- 3/4 cup (1 1/2 sticks) chilled unsalted butter, cut into 1/2-inch pieces
- 1/4 cup ice water
- 4 firm but ripe nectarines, halved, pitted, cut into 1/3-inch-thick wedges
- 4 firm but ripe plums, halved, pitted, cut into 1/3-inch-thick wedges
- 3 1/2 tbsps. sugar
- 6 blackberries
- 1/2 cup plum jelly

Direction

- To make pastry: in a processor, combine salt, sugar, and flour, then add the butter. Use on/off turns to cut in the mixture until it looks like a coarse meal. Add 1/4 cup of ice water, process with on/off turns until it forms moist clumps. Gather the dough and divide into 6 equal portions, then flatten into disks. Wrap each in plastic and chill until it becomes firm, a minimum of 1 hour to overnight.
- Place the rack in the middle of the oven and set the heat to 400 degrees Fahrenheit. Roll out each of the dough disks into 5 1/2 inch rounds on a floured surface. Move them to 4 1/2-inch tartlet pans that have removable bottoms. Press the dough up the pan sides and onto the bottoms, then place them onto a baking sheet.
- For the filling: Toss the sugar, plums, and nectarines in a big bowl, then place them in the crusts. Bake the tartlets for 10 minutes. Turn the heat down to 350 degrees Fahrenheit and continue to bake until the fruit is soft and starts to bubble and the crusts become golden, 40 minutes. Move the tartlets to a rack and completely cool, then place a berry in the middle of each.
- In a small heavy saucepan, stir the jelly over low heat to melt, then brush it over the tartlets. You can make this a day ahead, let them sit at room temperature.

Nutrition Information

- Calories: 553
- Total Carbohydrate: 81 g
- Cholesterol: 61 mg
- Total Fat: 24 g
- Fiber: 4 g
- Protein: 6 g
- Sodium: 61 mg
- Saturated Fat: 15 g

224. Nectarine Daiquiri

"A combination of plum wine and peel of nectarine for a sweet-tangy flavor."
Serving: Makes 6 servings

Ingredients

- 2 lbs. ripe nectarines (unpeeled), quartered, pitted
- 3/4 cup simple syrup
- 1 1/4 cups white rum
- 1 cup plum wine
- 2/3 cup fresh lime juice
- 3 cups ice cubes
- Fresh plum wedges (optional)

Direction

- In a processor, mix the simple syrup and nectarines; process until smooth. Strain the mixture over a big pitcher, extracting all liquid as possible by pressing the solids in the strainer. Throw away the solids. Pour into the pitcher the plum wine, lime juice, and rum. Mix until well blended. (Can be done 6 hours ahead and keep in refrigerator).
- Put 3 cups of ice cubes into the pitcher. Pour the daiquiri to cocktail glasses. If desired, you can garnish each rims glass using a plum wedge. Serve.

Nutrition Information

- Calories: 225
- Total Carbohydrate: 22 g
- Total Fat: 1 g
- Fiber: 3 g
- Protein: 2 g
- Sodium: 11 mg
- Saturated Fat: 0 g

225. North Carolina Coleslaw

"This coleslaw is tangy and made with no mayonnaise."
Serving: Makes 8 servings

Ingredients

- 3/4 cup coarsely grated onion (grated on large holes of box grater)
- 3/4 cup vegetable oil
- 1/4 cup ketchup
- 3 tbsps. apple cider vinegar
- 1 tbsp. sugar
- 1 1/2 tsps. celery seeds
- 1 medium head of green cabbage, cored, thinly sliced (about 10 cups)
- 2 cups coarsely grated peeled carrots (about 3 large)

Direction

- Whisk together the first 6 of the ingredients in a big bowl. Add in the carrots and cabbage, then toss and season with pepper and salt. Chill while covered for a minimum of 2 hours. You can make this 6 hours beforehand, keep it chilled, occasionally tossing. Serve the coleslaw chilled.

Nutrition Information

- Calories: 247
- Total Carbohydrate: 14 g
- Total Fat: 21 g
- Fiber: 4 g
- Protein: 2 g
- Sodium: 109 mg
- Saturated Fat: 1 g

226. Not Your Grandma's Chopped Chicken Liver

"At last, a recipe that can be shared after testing it for year. Those who isn't fond of livers would sure love this once tastes and paired with bagels, toast or homemade crackers. It will surely surprise everyone because of the minimized vermouth/bourbon deglazing step. Put cucumber slices or fresh herbs sprigs to garnish."
Serving: 16 | Prep: 15m | Ready in: 45m

Ingredients

- 3 tbsps. butter
- 1 large onion, halved and sliced
- 1 tbsp. white sugar
- 1 lb. chicken livers - rinsed, trimmed, and patted dry
- 2 fluid oz. bourbon
- 3 hard-boiled eggs, peeled
- 1 tsp. ground thyme
- 1/2 tsp. salt
- 1/2 tsp. freshly ground pepper

Direction

- Place a skillet pan on the stove and turn on to medium-high heat then put the butter in to melt. Add in the onions to fry for about 5 minutes until color becomes transparent. Stir in the sugar and fry for 5 minutes until onions turns into slightly brown and soft. Then put the onions in a food processor with the butter left in the pan as you can.
- Then sauté the livers in hot butter for about 4 minutes until slightly brown on 1 side. Rotate the livers and continue to cook for 3 to 4 minutes, until the middle of livers turns to light pink. Then put the livers to food processor with the onions.
- Use the same skillet and put the bourbon and make it boil while removing the color brown bits from bottom of pan using a wooden spoon. Continue to boil for about 6 minutes until texture becomes thick and decreased to half. Add the liquid to the processor.
- Mix together the pepper, salt, thyme and eggs in the food processor with the liver mixture. Blend well until texture becomes smooth.

Nutrition Information

- Calories: 80 calories;
- Total Carbohydrate: 2 g
- Cholesterol: 148 mg
- Total Fat: 4.4 g
- Protein: 5.8 g
- Sodium: 114 mg

227. Nut Butter

"You may use any kinds of nuts. Remove generous scoop of chopped nuts for chunky nut better from food processor before turning into powder; fold chopped nuts into nut butter prior to storing."
Serving: Makes approximately 1 cup / 250 ml

Ingredients

- 2 cups (about 280g) shelled raw nuts

Direction

- Preheat an oven to 180°C/300°F.
- In 1 layer, spread out nuts on baking sheet; toast for 20-30 minutes till slightly darker in color and aromatic. Bite one in half then check color in middle to check if they're ready; it should be golden in place of cream or white colored. Remove from oven. Rub together to remove bitter skins if using hazelnuts; fully cool.
- Put nuts in food processor; blend on high setting for 1-2 minutes till finely ground to powder. Stop to scrape container's sides down. Process for 1-2 minutes till oils begin to be released and runny, creamy and smooth paste forms. Time varies on machine and you do not need to put in any oil.
- Put nut butter into airtight glass container; keeps in fridge for 1 month.

Nutrition Information

- Calories: 208
- Total Carbohydrate: 9 g
- Total Fat: 18 g
- Fiber: 3 g
- Protein: 6 g
- Sodium: 4 mg
- Saturated Fat: 2 g

228. Onion Pie

"A fantastic recipe."
Serving: Makes 6 (light main course) servings | Prep: 25m

Ingredients

- 1 1/2 tbsps. unsalted butter
- 1 tbsp. olive oil
- 1 large onion (1 lb.), cut lengthwise into 12 wedges
- 1 tsp. fresh thyme leaves
- 1/2 tsp. salt
- 1/4 tsp. black pepper
- 3 oz. coarsely grated Gruyère (3/4 cup)

- 2 cups all-purpose flour
- 2 tsps. baking powder
- 1 tsp. baking soda
- 3/4 tsp. salt
- 2 oz. coarsely grated Gruyère (1/2 cup)
- 3/4 stick (6 tbsps.) cold unsalted butter, cut into pieces
- 3/4 cup well-shaken buttermilk
- 3/4 tsp. dry mustard

Direction

- Preheat an oven to 400°F.
- Onion topping: Heat oil and butter in a 12-in. heavy skillet till foam subsides on moderate heat; cook onion for approximately 25 minutes till golden brown, occasionally mixing. Take off the heat; mix in pepper, salt and thyme. Cool. Toss onion and cheese; spread on bottom of a deep-dish 9 1/2-in. glass pie plate.
- Crust: Blend salt, baking soda and powder and flour in a food processor then add cheese; pulse to combine for 3 or 4 times. Add butter; pulse till it looks like coarse meal.
- Whisk dry mustard and buttermilk in a small bowl; put into processor. Pulse till dough starts to clump and liquid is incorporated; don't let it make a ball.
- Turn out dough onto a lightly floured surface; fold over a few times on itself to knead lightly. Shape dough into a ball; stand for 10 minutes at room temperature, covered in plastic wrap.
- Roll out dough into a 10-in. round between 2 plastic wrap sheets. Remove top plastic wrap sheet; flip over dough onto onion. Peel off the leftover plastic; tuck dough inside the pie plate's rim.
- Bake pie in center of oven for 25-30 minutes till firm to touch and crust is golden brown; cool pie for 2 minutes on a rack. Invert a platter over pie; flip the pie onto platter then serve warm.

Nutrition Information

- Calories: 454
- Total Carbohydrate: 40 g
- Cholesterol: 70 mg
- Total Fat: 26 g
- Fiber: 2 g
- Protein: 15 g
- Sodium: 591 mg
- Saturated Fat: 15 g

229. Onion, Cheese, And Bacon Tart

Serving: Makes 6 servings

Ingredients

- 1 cup unbleached all purpose flour
- 1/4 tsp. salt
- 1/4 cup (1/2 stick) chilled unsalted butter, cut into 1/2-inch cubes
- 2 tbsps. chilled solid vegetable shortening, cut into 1/2-inch cubes
- 2 tbsps. (or more) ice water
- 3 thick-cut bacon slices, chopped
- 1 large onion, thinly sliced
- Pinch of sugar
- 1 cup whipping cream
- 1 large egg
- 1 large egg yolk
- 1/4 tsp. ground black pepper
- Generous pinch of salt
- Generous pinch of ground nutmeg
- 1/2 cup (packed) coarsely grated Gruyère cheese

Direction

- Crust: In processor, blend salt and flour. Add shortening and butter; cut in till it looks like coarse meal with on/off turns. Add 2 tbsp. of ice water; process till moist clumps form. If dough is dry, add extra ice water by teaspoonfuls. Gather dough to ball; flatten to disk. In plastic, wrap; chill for a minimum of 1 hour.
- Preheat an oven to 400°F. Roll dough out to 11-in. round on lightly floured surface. Put in 9-in. tart pan that has a removable bottom.

Press dough up sides and on bottom of pan; use fork to pierce crust all over. Freeze for 10 minutes. Line foil on crust; fill with pie weights/dried beans. Bake crust for 10 minutes. Remove beans and foil; bake for 15 minutes till partially cooked through and crust is set. While making filling, cool crust. Maintain the oven temperature.

- Filling: Sauté bacon till crisp for 4 minutes in medium skillet on medium heat. Put bacon on paper towels and drain. Put pinch sugar and onion in drippings in skillet; sauté for 20 minutes till onion gets deep golden brown. Whisk nutmeg, salt, pepper, egg yolk, egg and cream to blend in small bowl. Spread onion on baked crust's bottom; sprinkle bacon then cheese. Put cream mixture on top.
- Bake for 25 minutes till filling is set and tart is puffed; cool tart for 10 minutes on rack. Remove pan sides then serve at room temperature/warm.

Nutrition Information

- Calories: 433
- Total Carbohydrate: 20 g
- Cholesterol: 148 mg
- Total Fat: 35 g
- Fiber: 1 g
- Protein: 10 g
- Sodium: 327 mg
- Saturated Fat: 18 g

230. Paleo Chocolate Frosting

"This is a nice way to add a healthy frosting and fat to a dessert. Refrigerate to have a thicker frosting."
Serving: 10 | Prep: 10m | Ready in: 10m

Ingredients

- 2 avocados, peeled and pitted
- 1/2 cup cocoa powder
- 1/2 cup honey
- 2 tbsps. coconut oil
- 1 tsp. vanilla extract
- 1/2 tsp. salt

Direction

- In a food processor, blend together vanilla extract, avocados, salt, cocoa powder, coconut oil, and honey until the resulting mixture is smooth.

Nutrition Information

- Calories: 151 calories;
- Total Carbohydrate: 19.8 g
- Cholesterol: 0 mg
- Total Fat: 9.3 g
- Protein: 1.7 g
- Sodium: 121 mg

231. Parsley Pesto And Feta Phyllo Pizza

Serving: Serves 4 to 6 as an entrée or 8 to 10 as an hors d'oeuvre

Ingredients

- 3 cups packed fresh parsley leaves, preferably flat-leafed (about 3 bunches), rinsed and spun dry
- 2 large garlic cloves, chopped
- 1/3 cup freshly grated Parmesan cheese
- 1/3 cup pine nuts, toasted until golden and cooled
- 1/3 cup olive oil
- 3/4 stick (6 tbsps.) unsalted butter, melted and kept warm
- 10 sheets phyllo, stacked between 2 sheets of wax paper and covered with a kitchen towel
- 9 tbsps. freshly grated Parmesan cheese (about 2 oz.)
- 3/4 cup crumbled feta cheese (about 1/4 lb.)

Direction

- Preheat an oven to 400°F.

- Pesto: blend all pesto ingredients well in a food processor; you can make pesto 3 days ahead, chilled, surface covered in plastic wrap.
- Brush some butter on big baking sheet lightly; on butter, put 1 phyllo sheet. Brush some leftover butter on phyllo lightly; sprinkle 1 tbsp. parmesan. Push another phyllo sheet on cheese; firmly press to adhere to the bottom layer. Butter, sprinkle cheese, then layer leftover phyllo the same way, finishing with phyllo sheet. Brush leftover butter on top sheet lightly; fold all sides 1/4-in. in, pressing to top sheet. Fold 1/4-in. border up, crimping corners.
- On phyllo crust, spread pesto; spread with feta.
- In the middle of oven, bake pizza for 15 minutes till crust is golden.

Nutrition Information

- Calories: 708
- Total Carbohydrate: 31 g
- Cholesterol: 92 mg
- Total Fat: 58 g
- Fiber: 3 g
- Protein: 19 g
- Sodium: 830 mg
- Saturated Fat: 23 g

232. Pastry Dough

"You just need 4 ingredients and 15 minutes you make the ultimate pastry dough."
Serving: Makes 1 (9-to 9 1/2 inch) pie or tart shell | Prep: 15m

Ingredients

- 1 1/4 cups all-purpose flour
- 1 stick cold unsalted butter, cut into 1/2-inch pieces
- 1/4 tsp. salt
- 3 to 5 tbsps. ice water

Direction

- Use a pastry blender or your fingertips to blend together salt, butter and flour in bowl (or process in a food processor) just until the mixture is similar to a coarse meal and has a few roughly pea-sized butter lumps.
- Evenly sprinkle 3 tbsps. of ice water onto the mixture and gently mix with fork (or you can process in a processor) until blended.
- Squeeze a small handful: In case it does not pull together, pour in extra ice water, half a tbsp. at a time, while stirring (or pulsing) until well incorporated; test once again. Avoid overworking the dough since the pastry may become tough.
- Transfer the dough on a surface that is lightly floured and split into four portions. Spread each portion once or twice in forward motion using the heel of your hand to distribute the fat. Gather the dough together (you can use pastry scraper) and shape into a 5-inch disk. Refrigerate while wrapped in plastic wrap for at least 1 hour until firm.
- Note: You can chill the dough up to 3 days.

Nutrition Information

- Calories: 230
- Total Carbohydrate: 20 g
- Cholesterol: 40 mg
- Total Fat: 16 g
- Fiber: 1 g
- Protein: 3 g
- Sodium: 100 mg
- Saturated Fat: 10 g

233. Peach Bellini

""A fruity cocktail that everyone will surely enjoy under the summer heat!""
Serving: 1 | Prep: 5m | Ready in: 5m

Ingredients

- 1/4 cup pureed peaches

- 4 fluid oz. champagne
- 1 peach slice

Direction

- In a champagne flute, pour peach puree then add champagne. Garnish drink with a slice of peach.

Nutrition Information

- Calories: 131 calories;
- Total Carbohydrate: 11.1 g
- Cholesterol: 0 mg
- Total Fat: 0 g
- Protein: 0.1 g
- Sodium: 11 mg

234. Peach Curd

"A variation on lemon curd."
Serving: 48 | Prep: 20m | Ready in: 40m

Ingredients

- 3 fresh peaches, halved and pitted
- 4 cups white sugar
- 2 eggs
- 4 egg yolks
- 1 tbsp. lemon juice
- 1 tsp. rose water (optional)
- 3/4 cup butter

Direction

- Use a blender to process peach halves till smooth; remove to a big bowl.
- Whip rose water, lemon juice, egg yolks, eggs and sugar in peach puree to incorporate.
- In top of double boiler above simmering water, liquify the butter; mix in peach mixture, mixing continuously for 5 to 10 minutes, till curd thickens.
- Sterilize lids and jars for no less than 5 minutes in boiling water. Transfer peach curd into sterilized, hot jars, fill jars leaving quarter inch headspace. Run a thin spatula or a knife around inner of jars once filled to get rid of any air bubbles. Wipe clean the rims of jars using damp paper towel to get rid of any food residue. Put on lids, then screw on rings.
- Position one rack in big stockpot's bottom and pour in water, filling midway. Boil then put jars down in boiling water with holder. Space jars 2-inches apart. Add in extra boiling water if need be to come water level to no less than an-inch over the jars top. Let water come to rolling boil, put on pot cover, and process, about 10 minutes.
- Take jars out of stockpot, transfer to a wood or cloth-covered surface, spacing a few-inch apart, to cool down. Use finger to push top of every lid when cool, making sure that seal is secure (lid must not move down or up at all). Keep in dark and cool place.

Nutrition Information

- Calories: 99 calories;
- Total Carbohydrate: 17.1 g
- Cholesterol: 32 mg
- Total Fat: 3.5 g
- Protein: 0.5 g
- Sodium: 24 mg

235. Peanut Butter Tart With Caramel-peanut Glaze

"A divine recipe!"
Serving: Makes 12 servings

Ingredients

- 1 1/4 cups all purpose flour
- 3 tbsps. sugar
- 1/2 tsp. ground cinnamon
- 7 tbsps. chilled unsalted butter, cut into pieces
- 1 large egg yolk
- 2 tsps. whipping cream
- 3/4 tsp. vanilla extract
- 1/3 cup plus 2 tbsps. (packed) golden brown sugar
- 3 tbsps. plus 1/4 cup chilled whipping cream

- 2 tbsps. (1/4 stick) unsalted butter
- 3 oz. cream cheese, room temperature
- 1/4 cup creamy peanut butter, room temperature
- 1 tsp. vanilla extract
- 1/2 cup (packed) golden brown sugar
- 6 tbsps. (3/4 stick) unsalted butter
- 1/4 cup water
- 4 tbsps. whipping cream
- 2 tbsps. light corn syrup
- 3/4 cup chopped lightly salted roasted peanuts

Direction

- Crust: Blend initial 3 ingredients to mix in processor. Add butter; cut in till coarse meal form with on/off turns. Add vanilla extract, cream and egg yolk; process till moist clumps form. Bring dough to ball; flatten to disk. In plastic, wrap; chill for minimum of 1 hour – maximum of 1 day.
- Preheat an oven to 350°F. Roll dough out to 11-in. round on lightly floured surface. Put dough in 9-in. fluted tart pan that has removable bottom. To make double-thick sides, fold in overhang. Use fork to pierce dough all over; freeze for 15 minutes.
- Bake crust for 25 minutes till golden brown. Put on rack; fully cool. You can make it 1 day ahead; kept in room temperature, airtight.
- Filling: Mix butter, 3 tbsp. cream and 1/3 cup brown sugar till sugar is dissolved in medium saucepan on medium heat; fully cool.
- Beat vanilla, peanut butter and cream cheese using electric mixer till smooth in medium bowl; mix in the brown sugar mixture.
- Beat 1/4 cup cream and leftover 2 tbsp. brown sugar using electric mixer till peaks form in another medium bowl; fold into the peanut butter mixture. Put in curst; use spatula to smooth top. Chill for 3 hours till set.
- Caramel-peanut glaze: Mix corn syrup, 2 tbsp. cream, 1/4 cup water, butter and brown sugar till sugar is dissolved in medium heavy saucepan on medium heat. Put heat on high; boil without mixing for 7 minutes till candy thermometer reads 238°F. Take off heat. Mix in peanuts and leftover 2 tbsp. cream; cool for 15 minutes to lukewarm.
- Put glaze on filling; smooth using spatula. Chill tart for 30 minutes till set. You can make it 1 day ahead, kept chilled. Cut to wedges; serve.

Nutrition Information

- Calories: 413
- Total Carbohydrate: 35 g
- Cholesterol: 77 mg
- Total Fat: 29 g
- Fiber: 1 g
- Protein: 6 g
- Sodium: 43 mg
- Saturated Fat: 15 g

236. Pear And Maple Crumble

Serving: Serves 6 to 8

Ingredients

- 1 cup all purpose flour
- 1 cup walnuts
- 2/3 cup (packed) golden brown sugar
- 1/2 cup chilled unsalted butter, cut into small pieces
- 3 1/2 lbs. firm but ripe Anjou pears, peeled, cored, cut into 1/2-inch pieces
- 2/3 cup pure maple syrup
- 1/2 cup raisins
- 2 tbsps. all purpose flour
- 2 tbsps. fresh lemon juice
- 1 tbsp. finely chopped crystallized ginger
- Sour cream

Direction

- For topping: in processor, mix every ingredient. Blend till walnuts are roughly chopped and small moist lumps are created. In medium bowl, put the topping. Place cover on top and chill for an hour till firm.

- For pears: place the rack in middle of oven and preheat the oven to 350°F. In big bowl, toss every ingredient excluding sour cream to incorporate. Allow to sit for 15 minutes. Move the pear mixture to baking dish of 13x9x2-inch in size. Scatter topping on top of pears. Bake for half an hour till pears are soft, topping is golden and crisp, and juices bubble thickly. Allow to sit for a minimum of 10 minutes. Serve while warm together with sour cream.

Nutrition Information

- Calories: 655
- Total Carbohydrate: 120 g
- Cholesterol: 41 mg
- Total Fat: 19 g
- Fiber: 10 g
- Protein: 5 g
- Sodium: 20 mg
- Saturated Fat: 10 g

237. Pear And Raisin Mince Pie With Lattice Crust

"A quick recipe."
Serving: Makes 8 servings

Ingredients

- 2 1/2 cups all purpose flour
- 1 tsp. salt
- 1 tsp. sugar
- 1 cup (2 sticks) chilled unsalted butter, cut into 1-inch cubes
- 8 tbsps. (about) ice water
- 6 tbsps. orange marmalade
- 1/4 cup (packed) raisins
- 2 tbsps. sugar
- 2 tbsps. brandy
- 1/2 tsp. vanilla extract
- 1/2 tsp. ground cinnamon
- 1/8 tsp. ground cloves
- 2 1/4 lbs. firm Anjou or Bosc pears, peeled, cored, cut into 3/4-inch cubes
- 1 tbsp. cornstarch
- 1 egg yolk beaten with 2 tsps. milk (for glaze)

Direction

- Crust: blend sugar, salt and flour in processor. Add butter; process with on/off turns till butter is cut to 1/4-in. pieces then add 6 tbsp. ice water. Blend with on/off turns till dough comes together. If dough is dry, add extra water by tablespoonfuls. Gather dough to ball; divide to 2 pieces. Flatten them to disks; in plastic, wrap. Chill for minimum of 30 minutes – maximum of 1 day.
- Filling: In bowl, mix initial 7 ingredients; mix in cornstarch and pears. Put rack in middle of oven; preheat it to 400°F. Roll 1 dough disk out to 13-14-in. round on lightly floured surface. Put in 9-in. diameter glass pie dish; add filling. Roll 2nd dough disk out to 12-in. round; cut dough to 3/4-in. wide strips using ruler as aid. Lay strips on filling, 3/4-in. apart. At right angle, lay extra strips on first strips, making lattice. To 3/4-in., trim overhang. Fold strip and dough ends under; to seal, crimp. Brush yolk mixture on dough strips, not edge.
- Bake pie for 50 minutes till pears are tender and crust is golden; cool.

Nutrition Information

- Calories: 515
- Total Carbohydrate: 69 g
- Cholesterol: 79 mg
- Total Fat: 24 g
- Fiber: 5 g
- Protein: 5 g
- Sodium: 307 mg
- Saturated Fat: 15 g

238. Pear-mango Salsa

"This salsa is very refreshing and light that is outstanding when served together tortilla chips and Mexican dish. Even better, you can adjust this recipe to make your own taste."
Serving: 6 | Prep: 30m | Ready in: 30m

Ingredients

- 6 roma (plum) tomatoes, halved
- 1 large mango, peeled and pitted
- 1 onion, quartered
- 1/2 Asian pear, cored and cubed
- 1 banana pepper, seeded
- 2 jalapeno pepper, seeded
- 1/3 cup fresh cilantro leaves, or more to taste
- 1 lime, juiced
- 1/2 tsp. garlic powder
- 1/2 tsp. salt

Direction

- In a food processor, add salt, garlic powder, lime juice, cilantro, jalapeno pepper, banana pepper, Asian pear, onion, mango and tomatoes then pulse until gets wanted texture. Cover and chill until serving.

Nutrition Information

- Calories: 68 calories;
- Total Carbohydrate: 16.8 g
- Cholesterol: 0 mg
- Total Fat: 0.4 g
- Protein: 1.4 g
- Sodium: 201 mg

239. Pecan Fig Bourbon Cake

"A crowd pleaser."
Serving: Makes 12 to 16 servings | Prep: 40m

Ingredients

- 1 lb. dried Black Mission figs, hard tips discarded
- 2 cups water
- 1/2 cup bourbon
- 1 tsp. pure vanilla extract
- 3 cups sifted cake flour (not self-rising; sift before measuring)
- 2 tsps. baking powder
- 3/4 tsp. baking soda
- 3/4 tsp. salt
- 1/2 tsp. cinnamon
- 1/2 tsp. grated nutmeg
- 1 3/4 cups pecans (7 oz.)
- 2 cups packed light brown sugar
- 1 cup vegetable oil
- 3 large eggs, at room temperature 30 minutes
- 1 cup confectioners sugar
- 4 1/2 tbsps. heavy cream
- 2 tsps. bourbon
- 1/4 tsp. pure vanilla extract
- Equipment: a 12-cup bundt pan

Direction

- Cake: Simmer figs in the water for 35-40 minutes in medium heavy saucepan, with a cover, till most liquid is absorbed and figs are tender; puree with vanilla and bourbon in a food processor. Cool to warm.
- Preheat an oven with rack in center for 350°F. Butter then flour Bundt pan; knock extra flour out.
- Sift nutmeg, cinnamon, salt, baking soda, baking powder and flour as oven preheats.
- Toast pecans lightly for 8-10 minutes in shallow baking pan in the oven. Cool; chop coarsely. Leave oven on.
- Using electric mixer, beat eggs, oil and brown sugar for 3 minutes till creamy and thick in a big bowl. Mix in fig mixture; mix in flour mixture on low speed till incorporated. Fold in pecans.
- Put batter in Bundt pan; bake for 1-1 1/4 hours till inserted wooden pick in middle exits clean. Fully cool cake in pan on the rack; invert onto plate.
- Icing: Into bowl, sift confectioners' sugar; whisk in leftover icing ingredients till smooth. Drizzle on cake.

Nutrition Information

- Calories: 578
- Total Carbohydrate: 71 g
- Cholesterol: 46 mg
- Total Fat: 29 g
- Fiber: 3 g
- Protein: 5 g
- Sodium: 272 mg
- Saturated Fat: 3 g

240. Pecan, Caramel And Fudge Pie

"A super simple dessert."
Serving: Serves 8 to 10

Ingredients

- 1 1/2 cups chocolate wafer cookie crumbs (about 7 oz.)
- 5 tbsps. butter, melted
- 1/2 tsp. vanilla extract
- 3/4 cup unsalted butter
- 3/4 cup (packed) golden brown sugar
- 6 tbsps. light corn syrup
- 3 cups pecan halves (about 10 oz.)
- 3 tbsps. whipping cream
- 2 oz. unsweetened chocolate, chopped

Direction

- Crust: In a processor, blend all ingredients; press crumb mixture up the sides and on bottom of 9-in. diameter glass pie dish and cover crust; while prepping filling, freeze. You can make it 1 week ahead, kept frozen.
- Filling: Preheat an oven to 350°F. Boil corn syrup, brown sugar and butter in medium heavy saucepan for 1 minute, mixing often; mix in cream and nuts. Boil for 3 minutes till it slightly thickens; take off from the heat. Add chocolate; mix till it is blended well and chocolate melts.
- Put hot filling into the crust; evenly distribute nuts using a spoon. Bake for 10 minutes till filling bubbles all over. Put pie on rack; cool.

Nutrition Information

- Calories: 756
- Total Carbohydrate: 58 g
- Cholesterol: 72 mg
- Total Fat: 59 g
- Fiber: 5 g
- Protein: 6 g
- Sodium: 167 mg
- Saturated Fat: 22 g

241. Penne With Butternut-sage Sauce

"An amazing Italian recipe."
Serving: Makes 4 to 6 servings | Prep: 10m

Ingredients

- 1 lb peeled butternut squash pieces
- 1 small onion, quartered
- 1/2 stick (1/4 cup) unsalted butter
- 1 tbsp. finely chopped fresh sage
- 1 1/2 cups water
- 3/4 tsp. salt
- 1/2 tsp. black pepper
- 2 oz finely grated Parmigiano-Reggiano (1 cup) plus additional for serving
- 1 lb penne rigate

Direction

- Process onion and squash for 1 minute till finely chopped in a food processor.
- Heat butter till foam subsides in 5-6-qt. heavy pot on medium high heat. Add sage; cook for 15 seconds till fragrant. Add pepper, salt, water and chopped squash mixture; simmer for 8-10 minutes till squash is very tender and water is evaporated, occasionally mixing, uncovered. Mix in Parmigiano-Reggiano; take off heat.

- Cook penne till al dente in 6-8-qt. pot with boiling salted water as squash mixture simmers. Keep 1 cup of pasta cooking water; in colander, drain pasta. Put 1/2 cup cooking water in squash mixture. Add drained pasta; toss to mix.
- As desired, use extra cooking water to thin sauce; serve pasta with extra cheese alongside.

242. Penne With Pea Pesto

"A versatile recipe."
Serving: Makes 4 to 6 servings | Prep: 10m

Ingredients

- 1 (10-oz.) package frozen peas
- 2 large garlic cloves
- 1/2 cup pine nuts (2 oz.)
- 1/2 cup grated Parmigiano-Reggiano plus additional for serving
- 1/3 cup olive oil
- 1 lb. penne

Direction

- Follow package directions to cook peas in a microwave/on stove; drain well.
- Drop in garlic as food processor runs; chop finely. Turn off the motor. Add 1/2 tsp. pepper, 1/2 tsp. salt, cheese, nuts and peas; process till chopped finely. Add oil as motor runs; blend till incorporated.
- Meanwhile, cook pasta till al dente in a big pasta pot with boiling salted water; 6-qt. water to 3 tbsp. salt. Keep 1 cup of pasta-cooking water; in a colander, drain pasta.
- Toss pea pesto and pasta; as desired, thin using reserved cooking water. Season using freshly ground pepper.

Nutrition Information

- Calories: 734
- Total Carbohydrate: 97 g
- Total Fat: 30 g
- Fiber: 7 g
- Protein: 21 g
- Sodium: 84 mg
- Saturated Fat: 4 g

243. Perfect Coconut Macaroons

"An amazing recipe!"
Serving: 18 | Prep: 20m | Ready in: 1h20m

Ingredients

- 1 (14 oz.) package sweetened, flaked coconut
- 1/3 cup white sugar
- 1 tbsp. all-purpose flour
- 1/2 tsp. vanilla extract
- 1/2 tsp. almond extract
- 1 pinch salt
- 3 egg whites, room temperature
- 8 oz. semisweet chocolate chips

Direction

- Preheat an oven to 175°C/350°F.
- Line parchment paper on baking sheet.
- Blend salt, almond extract, vanilla extract, flour, sugar and coconut for 30 seconds till combined in a food processor.
- Beat egg whites till soft peaks form in a bowl.
- Fold coconut mixture into the egg whites just till combined.
- Wet your hands. Between palms, roll spoonfuls coconut mixture to golf ball-sized cookies; put on prepped baking sheet.
- In the preheated oven, bake cookies for 15 minutes till coconut is toasted and slightly golden. Put on wire rack; cool for 30 minutes.
- Line new parchment paper piece on baking sheet.
- Melt chocolate chips on top of double boiler above just-barely simmering water, scraping down sides to avoid scorching with a rubber spatula, frequently mixing.
- In chocolate, dip 1/2 of every cookie; put on prepped baking sheet. Put in fridge for 15 minutes till chocolate is set.

Nutrition Information

- Calories: 178 calories;
- Total Carbohydrate: 23.2 g
- Cholesterol: 0 mg
- Total Fat: 9.8 g
- Protein: 1.9 g
- Sodium: 73 mg

244. Pimiento Mac And Cheese

"Upgraded mac and cheese made with sweet-tangy Peppadew peppers, bell pepper, cheddar and Parmesan topped with Panko."
Serving: Makes 6 servings | Prep: 45m

Ingredients

- 1 7- to 8-oz. red bell pepper, seeded, cut into 1-inch pieces
- 2 garlic cloves, halved, divided
- 1/2 cup panko (Japanese breadcrumbs)
- 3 tbsps. unsalted butter, room temperature, divided
- 1/2 cup freshly grated Parmesan cheese, divided
- 3/4 cup drained mild Peppadew peppers in brine, 1 tbsp. brine reserved
- 1/4 tsp. ground ancho chiles
- 1 1/4 cups (packed) coarsely grated extra-sharp cheddar cheese
- 1 cup (packed) coarsely grated whole-milk mozzarella
- 8 oz. medium shell pasta or gemelli
- Look for panko at supermarkets and at Asian markets. Ground ancho chiles are available in the spice section of supermarkets and at Latin markets.

Direction

- To prepare: In a small saucepan, boil the 1 1/2 garlic cloves, bell pepper and 1/2 cup water. Put on cover and turn down the heat to medium-low. Let simmer for around 15 minutes, until the pepper becomes soft.
- In a frying pan, toast the panko on medium-high heat for 5-6 minutes, mixing frequently until it turns golden. Move to a bowl and allow it to cool to lukewarm. Rub the crumbs with 1 tbsp butter until coated. Stir in 1/4 cup Parmesan.
- Move the bell pepper mixture into a processor. Add the 1/2 garlic clove, ground chilies, 2 tbsp butter, 1 tbsp brine and Peppadews, then add the 1/4 cup Parmesan and cheddar and blend until the sauce becomes smooth, then sprinkle with pepper and salt to season.
- Set an oven to 400 degrees F to preheat. Butter 6 individual dishes or 8-cup baking dish. In the pot of boiling salted water, cook the pasta until it becomes tender yet still firm to the bite. Let it drain and put it back into the pot. Mix the mozzarella and sauce into the pasta. Sprinkle with pepper and salt to season. Scoop the pasta into the dish and sprinkle with crumb topping.
- Let the pasta bake for around 25 minutes (15 for individual), until the sauce becomes bubbly and the topping becomes crisp. Allow to stand for 10 minutes.

Nutrition Information

- Calories: 413
- Total Carbohydrate: 36 g
- Cholesterol: 60 mg
- Total Fat: 21 g
- Fiber: 2 g
- Protein: 19 g
- Sodium: 411 mg
- Saturated Fat: 12 g

245. Pistachio Brittle Cheesecake

"A great dessert."
Serving: Makes 10 to 12 servings

Ingredients

- 1 (5 1/2-oz.) package shortbread cookies
- 1/2 cup natural unsalted pistachios

- 1/4 cup sugar
- 1/4 cup (1/2 stick) chilled unsalted butter, diced
- 3 (8-oz.) packages cream cheese, room temperature
- 1 1/4 cups sugar
- 1 tsp. ground cardamom
- 4 large eggs, room temperature
- 2 1/4 cups sour cream
- 1/2 cup pear nectar
- 2 tbsps. all purpose flour
- 2 tsps. vanilla extract
- 5 oz. good-quality white chocolate (such as Lindt or Baker's), finely chopped
- Pistachio Brittle

Direction

- Crust: Preheat an oven to 350°F. Blend sugar, nuts and shortbread till nuts are finely ground in processor then add butter; process till moist clumps form. On bottom of 9-in. diameter springform pan that has 2 3/4-in. high sides, press. Use foil to wrap outside of pan; bake crust for 15 minutes till golden. Cool crust.
- Filling and topping: Beat cardamom, sugar and cream cheese till smooth in big bowl; one by one, beat in eggs. Add vanilla, flour, pear nectar and 1 cup sour cream; beat till blended. Put filling on crust.
- Bake cheesecake for 1 hour 5 minutes till softly set in middle and puffed at edges. Put cheesecake on rack; cool for 10 minutes.
- Meanwhile, mix white chocolate on top of double boiler above barely simmering water till smooth; don't let bowl's bottom touch water. Cool the chocolate to lukewarm then whisk in leftover 1 1/4 cups of sour cream.
- Spread topping on warm filling; refrigerate the cake overnight, uncovered. Cut around pans sides and release pan sides. Put cake on platter. On edge, stand brittle pieces in topping on cheesecake.

Nutrition Information

- Calories: 725
- Total Carbohydrate: 58 g
- Cholesterol: 191 mg
- Total Fat: 51 g
- Fiber: 1 g
- Protein: 11 g
- Sodium: 370 mg
- Saturated Fat: 27 g

246. Pistachio-crusted Rack Of Lamb

"Elegant and easy."
Serving: Makes 4 servings | Prep: 25m

Ingredients

- 1 cup pomegranate juice
- 1/4 cup dried currants
- 1 garlic clove, peeled
- 3 tbsps. chilled butter, cut into 1/2-inch cubes
- 1/2 tsp. ground cinnamon
- 1/4 tsp. ground cumin
- 1 large rack of lamb (2 1/4 lbs.), well trimmed
- 1/4 cup chopped natural unsalted pistachios
- 1/4 cup panko (Japanese breadcrumbs)*

Direction

- Preheat an oven to 400°F. Boil garlic, currants and pomegranate juice for 10 minutes till reduced to 1/4 cup and liquid is syrupy in medium skillet, mixing often. Put mixture in mini processor. Add cumin, cinnamon and butter; blend till coarse puree foams. Put processor bowl in freeze to slightly firm butter for 10 minutes.
- Line foil on small rimmed baking sheet. Put lamb on sheet, bone side down; sprinkle pepper and salt. Spread over with pomegranate butter; sprinkle panko and pistachios, pressing to adhere.
- Roast the rack of lamb for 30 minutes till inserted instant-read thermometer into side reads 135°F for medium rare. Put on work surface; rest for 10 minutes. Between bones, cut lamb; drizzle juices from foil.

247. Pistou

"You can make this in under 1 hour."
Serving: Makes about 1 cup

Ingredients

- 8 cups packed fresh basil leaves, rinsed and spun dry
- 2 garlic cloves, chopped fine
- 1/2 cup olive oil
- 1/4 cup freshly grated Parmesan

Direction

- Puree garlic and basil in a food processor. Add pepper and salt to taste, parmesan and oil; blend pistou till smooth. Mix pistou into soups/toss with cooked veggies/pasta. You can make pistou 1 week ahead, kept in an airtight container, chilled.

Nutrition Information

- Calories: 280
- Total Carbohydrate: 2 g
- Cholesterol: 5 mg
- Total Fat: 29 g
- Fiber: 1 g
- Protein: 4 g
- Sodium: 100 mg
- Saturated Fat: 5 g

248. Plantain Veggie Burgers

"A pleasant recipe."
Serving: 6 | Prep: 15m | Ready in: 30m

Ingredients

- 2 plantains, peeled and chopped
- 1/2 cup spinach
- 1/4 cup bread crumbs
- 1/4 cup cornmeal
- 1/4 cup shiitake mushrooms
- 1/4 cup black olives
- 1 clove garlic
- 1 1/2 tbsps. paprika
- 1 tbsp. fresh oregano
- 3 tbsps. butter
- salt and ground black pepper to taste

Direction

- Blend oregano, paprika, garlic, olives, mushrooms, cornmeal, breadcrumbs, spinach and plantains till moldable batter forms in a food processor; shape to patties.
- Melt butter on medium heat in a skillet; pan-fry patties for 6-8 minutes per side till golden brown. Season with pepper and salt.

Nutrition Information

- Calories: 179 calories;
- Total Carbohydrate: 28.8 g
- Cholesterol: 15 mg
- Total Fat: 7.2 g
- Protein: 2.4 g
- Sodium: 132 mg

249. Plum Granita With Summer Fruit

"This allspice and cinnamon flavored fruit ice is garnished with nectarine, plums, and peaches. Any seasonal fruit will also work for this yummy cold dessert.""
Serving: Makes 4 servings

Ingredients

- 3/4 cup water
- 1/2 cup sugar
- 2 whole allspice
- 1 cinnamon stick
- 1/2 vanilla bean, split lengthwise
- 1 1/2 lbs. plums, preferably red-fleshed (about 7 large), pitted, cut into 3/4-inch pieces
- 1 peach, pitted, thinly sliced
- 1 nectarine, pitted, thinly sliced
- 1 plum, pitted, thinly sliced

Direction

- In a small heavy saucepan, combine cinnamon, allspice, sugar, and water. Scrape the seeds from the vanilla bean and add into the mixture and bring to a boil, stirring until the sugar is dissolved. Reduce heat and simmer for about 2 minutes until the liquid has reduced to 3/4 cup. Cool syrup completely.
- In a processor, puree 1 1/2 lbs. of plums then, press enough of the puree through a sieve to measure up to 1 1/2 cups. Strain the syrup onto the puree and blend. Transfer to a 9x5x3-inch glass loaf dish. Freeze the plum mixture for about 4 hours, stirring every 30 minutes, until flaky crystals form. (You can make this a week ahead if you keep covered and frozen.)
- Spoon the granita onto 4 glass goblets and top with plum, nectarine, and peach slices. Serve immediately.

250. Plum Streusel Coffeecake

Ingredients

- 1 cup all-purpose flour
- 1/2 cup firmly packed light brown sugar
- 1/2 cup walnuts
- 3/4 stick (6 tbsps.) unsalted butter, cut into pieces and softened
- 1 tsp. cinnamon
- 1/4 tsp. freshly grated nutmeg
- 1 stick (1/2 cup) unsalted butter, softened
- 3/4 cup granulated sugar
- 2 large eggs
- 1 tsp. vanilla
- 1 1/4 cups all-purpose flour
- 1 tsp. baking powder
- 1/2 tsp. salt
- 3/4 lb. plums (4 to 5 medium), sliced
- confectioners' sugar for sifting over cake

Direction

- Preheat an oven to 350°F, and butter and flour a square or round baking pan, 9-inch across at a minimum of 2-inch deep.
- For streusel: pulse together streusel ingredient in food processor till crumbly and mixed thoroughly.
- For cake batter: beat sugar and butter in bowl using electric mixer till fluffy and light and put eggs, one by one, beating thoroughly after every addition, and the vanilla. Sift in salt, baking powder and flour, and beat till barely blended.
- In pan, scatter the cake batter, leveling surface, and set slices of plum on top, lightly overlapping concentric rounds. Scatter streusel on top of slices of plum and let the cake bake in center of the oven for an hour, or till a tester gets out clean. Coffeecake can be done a week in advance: In pan on rack, cool the cake fully, nicely wrap using plastic wrap and foil and put in freezer. Reheat the cake for 35 to 40 minutes without wrap but not defrost, in prepped 350°F oven till heated completely. Let the cake cool slightly on rack and sift confectioners' sugar on top. Serve coffeecake at room temperature or while warm.

Nutrition Information

- Calories: 280
- Total Carbohydrate: 38 g
- Cholesterol: 57 mg
- Total Fat: 13 g
- Fiber: 1 g
- Protein: 3 g
- Sodium: 123 mg
- Saturated Fat: 8 g

251. Pork Chops With Mango Pineapple Sauce

Serving: Makes 4 servings | Prep: 30m

Ingredients

- 4 (3/4-inch-thick) loin pork chops
- 2 tsps. salt
- 1 3/4 tsps. black pepper
- 1 (1-lb) firm-ripe mango, peeled and coarsely chopped
- 2 tbsps. unsalted butter
- 1 cup drained canned pineapple chunks (from a 14-oz can)
- 1 cup mango nectar
- 1/4 cup packed light brown sugar
- 2 tbsps. Dijon mustard
- 4 whole cloves
- 2 tbsps. olive oil
- 1 large onion, coarsely chopped
- 1 garlic clove, finely chopped
- 1/3 cup fresh cilantro leaves

Direction

- Scatter a total of 3/4 tsp. of pepper and a tsp. salt on pork chops' both sides; refrigerate with cover, for no less than 4 hours to let meat adsorb the seasoning.
- Use a food processor to purée chopped mango till smooth, then pass through sieve right in bowl. In a heavy, 1 1/2- to 2-quart saucepan, boil cloves, mustard, brown sugar, mango nectar, pineapple, butter, mango purée, and leftover tsp. pepper and leftover tsp. salt, mix till butter melts; let simmer for 12 to 15 minutes, with no cover, mixing from time to time, till thicken. Get rid of cloves.
- Blot pork chops dry. In a heavy, 12-inch skillet, heat the oil on medium high heat till hot yet do not let smoke, then let chops brown for approximately 1 1/2 minutes per side in two batches. Turn onto plate once chops become brown.
- Drain all except approximately 1 1/2 tbsps. of fat from skillet; on medium heat, cook onion for 3 minutes while mixing, till soften. Put in garlic; cook for a minute while mixing. Put in pork chops including any juices and sauce, let simmer with no cover for 6 to 8 minutes, flipping chops one time, till barely cooked fully. Scatter cilantro over.
- Note: You may refrigerate seasoned yet not cooked pork chops for maximum of 10 hours.

Nutrition Information

- Calories: 627
- Total Carbohydrate: 44 g
- Cholesterol: 153 mg
- Total Fat: 31 g
- Fiber: 3 g
- Protein: 43 g
- Sodium: 1145 mg
- Saturated Fat: 11 g

252. Potato And Leek Purée

"You can serve this in room temperature/warm."
Serving: Makes 1 1/2 cups

Ingredients

- 1 lb. Yukon gold potatoes, peeled, washed, and quartered
- 2 leeks, trimmed, cleaned, and cut into 1-inch pieces
- 2 tbsps. unsalted butter
- 1/2 cup whole milk

Direction

- Boil leeks and potatoes in water to just cover in a big pot till potatoes are pierced easily with knife's tip and tender for 30 minutes. Drain; keep water. Remove potatoes. Pass through ricer; put aside.
- Put leeks in a food processor with a steel blade; puree.
- Melt butter on medium heat in a heavy saucepan. Add riced potatoes; mix in milk slowly, beating till creamy with a wooden spoon. Mix in pureed leeks; mix in some

reserved potato water to get more liquid consistency.
- Immediately serve; freeze any leftover puree that won't get consumed the next day.

Nutrition Information

- Calories: 184
- Total Carbohydrate: 28 g
- Cholesterol: 18 mg
- Total Fat: 7 g
- Fiber: 3 g
- Protein: 4 g
- Sodium: 30 mg
- Saturated Fat: 4 g

253. Potato Latkes

"It's complicated but good."
Serving: Makes 18 to 20 latkes

Ingredients

- 2 1/2 lbs. Idaho russet potatoes
- 1 medium onion
- 2 large eggs, separated
- 1/2 cup finely chopped scallions (white and green parts)
- 1/4 cup potato flour or matzo meal
- 3 tbsps. unsalted butter, melted
- 2 tsps. kosher salt
- 1/2 tsp. freshly ground black pepper
- 1/4 tsp. baking powder
- Canola or vegetable oil, for frying
- Sour cream, for serving
- Applesauce, for serving

Direction

- Over a large bowl, place a large strainer. Grate some of the potatoes, then some of the onion into the strainer using the large holes of a box grater. Repeat the process until all of the onion and potatoes are used up. (Alternating the onion and potatoes will prevent the potatoes from discoloring.) Press or squeeze out the liquid as much as possible. In another bowl, let the accumulated liquid to sit for 2-3 minutes. Then pour the watery part off but store the starchy, thick paste at the bottom.
- Move the potato-onion mixture to a large, clean bowl. Add the starchy paste, baking powder, pepper, salt, butter, matzo meal or potato flour, scallions, and egg yolks; mix well. Use an electric mixer to beat the egg whites in another medium bowl, until shiny, stiff peaks form. Next, add the egg whites to the potato mixture and fold.
- In a large frying pan, heat a thin layer of oil over medium-high heat. For each pancake, scoop 1/4 cup of the potato mixture into the pan, doing in batches. Use a spatula to gently flatten. Fry about 4 minutes per side, or until the pancakes are golden brown and crisp.
- Immediately serve or reheat for about 6 minutes in a 350 degrees F oven. Enjoy with applesauce and sour cream.

Nutrition Information

- Calories: 193
- Total Carbohydrate: 14 g
- Cholesterol: 26 mg
- Total Fat: 15 g
- Fiber: 1 g
- Protein: 2 g
- Sodium: 219 mg
- Saturated Fat: 2 g

254. Potato, Carrot And Parsnip Soup

Serving: Makes 8 servings

Ingredients

- 1/4 cup (1/2 stick) butter
- 2 large onions, halved and sliced (about 5 cups)
- 4 carrots, peeled, cut into 1/2-inch pieces (about 2 cups)

- 4 parsnips, peeled, cut into 1/2-inch pieces (about 1 cups)
- 2 14 1/2 oz. cans (or more) low-salt chicken broth
- 3 large red potatoes, cut into 1/2-inch pieces (about 2 1/2 cups)
- 1/4 cup chopped fresh parsley
- 1 tsp. fresh thyme
- 1 1/4 cups half and half
- 1/4 cup Sherry

Direction

- Place the butter in a heavy large pot and melt it over medium-high heat. Add the onions and cook it for 15 minutes until golden. Add the parsnips and carrots. Let it cook for 10 minutes. Add the parsley, potatoes, 2 cans of broth, and thyme. Cover the pot and let it simmer for 30 minutes, stirring occasionally until the potatoes are tender.
- In a food processor, puree half of the soup. Pour the puree into the pot with the remaining soup. Stir in Sherry and half-and-half. Season it with salt and pepper to taste. Take note that this can be prepared a day ahead. Just keep it covered and refrigerated.
- Before serving, simmer the soup and if desired, thin it with additional broth. Spoon into the bowls and serve.

Nutrition Information

- Calories: 326
- Total Carbohydrate: 51 g
- Cholesterol: 29 mg
- Total Fat: 11 g
- Fiber: 8 g
- Protein: 8 g
- Sodium: 106 mg
- Saturated Fat: 7 g

255. Potato, Corn, And Cherry Tomato Salad With Basil Dressing

"You can make this recipe in less than 45 minutes."
Serving: Serves 8

Ingredients

- 2 tbsps. white-wine vinegar
- 1/2 cup olive oil
- 1 cup packed fresh basil leaves
- 2 1/2 lbs. small red potatoes
- the kernels cut from 6 cooked ears of corn
- 1/2 lb. cherry tomatoes, halved

Direction

- Blend together basil, oil, and vinegar with pepper and salt to taste using a food processor or blender until the dressing becomes emulsified. In a big saucepan, combine potatoes with enough cold water to cover by 2 inches and boil, then simmer until potatoes are tender, 15 minutes. Drain, cool, and quarter the potatoes. In a big bowl, combine dressing, tomatoes, potatoes, and corn with pepper and salt to taste, then gently toss the salad.

256. Powdered Sugar

"A powdered sugar recipe."
Serving: 192 | Prep: 5m | Ready in: 5m

Ingredients

- 4 cups white sugar
- 1/2 cup cornstarch

Direction

- Process cornstarch and sugar for 2-3 minutes till powdery and fine in a food processor's work bowl.

Nutrition Information

- Calories: 17 calories;

- Total Carbohydrate: 4.5 g
- Cholesterol: 0 mg
- Total Fat: 0 g
- Protein: 0 g
- Sodium: < 1 mg

257. Provencal Vegetable And Goat Cheese Terrine

Serving: Serves 6

Ingredients

- 2 red bell peppers
- 1 large eggplant, cut lengthwise into 3/8-inch-thick slices
- Olive oil
- 2 large zucchini, cut lengthwise into 1/4-inch-thick slices
- 1 11-oz. package soft mild goat cheese (such as Montrachet), room temperature
- 3 tbsps. olive oil
- 2 tbsps. chopped fresh thyme
- 1 large bunch fresh arugula, chopped
- 1/2 cup chopped pitted brine-cured olives (such as Niçoise or Kalamata)
- Fresh arugula leaves
- French bread

Direction

- Char peppers till blackened on all sides in broiler/above gas flame. Put in bag; stand for 10 minutes. Peel then seed peppers; cut to 1/2-in. pieces.
- Preheat broiler. Brush oil on both eggplant sides; season with pepper and salt. Broil for 3 minutes per side till golden and cooked through; on paper towels, drain. Brush oil on both zucchini sides; season with pepper and salt. Broil for 3 minutes per side till cooked through; on paper towels, drain.
- Puree cheese till smooth in processor. Through feed tube, add 3 tbsp. oil as machine runs. Add bell peppers; with on/off turns, process till cheese starts to color and peppers are chopped coarsely. Add thyme; season using pepper and salt.
- Line plastic on 9x5-in. glass loaf pan; leave 4-in. overhang. Put 1 layer of zucchini on bottom of pan, fully covering, trimming to fit. On it, spread 1/3 cheese mixture; top with 1/3 olives and 1/3 chopped arugula. Cover using 1 eggplant layer, trimming to fit. On top, spread 1/3 cheese; put 1/3 olives and 1/3 chopped arugula on top. Repeat using leftover olives, chopped arugula, cheese and zucchini. Finish with eggplant layer. To cover, fold plastic over; gently press down on eggplant and cover; chill for minimum of 6 hours till firm. You can make it 2 days ahead, kept chilled. Stand before serving for 30 minutes in room temperature.
- Line arugula leaves on platter. On top of terrine, open plastic wrap. Unmold terrine on platter and lift off pan; peel off plastic then serve with bread.

Nutrition Information

- Calories: 328
- Total Carbohydrate: 15 g
- Cholesterol: 24 mg
- Total Fat: 25 g
- Fiber: 7 g
- Protein: 14 g
- Sodium: 338 mg
- Saturated Fat: 10 g

258. Pumpkin Clafouti

"Use puréed pumpkin to mix into the batter to make this clafouti particularly creamy and silken."
Serving: Makes 8 servings

Ingredients

- 1 4- to 5- lb. cheese pumpkin or butternut or Hubbard squash
- 5 large eggs
- 3/4 cup plus 2 tbsps. sugar
- 1/2 cup milk

- 1/2 cup heavy cream
- 1 tsp. vanilla extract
- 1-inch piece of vanilla bean, split lengthwise, pulp scraped
- Pinch of salt
- 1/4 cup all-purpose flour
- 1 tbsp. unsalted butter, melted
- 1/3 chopped toasted hazelnuts

Direction

- Preheat an oven to 350°F. Halve squash or pumpkin and scoop the seeds out. On a baking sheet, put the halves, cut side facing up, and bake for 90 minutes.
- Once cool enough to touch, into food processor, scoop the flesh and process into a smooth purée. Line a double thickness of cheesecloth or a clean kitchen towel on a sieve and put on top a bowl. Into the lined sieve, scoop the purée, then refrigerate overnight to allow to drain. The following day, through a fine sieve, pour the drained purée to measure 2/3 cup, use any leftover purée for other purpose.
- In a food processor or blender, put the salt, vanilla pulp, vanilla extract, cream, milk, 3/4 cup of sugar and eggs. Pulse or blend mixture for 30 seconds till extremely smooth. Put in the pumpkin purée and process thoroughly. Put in the flour and blend till thoroughly incorporated.
- Through a fine sieve, pour the batter, then allow to sit for 30 minutes at room temperature.
- Preheat an oven to 425°F. With melted butter, brush a pie plate or quiche, 9 inches in size; scatter the leftover 2 tbsps. sugar over. In the pan, scatter the hazelnuts. On top of nuts, put the batter. Let the clafouti bake for 15 minutes, then reduce the temperature to 375°F and bake for 12 minutes till the middle is just firm. Serve right away.

Nutrition Information

- Calories: 246
- Total Carbohydrate: 31 g
- Cholesterol: 142 mg
- Total Fat: 10 g
- Fiber: 0 g
- Protein: 6 g
- Sodium: 94 mg
- Saturated Fat: 6 g

259. Quiche With Leeks, Mushrooms And Sweet Potatoes

"This vegetarian quiche is a perfect dish for a light breakfast with your family."
Serving: 6 | Prep: 20m | Ready in: 1h35m

Ingredients

- 2 tsps. olive oil
- 1 onion, chopped
- 1/2 tsp. dried thyme
- 2 leeks, white part only, chopped
- 6 oz. mushrooms, chopped
- 1/2 sweet potato, peeled and diced
- 5 eggs
- 1/3 cup sour cream
- 1/2 tsp. salt
- 1 cup heavy whipping cream
- 1 tbsp. finely shredded Asiago cheese

Direction

- Set the oven to 175°C (350°F) to preheat. Lightly coat a 9-inch pie dish with oil.
- Over medium heat, put olive oil in a skillet and add in onion. Cook while stirring them for around 2 minutes then put in mushrooms and leeks, and thyme. Continue stirring and cooking for 5 to 8 minutes, or until the onions are well cooked.
- Put in sweet potato, cook while stirring for about 15 minutes or until the sweet potato softens. Put the mixture in the greased pie dish.
- In a food processor, add cream, salt, sour cream and eggs; blend them well together

until smooth. Transfer them to the pie dish and gently pour over the onion mixture. Put on top some Asiago cheese.
- Bake the quiche for 45-50 minutes in the preheated oven, or until the outside is golden brown and the center feel gently firm. Set aside to warm for a few minutes. Cut into pieces and serve.

Nutrition Information

- Calories: 298 calories;
- Total Carbohydrate: 14.5 g
- Cholesterol: 216 mg
- Total Fat: 23.6 g
- Protein: 8.8 g
- Sodium: 307 mg

260. Quick Puff Pastry

Serving: Makes 2 1/2 lbs.

Ingredients

- 4 cups all-purpose flour
- 1 1/2 tsps. salt
- 6 1/2 sticks (3 1/4 cups) unsalted butter, cut into 1/2-inch cubes, chilled
- 1 cup cold water

Direction

- Sift salt and flour in a food processor bowl with blade attachment.
- Add diced, chilled butter; pulse 3-5 times till butter pieces are lima bean sized. Add water to mixture; pulse 3 times. On a lightly floured work surface, invert crumbly mass.
- Shape mass to long rectangle with bench scraper and rolling pin. Flip 1/3 rectangle toward center using bench scraper; flip other end to middle like a business letter. Rotate dough 90°.
- Reshape then roll dough to rectangle; repeat folding and rotating procedure thrice for 4 turns total. Immediately refrigerate till firm if dough is sticky or soft during the process.
- Wrap dough in plastic wrap after 4 turns; create 4 indentations in dough with a finger, one for each time dough was turned. Refrigerate dough till firm or for 45 minutes minimum.
- Unwrap and discard plastic when dough was refrigerated for 45 minutes; keep rolling pin and work surface well-floured. To seal the shape, press down on each of 4 dough sides.
- Roll away from you, stating with rolling pin at middle; return to middle then roll toward you. Repeat folding and rotating dough process twice for 6 times total.
- Wrap finished dough in plastic wrap after 6th turn; refrigerate before baking till well-chilled. Quick puff pastry keeps for up to 3 days or for a few months frozen.

Nutrition Information

- Calories: 323
- Total Carbohydrate: 17 g
- Cholesterol: 72 mg
- Total Fat: 27 g
- Fiber: 1 g
- Protein: 3 g
- Sodium: 156 mg
- Saturated Fat: 17 g

261. Quick Sun-dried Tomato And Basil Hummus

"This easy to whip hummus is great with sandwiches and burgers, and best served with crackers, pita wedges and chips."
Serving: 20 | Prep: 15m | Ready in: 15m

Ingredients

- 1 (15.5 oz.) can garbanzo beans, drained (reserve liquid) and rinsed
- 1/2 cup chopped sun-dried tomatoes (not oil-packed)
- 3 cloves garlic
- 2 tbsps. chopped fresh basil leaves
- 1/4 cup grated Parmesan cheese

- 1/4 cup olive oil
- salt and pepper to taste

Direction

- In a food processor, grind together the Parmesan cheese, basil, garlic, sun-dried tomatoes and garbanzo beans for 15 seconds.
- Stir in about 1/4 of the reserved liquid, then grind for 15 seconds more. Put in enough additional reserved liquid a small amount at a time then grind. Redo until you reach a chunky peanut butter consistency.
- Put in olive oil and grind for 15 seconds more. Put pepper and salt to season.

Nutrition Information

- Calories: 59 calories;
- Total Carbohydrate: 5.9 g
- Cholesterol: < 1 mg
- Total Fat: 3.3 g
- Protein: 1.7 g
- Sodium: 110 mg

262. Quick Sweet Potato Bisque

"A dish made with sweet potatoes and milk, then served with a sprinkling of pepitas."
Serving: 12 | Prep: 20m | Ready in: 40m

Ingredients

- 6 cups skim milk
- 5 large sweet potatoes, peeled and chopped
- 3 apples - peeled, cored, and chopped
- 1 large onion, sliced
- 3 carrots, chopped
- 3 stalks celery, chopped
- 6 cloves garlic, chopped
- 1 tsp. salt
- 1/2 tsp. ground nutmeg
- 1/2 tsp. cayenne pepper
- 8 black peppercorns

Direction

- In a big pot, mix together the peppercorns, cayenne pepper, nutmeg, salt, garlic, celery, carrots, onion, apples, sweet potatoes and milk, then boil. Lower the heat to low, cover the pot and let it simmer for 20-30 minutes, mixing from time to time, until the potatoes become tender.
- In a blender or food processor, pour the soup not more than halfway full. Put cover and hold the lid down, then pulse several times prior to leaving it on to blend. Puree in batches until it has a smooth consistency.

Nutrition Information

- Calories: 240 calories;
- Total Carbohydrate: 52.9 g
- Cholesterol: 2 mg
- Total Fat: 0.4 g
- Protein: 7.7 g
- Sodium: 369 mg

263. Quince Apple Strudels With Quince Syrup

"This fruit-filled dessert has a strudel dough that seems more difficult than it is to make. It also has a dough made with bread flour to allow more stretch."
Serving: Makes 2 (10-inch) strudels | Prep: 1.75h

Ingredients

- 2 lbs. quinces (4 or 5), peeled, quartered, cored, and cut into 3/4-inch pieces
- Reserved syrup from star-fruit chips
- 1/2 vanilla bean, halved lengthwise
- 1 (4- by 1-inch) strip fresh lemon zest plus 1 tsp. finely grated
- 2 lbs. Gala apples (4 or 5), peeled, cored, and cut into 3/4-inch pieces
- 1/2 stick (1/4 cup) unsalted butter, melted
- 1/4 tsp. salt
- 1/2 cup sugar
- 1 cup soft dried tart cherries (6 oz.)

- 1 tbsp. fresh lemon juice
- 1 slice firm white sandwich bread
- 1/2 cup slivered almonds (2 oz.), lightly toasted
- 2 cups bread flour
- 1 tbsp. granulated sugar
- 1/2 tsp. salt
- 1 large egg yolk
- 3/4 cup lukewarm water
- 1 1/4 sticks (10 tbsps.) unsalted butter, melted and cooled slightly
- About 1/2 cup all-purpose flour for rubbing into cloth
- 1/4 cup confectioners sugar
- Accompaniment: 1 qt store-bought premium vanilla ice cream; star-fruit chips
- a stand mixer fitted with paddle attachment; parchment paper; a (36-inch) round or square work table; a cotton sheet or smooth, lint-free tablecloth large enough to hang over edge of table; a small blowtorch (optional)

Direction

- To make the filling and quince syrup: In a heavy 3 quart saucepan, combine reserved star-fruit syrup with quince and boil, stirring until the sugar dissolves. Scrape in the vanilla bean seeds and add a strip of zest and the vanilla pod. Turn the heat down and simmer, covered partially, until the quince is really tender and starts to turn pinkish, roughly 50-60 minutes.
- As the quince simmers, place a rack in the middle of the oven and set the temperature to 400 degrees Fahrenheit.
- At the same time, toss the apples with 1/4 cup of sugar, salt, finely grated zest, and butter in a shallow big baking pan until well coated, spreading it out evenly in a layer. Roast, stirring sometimes, until the apples become really tender and the liquid released evaporates, around 45 minutes up to 1 hour.
- Pour the quince mixture in a big sieve set atop a bowl, throwing out the pod and zest, set the syrup aside. If the syrup is more than a cup, place back to the saucepan and boil to reduce it to 1 cup. If less, add more water to make 1 cup. Completely cool the syrup.
- In a big bowl, stir together the cherries and quince, then fold in the lemon juice and roasted apples, then cool to room temperature, occasionally stirring, around 30 minutes.
- Use a food processor or blender to pulse the bread into fine crumbs and add the remaining 1/4 cup of sugar and nuts, pulse until chopped finely, then put aside.
- As the apples roast, make the dough: In a mixer bowl, stir together salt, granulated sugar, and bread flour, then make a well in the middle and add 2 tbsps. of melted butter, lukewarm water, and yolk. Beat it at medium speed until the dough is elastic and silky, then forms into a sticky soft ball that comes away from the sides of the bowl, 8-10 minutes.
- Turn out the dough on a lightly floured work surface and form into a ball. Brush lightly with melted butter and cover with an inverted warmed bowl (rinse the bowl with hot water to warm it up and dry) and let sit for 1 - 1 1/4 hours to allow the gluten to relax and make the stretching easier.
- To stretch the dough: Place the rack in the middle of the oven and set the oven to 375 degrees Fahrenheit. Use parchment paper to line a big 17x13-inch big baking sheet. Use a sheet to cover a work table in a draft-free room and rub all over with all-purpose flour, leaving out the overhang.
- Place the dough in the middle of the table and stretch to a 12-inch round using your fingers. Using the floured back of your hands (without any jewelry), reach under the dough and gently start to stretch and thin the dough from the center out to the edges, moving around the table as you work, intermittently stretching, and slightly thinning the thicker edges. Slowly stretch the dough paper-thin into a minimum of 36-inch square (it will hang over the edge of the table), letting it sit for a few minutes when it resist stretching and re-flouring your hands occasionally. This may take around 20 minutes and try not to make holes in the dough, if it does, cut out pieces from the overhang to

patch. Allow the dough to sit to dry for 5 minutes.
- To assemble strudel: Really gently brush the dough with 1/3 cup of melted butter and evenly sprinkle with reserved almond mixture. Mound the filling in two 11x3-inch strips, from one end to the other, along the dough edge nearest you, leaving 3 inch gap between the strips and a 4-inch border along the sides and edge of the dough nearest to you. Cut the dough overhang off to the table edge using kitchen shears. Fold the dough edge nearest you over the filing. As you hold the sheet tautly, use the sheet to allow the dough to roll over the filling and away from you.
- Brush all over the strudel with the leftover melted butter and cut into 2 pieces through the space between the mounds. Use 2 metal spatulas to transfer the strudels carefully to a baking sheet, placing them 4 inches apart, and sprinkle with 2 tbsps. of confectioners' sugar. Cut out 3-4 steam vents, 2 inches apart, in top of each of the strudels and bake until they turn golden, 40-45 minutes. Cool them for 10 minutes on a sheet on a rack, then move carefully to the rack and cool to room temperature or warm, roughly 30 minutes. Evenly dust with the leftover 2 tbsps. of confectioners' sugar. If you want, you can move the blowtorch flame carefully and evenly back and forth above the sugar until it melts and caramelizes.
- Cut the strudel into pieces that are 2 inches wide and serve along with star-fruit chips and ice cream. Drizzle with the reserved quince syrup.
- To make the syrup, use a 3-quart heavy saucepan to boil 2 cups of sugar and 2 cups of water, stirring until the sugar dissolves, then add the quince and proceed.
- You can make the filling and quince syrup (including cherries and apples) 3 days ahead, completely cool without a cover, then chill while covered. Bring it to room temperature before use.
- You can make the nut mixture 2 days beforehand, keep at room temperature in an airtight container.
- Strudel is best eaten the same day you make it but you can make it a day before, keeping it covered at room temperature. Reheat it in a preheated oven at 350 degrees Fahrenheit for 15 minutes.
- You can assemble but not bake the strudel then freeze it on a baking sheet, tightly covered with foil, until it is frozen hard and keep frozen, wrapped in parchment then foil, 2 weeks beforehand. Thaw while uncovered on a baking sheet for a minimum of 1 hour before you bake it.

Nutrition Information

- Calories: 2634
- Total Carbohydrate: 409 g
- Cholesterol: 306 mg
- Total Fat: 102 g
- Fiber: 30 g
- Protein: 33 g
- Sodium: 1003 mg
- Saturated Fat: 54 g

264. Quince Tarte Tatin

"A classic dessert."
Serving: Makes 8 to 10 servings

Ingredients

- 1 1/2 cups all purpose flour
- 1 1/2 tbsps. sugar
- 1 tsp. salt
- 1/2 cup (1 stick) chilled unsalted butter, cut into 1/2-inch cubes
- 3 tbsps. (or more) ice water
- 1 1/2 tsps. cider vinegar
- 1 cup sugar
- 1/4 cup water
- 1 tbsp. honey
- 5 tbsps. unsalted butter, room temperature
- 1/2 tsp. ground cinnamon

- 8 small quinces (about 3 1/4 lbs.), peeled, each cut into 1–inch–wide wedges, cored

Direction

- Crust: In a processor, mix initial 3 ingredients. Cut in butter till it looks like coarse meal with on/off turns. Mix vinegar and 3 tbsp. ice water in a small bowl; put into the processor. Blend till moist clumps form; if dough is dry, add extra ice water by teaspoonfuls. Bring the dough into a ball; flatten into a disk. In plastic, wrap; refrigerate for at least 1 hour. You can make it 1 day ahead, kept refrigerated. Before rolling out, slightly soften at room temperature.
- Filling: Use ice cubes to fill big skillet; put aside.
- Mix initial 3 ingredients in 11-in. diameter heavy ovenproof skillet; mix till sugar melts on medium heat. Put heat on medium high; boil for 8 minutes till caramel is deep amber color, swirling skillet, brushing sides of skillet down using wet pastry brush occasionally. Take off from the heat. Mix in cinnamon and butter; put skillet with caramel immediately on ice in a big skillet. Stand for 30 minutes till caramel is hard and cold; take the skillet from ice.
- In the middle of oven, put rack; preheat to 400°F. Tightly together, put quince wedges in concentric circles on top of caramel in the skillet, rounded side down. Fill the middle with any broken quince pieces. Roll the dough out to 12 1/2-in. round on a lightly floured surface. Put the dough on top of quinces; tuck dough edges down around the quinces sides. In the middle of the dough, create 3 2-in. long cuts to let the steam escape while baking. On rimmed baking sheet, put skillet; bake for 1 hour 15 minutes till crust is deep golden brown and quinces are tender. Take out from the oven; cool for 30 minutes.
- Put a big platter on the skillet. Firmly hold skillet and platter together using oven mitts; invert, letting tart slide onto the platter. If needed, rearrange any dislodged quince wedges. Serve warm or at room temperature.

Nutrition Information

- Calories: 429
- Total Carbohydrate: 65 g
- Cholesterol: 50 mg
- Total Fat: 19 g
- Fiber: 3 g
- Protein: 3 g
- Sodium: 299 mg
- Saturated Fat: 12 g

265. Raspberry And Lime Custard Tart

"You need 13x4-in. rectangular tart pan that has removable fluted rim for this recipe."
Serving: Makes 1 tart

Ingredients

- 1 1/4 cups all-purpose flour
- 3/4 stick (6 tbsps.) cold unsalted butter, cut into bits
- 2 tbsps. cold vegetable shortening
- 1/4 tsp. salt
- 2 to 4 tbsps. ice water
- pie weights or raw rice for weighting shell
- 1/2 cup sugar
- 1/2 cup heavy cream
- 3 large eggs
- 1/3 cup fresh lime juice
- 4 tsps. finely grated fresh lime zest
- 3 cups picked-over raspberries
- 1/4 cup sugar

Direction

- Shell: Pulse/blend salt, shortening butter and flour till it looks like coarse meal in a food processor or pastry blender in a bowl. Add 2 tbsp. ice water; pulse/toss till incorporated; 1 tbsp. at a time, add leftover ice water, pulsing/tossing with fork to incorporate to make dough. With heel of hand, smear dough on work surface in 3-4 forward motions so dough is easy to work with. Shape dough to

ball; flatten to make disk. Chill dough for minimum of 1- maximum of 24 hours, wrapped in plastic wrap.
- Roll dough out with floured rolling pin to 16x7-in. 1/8-in. thick rectangle on lightly floured surface; fit dough in 13x4-in. rectangular tart pan that has removeable fluted rim. Chill the shell for 1 hour till firm, covered.
- Preheat an oven to 400°F.
- Line foil on shell; fill with raw rice/pie weights. Bake shell for 10 minutes in center of oven. Remove foil and rice/weights. Bake shell for 5 minutes till pale golden; cool shell in the pan on rack. You can make shell 2 days ahead, kept in pan in room temperature, covered.
- Lower temperature to 250°F. Put pan on baking sheet.
- Custard: Whisk custard ingredients.
- Put custard in tart shell; bake tart on the baking sheet for 30 minutes in center of oven. Put on rack; cool. Custard sets as tart cools. Up to this point, you can prep tart 1 day ahead, chilled, covered.
- Cook sugar and 1 cup raspberries in small saucepan on medium low heat for 5 minutes, occasionally mixing, mashing with fork. Through fine sieve, put into small bowl; press on solids hard. Discard solids; cool raspberry mixture. Remove tart pan's rim; put tart on platter. Put cooked raspberry mixture on custard; put leftover 2 cups raspberries over.

Nutrition Information

- Calories: 2827
- Total Carbohydrate: 326 g
- Cholesterol: 904 mg
- Total Fat: 157 g
- Fiber: 29 g
- Protein: 43 g
- Sodium: 862 mg
- Saturated Fat: 83 g

266. Raspberry Jam Tart With Almond Crumble

"An easy dessert."
Serving: Makes 8 servings | Prep: 15m

Ingredients

- 2 cups sliced natural almonds
- 2/3 cup sugar
- 1 1/4 sticks (1/2 cup plus 2 tbsps.) cold unsalted butter, cut into pieces
- 11/4 cups all-purpose flour
- 1 rounded 1/4 tsp. salt
- 2 tbsps. beaten egg
- 1 cup raspberry jam

Direction

- Preheat an oven to 400°F.
- Keep 1/4 cup almonds for topping in a bowl. Grind sugar and leftover 1 3/4 cups nuts finely in food processor.
- Add salt, flour and butter; process till it looks like sand. Put 1 cup flour mixture in reserved almonds. Put beaten egg in leftover flour mixture; pulse till it clumps together.
- From processor, put mixture in 9x1-in. round tart pan that has removable bottom; use floured fingers to press mixture up pan's sides and bottom of pan. Bake for 15 minutes in center of oven.
- Meanwhile, to loosen, mix raspberry jam. Rub the reserved almond mixture in the bowl between palms to make small clumps.
- Take tart shell from oven; spread jam on bottom. On jam, sprinkle almond mixture; bake tart for 15 minutes. Cool the tart in pan on the rack. Use a knife to loosen side of pan; remove it.
- You can make it 1 day ahead; before chilling, cool, covered. Before serving, bring to room temperature.

Nutrition Information

- Calories: 592
- Total Carbohydrate: 82 g

- Cholesterol: 39 mg
- Total Fat: 26 g
- Fiber: 4 g
- Protein: 10 g
- Sodium: 307 mg
- Saturated Fat: 10 g

267. Raspberry Linzer Tart

"A terrific cake."
Serving: Serves 8

Ingredients

- 2/3 cup (packed)golden brown sugar
- 1/2 cup (1 stick) unsalted butter, room temperature
- 1 large egg
- 1 1/2 cups all purpose flour
- 1/2 cup ground toasted blanched almonds (about 2 1/2 oz.)
- 3/4 tsp. ground cinnamon
- 1/2 tsp. baking powder
- 1/2 tsp. salt
- 6 oz. semisweet chocolate chips (about 1 cup)
- 1 1/2-pint basket raspberries
- 1/2 cup seedless raspberry jam
- Powdered sugar
- Lightly sweetened whipped cream

Direction

- Crust: Beat egg, butter and sugar using electric mixer till creamy in medium bowl. Add salt, baking powder, cinnamon, almonds and flour; beat till just blended well. Get 3/4 cup dough; flatten to disk. In plastic, wrap; chill. Press leftover dough up sides and on bottom of 9-in. diameter tart pan that has removable bottom using floured fingertips. Use a fork to pierce dough in few places; chill for minimum of 1 hour. You can make it 1 day ahead, kept chilled.
- Preheat an oven to 375°F. Bake the crust for 15 minutes till light golden; if crust bubbles, pierce with toothpick. Put on rack; cool. Maintain the oven temperature.
- Roll chilled dough disk out to 1/8-in. thick on generously floured surface. Use 2 and 3-in. star cookie cutters to cut dough to starts; put cookies on baking sheet. Bake for 6 minutes till cookies are light golden. Put cookies on rack; cool. Maintain the oven temperature.
- Filling: Melt the chocolate chips on top of double boiler above simmering water, mixing till smooth; cool for 5 minutes. Spread chocolate on bottom of crust. Put berries on chocolate, evenly spacing. Mix jam in small heavy saucepan on low heat till smooth and melted. Put jam on raspberries.
- Bake tart for 35 minutes till crust is golden brown; filling might look slightly liquid, it'll set as tart cools. Put tart on rack; cool. Put stars on tart, overlapping points. Use powdered sugar to dust; serve with whipped cream.

Nutrition Information

- Calories: 517
- Total Carbohydrate: 74 g
- Cholesterol: 54 mg
- Total Fat: 24 g
- Fiber: 7 g
- Protein: 7 g
- Sodium: 195 mg
- Saturated Fat: 12 g

268. Raw Cucumber Soup (Gluten And Dairy-free)

""This recipe will be loved by those who are looking for taste that would satisfy them or for those who are conscious in diet! Present this warmed up or cool, so fast and easy to make while still contributing the benefits of raw food. Wonderfully topped with a slice of lime or a mint leaf. Have fun!""
Serving: 4 | Prep: 20m | Ready in: 20m

Ingredients

- 2 cups chopped cucumber

- 1 cup chopped zucchini
- 1 cup peeled and chopped avocado
- 1 clove garlic, minced
- 2 cups lukewarm water
- 1/2 large lemon, juiced
- 2 tbsps. olive oil
- 1/2 tsp. salt

Direction

- In a blender or food processor, put garlic, avocado, zucchini and cucumber then blend for about 30 minutes until very finely chopped.
- Mix together in a bowl the salt, olive oil, lemon juice and water.
- Start the food processor and put water mixture slowly through the food processor's feed tube while blending cucumber mixture. Blend for about 1 minute until it turns smooth.

Nutrition Information

- Calories: 137 calories;
- Total Carbohydrate: 7.4 g
- Cholesterol: 0 mg
- Total Fat: 12.4 g
- Protein: 1.6 g
- Sodium: 302 mg

269. Raw Pasta Sauce

"This pasta sauce is sugar-free, vegan and uncooked. It has a nice flavor without the need of cooking all the nutrients. Ideal for raw foods when served on top of uncooked spaghetti squash."
Serving: 2 | Prep: 20m | Ready in: 50m

Ingredients

- 2 tomatoes, chopped
- 1/4 cup chopped green bell pepper
- 1/4 cup chopped onion
- 1 1/2 tsps. lime juice
- 1 clove garlic, minced
- 1/8 tsp. sea salt
- 1/8 tsp. dried oregano
- 1/8 tsp. dried rosemary

Direction

- In a blender or food processor, puree the tomatoes along with its juice and seeds. Pour into a lidded two-cup container.
- Mix rosemary, green bell pepper, lime juice, oregano, onion, garlic, and sea salt into the pureed tomatoes. Cover the container with the lid and chill for at least half an hour.

Nutrition Information

- Calories: 38 calories;
- Total Carbohydrate: 8.5 g
- Cholesterol: 0 mg
- Total Fat: 0.3 g
- Protein: 1.6 g
- Sodium: 118 mg

270. Red Bean And Sausage Cakes With Poached Eggs And Cilantro Salsa

"A great breakfast recipe."
Serving: Makes 4 servings

Ingredients

- 1 cup fresh cilantro leaves plus 2 tbsps. chopped cilantro
- 1/3 cup bottled green taco sauce
- 5 oz. breakfast sausage roll
- 1 15-to 16-oz. can kidney beans, drained well
- 1 tsp. chili powder
- 1 tsp. ground cumin
- 1/4 tsp. (scant) salt plus additional for poaching liquid
- Nonstick vegetable oil spray
- 4 large eggs
- 3/4 cup chopped seeded plum tomatoes

Direction

- Puree taco sauce and 1 cup cilantro leaves till nearly smooth in mini processor. Sauté sausage till cooked through in big skillet on medium high heat for 4-5 minutes, finely breaking up sausage. Put in a small bowl; keep skillet.
- Blend 2 tbsp. chopped cilantro, scant 1/4 tsp. salt, cumin, chili powder and beans with on/off turns till most beans are chopped in processor. Add sausage; with 4-5 on/off turns, blend, some chunky texture should be left. By generous 1/3 cupfuls, form mixture using wet hands to 4 3-in. diameter patties.
- Use nonstick spray to coat reserved skillet; heat on medium high heat then add patties. Cook for 3 minutes per side till brown.
- In another big skillet, add 2-in. water. Add salt; boil. Lower heat to medium low. Into water, crack eggs; simmer 2-3 minutes to get runny yolks and whites are firm.
- On plates, put patties; sprinkle tomatoes. Put 1 egg over each then salsa.

271. Red Chili And Honey-glazed Turkey With Ancho Pan Gravy

"This is a rich and spicy gravy that is reminiscent of mole poblano, the great Mexican sauce. The gravy is based on the puréed ancho chilies and often known to have a chocolatey quality. In this recipe, it's reinforced with addition of a little amount of unsweetened chocolate."
Serving: Makes 10 servings

Ingredients

- 3 1/2 cups water
- 4 oz. dried ancho chilies,* stemmed, seeded, torn into small pieces
- 1 lb. plum tomatoes, halved
- 5 large heads of garlic
- 2 tbsps. plus 2 1/3 cups (about) canned low-salt chicken broth
- 1 tbsp. olive oil
- 1/4 cup (1/2 stick) unsalted butter, room temperature
- 2 tbsps. chili powder
- 2 tbsps. honey
- 1 14-lb. turkey, wing tips cut off; neck, heart, gizzard and wing tips reserved for stock
- 1/2 cup fresh orange juice
- 5 1/2 cupsGiblet Stock
- 1/2 oz. unsweetened chocolate

Direction

- Over high heat, heat 3 1/2 cups of water to boil in a medium saucepan. Take out from the heat. Pour in ancho chilies and leave to sit for one hour. Drain and save 2/3 cup of liquid. In a processor, mix the reserved liquid and chilies and process to form a smooth thick paste. Press ancho paste through a strainer using a rubber spatula and get rid of the solids in the strainer. Reserve.
- Set the rack in the middle of oven and then preheat to 400 degrees F. Spread a single layer the tomatoes in a 13x9-inch baking pan that is oiled. Cut top 1/4 off heads of garlic and get rid of tops. Spread garlic in single layer in a small glass baking dish with the cut side up. Sprinkle with oil and two tbsps. of chicken broth. Tightly cover the baking dish with foil. Transfer the garlic and tomatoes into the oven and roast tomatoes, flipping once, for about 30 minutes until lightly browned and softened. Bake the garlic for about 1 hour until it's tender when pierced with a skewer. In a processor, put the tomatoes and then blend to form a smooth purée. Let the garlic cool, and then squeeze the garlic cloves from skins into a small bowl. Use a fork to mash the garlic to form a smooth purée. (You can make tomato purée, garlic purée and ancho paste one day ahead. Then cover separately and refrigerate).
- Set the rack on the bottom third of oven and then preheat to 325 degrees F. In a small bowl, combine 1 tbsp. of honey, 3 tbsps. of garlic purée, chili powder and butter until blended well. Add pepper and salt to taste. Rinse the turkey inside and outside and pat dry.

Beginning from the neck end, gently slide your hand between the skin and breast meat to loosen the skin. Smear all except two tbsps. of garlic-chili butter below the turkey skin. Brush the outside of the turkey with the rest of the garlic-chili butter. Transfer the turkey onto a rack set in a large roasting pan and roast for an hour. Mix 2/3 cup of chicken broth with orange juice. Spread the mixture on top of turkey. Continue to roast for about 3 hours more while basting with the pan juices after every 20 minutes and adding extra broth as required in case the pan juices evaporate, until the temperature at the thickest part of thigh is 180 degrees F on a thermometer. Place the turkey into a platter. Enclose with foil to keep it warm.

- Pour one cup of chicken broth into the pan juices and heat to boil while scraping up the browned bits. Then strain the pan juices into a heavy large saucepan and get rid of solids in the strainer. Scoop off fat on top and discard it. Add 5 1/2 cups of Giblet Stock, ancho paste, remaining garlic purée and tomato purée. Heat to boil on medium-high heat. Decrease the heat to medium and let to simmer uncovered while stirring often for about 10 minutes until thickened slightly. Stir in chocolate until smooth. Stir in the remaining one tbsp. of honey. Add pepper and salt to taste. You can serve the gravy together with turkey.

Nutrition Information

- Calories: 457
- Total Carbohydrate: 52 g
- Cholesterol: 35 mg
- Total Fat: 18 g
- Fiber: 4 g
- Protein: 25 g
- Sodium: 1177 mg
- Saturated Fat: 6 g

272. Red Lentil Dal

"A traditional dish from India."
Serving: Serves 4

Ingredients

- 1 tbsp. vegetable oil
- 2 cups chopped onions
- 3 garlic cloves, minced
- 3 cups water
- 1 cup dried red lentils*
- 3/4 tsp. turmeric
- 3/4 tsp. ground cumin
- 1/2 tsp. ground ginger
- 1 cup basmati rice,* cooked according to package directions
- 2 plum tomatoes, seeded, chopped
- 1/4 cup chopped fresh cilantro
- 1 jalapeño chili, seeded, chopped
- *Available at Indian markets and in many supermarkets.

Direction

- Heat oil on medium heat in medium skillet. Add 1 minced garlic clove and 1 cup onion; sauté for 10 minutes till golden brown and tender; put aside. Boil ginger, cumin, turmeric, 2 minced garlic cloves, leftover 1 cup onion, lentils and 3 cups water in medium heavy saucepan. Lower heat; cover. Simmer for 15 minutes till lentils are tender. Put 1/2 lentil mixture in processor; puree till smooth. Put puree in same saucepan; stir in sautéed onion mixture and simmer to blend flavors for 5 minutes. Season with pepper and salt to taste.
- In bowls, put rice; put dal on top. Top with chili, cilantro and tomatoes.

273. Red-fruit Puddings

"Tart small puddings!"
Serving: Makes 8 to 12 servings | Prep: 25m

Ingredients

- 3 (12-oz.) packages unsweetened frozen raspberries, thawed
- 2 (1/4-oz.) packages unflavored gelatin
- 1 cup bottled pomegranate juice
- 2 cups bottled wild lingonberry sauce or lingonberries (from two 14-oz. jars)
- 1/2 cup sugar
- Accompaniment: lightly sweetened whipped cream

Direction

- In food processor, puree raspberries with juices. Through fine-mesh sieve, force into bowl; discard solids.
- Sprinkle gelatin on pomegranate juice and stand to soften for 1 minute in a medium saucepan; cook on low heat till gelatin dissolves, mixing. Mix in sugar and lingonberry sauce; cook till sauce melts and sugar dissolves, mixing. Mix into berry puree.
- In ice bath, quick chill for 30 minutes till it starts to mound, occasionally mixing. Put into glasses/dishes; chill for minimum of 3 hours till set.
- You can chill puddings for maximum of 3 days.

274. Ricotta- And Walnut-stuffed Artichokes

"Such a lovely recipe!"
Serving: Makes 6 servings

Ingredients

- 1/3 cup fresh lemon juice
- 6 large artichokes
- 1 cup plus 2 tbsps. walnuts, toasted
- 1 16-oz. container whole-milk ricotta cheese
- 1/2 cup extra-virgin olive oil, divided
- 1 garlic clove, chopped
- 1 tsp. salt
- 1/4 tsp. ground white pepper
- 1/4 tsp. ground nutmeg
- 1/4 cup coarsely chopped fresh Italian parsley
- 3/4 cup water
- 1/2 cup dry white wine

Direction

- Use cold water to fill big bowl; add lemon juice. Cut off top 2-in. and stem from 1 artichoke. Cut off the point ends of the outer artichoke leaves using scissors. Scoop out the fuzzy choke from middle of artichoke using melon baller, making opening. Put artichoke into lemon water. Repeat using leftover artichokes. Boil a big pot of salted water. Add artichokes; cook for 15 minutes till tender when metal skewer pierces hearts of artichoke. Drain and cool them to room temperature.
- Chop walnuts coarsely in processor. Put 2 tbsp. chopped walnuts in small bowl; put aside. Put nutmeg, white pepper, salt, garlic, 1/4 cup olive oil and ricotta cheese to walnuts in processor and process till well blended. Put ricotta mixture in bowl; mix in parsley. Season with white pepper and extra salt to taste. Put ricotta mixture in middle of each artichoke using fingertips and tsp. as aids; between artichoke leaves, put some mixture. Put leftover 1/4 cup olive oil in 13x9x2-in. ceramic/glass dish. In dish, put stuffed artichokes. You can make it 6 hours ahead then cover; refrigerate.
- Preheat an oven to 375°F. Put wine and 3/4 cup water on bottom of dish with the artichokes. Use foil to cover dish; bake for 40 minutes till stuffing is slightly firm and artichokes are very tender. Uncover; sprinkle reserved 2 tbsp. chopped walnuts on artichokes. Bake for 10 minutes, uncovered. Stand for 10 minutes; serve.

Nutrition Information

- Calories: 428
- Total Carbohydrate: 22 g
- Cholesterol: 39 mg
- Total Fat: 33 g
- Fiber: 9 g
- Protein: 15 g
- Sodium: 607 mg
- Saturated Fat: 9 g

275. Ripley's Bloody Mary Mix For Canning

"Start the morning right with this bloody mary made from fresh ingredients."
Serving: 32 | Prep: 2h | Ready in: 11h5m

Ingredients

- 4 dried chile de arbol peppers
- 20 lbs. tomatoes, chopped
- 2 lbs. onions, chopped
- 4 green bell peppers, chopped
- 4 carrots, chopped
- 1 jalapeno pepper, chopped
- 4 cloves garlic, minced
- 2 (8 oz.) cans tomato sauce
- 1 cup vinegar
- 6 tbsps. prepared horseradish
- 4 tsps. kosher salt
- 4 tsps. Worcestershire sauce
- 2 tsps. freshly ground black pepper
- 5 bay leaves
- 1 tsp. celery seed
- 1 tsp. seafood seasoning (such as Old Bay®)
- 1 tsp. hot pepper sauce (such as Tabasco®)
- 1 cup lemon juice
- 8 (1 quart) sterilized canning jars with lids and rings

Direction

- In a mortar and pestle, pulverize chile de arbol peppers.
- In a food processor, process garlic, tomatoes, jalapeno pepper, onions, carrots, and green bell peppers. Work in batches until vegetables are finely chopped. Move mixture in a large pot.
- In the pot of vegetables, mix in hot pepper sauce, tomato sauce, seafood seasoning, vinegar, celery seeds, horseradish, bay leaves, ground chile de arbol peppers, black pepper, kosher salt, and Worcestershire sauce. Bring mixture to a boil. Lower heat and let it simmer for half an hour until the veggies are tender, stir constantly. Take out the bay leaves.
- In a vegetable juicer, blend the mixture in batches. If desired, strain the excess pulp from the mixture. On medium heat, pour juice to a large pot and heat until almost boiling. Mix in lemon juice.
- In boiling water, place jars and lids to sterilize for at least 5 minutes. Pour bloody mary mix in the hot and sterilized jars until a quarter inch from the top. To get rid of the air bubbles, slide a thin spatula or knife around the interior of the jars. Remove the residue from the jars' rims with a moist paper towel. Secure the lid and screw rings.
- Arrange a rack at the base of a canning kettle or a large stockpot. Pour in water until halfway full then boil. With a holder, place jars 2 inches apart in the boiling water. If needed, add more boiling water to keep the water level an inch over the jars' tops. Bring the water to a boil, cover the pot, and process for 40 minutes.
- Take the jars out of the pot and place them on a wood or cloth-covered surface giving a few inches of space in between allowing them to cool. With a finger, push the top of every lid to make sure that they don't move and are sealed tight. Place in a dark and cool place.

Nutrition Information

- Calories: 78 calories;
- Total Carbohydrate: 17.4 g
- Cholesterol: 0 mg
- Total Fat: 0.7 g
- Protein: 3.3 g

- Sodium: 371 mg

276. Roasted Cornish Hens With Black-olive Butter

"A savory recipe."
Serving: Makes 8 (main course) servings | Prep: 30m

Ingredients

- 2 garlic cloves
- 2 tbsps. coarsely chopped shallot
- 1 stick (1/2 cup) unsalted butter, softened
- 1/2 tsp. black pepper
- 1 tsp. salt
- 1 tbsp. coarsely chopped pitted Kalamata or other brine-cured black olives
- 1 tbsp. drained capers (in brine)
- 1 tbsp. olive oil
- 4 (1 1/4- to 1 1/2-lb) Cornish hens (not frozen), halved lengthwise
- 1/4 cup dry white wine
- a 17- by 13-inch heavy shallow metal baking pan

Direction

- In upper oven third, put oven rack; preheat an oven to 500°F.
- Drop garlic cloves in processor as food processor's motor runs; chop finely. Add shallot; pulse till finely chopped. Heat 1 tbsp. butter till foam subsides in a small skillet on medium heat. Add garlic mixture (don't wash food processor's bowl), 1/4 tsp. salt and pepper; cook for 3 minutes till garlic starts to be golden, occasionally mixing. Put garlic mixture in food processor; add capers and olives. Pulse till capers and olives are chopped finely. Add 5 tbsp. butter; pulse till smooth.
- Brush 1 tbsp. oil on baking pan.
- Slide index finger under skin around legs and on every breast, including drumsticks, without tearing skin, doing 1 hen half at 1 time; put 1 tbsp. olive butter under the skin on every half hen. Massage skin on breast, drumstick and thigh to distribute butter.
- Put hen halves in baking pan, skin sides up. Melt leftover 2 tbsp. butter in a small skillet; evenly brush on hen's skins. Evenly sprinkle leftover 3/4 tsp. salt.
- Roast hens for 30 minutes till cooked through and golden.
- Put hens on platter. Straddle baking pan above 2 burners; add wine. Simmer on low heat to deglaze pan for 2 minutes, mixing, scraping brown bits up with wooden spoon. Put pan sauce in small serving bowl; use spoon to skim fat. Serve sauce with hens.
- You can make olive butter 1 day ahead, covered, chilled. Before using, bring to room temperature.
- You can stuff hens with olive butter about 4 hours ahead, covered in plastic wrap, chilled in baking pan.

Nutrition Information

- Calories: 506
- Total Carbohydrate: 1 g
- Cholesterol: 223 mg
- Total Fat: 40 g
- Fiber: 0 g
- Protein: 33 g
- Sodium: 442 mg
- Saturated Fat: 15 g

277. Roasted Garlic, Brie And Grape Crostini

"An inventive appetizer."
Serving: Makes 24

Ingredients

- 30 garlic cloves, peeled
- 1/2 cup olive oil
- 3/4 tsp. ground thyme
- 1 1/2 cups seedless grapes, halved
- 1/4 cup ruby Port
- 1 tsp. chopped fresh rosemary

- 1 baguette, cut diagonally into 24 slices, toasted
- 8 oz. Brie cheese, rind removed, room temperature
- Fresh rosemary sprigs

Direction

- Preheat an oven to 325°F. In small baking dish, mix oil and garlic; bake for 30 minutes till garlic is tender. Drain; keep 3 tbsp. oil. Put garlic in processor. Add reserved oil and thyme; puree. You can make it 1 day ahead then chill; before using, bring to room temperature.
- Mix 1 tsp. rosemary, Port and grapes in bowl; stand for 15 minutes.
- Spread 1 tsp. garlic on each toast slice; spread 2 tsp. brie. Put herb sprigs and grapes over.

278. Roasted Salsa

""This salsa is made more flavorful because of the peppers and charred tomatoes.""
Serving: 32 | Prep: 15m | Ready in: 1h5m

Ingredients

- olive oil cooking spray
- 7 roma tomatoes, halved and cored, or more to taste
- 2 Anaheim chile peppers, halved lengthwise and seeded
- 2 jalapeno peppers
- 1 poblano chile pepper, halved lengthwise and seeded
- 2 onions, quartered
- 2 garlic cloves, peeled
- 1 lime, juiced
- 2 tbsps. chopped fresh cilantro, or more to taste
- 2 tbsps. cider vinegar, or more to taste
- 3/4 tsp. dried oregano, or more to taste
- 3/4 tsp. ground cumin, or more to taste
- 3/4 tsp. kosher salt, or more to taste
- 3/4 tsp. ground black pepper, or more to taste
- 1/2 tsp. celery salt, or more to taste

Direction

- Set the oven to 450°F or 230°C. Line a baking sheet with foil then apply cooking spray.
- Put the tomatoes in the baking sheet with the cut sides facing down. Add in the jalapeno peppers, Anaheim chile peppers and poblano peppers, all skin side facing up. Add in the garlic and onions; spray with cooking spray.
- Let it roast in the oven for about 40-45 minutes until the chile pepper and tomato skins are charred and blistering. Remove from the oven and let it cool 10-15 minutes. Keep the skins on the child peppers and tomatoes
- Transfer the mixture into a food processor and add cilantro, lime juice, oregano, cider vinegar, kosher salt, cumin, celery salt and black pepper. Process in quick pulses until you reach the desired consistency. Transfer to an airtight container and refrigerate.

Nutrition Information

- Calories: 12 calories;
- Total Carbohydrate: 2.6 g
- Cholesterol: 0 mg
- Total Fat: 0.1 g
- Protein: 0.4 g
- Sodium: 70 mg

279. Roasted Vegetables With Pecan Gremolata

"Parmesan and pecans add texture and richness to the traditional gremolata."
Serving: Makes 8 servings

Ingredients

- 1 lb. medium carrots, peeled, halved lengthwise, then crosswise
- 1 lb. medium parsnips, peeled, cut in half lengthwise, then crosswise

- 1 lb. turnips, peeled, halved, cut into 1-inch-thick wedges
- 1 1/4 lbs. brussels sprouts, trimmed, halved
- 6 tbsps. olive oil, divided
- 3/4 cup pecans
- 1/4 cup grated Parmesan cheese (about 1 oz.)
- 1/4 cup finely chopped fresh parsley
- 2 tbsps. fresh lemon juice, divided
- 1 tbsp. finely grated lemon peel
- 1 small garlic clove, minced

Direction

- Preheat an oven to 425 degrees Fahrenheit. In a large bowl, toss brussels sprouts, turnips, parsnips, and carrots with 3 tbsp. oil. Transfer the mixture onto a rimmed baking sheet and season with salt and pepper. Roast for about 1 hour, tossing often, until vegetables are tender and transfer to a large platter to cool.
- In a processor, use on/off turns to chop pecans until ground coarsely. Transfer to a small bowl and stir in 1 tbsp. oil, garlic, lemon peel, 1 tbsp. lemon juice, parsley, and grated cheese. Season the gremolata with salt to taste. Drizzle vegetables with remaining 1 tbsp. lemon juice and 2 tbsp. oil. Before serving, sprinkle gremolata over vegetables.

Nutrition Information

- Calories: 282
- Total Carbohydrate: 28 g
- Cholesterol: 2 mg
- Total Fat: 18 g
- Fiber: 9 g
- Protein: 6 g
- Sodium: 151 mg
- Saturated Fat: 3 g

280. Roasted-almond Ricotta Pesto With Olives

Serving: Makes 4 to 6 servings | Prep: 15m

Ingredients

- 1 small garlic clove
- 2/3 cup roasted unsalted almonds
- 4 cups basil leaves
- 1 tsp. fresh lemon juice
- 1/4 cup grated Parmigiano-Reggiano
- 1/4 cup extra-virgin olive oil
- 3/4 cup ricotta (preferably fresh)
- 1/2 cup chopped pitted Kalamata olives
- Accompaniment: 1 lb. spaghetti, cooked and drained, reserving 1 cup cooking water

Direction

- Drop in garlic as food processor runs; chop finely. Stop motor; add 1/2 tsp. pepper, 1/4 tsp. salt, parmesan, lemon juice, basil and almonds. Process till chopped finely. Add oil as motor runs, blending till incorporated.
- Put into a big bowl; mix in olives and ricotta. Season using salt.
- Toss pesto with hot spaghetti; use some cooking water to thin.

Nutrition Information

- Calories: 390
- Total Carbohydrate: 9 g
- Cholesterol: 29 mg
- Total Fat: 35 g
- Fiber: 4 g
- Protein: 14 g
- Sodium: 248 mg
- Saturated Fat: 8 g

281. Roasted-pepper And Almond Mayonnaise

"Great sauce for burgers or grilled veggies or fish."
Serving: Makes about 1 cup | Prep: 10m

Ingredients

- 1/2 cup mayonnaise
- 1/4 cup drained bottled roasted red peppers, chopped
- 1/4 cup salted roasted almonds
- 1 garlic clove, smashed
- 2 tsps. Sherry vinegar, or to taste
- 1/8 tsp. cayenne

Direction

- Blend all ingredients till smooth in a food processor or blender; chill for 1 hour to develop flavors, covered.

Nutrition Information

- Calories: 128
- Total Carbohydrate: 1 g
- Cholesterol: 6 mg
- Total Fat: 13 g
- Fiber: 1 g
- Protein: 1 g
- Sodium: 105 mg
- Saturated Fat: 2 g

282. Roman Garlic And Anchovy Salad Dressing

"Whole packed anchovies are best, bottled anchovies are good too, but canned should be your last choice. Don't use anchovy paste."
Serving: Makes about 1/2 cup

Ingredients

- 3 whole anchovies packed in salt or 6 bottled or canned flat anchovy fillets
- 1/4 cup plus 2 tbsps. red-wine vinegar
- 2 to 3 garlic cloves
- 1/2 cup extra-virgin olive oil
- fine sea salt to taste
- freshly ground black pepper to taste

Direction

- Mix 1/4 cup vinegar and anchovies in a bowl; stand for 2 hours if using canned/bottle or 6 hours for salted anchovies. Drain anchovies; if using salted, debone. Rinse well. Between paper towels, pat dry anchovies then blend with garlic till garlic is minced in a small food processor. Add pepper, salt, leftover 2 tbsp. vinegar and oil; blend dressing till emulsified and smooth. Dressing keeps for 1 week, chilled, covered.

Nutrition Information

- Calories: 252
- Total Carbohydrate: 1 g
- Cholesterol: 3 mg
- Total Fat: 27 g
- Fiber: 0 g
- Protein: 1 g
- Sodium: 127 mg
- Saturated Fat: 4 g

283. Rudy's Garlic Scape Pesto

"Pesto freezes well. Fantastic with chilled pasta salad and grilled chicken."
Serving: 16 | Prep: 10m | Ready in: 10m

Ingredients

- 6 garlic scapes, chopped
- 1/2 cup freshly grated Parmesan cheese
- 1/2 cup freshly grated Asiago cheese
- 1 tbsp. fresh lemon juice
- 1/4 cup pine nuts
- 3/4 cup extra-virgin olive oil
- salt and pepper to taste

Direction

- In a food processor, put pine nuts, lemon juice, Asiago cheese, parmesan cheese and garlic scapes. Drizzle olive oil on the mixture. Blend until smooth and bright green in color. Season with pepper and salt.

Nutrition Information

- Calories: 138 calories;
- Total Carbohydrate: 2.3 g
- Cholesterol: 5 mg
- Total Fat: 13.3 g
- Protein: 2.7 g
- Sodium: 80 mg

284. Rum Balls

"Good rum ball."
Serving: 24 | Prep: 20m | Ready in: 1h10m

Ingredients

- 1 (12 oz.) box vanilla wafer cookies (such as Nilla®)
- 1 cup semisweet chocolate chips
- 1/4 cup light corn syrup
- 3/4 cup dark rum (such as Meyer's®)
- 1 cup confectioners' sugar, plus more for dusting

Direction

- In food processor, put the vanilla cookies and pulse till fine crumbs form.
- In saucepan, heat corn syrup and chocolate chips on low heat. Cook for 5 minutes, mixing frequently, till chocolate melts and smoothen. Take off from heat and mix in confectioners' sugar and rum till smooth. Fold cookie crumbs in; dough will become gooey.
- Put the saucepan in fridge for 15 minutes, till dough firms and becomes easy to form. Use waxed paper to cover two plates; sprinkle confectioners' sugar over.
- Form the dough making an-inch balls; put onto prepped plates. Sprinkle confectioners' sugar on rum balls. Chill for half an hour, till set.
- Take rum balls out of the fridge and place into a sealable bag, put in additional confectioners' sugar. Enclose bag and shake to cover rum balls fully in confectioners' sugar.

Nutrition Information

- Calories: 148 calories;
- Total Carbohydrate: 22.3 g
- Cholesterol: 0 mg
- Total Fat: 4.9 g
- Protein: 0.9 g
- Sodium: 46 mg

285. Rutabaga Purée

"Great to go with pork tenderloin."
Serving: Makes 6 servings

Ingredients

- 3 lbs. rutabagas, peeled, cut into 1-inch cubes
- 3 tbsps. butter

Direction

- In a big pot of boiling salted water, cook rutabagas for 45 minutes until very tender. Drain well. Put in processor. Puree it until smooth. Return in pot. Mix until extra liquid evaporates on medium heat. Stir in butter until melted. Season with pepper and salt. You can make this 2 hours in advance, standing at room temperature, uncovered. Rewarm again on medium heat, mixing often.

Nutrition Information

- Calories: 135
- Total Carbohydrate: 20 g
- Cholesterol: 15 mg
- Total Fat: 6 g
- Fiber: 5 g

- Protein: 3 g
- Sodium: 28 mg
- Saturated Fat: 4 g

286. Salmon Rillettes

"A lovely recipe."
Serving: Makes around 1 1/2 cups or around 8 servings | Prep: 15m

Ingredients

- 1 celery stalk, sliced thin
- 1 onion, sliced thin
- 1 leek, sliced thin
- 1 tsp. whole peppercorns
- 1 bay leaf
- 1 cup white wine
- 1 lemon, halved
- 6 oz. king salmon filet
- 2 oz. crème fraîche (budget partiers can substitute sour cream or a cream and sour cream combo)
- 2 tbsps. minced chives
- 3 tbsps. lemon extra virgin olive oil
- salt and freshly ground black pepper

Direction

- Simmer big pot of water. Add lemon, wine, bay leaf, peppercorns, leek, onion and celery; simmer for 25 minutes.
- Add salmon; cover pot. Take off heat; stand for 10 minutes.
- Take out salmon; chill in the fridge. Discard veggie water.
- Whip salmon with olive oil, chives and crème fraiche by hand/in food processor. To taste, add pepper and salt; keep spread chilled till serving.

Nutrition Information

- Calories: 129
- Total Carbohydrate: 3 g
- Cholesterol: 15 mg
- Total Fat: 9 g
- Fiber: 1 g
- Protein: 5 g
- Sodium: 177 mg
- Saturated Fat: 2 g

287. Salsa Quemada (roasted Tomato Salsa)

"A great salsa recipe."
Serving: Makes 2 1/2 cups

Ingredients

- 5 large Roma tomatoes, whole, not cored or cut in any way
- 1 serrano or jalapeño chile
- 2 cloves garlic, skin on
- 1/4 cup minced white onion
- 1 tsp. salt, or to taste
- 1/2 bunch cilantro

Direction

- Be sure the kitchen is ventilated well. Put aluminum foil piece in a heavy, cast-iron is best, sauté pan; put on medium high heat. Put garlic cloves, chile and whole tomatoes in the pan; dry-roast on all sides till soft and well charred. Tomatoes might take around 10 minutes to cook; chiles and garlic cook quickly.
- Peel garlic; stem chile. Put cilantro, salt, onion, chile, garlic and tomatoes in a food processor; pulse till salsa is smooth. Taste for seasoning. Salsa keeps for a few days, refrigerated. Before use, reseason.

Nutrition Information

- Calories: 21
- Total Carbohydrate: 4 g
- Total Fat: 0 g
- Fiber: 1 g
- Protein: 1 g
- Sodium: 217 mg

- Saturated Fat: 0 g

288. Sarson Ka Saag (Indian Mustard Greens)

"This dish is North Indian vegetarian recipe. Using and Indian butter made from cow's milk known as ghee is essential, since ghee produces that distinct savor."
Serving: 6 | Prep: 25m | Ready in: 45m

Ingredients

- 2 large dried red chile peppers (optional)
- 2 bunches fresh spinach, washed and chopped
- 1 bunch mustard greens, washed and chopped
- 2 tbsps. ghee (clarified butter)
- 1/2 tsp. cumin seeds
- 1/4 cup finely chopped onion
- 1/2 tsp. ginger paste
- 2 tsps. garlic paste
- 1/2 tomato, chopped
- salt to taste
- 1/2 tsp. white sugar, or to taste
- 1/4 cup water (optional)

Direction

- Put the chiles in a dry skillet and set it over medium heat. Stir while the chiles cook for 1 to 2 minutes until turns dark red-brown in color and aromatic. Take off from heat and let the chiles cool. Get rid of the stems and shake out seeds, tear the flesh of the roasted chiles into bits. Put aside.
- Put the spinach in a saucepan set over medium heat; place the mustard greens in a different saucepan. If leaves appears dry, mix in 1 or 2 tbsps. of water. If leaves looks wet, just cover the pans and make it to simmer for about 10 minutes until the greens have softened. Let the leaves cool.
- Put the greens together in the work bowl of a food processor. Pulse for quite a few times to break up the greens the process for about 1 minute to form a paste.
- Put the ghee in a big saucepan set over medium heat. Add the cumin seeds, keep stirring for about half a minute or until the seeds turn darker brown and sizzles. Add the onion, sauté for roughly 3 minutes until it turns lightly browned; stir in the ginger paste, roasted peppers, tomato and garlic paste. Stir in the pureed greens and make it to simmer; spice it up with salt and sugar. If the dish turns out too thick, stir in about a quarter cup of water, a tbsp. at a time. Mix until the desired consistency of the greens has achieved.

Nutrition Information

- Calories: 89 calories;
- Total Carbohydrate: 8.5 g
- Cholesterol: 11 mg
- Total Fat: 4.9 g
- Protein: 4.8 g
- Sodium: 160 mg

289. Sauerkraut Pierogi Filling

"A conventional filling recipe with onion, mushroom and sauerkraut."
Serving: 24 | Prep: 5m | Ready in: 37m

Ingredients

- 16 oz. sauerkraut
- 1/2 cup butter
- 1 onion, chopped
- 1 cup chopped mushrooms (optional)
- salt and ground black pepper to taste

Direction

- In a food processor, grind the sauerkraut, then move it into a pan. Cook and stir for about 10 minutes on medium heat until it becomes soft; use a colander to drain.
- In a pan, heat the butter on medium heat. Mix in the mushrooms and onions. Cook and stir for about 10 minutes until the onion becomes translucent and soft.

- Mix the onion mixture with the sauerkraut and put pepper and salt; cook for 2 minutes. Spread it on a plate to fully cool.

Nutrition Information

- Calories: 42 calories;
- Total Carbohydrate: 1.8 g
- Cholesterol: 10 mg
- Total Fat: 3.9 g
- Protein: 0.4 g
- Sodium: 158 mg

290. Sautéed Striped Bass With Mint Pesto And Spiced Carrots

"So tasty!"
Serving: Makes 4 servings

Ingredients

- 1/4 cup (packed) fresh mint leaves
- 1/4 cup lightly toasted shelled unsalted natural pistachios
- 1/4 cup extra-virgin olive oil
- 1 garlic clove, peeled
- Coarse kosher salt
- 1 tbsp. extra-virgin olive oil
- 2 tbsps. chopped fresh mint
- 1 tbsp. chopped fresh thyme
- 4 (6- to 8-oz.) striped bass fillets (with or without skin)
- 1/2 tsp. coriander seeds
- 1/2 tsp. cumin seeds
- 1/2 tsp. fennel seeds
- 3 tbsps. extra-virgin olive oil, divided
- 12 oz. medium carrots, peeled, thinly sliced into rounds
- 1/8 tsp. dried crushed red pepper
- 1 cup low-salt chicken broth
- 3 tbsps. fresh lemon juice

Direction

- Pesto: Blend garlic, olive oil, pistachios and mint leaves till coarse puree forms in processor; season using coarse salt. You can make it 1 day ahead, chilled, covered. Before using, bring to room temperature and mix.
- Fish: In small bowl, mix thyme, mint and olive oil. Spread herb mixture on both fish fillet's side all over; cover. Refrigerate fish for minimum of 3- maximum of 5 hours.
- Spiced carrots: mix all seeds in dry small skillet on medium heat for 2 minutes till fragrant. Put seeds in a mortar/spice mill; coarsely grind.
- Heat 1 tbsp. oil on medium high heat in heavy big skillet. Add ground seeds, crushed red pepper and carrots; sauté for 5 minutes till carrots start to brown in spots. Add lemon juice and broth; boil. Lower heat to medium low and cover; simmer for 6 minutes till carrots are tender. Season with pepper and salt to taste. You can make it 2 hours ahead, standing in room temperature.
- Sprinkle pepper and salt on fish. Heat 1 tbsp. oil in each of 2 big nonstick skillets on medium high heat then add fish; cook for 5 minutes total till opaque in middle and both sides are browned.
- Rewarm carrots till just heated through. Divide juices and carrots to 4 plates. Put 1 fish fillet on each serving; put pesto over.

Nutrition Information

- Calories: 530
- Total Carbohydrate: 13 g
- Cholesterol: 159 mg
- Total Fat: 36 g
- Fiber: 4 g
- Protein: 39 g
- Sodium: 927 mg
- Saturated Fat: 5 g

291. Scott's Holiday Cranberry Salad

"Make the dressing with cream cheese, Cool Whip® and Miracle Whip® to complement this wonderful fresh uncooked cranberry salad."
Serving: 10 | Prep: 25m | Ready in: 8h25m

Ingredients

- Cranberry Salad:
- 1 tbsp. creamy salad dressing (such as Miracle Whip®), or as needed
- 2 oranges
- 1 (12 oz.) bag fresh cranberries
- 2 apples, unpeeled and cored
- 2 1/2 cups boiling water, or as needed
- 1 (.25 oz.) package unflavored gelatin (such as Knox ®)
- 1/2 cup cold water
- 1 (6 oz.) package raspberry-flavored gelatin mix (such as Jell-O®)
- 2 cups white sugar
- 2 cups halved seedless grapes
- 2 cups chopped pecans
- Dressing:
- 1 1/2 cups frozen whipped topping (such as Cool Whip®), thawed
- 1 (8 oz.) package cream cheese, softened
- 3 tbsps. creamy salad dressing (such as Miracle Whip®)
- 2 tsps. white sugar
- 1 sprig fresh parsley

Direction

- Use 1 tbsp. of creamy salad dressing to grease a ring mold. Zest 1 orange and remove the peel of both oranges.
- In the bowl of a food processor, place apples, cranberries, orange zest and oranges together then pulse to chop coarsely. Strain juice from the fruit pieces and save in a measuring cup with quart size. Measure 3 cups of liquid by pouring enough boiling water.
- In a large bowl, let unflavored gelatin dissolve in cold water then pour over with juice-water mixture. Stir in 2 cups of sugar and raspberry gelatin till completely dissolved. Stir in pecans, grapes and fruit mixture. In the prepped ring mold, place the gelatin mixture and let chill for 8 hours or overnight.
- In a bowl, mix 2 tsp of sugar, 3 tbsp. of creamy salad dressing, cream cheese and whipped topping together till smooth.
- Loosen the gelatin mold by dipping the chilled mold a few inches into the hot water. Turn out and place on serving platter. Add parsley for garnish. Enjoy with dressing.

Nutrition Information

- Calories: 556 calories;
- Total Carbohydrate: 76.1 g
- Cholesterol: 27 mg
- Total Fat: 28.1 g
- Protein: 6.5 g
- Sodium: 184 mg

292. Sea Bass With Red Pepper And Olive Tapenade

Serving: Makes 6 servings

Ingredients

- 1/2 cup fresh breadcrumbs made from soft white bread
- 1/3 cup Kalamata olives or other brine-cured black olives, pitted
- 1/3 cup roasted red peppers from jar, drained
- 3 tbsps. purchased pesto
- 3 1/2 tbsps. olive oil
- 6 6-oz. sea bass fillets
- Lemon wedges
- Fresh parsley sprigs (optional)

Direction

- In a processor, mix the initial four ingredients. Pour in 2 tbsps. of oil; puree till nearly smooth. Season with pepper and salt to taste.

(Tapenade may be done 3 days in advance. Refrigerate with cover.)
- Heat an oven to 400 degrees F. In a big, heavy skillet, heat leftover 1 1/2 tbsps. of oil on high heat. Scatter pepper and salt on sea bass. Put fish in to skillet, in batches if need be, and cook about 2 minutes on each side. Turn onto a baking sheet with rim. Smear 2 tbsps. of tapenade over every fish fillet. Let fish bake approximately 8 minutes, till opaque in the middle. Turn onto plates. Jazz up using parsley sprigs if wished and lemon wedges.

Nutrition Information

- Calories: 356
- Total Carbohydrate: 8 g
- Cholesterol: 72 mg
- Total Fat: 20 g
- Fiber: 1 g
- Protein: 34 g
- Sodium: 347 mg
- Saturated Fat: 4 g

293. Sesame Balls With Drunken Fig Filling

"Sesame balls."
Serving: Makes 25 balls

Ingredients

- 2 1/4 cups (15 3/4 oz./448grams) dried figs, preferably Black Mission, stemmed and quartered
- 1/2 cup (3 1/2 oz./98 grams) sugar
- 1 tsp. salt
- 1/4 cup (2 oz./56 grams) cognac or dark rum
- 1 cup (7 oz./200 grams) sugar
- 1 tbsp. salt
- 1 1/2 tsps. baking soda
- 5 1/3 oz. (150 grams) taro, deeply peeled and cut crosswise into 1/2-inch slices
- 3 1/2 cups (16 1/8 oz./462 grams) glutinous rice flour
- Canola, vegetable, or other neutral oil for deep-frying
- 1 cup (3 3/8 oz./96 grams) white sesame seeds

Direction

- Prepare drunken fig filling: in a big mixing bowl place every ingredient and mix thoroughly to cover figs in sugar. Put aside with cover at room temperature for no less than half an hour up to overnight.
- Remove figs including the liquid into bowl of an electric mixer equipped with paddle attachment or a food processor. Blend or whip mixture till crushed into paste. (You may even crush mixture by hand using fork.) Chill with cover till set to use; you may store filling for maximum of 2 weeks.
- Prep sesame balls: in an electric mixer's bowl equipped with paddle attachment, put salt, baking soda and sugar, and combine thoroughly; put aside.
- Pour water into a big saucepan equipped with rack or steamer basket, filling it to 2-inch depth then let come to a rolling boil. Place taro into the basket; let steam for 10 minutes, till extremely tender; it must fall apart once puncture with knife. Put taro into sugar mixture immediately, and whip for 5 minutes on moderate speed till pasty and smooth.
- Meantime, boil a cup plus two tbsps. of water.
- Switch the speed of mixer to low; put in glutinous rice flour. Pour in all boiling water once mixture is crumbly. (The water should be boiling one poured in.) Keep on whipping till dough becomes soft and just a bit sticky. Press dough to ball, use plastic wrap to encase it, then put aside till it reaches a room temperature.
- Form dough to an-inch log, and slice log making 2-inches-long portions. Pat every dough piece one by one using your palm making a 4-inch across with quarter-inch-thick circle. Place a tbsp. cold fig filling in the middle of circle, then gather edges making half-moon and press to enclose. Tear off extra

dough at both ends and form filled dumpling making ball. Put aside.
- Pour oil into a heavy, deep saucepan filling it no less than 3-inch depth oil and heat to 300 degrees F. Pour water into a shallow dish filling it 1/8-inch then with sesame seeds into a different shallow dish. Roll one sesame ball into water, sufficient just to moisten, then in sesame seeds till covered thoroughly. Push the seeds to make them adhere to balls, if need be. Put covered ball down in oil carefully; cook for 5 minutes, without mixing, till it rises and becomes pale golden brown and crispy. You may cook approximately eight balls at one time, yet avoid overcrowding the pan. Take out of oil cautiously and transfer onto paper towels to drain. Redo with the rest of the balls. Serve at room temperature or while hot.

Nutrition Information

- Calories: 168
- Total Carbohydrate: 32 g
- Total Fat: 3 g
- Fiber: 2 g
- Protein: 2 g
- Sodium: 143 mg
- Saturated Fat: 0 g

294. Shrimp And Artichokes In Peppery Butter Sauce

Serving: Serves 2

Ingredients

- 2 large artichokes (each about 3/4 lb.)
- 1 large garlic clove
- 1 tbsp. fresh lemon juice or to taste
- 1 tbsp. freshly ground black pepper
- 2 tsps. Worcestershire sauce
- 1/2 tsp. Tabasco
- 1/2 tsp. dried basil, crumbled
- 1/2 tsp. salt, or to taste
- 1/4 tsp. dried oregano, crumbled
- 1/4 tsp. cayenne
- 1 stick (1/2 cup) cold unsalted butter, cut into bits
- 1/2 lb. small shrimp in their shells, preferably with heads (about 24)
- 3 scallions, minced
- Accompaniments: crusty bread and lemon wedges

Direction

- Use a serrated knife to cut out the artichoke stems and throw away. Use scissors to trim off the leaf tips. In a big saucepan with boiling salted water, cook the artichokes until the bottoms become tender once pierced with a knife, around 30-45 minutes.
- As the artichokes cook, set the oven to 500 degrees Fahrenheit.
- Drop the garlic in a running food processor and mince. Turn the machine off and add cayenne, oregano, salt, basil, Tabasco, Worcestershire sauce, black pepper, and lemon juice, then pulse to blend. Add the butter and blend until well combined.
- Spread the shrimp in a shallow 3 cup baking dish that's big enough to hold them in a single layer and sprinkle with the scallions. Drop the butter mixture by spoonfuls evenly on top and bake, stirring one or two times, until the shrimps are cooked through, roughly 5 minutes.
- Invert the artichokes onto paper towels to drain. Divide the shrimp and artichokes with the sauce among the soup plates and serve along with lemon wedges and crusty bread.

Nutrition Information

- Calories: 591
- Total Carbohydrate: 25 g
- Cholesterol: 265 mg
- Total Fat: 48 g
- Fiber: 10 g
- Protein: 22 g
- Sodium: 872 mg
- Saturated Fat: 30 g

295. Simple Basil-spinach Pesto

"Spinach and basil can be switches for 2 kinds of pesto or mix them both together."
Serving: 4 | Prep: 5m | Ready in: 5m

Ingredients

- 1/2 cup fresh basil leaves, packed
- 1/2 cup fresh spinach leaves
- 1/4 cup pine nuts
- 2 cloves garlic, minced
- 1/2 cup extra-virgin olive oil
- 1/4 cup freshly grated Parmesan cheese

Direction

- In a food processor, blend pine nuts, spinach and basil for about 30 seconds until chopped finely. Pulse garlic in for 15-30 seconds. Slowly add oil as processor runs. Stop and scrape sides using a rubber spatula when needed. Add parmesan cheese. Pulse until combined.

Nutrition Information

- Calories: 326 calories;
- Total Carbohydrate: 2.2 g
- Cholesterol: 4 mg
- Total Fat: 33.8 g
- Protein: 4.3 g
- Sodium: 80 mg

296. Simple Sweet Potato Soup

"It's a delicious soup made of six ingredients."
Serving: 8 | Prep: 15m | Ready in: 50m

Ingredients

- 6 medium sweet potatoes, peeled and chopped
- 1 tbsp. minced fresh ginger
- 2 cups chicken or vegetable stock
- 1 cup water, or as needed
- 1 lime, juiced
- 2 cups milk or cream, or as needed

Direction

- In a big saucepan, add ginger and potatoes. Put in water and chicken stock, then bring to a boil on high heat. Lower heat to moderately low, place a cover and simmer for a half hour, until potatoes are soft. In a food processor or a hand blender, puree the lime juice and potatoes together until smooth. Turn the soup back to saucepan and stir in cream or milk as wanted. Heat until warmed through.

Nutrition Information

- Calories: 187 calories;
- Total Carbohydrate: 37.8 g
- Cholesterol: 6 mg
- Total Fat: 2.2 g
- Protein: 4.8 g
- Sodium: 291 mg

297. Simple Vegan Tzatziki Sauce

"It's a mild, great and refreshing tzatziki sauce for vegans that is great to serve as a dip or cooling sauce."
Serving: 16 | Prep: 10m | Ready in: 10m

Ingredients

- 1 (14 oz.) package soft tofu, chilled
- 1 cucumber, peeled and quartered
- 1/4 tsp. orange zest, or to taste

Direction

- In a food processor, puree together orange zest, cucumber and tofu until smooth.

Nutrition Information

- Calories: 21 calories;
- Total Carbohydrate: 1.1 g
- Cholesterol: 0 mg
- Total Fat: 1.2 g
- Protein: 2.1 g
- Sodium: 2 mg

298. Small Pear And Almond Cakes

"Cute and yummy."
Serving: Makes 12 servings | Prep: 45m

Ingredients

- 12 firm small Seckel pears (2 to 3 inches long)
- 1 tbsp. fresh lemon juice
- 2 cups Essencia or other Muscat wine
- 1/2 tbsp. unsalted butter
- 1 1/2 cups whole blanched almonds (1/2 lb)
- 1 cup plus 1 tbsp. sugar
- 2 sticks (1 cup) unsalted butter, softened, plus additional for greasing ramekins
- 1 tsp. pure vanilla extract
- 4 large eggs
- 2/3 cup all-purpose flour plus additional for dusting
- 3/8 tsp. salt
- a small melon-ball cutter; 12 (4-oz) ramekins or 2 muffin pans with 6 large (1-cup) muffin cups

Direction

- Poach pears: Leaving stems intact, peel pears; core from bottom using melon-ball cutter. As peeled, toss lemon juice and pears in a bowl; put in 10-in. heavy skillet on their sides. Add lemon juice from bowl, butter and wine; liquid won't cover pears. Boil; lower heat. Simmer for 10-20 minutes till pears are tender, covered. Put pears in a dish with slotted spoon; boil poaching liquid with no cover for 12-15 minutes till reduced to 1/4 cup and syrupy. Put syrup on pears; cool for 10 minutes to room temperature, occasionally mixing.
- Prep cakes: In center position, put oven rack; preheat the oven to 400°F.
- Pulse 1/2 cup sugar and almonds till finely ground in a food processor; put in bowl. Don't clean processor.
- Process 1/2 cup sugar and butter till creamy and pale in processor; pulse in vanilla. One by one, add eggs; blend well after each. Pulse in salt, flour and almond mixture just till combined.
- Lightly butter then flour ramekins; knock out extra flour. Put in baking pan. Divide batter to ramekins; slightly rounded 1/2 cup for each ramekin. Nestle a pear into batter in middle of every cake gently, slightly leaning it, very lightly pressing it. Cakes rise around pears while baking. Keep reduced poaching liquid for another time. Sprinkle leftover tbsp. sugar on tops of cakes and pears.
- Bake for 20 minutes till cakes are pale golden and just firm while edges are slightly darker, rotating the pan halfway through baking.
- Put ramekins on rack; cool for 10 minutes. Run thin knife around each cake's edge; invert onto plate. Flip cakes right side up; serve at room temperature/warm.
- Use 6 peeled, cored then lengthwise halved Forelle pears if you can't find the others.
- You can poach pears 2 days ahead, covered, chilled.
- You can bake cake 8 hours ahead, fully cooled, uncovered, then kept in room temperature, covered with plastic wrap loosely.

Nutrition Information

- Calories: 523
- Total Carbohydrate: 58 g
- Cholesterol: 106 mg
- Total Fat: 28 g
- Fiber: 8 g
- Protein: 8 g
- Sodium: 128 mg
- Saturated Fat: 11 g

299. Smoked Salmon Rillettes On Tortilla Wafers

"A delicious recipe."
Serving: Makes about 40

Ingredients

- 5 8-inch-diameter flour tortillas

- Olive oil
- 3 tbsps. water
- 1 9-oz. salmon fillet with skin
- 1/2 lb. thinly sliced smoked salmon, coarsely chopped
- 1/3 cup crème fraîche or sour cream
- 1/4 cup (1/2 stick) butter, room temperature
- 1 tbsp. minced fresh tarragon
- 1 tbsp. fresh lemon juice
- 1 1/2 tsps. grated lemon peel
- Finely chopped fresh chives

Direction

- Preheat an oven to 375°F. Cut 8 rounds out from every tortilla with 2-in. diameter cookie cutter. Put rounds onto big heavy baking sheet; brush olive oil on both sides of the tortilla rounds. Bake for 9 minutes till rounds are crisp and golden; put aside tortilla wafers.
- Preheat an oven to 400°F. On a heavy rimmed baking sheet, sprinkle 3 tbsp. water. Put salmon fillet on baking sheet, skin side down; sprinkle with pepper and salt. Bake for 15 minutes till salmon is opaque in middle; fully cool. From salmon, remove the skin. Coarsely flake salmon to into big bowl.
- With on/off turns, blend butter, crème fraiche, smoked salmon and flaked salmon till coarse paste forms in a food processor; don't over process.
- Put salmon mixture in a medium bowl; mix in lemon peel, lemon juice and tarragon. Season rillettes with pepper and salt to taste; cover. Refrigerate for 2 hours till firm. You can make it 2 days ahead; keep wafers in room temperature, airtight. Keep rillettes refrigerated.
- Spread tortilla wafers over rillettes; put wafers onto platters. Sprinkle with chives; serve.

Nutrition Information

- Calories: 55
- Total Carbohydrate: 3 g
- Cholesterol: 9 mg
- Total Fat: 3 g
- Fiber: 0 g
- Protein: 3 g
- Sodium: 88 mg
- Saturated Fat: 1 g

300. Smoked Trout Soufflé In A Phyllo Crust

Serving: Serves 6 as a main course

Ingredients

- eight 17- by 12-inch phyllo sheets
- 5 1/2 tbsps. unsalted butter
- 1 1/2 tbsps. all-purpose flour
- 1/2 cup whole milk
- 1/2 cup heavy cream
- 2 smoked trout fillets* (about 1/2 lb. total)
- 6 large eggs
- 1 1/2 tsps. drained bottled horseradish
- 2 tbsps. fresh dill leaves
- *available at fish markets, the deli counter of many supermarkets

Direction

- With overlapping plastic wrap sheets, cover phyllo stack then with a damp kitchen towel.
- Melt 4 tbsp. butter. On a work surface, put 1 phyllo sheet. Brush some melted butter on. Put an extra sheet to overlap the original one. Make a 17-in. square. Brush butter on it. Keep layering with butter and remaining 6 sheets. Over a 10-in. tart pan that has a removable bottom, drape phyllo stack and fit phyllo in the pan. Crumple the overhang against the rim's inside edges to make a ragged edge that is 1-in. above the rim. Chill shell for at least 3 hours until firm while loosely covered.
- Preheat the oven to 375 degrees F.
- Use a fork to prick the shell's bottom all over. Bake for 15 minutes in the center of the oven until it's golden. On a rack, cool shell in pan. You can make this 1 day in advance, covered in cool room temperature.
- Melt remaining 1 1/2 tbsp. butter in a saucepan on medium low heat. Whisk flour in.

Cook roux for 3 minutes, stirring, and mix in cream and milk. Boil mixture, constantly whisking, then simmer for 3 minutes, occasionally whisking. Season pepper and salt into mixture. Cool.

- Throw trout bones and skin. Break fish to small pieces. Separate the eggs. Pulse dill, horseradish, yolks, trout and milk mixture in a food processor until smooth. Put in a big bowl.
- Use an electric mixer to beat a pinch of salt and whites in another big bowl just until they hold stiff peaks. Mix 1/4 whites in the trout mixture to lighten. Fold remaining whites thoroughly but gently.
- Put soufflé mixture in the shell. Run a knife's tip around the souffle's edge to aid in rising. Bake soufflé for 25 minutes on a baking sheet on the lower third of the oven until golden brown and puffed. Immediately serve soufflé.

Nutrition Information

- Calories: 395
- Total Carbohydrate: 17 g
- Cholesterol: 271 mg
- Total Fat: 28 g
- Fiber: 1 g
- Protein: 19 g
- Sodium: 241 mg
- Saturated Fat: 14 g

301. Smoky Black Bean Dip

Serving: Makes about 4 cups

Ingredients

- 4 bacon slices
- 1 medium onion, chopped
- 1 small red bell pepper, seeded, chopped
- 1/2 tsp. ground cumin
- 1/2 tsp. dried oregano
- 2 15-oz. cans black beans, undrained
- 1 tsp. chopped seeded canned chipotle chilies*
- 1/2 cup sour cream
- 2 tbsps. chopped fresh cilantro

Direction

- Over medium heat, cook bacon in a heavy large skillet for about 6 minutes until crisp. Drain with paper towels. Chop the bacon coarsely. Drain off all except one tbsp. of drippings from the skillet. Add bell pepper and onion. Sauté for about 6 minutes until the onion becomes soft. Add oregano and cumin and then sauté for one minute. Pour in chipotles and beans along with their liquid. Let to simmer while stirring often on medium-low heat for about 5 minutes until thickened slightly.
- Pour one cup of the bean mixture into the processor and then blend until the resulting mix is smooth. Mix the blended mixture into the remaining bean mixture. Add pepper and salt to taste. Pour into a bowl. Cover the bowl and chill for two hours. (You can make two days ahead. Then refrigerate bacon and dip separately). Mix half of the bacon into the dip. Add sour cream on top. Drizzle with the remaining bacon and cilantro. Can serve the dip at lukewarm or chilled.

Nutrition Information

- Calories: 192
- Total Carbohydrate: 20 g
- Cholesterol: 17 mg
- Total Fat: 9 g
- Fiber: 8 g
- Protein: 9 g
- Sodium: 255 mg
- Saturated Fat: 4 g

302. Sour Cream Chocolate-chip Cake

"Easy and yummy."
Serving: Makes 12 servings

Ingredients

- 1 cup finely chopped pecans

- 1/4 cup whole pecans
- 1 12-oz. package of chocolate chips
- 1/4 cup packed brown sugar
- 2 tsps. cinnamon
- 2 cups flour
- 1 cup sugar
- 1/2 cup (1 stick) butter
- 2 eggs
- 1 cup sour cream
- 2 tsps. vanilla
- 1 1/2 tsps. baking powder
- 1 tsp. baking soda
- 1 tsp. cinnamon
- 1/4 cup powdered sugar (optional)

Direction

- Preheat an oven to 350°F. Butter the 10- to 12-cup Bundt pan and dust with flour.
- Topping: Mix cinnamon, chopped pecans, chocolate chips and brown sugar in medium bowl; put aside.
- Batter: Sift baking soda, baking powder and flour into a medium bowl; put aside.
- Cream sugar and butter using an electric mixer till blended fully. Beat in eggs then sour cream till smooth and creamy; add sifted dry ingredients slowly, being sure to scrape bowl's sides into mixture. Mix in vanilla and cinnamon; mix till batter is blended well.
- Sprinkle bottom of prepped pan with whole pecans; distribute 1/4 cup topping evenly in pan. Fold leftover topping into batter till well mixed. Put batter into pan; evenly spread. Bake for 35-40 minutes. Insert tester, like a toothpick, into middle to test cake; if done, it should exit clean without batter sticking on it.
- Cool cake in pan for minimum of 20 minutes. Put a serving piece/plate upside down over top of cake pan when cake is cool so plate's face covers open portion of cake pan fully. Invert pan and plate at the same time; put onto flat surface. Raise pan slowly using pot holders so cake stands upright on serving plate. To decorate, sprinkle powdered sugar.
- Cake freezes well; you can make it maximum of 2 days ahead.

Nutrition Information

- Calories: 503
- Total Carbohydrate: 59 g
- Cholesterol: 61 mg
- Total Fat: 28 g
- Fiber: 3 g
- Protein: 6 g
- Sodium: 192 mg
- Saturated Fat: 12 g

303. Southern Style Honey Butter

"A great butter recipe."
Serving: 16 | Prep: 5m | Ready in: 5m

Ingredients

- 1/2 cup softened butter
- 2 tbsps. sweetened condensed milk
- 5 tbsps. honey, or to taste

Direction

- Process honey, milk and butter till its light cream color and smooth in a blender/food processor; refrigerate till serving.

Nutrition Information

- Calories: 78 calories;
- Total Carbohydrate: 6.7 g
- Cholesterol: 16 mg
- Total Fat: 6 g
- Protein: 0.3 g
- Sodium: 44 mg

304. Spaghetti And Meatballs All'amatriciana

"A fun recipe."
Serving: Makes 8 servings

Ingredients

- 6 oz. uncured applewood-smoked bacon (about 6 slices), diced
- 2 large garlic cloves, peeled
- 2 lbs. ground beef (15% fat)
- 2/3 cup chopped drained roasted red peppers from jar
- 2/3 cup panko (Japanese breadcrumbs)*
- 2 large eggs
- 1/2 cup coarsely grated onion
- 1/2 cup freshly grated Parmesan cheese
- 1 tbsp. minced fresh marjoram
- 2 tsps. dried crushed red pepper
- 1/2 tsp. coarse kosher salt
- 1/2 tsp. freshly ground black pepper
- 2 28-oz. cans diced tomatoes in juice (preferably San Marzano)
- 2 large garlic cloves, peeled
- 6 oz. uncured applewood-smoked bacon (about 6 slices), cut crosswise into thin strips
- 1 tbsp. (or more) extra-virgin olive oil
- 3 cups finely chopped onions
- 1 1/2 tsps. dried crushed red pepper
- 2 cups dry white wine
- 1 tbsp. minced fresh marjoram
- 1 1/2 lbs. spaghetti
- 2 to 3 tbsps. extra-virgin olive oil
- 1 1/2 tbsps. minced fresh marjoram
- Freshly grated Parmesan cheese

Direction

- Meatballs: Use on/off turns to grind bacon to coarse paste in a processor; put into a big bowl. Squeeze in garlic using garlic press; mix in beef gently and all leftover ingredients. Stand for 15 minutes.
- Line plastic wrap on a big rimmed baking sheet. For each, use scant 2 tbsp. and moistened hands to roll the meat mixture into 1 1/2-in. meatballs; put onto sheet. You can make it 1 day ahead, chilled, covered in plastic wrap.
- Sauce: In batches, puree garlic and tomatoes with juices till smooth in a blender.
- Cook bacon till crisp in a big pot on medium heat; put bacon on a plate.
- Put 1 tbsp. oil in drippings in pot; heat on medium heat. Add 1/2 meatballs; cook for 9 minutes, carefully flipping with small metal spatula, till all sides are brown. Put meatballs on a baking sheet. If needed, add more oil in the pot; repeat using leftover meatballs.
- Put heat on medium high then add crushed red pepper and onions into the pot.
- Sauté for 6 minutes till golden. Add wine; boil for 8 minutes, mixing up browned bits, till reduced by half. Add marjoram and tomato puree; boil for 8 minutes till sauce slightly thickens, occasionally mixing. Season with pepper and salt. Stir bacon into the sauce then add meatballs; simmer. Lower the heat to low; cover. Simmer for 10-15 minutes till meatballs are tender and heated through; season sauce with pepper and salt.
- Pasta: Meanwhile, cook the spaghetti till tender yet firm to chew in a pot with boiling salted water, occasionally mixing. Drain; put into a big bowl. Toss with marjoram and 2 tbsp. oil; if desired, add extra oil to moisten. Divide spaghetti into bowls; put sauce and meatballs on top. Sprinkle with cheese; serve with extra cheese separately.

305. Spaghetti With Cauliflower, Green Olives, And Almonds

"Cauliflower, enhanced with a briny parsley-olive mixture and toasty almonds."
Serving: Makes 4 (main course) servings | Prep: 35m

Ingredients

- 1 1/4 cups pitted brine-cured green olives (plain or stuffed)
- 1/2 cup chopped fresh flat-leaf parsley

- 1/2 cup olive oil
- 1 (2 1/2-lb.) head cauliflower, cut into 1-inch-wide florets (8 cups)
- 1/2 tsp. salt
- 3 garlic cloves, finely chopped
- Scant 1/2 tsp. dried hot red-pepper flakes
- 1/4 cup water
- 3/4 lb. dried spaghetti or linguine
- 1 oz. finely grated Pecorino Romano or Parmigiano-Reggiano (1/2 cup) plus additional for serving
- 3/4 cup whole almonds with skin (3 3/4 oz.), toasted and coarsely chopped

Direction

- In food processor, pulse parsley and olives till chopped coarsely. Remove to bowl.
- In a heavy, 12-inch skillet, heat the oil on medium heat till hot yet do not let smoke, then let cauliflower cook along with salt for 8 minutes, mixing from time to time, till golden brown. Put in red-pepper flakes and garlic; cook for 3 to 5 minutes, mixing from time to time, till garlic turn golden and cauliflower soften.
- Mix in water; boil for a minute. Put in olive mixture then cook for 2 minutes, mixing, till heated fully.
- Meantime, let pasta cook in a 6-quart to 8-quart pot with salted, boiling water, mixing from time to time, till al dente. Put aside a cup pasta-cooking liquid. Strain using colander and bring back to pot.
- Put in mixture of cauliflower; toss thoroughly, then put in cheese and toss once more. Add some of the reserved cooking liquid to moisten in case pasta is dry.
- Scatter almonds on pasta and serve right away, with extra cheese alongside.

Nutrition Information

- Calories: 841
- Total Carbohydrate: 86 g
- Total Fat: 48 g
- Fiber: 13 g
- Protein: 23 g
- Sodium: 970 mg
- Saturated Fat: 6 g

306. Spiced Carrot Spread

Serving: Makes about 1 1/4 cups

Ingredients

- 1 tbsp. sesame seeds
- 1/2 tbsp. yellow mustard seeds
- 1/4 tsp. cumin seeds
- 1/4 cup water
- 1 lb. carrots, thinly sliced
- 3/4 tsp. salt
- 1/8 tsp. cayenne, or to taste
- 4 tbsps. olive oil

Direction

- Use a heavy dry 2-3 quart saucepan to toast together the cumin, mustard, and sesame seeds over moderate heat while stirring until they turn 1-2 shades darker and become fragrant, roughly 2-3 minutes. Stir in 2 tbsps. of oil, cayenne, salt, carrots, and water, then cook while covered over low heat, occasionally stirring, until the carrots are really tender, 20-30 minutes.
- Use a food processor to puree the mixture with the leftover 2 tbsps. of oil until the carrots are smooth while the spices are still a bit coarse.

Nutrition Information

- Calories: 183
- Total Carbohydrate: 12 g
- Total Fat: 15 g
- Fiber: 4 g
- Protein: 2 g
- Sodium: 337 mg
- Saturated Fat: 2 g

307. Spiced Streusel Apple Pie

Serving: Makes 8 servings

Ingredients

- 2/3 cup walnuts
- 1/2 cup (packed) golden brown sugar
- 1/4 cup yellow cornmeal
- 1/4 cup all purpose flour
- 3/4 tsp. ground cinnamon
- 1/2 tsp. ground nutmeg
- 5 tbsps. chilled unsalted butter, cut into small pieces
- 2 1/4 lbs. Granny Smith apples (about 6 medium), peeled, quartered, cored, cut into 1/2-inch-thick wedges
- 1/2 cup sour cream
- 1/4 cup sugar
- 2 tbsps. all purpose flour
- 1 1/2 tsps. ground cinnamon
- 3/4 tsp. ground nutmeg
- 1/4 tsp. ground cloves
- 1 Flaky Pie Crust
- Vanilla ice cream

Direction

- Streusel: Process nutmeg, cinnamon, flour, cornmeal, brown sugar and nuts till nuts are chopped finely with on/off turns in processor. Add butter; process till small moist clumps form. You can make it 1 day ahead, refrigerated, covered.
- Filling: In middle of oven, put rack; preheat 375°F. Toss sour cream and apples to coat in big bowl. Mix cloves, nutmeg, cinnamon, flour and sugar in small bowl; sprinkle it on apples. Toss till coated.
- Put filling in prepped crust. Sprinkle streusel on apples, fully covering. Bake pie for 1 hour till streusel is golden and apples are tender; if streusel browns quickly, tent pie with foil. Put pie on rack; slightly cool.
- Serve pie in room temperature/slightly warm with vanilla ice cream.

Nutrition Information

- Calories: 428
- Total Carbohydrate: 62 g
- Cholesterol: 27 mg
- Total Fat: 19 g
- Fiber: 5 g
- Protein: 3 g
- Sodium: 131 mg
- Saturated Fat: 9 g

308. Spicy Chipotle Grilled Chicken

"This recipe has the right amount of heat. Be sure to begin making this dish 1 day ahead because you will need to marinate the chicken overnight."
Serving: Makes 4 servings

Ingredients

- 1/4 cup canned chipotle chiles in adobo*
- 3 tbsps. olive oil
- 2 garlic cloves, pressed
- 1/2 onion, coarsely chopped
- 2 tbsps. chopped fresh cilantro
- 1 tbsp. paprika
- 1 tsp. ground cumin
- 1 tsp. chili powder
- 1 tsp. salt
- 1 3 1/2-lb. chicken, cut into 8 pieces
- Nonstick vegetable oil spray

Direction

- In a processor, mix chipotles in adobo, garlic cloves and olive oil. Puree until a paste is formed. Add chili powder, chopped onion, paprika, salt, chopped cilantro and ground cumin. Process until the onion is chopped finely. Pour 1/4 cup of chipotle mixture into a small bowl, cover and chill. Lay pieces of chicken in an 11x7x2-inch glass baking dish. Pour the remaining chipotle mixture on top of the chicken pieces. Cover and chill overnight.
- Use nonstick spray to spritz a grill rack. Assemble the barbecue (medium heat). Then

grill the chicken for about 30 minutes until cooked through. Ensure to move to the cooler part of grill as needed to avoid burning and rub with the reserved marinade during final five minutes of grilling. Place the chicken onto a platter and then serve.

Nutrition Information

- Calories: 742
- Total Carbohydrate: 4 g
- Cholesterol: 202 mg
- Total Fat: 57 g
- Fiber: 1 g
- Protein: 51 g
- Sodium: 893 mg
- Saturated Fat: 13 g

309. Spicy Feta Dip

"It's a spicy Greek dip made with roasted red peppers, feta, pepperoncini, and ricotta cheese."
Serving: 8 | Prep: 15m | Ready in: 2h15m

Ingredients

- 1 cup crumbled feta cheese
- 1/2 cup chopped roasted red peppers
- 4 pepperoncini peppers, drained and stemmed
- 1 tsp. cayenne pepper, or more to taste
- 1 cup ricotta cheese
- 1 tsp. lemon juice

Direction

- In a food processor, pulse the feta cheese just enough to get uniformly small crumbles, then remove to a bowl.
- In the food processor, puree together cayenne pepper, pepperoncini peppers and red peppers until smooth. Combine into the feta cheese with lemon juice, ricotta cheese and pepper puree until the dip has an even texture and color. Remove to a sealed container and chill for 2 hours or overnight.

Nutrition Information

- Calories: 134 calories;
- Total Carbohydrate: 4.2 g
- Cholesterol: 38 mg
- Total Fat: 9.3 g
- Protein: 8.3 g
- Sodium: 734 mg

310. Spicy Roasted Red Pepper And Feta Hummus

"This finely seasoned hummus is good to serve with pita chips, sliced veggies or chips."
Serving: 8 | Prep: 10m | Ready in: 10m

Ingredients

- 1 (15 oz.) can garbanzo beans, drained
- 1/2 cup crumbled feta cheese
- 1 (4 oz.) jar roasted red bell peppers, drained
- 3 tbsps. lemon juice
- 1 tbsp. chopped fresh parsley
- 1/2 tsp. cayenne pepper
- 1/4 tsp. salt

Direction

- In the bowl of a food processor, blend the salt, cayenne pepper, parsley, lemon juice, drained red peppers, feta cheese and garbanzo beans until it becomes smooth.

Nutrition Information

- Calories: 90 calories;
- Total Carbohydrate: 9.9 g
- Cholesterol: 14 mg
- Total Fat: 3.9 g
- Protein: 4.2 g
- Sodium: 405 mg

311. Spicy Sweet Potato Spread

"Just 10 or 12 minutes in a microwave and the sweet potatoes are done! This meal can be served with root vegetable chips."
Serving: Makes about 2 cups

Ingredients

- 2 or 3 small to medium sweet potatoes (about 12 oz.)
- 2 large garlic cloves, minced
- 1 tsp. hot red pepper sauce
- 1/2 tsp. salt
- 1/4 tsp. cayenne pepper
- 1/4 cup juice from 2 limes
- 2/3 cup olive oil
- 1/3 cup canned chicken broth

Direction

- 1. Cook the potatoes in the microwave for 10 to 12 minutes on high until veggies are soft. Using an oven mitt, hold the potatoes while peeling or let the potatoes cool and then peel them.
- 2. Put the potatoes, pepper sauce, garlic, cayenne, salt, and lime juice in the food processor fitted with the metal blade and process until puréed. Add oil gradually through the feeder tube while the food processor is running. Carry on with blending until the mixture is silky and light, gradually pouring the broth through the feeder tube. Place in a serving bowl.

Nutrition Information

- Calories: 253
- Total Carbohydrate: 10 g
- Total Fat: 24 g
- Fiber: 2 g
- Protein: 1 g
- Sodium: 246 mg
- Saturated Fat: 3 g

312. Spinach And Garlic Dip With Pita Triangles And Vegetables

"A lovely dip!"
Serving: Makes 6 servings

Ingredients

- 1 1/2 tsps. plus 2 tbsps. olive oil
- 2 tsps. finely chopped garlic
- 8 cups (packed) fresh spinach leaves (about 5 oz.)
- 1/2 cup chopped green onions
- 1 cup sour cream
- 1 tsp. fresh lemon juice
- 2 6-inch-diameter pita breads
- Assorted raw vegetables

Direction

- Heat 1 1/2 tsp. oil on medium high heat in big nonstick skillet. Add garlic; sauté for 10 seconds. Add the spinach; sauté for 2 minutes till tender and wilted. Cool.
- Puree green onions and spinach in processor; put in medium bowl. Stir in lemon juice and sour cream; season with pepper and salt. Cover; chill.
- Preheat broiler. Horizontally halve each pita bread, making 2 circles. Cut every circle to 4 triangles. In 1 layer, put triangles on baking sheet; brush 2 tbsp. oil on pita triangles lightly. Sprinkle with pepper. Broil for 2 minutes till golden, moving triangles on the baking sheet to evenly brown, closely watching to prevent burning. Cool. You can make pita triangles and dip 1 day ahead; keep the dip chilled. Keep pita in an airtight container.
- Serve dip with assorted raw veggies and pita triangles.

313. Spinach And Garlic Scape Pesto

"I use this sauce on almost anything! From spreads to salads to pastas."
Serving: 16 | Prep: 10m | Ready in: 10m

Ingredients

- 4 cups fresh spinach
- 1 lb. garlic scapes, minced
- 1 1/2 cups Parmesan cheese
- 1 1/2 cups olive oil
- 2 tbsps. pine nuts, or to taste (optional)
- salt and ground black pepper to taste

Direction

- In a food processor, blend pine nuts, olive oil, parmesan cheese, garlic scapes and spinach until smooth. Season using pepper and salt.

Nutrition Information

- Calories: 261 calories;
- Total Carbohydrate: 10.1 g
- Cholesterol: 7 mg
- Total Fat: 23.1 g
- Protein: 5.2 g
- Sodium: 126 mg

314. Spinach And Tofu Paneer

"An easy dish to make, serve it over rice and sprinkle toasted black sesame seeds."
Serving: serves 3-4

Ingredients

- 1 carton firm or soft tofu
- Salt
- 1 large bunch spinach, stems discarded, leaves well washed
- 1 jalapeño chile, seeded and coarsely chopped
- 1 serrano chile, coarsely chopped
- 1-inch knob ginger, peeled and diced
- 3 garlic cloves, coarsely chopped
- 1 cup diced onion
- 2 tbsps. ghee, butter, or vegetable oil
- 1 1/2 tsps. ground cumin
- 1/8 tsp. nutmeg, plus a pinch
- 1/8 tsp. cayenne pepper
- 1/2 cup half-and-half
- 1/3 cup yogurt

Direction

- Cube tofu into portions approximately the size of sugar cube or a bit smaller. Boil 6 cups water, put a tsp. salt and reduce heat to a simmer. Put tofu, switch off the heat, and let rest for 4 or 5 minutes. Put into colander to let drain. Take it off using a slotted spoon in case you use soft tofu. Reserve.
- Let the spinach steam till wilted, then take off to a chopping board and slice. Once cool enough to handle, press out extra water.
- In a food processor, place the onion, garlic, ginger and chilies, and blend till finely chopped. In a nonstick skillet, heat butter or ghee, put the onion mixture and allow to cook for 5 minutes over medium heat, mixing often.
- Put 1 cup water, cayenne, nutmeg, cumin and 1 tsp. salt. Allow to simmer for 5 minutes, then put the mixture back to food processor, put the spinach, and puree.
- Put the mixture back to skillet, put tofu and half-and-half, and allow to simmer for approximately 5 minutes. Switch off the heat and mix in yogurt. Serve on top of basmati rice.

315. Standing Rib Roast With Winter-vegetable Crust

"An easy entrée."
Serving: Makes 8 Servings

Ingredients

- 1 large onion, peeled, quartered

- 1 large carrot, peeled, coarsely chopped
- 1 celery stalk, coarsely chopped
- 10 garlic cloves, peeled
- 1/4 cup olive oil
- 3 tbsps. all purpose flour
- 2 tbsps. chopped fresh rosemary
- 1 tbsp. salt
- 1 1/2 tsps. ground black pepper
- 1 3/4-lb. standing rib roast

Direction

- Puree pepper, salt, rosemary, flour, oil, garlic cloves, celery, carrot and onion in processor. In roasting pan, put beef; rub herb and veggie puree on beef, fully covering. Stand beef in room temperature for 1 hour.
- Preheat an oven to 500°F and roast beef for 20 minutes. Lower oven temperature down to 375°F. Roast beef for 1 hour 45 minutes till inserted thermometer in middle reads 125°F. Take roast from oven; stand for 20 minutes. Cut roast; serve.

Nutrition Information

- Calories: 409
- Total Carbohydrate: 7 g
- Cholesterol: 70 mg
- Total Fat: 35 g
- Fiber: 1 g
- Protein: 17 g
- Sodium: 340 mg
- Saturated Fat: 12 g

316. Steamed Vegetables With Basil Pecan Pesto

Serving: Serves 6 as a main course

Ingredients

- 6 medium carrots, cut diagonally into 1/8-inch-thick slices
- 2 fennel bulbs (sometimes called anise), stalks trimmed flush with bulb and bulb cut lengthwise into 1/8-inch-thick slices
- 1 1/2 lbs. small red potatoes, cut into 1/4-inch-thick slices
- 1 1/2 lbs. green beans, trimmed
- 3 to 4 tbsps. hot water
- 1 1/4 cups basil pecan pesto
- 2 cups packed fresh basil leaves, washed well and spun dry
- 2/3 cup olive oil
- 1/2 cup pecans, toasted golden brown and cooled
- 1/3 cup freshly grated Parmesan
- 2 large garlic cloves, chopped and mashed to a paste with 1/2 tsp. salt

Direction

- Veggies: layer carrots, fennel then potatoes on a big steamer rack; steam above boiling water for 10 minutes till potatoes are tender, covered. Put steamed veggies on a platter. Steam the beans for 10 minutes till just tender, covered. Put on platter. Blend 3 tbsp. hot water and pesto in a food processor; if needed, add extra hot water to get preferred consistency.
- Serve veggies with pesto in room temperature/warm.
- Pesto: blend all ingredients with pepper and salt to taste till smooth in a food processor. Pesto keeps for 1 week, chilled, surface covered in plastic wrap. Creates 1 1/4 cups.

Nutrition Information

- Calories: 1015
- Total Carbohydrate: 46 g
- Cholesterol: 21 mg
- Total Fat: 89 g
- Fiber: 13 g
- Protein: 19 g
- Sodium: 1292 mg
- Saturated Fat: 15 g

317. Strawberry Buttermilk Ice

"Quick and low-fat."
Serving: Serves 8

Ingredients

- 2 12-oz. baskets strawberries, hulled, halved
- 1/2 cup sugar
- 1 cup low-fat buttermilk

Direction

- Puree sugar and strawberries in processor. Add buttermilk; process till smooth. Put in 8x8x2-in. glass dish. Put in freezer; freeze for 3 hours till firm.
- Put mixture in processor; process till smooth. Put mixture in plastic container; tightly cover. Freeze for 3 hours till firm. You can make ice 2 days ahead, kept frozen. Soften ice 5 minutes before serving in room temperature.

318. Strawberry Cup

Serving: Makes about 20 drinks

Ingredients

- 2 3/4 lbs. strawberries (about 5 pints), trimmed and hulled
- 1 cup distilled white vinegar
- 2 cups sugar, or to taste
- 3 quart cold water or club soda (96 fluid oz.)
- Ice cubes
- a 2-quart pitcher

Direction

- Pulse strawberries till coarsely chopped in a food processor. Put in a big bowl; mix in vinegar. Chill for 12 hours, covered.
- Put into fine-mesh sieve above a big bowl; drain for 25-30 minutes till juice in bowl is 3 1/2-4 cups, frequently gently mixing, pressing without forcing pulp through sieve. Discard pulp.
- Put juice in 3-qt. heavy nonreactive saucepan; mix in 2 cups sugar. Cook on medium heat for 5-6 minutes till sugar dissolves, mixing. Add extra sugar to taste, if desired. Cool syrup for 30 minutes; you'll get 4 cups.
- Mix 3 cups water/soda and 1 cup syrup in pitcher, for every pitcherful, then add ice to fill.
- Syrup keeps for 1 week, chilled, covered.

319. Strawberry Panachee

"You can use any cookies."
Serving: Makes 4 servings

Ingredients

- 2 1/2 cups ripe strawberries
- 1/4 cup jam (raspberry, currant, or strawberry are good)
- 4 shortbread cookies
- 1/3 cup crème fraîche or sour cream, plus additional for garnish
- 4 sprigs mint or basil

Direction

- Cut off top and bottom of every berry to get 1 1/4 cups. Slice middle of berries; put aside. Push bottoms and tops of berry and jam through food mill/process in mini food processor till pureed. Mix sliced berries into puree; use plastic wrap to cover. Refrigerate till needed.
- Put cookies into plastic bag at serving time; coarsely crush using rolling pin. Divide crumbs to 4 goblets or bowls. Put 1/2 berry mixture over cookies; to loosen it, mix crème fraiche/sour cream then put over berries. Put leftover berry mixture over; garnish every dessert with mint sprig. If desired, pass with some sour cream/crème fraiche.

Nutrition Information

- Calories: 148
- Total Carbohydrate: 29 g

- Total Fat: 3 g
- Fiber: 2 g
- Protein: 1 g
- Sodium: 50 mg
- Saturated Fat: 1 g

320. Strawberry Vinegar

"A flavorful recipe."
Serving: Makes about 2 cups

Ingredients

- 1 lb. strawberries, hulled, quartered
- 1 cup white wine vinegar
- 1/2 cup unseasoned rice vinegar
- 1/4 cup sugar
- A sieve lined with cheesecloth or a coffee filter, clean glass jar

Direction

- In a big glass jar, mix 1/4 cup sugar, 1/2 cup of unseasoned rice vinegar, 1 cup of white wine vinegar, 1-lb strawberries, hulled and quartered; cover. Chill for 1-2 days. Through a cheesecloth/coffee filter-lined sieve, strain into clean glass jar and cover; chill.
- You can make it 3 months ahead, kept chilled.
- You can also make it with sour cherries, raspberries and currants.

Nutrition Information

- Calories: 203
- Total Carbohydrate: 42 g
- Total Fat: 1 g
- Fiber: 5 g
- Protein: 2 g
- Sodium: 8 mg
- Saturated Fat: 0 g

321. Strawberry-cheesecake Ice Cream

Ingredients

- 3/4 lb. (1 quart) strawberries
- 8 oz. softened cream cheese
- 3/4 cup sugar
- 1 cup milk
- 1 tbsp. lemon juice
- a pinch of salt
- 1/2 cup heavy cream

Direction

- Ice cream: puree salt, lemon juice, milk, cream cheese and strawberries; mix heavy cream in. Thoroughly chill; freeze in ice-cream maker.

Nutrition Information

- Calories: 253
- Total Carbohydrate: 25 g
- Cholesterol: 55 mg
- Total Fat: 16 g
- Fiber: 1 g
- Protein: 3 g
- Sodium: 159 mg
- Saturated Fat: 9 g

322. Strawberry-kiwi Sangria With Rosé Geranium

"Refreshing!"
Serving: Serves 12

Ingredients

- 8 cups water
- 8 wild-berry tea bags
- 2 cups sugar
- 4 1-pint baskets strawberries, hulled
- 2 25.4-oz. (750-ml) bottles chilled sparkling apple cider

- 6 kiwis, peeled, cut into 1/2-inch cubes
- 16 fresh rose geranium leaves, crushed slightly, or 3/4 tsp. rose water*
- 4 cups ice cubes

Direction

- Boil 4 cups water in big saucepan. Add the tea bags; cover. Steep for 10 minutes. Throw tea bags. Put sugar in hot tea; mix till dissolves. Mix in leftover 4 cups water; chill the tea for 3 hours till cold. You can make it 1 day ahead, kept chilled, covered.
- In processor, puree 2 baskets strawberries. Slice leftover 2 baskets strawberries. Put sliced and purred strawberries in big pitcher/divide to 2 pitches. Add all leftover ingredients and tea; mix. Serve.

Nutrition Information

- Calories: 1062
- Total Carbohydrate: 88 g
- Total Fat: 1 g
- Fiber: 6 g
- Protein: 2 g
- Sodium: 63 mg
- Saturated Fat: 0 g

323. Strawberry-orange Sorbet

"Refreshing and yummy."
Serving: Makes 6 servings

Ingredients

- 1 cup water
- 2/3 cup sugar
- 2 3/4 cups sliced hulled strawberries (about 1 1/2 one-pint baskets)
- 1/2 cup fresh orange juice
- 1/2 tsp. grated orange peel

Direction

- Boil sugar and 1 cup water till sugar melts in small saucepan on medium heat; chill sugar syrup for 1 hour till cold.
- Puree orange peel, fresh orange juice and sliced strawberries till smooth in a processor. Add chilled sugar syrup slowly as processor runs; process till blended well. Put sorbet mixture in a 13x9x2-in. glass dish and freeze for 3 hours total, mixing every 30 minutes, till sorbet is firm. Put frozen sorbet in a processor; puree till smooth. Put into dessert glasses; immediately serve/ freeze for 3 days in a covered container.

324. Summer Herb Pesto

"You can keep this frozen for 1 month or in an airtight container in the fridge for 1 week."
Serving: 12 | Prep: 10m | Ready in: 10m

Ingredients

- 2 garlic cloves, minced
- 1 cup fresh basil leaves
- 1 cup fresh flat-leaf parsley leaves
- 1 cup fresh spinach leaves
- 1/2 cup chopped fresh oregano
- 1/2 cup toasted pine nuts
- 1/2 cup grated Parmesan cheese
- 1 pinch salt and freshly ground black pepper to taste
- 3/4 cup olive oil

Direction

- In a food processor/blender, blend olive oil, pepper, salt, parmesan cheese, pine nuts, oregano, spinach, parsley, basil and garlic until smooth.

Nutrition Information

- Calories: 172 calories;
- Total Carbohydrate: 2 g
- Cholesterol: 3 mg
- Total Fat: 17.5 g

- Protein: 3.1 g
- Sodium: 57 mg

325. Summer Peach Pie With Vanilla And Cardamom

"Rub off peach fuzz gently with a kitchen towel; you don't have to peel the peaches."
Serving: Makes 8 servings

Ingredients

- 2/3 cup plus 2 tsps. sugar
- 1/2 vanilla bean, cut crosswise into 1/2-inch pieces
- 3 tbsps. unbleached all purpose flour
- 1 tsp. (scant) ground cardamom
- 3 3/4 lbs. firm but ripe unpeeled peaches, halved, pitted, each half cut into 4 slices (about 10 cups)
- 2 Best-Ever Pie Crust dough disks
- 2 tbsps. (1/4 stick) unsalted butter, cut into 1/2-inch cubes
- Whipping cream (for glaze)
- Vanilla ice cream

Direction

- On the bottom third of oven, put rack; preheat it to 400°F. Blend vanilla bean and 2/3 cup sugar till vanilla bean is minced very finely in a processor. Through a strainer, sift vanilla sugar into a big bowl; in a strainer, discard any big bits. Mix cardamom and flour into vanilla sugar. Put peaches in flour-sugar mixture; gently toss to coat.
- Roll 1 pie crust disk out to 12-in. round on a floured surface; put in 9-in. diameter glass pie dish. To 1/2-in., trim dough overhang. Put peach mixture into the crust; dot using butter. Roll 2nd pie crust disk out to 12-in. round on a lightly floured surface. Drape the dough on peach filling; to 1 1/2-in., trim overhang. Fold bottom and top edges under; to seal, press together. Decoratively crimp the edges. Cut 2-in. long X in the middle of top crust using a small sharp knife to let steam escape. Lightly brush whipping cream on crust; sprinkle with leftover 2 tsp. sugar.
- On rimmed baking sheet, put pie; bake for 1 hour 15 minutes till juices thickly bubble through cut on top crust, peaches are tender and crust is golden. Put pie on rack; cool for 2 hours till lukewarm.
- Serve pie with vanilla ice cream at room temperature/lukewarm.

326. Sun-dried Tomato Hummus

"This is a creamy hummus made with pureed garbanzo beans and tahini (sesame seed paste), seasoned with garlic and lemon juice."
Serving: 16 | Prep: 15m | Ready in: 1h15m

Ingredients

- 4 cloves garlic
- 1 tsp. salt
- 3 tbsps. tahini paste
- 1/4 cup fresh lemon juice
- 2 (15.5 oz.) cans garbanzo beans, drained
- 1/2 cup olive oil
- 1/2 cup oil-packed sun-dried tomatoes, drained
- 1/4 cup finely shredded fresh basil
- 2 tbsps. olive oil
- 1/8 tsp. paprika (optional)

Direction

- In a food processor, process the lemon juice, tahini, salt and garlic until it becomes smooth. Stir in 1/2 cup of olive oil and garbanzo beans then blend until it becomes smooth again; occasionally scrape the bowl's side. Stir in the sun-dried tomatoes when the mixture is already smooth, then process until chopped to very fine pieces and combined well into the hummus. Lastly, put the basil and process several times until incorporated.
- In a shallow serving dish, spread the hummus and form several decorative grooves on the top. Let it chill in the fridge for a minimum of

1 hour, then trickle with 2 tbsps. of olive oil and sprinkle paprika on top prior to serving.

Nutrition Information

- Calories: 163 calories;
- Total Carbohydrate: 14.6 g
- Cholesterol: 0 mg
- Total Fat: 10.6 g
- Protein: 3.5 g
- Sodium: 349 mg

327. Sweet Potato Hummus

"A sweet and savory hummus served with sliced veggies, crackers or pita wedges."
Serving: 20 | Prep: 20m | Ready in: 1h20m

Ingredients

- 3 sweet potatoes
- 1 (15 oz.) can garbanzo beans, drained (reserve liquid) and rinsed
- 2 tbsps. extra-virgin olive oil
- 2 tbsps. tahini
- 2 tbsps. lemon juice
- 1/2 tsp. lemon zest
- 1/4 tsp. ground cumin
- 1/4 tsp. ground coriander
- 1/4 tsp. ground white pepper
- sea salt to taste

Direction

- Set an oven to preheat at 200°C (400°F).
- Using a fork, prick the sweet potatoes all over to make holes.
- In the preheated oven, roast the sweet potatoes for about 45 minutes until tender and let it cool. Halve the sweet potatoes lengthwise.
- In a blender, mix olive oil and garbanzo beans then pulse a few times to puree. Scoop out the flesh of sweet potato peels and put it in the blender, then process to blend. Stir into mixture the sea salt, white pepper, coriander, cumin, lemon zest, lemon juice and tahini, then process until it becomes smooth. If

necessary, add reserved garbanzo bean liquid to create a creamy and smooth hummus.

Nutrition Information

- Calories: 75 calories;
- Total Carbohydrate: 12.2 g
- Cholesterol: 0 mg
- Total Fat: 2.3 g
- Protein: 1.6 g
- Sodium: 83 mg

328. Sweet Potato Purée With Ginger And Cider

"Sweet and spicy."
Serving: Makes 6 servings

Ingredients

- 2 1/2 lbs. sweet potatoes (about 3 medium)
- 4 cups apple cider
- 1/4 cup minced peeled fresh ginger
- 2 tbsps. (1/4 stick) butter

Direction

- Cover potatoes by 2-in. water in a big pot; boil on high heat. Lower heat to medium low and simmer for 40 minutes till potatoes are very tender; drain. Cool. Peel and cut to big chunks; put into processor.
- Boil cider in a medium heavy saucepan on high heat. Lower heat to medium low and simmer for 30 minutes till cider reduces to 1 cup. Put butter, ginger and cider in processor with potatoes; process till very smooth. Season with pepper and salt. You can make it 4 hours ahead. Put in a medium saucepan and cover; chill. To rewarm, mix on medium heat before serving.

Nutrition Information

- Calories: 276
- Total Carbohydrate: 57 g
- Cholesterol: 10 mg

- Total Fat: 4 g
- Fiber: 6 g
- Protein: 3 g
- Sodium: 112 mg
- Saturated Fat: 3 g

329. Sweet-pea Canapes

Serving: Makes about 48 hors d'oeuvres | Prep: 25m

Ingredients

- 1 (10-oz.) box frozen baby peas (2 1/4 cups)
- 1/4 cup water
- 1/2 cup chilled heavy cream
- 1/4 tsp. salt
- 1/8 tsp. black pepper
- 1 tbsp. finely grated Parmigiano-Reggiano
- 1/2 baguette
- 1/4 lb. very thinly sliced baked ham

Direction

- Place the rack in the middle part of the oven then preheat to 375 degrees F.
- In a 1 1/2-2 qt. pot with water, simmer peas for 5 minutes with a cover until tender. In a food processor, purée peas with water until very smooth, avoid using a blender. Press the pureed peas over a bowl with fine-mesh sieve then remove the solids; refrigerate until cold. In a separate bowl, whisk pepper, salt and cream until stiff peaks form; mix in cheese and pea puree until blended. Cover then refrigerate the pea mousse while preparing the toasts.
- Cut twenty-four very thin baguette slices; halve each slice. Arrange the slices on a baking sheet in one layer; toast for 7-9mins in the oven until the sides are golden. Place toasts on a rack to fully cool.
- Scoop a dollop of the mousse on top of each toast; add a small piece of ham torn from a slice on top. Serve right away.
- The pea mousse can be placed in the refrigerator for up to 8hrs.
- The toasts can be prepared a day in advance then cooled. Store at room temperature in an airtight container.

Nutrition Information

- Calories: 28
- Total Carbohydrate: 3 g
- Cholesterol: 5 mg
- Total Fat: 1 g
- Fiber: 1 g
- Protein: 1 g
- Sodium: 73 mg
- Saturated Fat: 1 g

330. Tangy Rhubarb Salsa

"You can adjust ingredients to your preference, like omitting jalapenos. Mix and match peppers as desired; just use 3 peppers."
Serving: 12 | Prep: 30m | Ready in: 3h35m

Ingredients

- 2 cups thinly sliced rhubarb
- 1 small red onion, coarsely chopped
- 1 large green bell pepper, seeded and coarsely chopped
- 1 large red bell pepper, seeded and coarsely chopped
- 1 large yellow bell pepper, seeded and coarsely chopped
- 1 jalapeno pepper, seeded and coarsely chopped - or to taste
- 1/2 cup chopped fresh cilantro
- 3 roma (plum) tomatoes, finely diced
- 2 tsps. brown sugar
- 5 tbsps. Key lime juice
- 2 tsps. coarse salt
- 1 pinch garlic powder, or to taste
- ground black pepper to taste

Direction

- Mix rhubarb into big pot with boiling water; cook for 10 seconds. Drain rhubarb quickly;

rinse in cold water till cool. Put rhubarb in a big bowl.
- Pulse cilantro, jalapeno pepper, red onion and yellow, red and green bell peppers 3-4 times to chop finely in a food processor; put pepper mixture in bowl with rhubarb. Mix in roma tomatoes.
- In a bowl, dissolve brown sugar in the Key lime juice; mix lime juice mixture lightly into rhubarb mixture. Sprinkle salsa using black pepper, garlic powder and salt; mix salsa. Refrigerate to blend flavors for minimum of 3 hours.

Nutrition Information

- Calories: 26 calories;
- Total Carbohydrate: 6.1 g
- Cholesterol: 0 mg
- Total Fat: 0.2 g
- Protein: 0.9 g
- Sodium: 392 mg

331. Thai Shrimp Curry

"You can cook Thai food at your home. This slightly spicy curry is a cross between a stew and a soup. It's simple to prepare and will impress your guests. Start your dinner with some frozen egg rolls or order from a Chinese restaurant and then complete with sorbet or ice cream topped with sliced tropical fruit."
Serving: Serves 6

Ingredients

- 1/2 cup chopped onion
- 3 large shallots, chopped
- 3 tbsps. chopped lemongrass* (from bottom 3 inches of about 5 peeled stalks)
- 3 tbsps. chopped cilantro stems
- 3 tbsps. chopped peeled fresh ginger
- 1 tbsp. turmeric
- 2 tsps. ground cumin
- 1 tsp. dried crushed red pepper
- 2 cups canned unsweetened coconut milk**
- 2 8-oz. bottles clam juice
- 2 tbsps. vegetable oil
- 2 lbs. large uncooked shrimp, peeled, deveined
- 1 head bok choy (about 1 1/2 lbs.), white part cut crosswise into 1/4-inch-thick slices, dark green part cut crosswise into 1-inch-wide slices
- 1 lb. snow peas, stringed
- 2 3.5-oz. packages enoki mushrooms, trimmed
- fresh basil
- Cooked rice
- *Chopped lemon grass is available at Southeast Asian markets and in the produce section of some markets.
- **Canned unsweetened coconut milk available at Indian, Southeast Asian or Latin American markets and many supermarkets nationwide.

Direction

- In a processor, puree the first nine ingredients, scraping the sides of bowl from time to time until you have a paste. Pour the curry paste into a bowl. (You can make four days ahead, cover and refrigerate).
- In a heavy large saucepan, boil clam juice and coconut milk for about 20 minutes until decreased to 2 cups. (You can make one day ahead, then cover and chill).
- Over high heat, heat oil in a heavy large skillet and add six tbsps. of curry paste. Then mix for 1 minute. Place in shrimp and sauté for about 2 minutes until starting to become pink. Transfer the shrimp onto a plate using a slotted spoon. Pour the reduced coconut milk mixture into the same skillet and then boil while stirring from time to time for about 7 minutes until the mixture thickly coats the spoon. Place in the white part of bok choy and let boil for about 2 minutes until starting to soften. Stir in snow peas for about 1 minute until crisp-tender. Place the shrimp back into sauce. Then add mushrooms and green part of bok choy. Mix for about 5 minutes until heated through. Scatter with basil. Serve on top of rice.

332. Three Basil Pesto

"A fun recipe."
Serving: Makes about 2 1/2 cups | Prep: 45m

Ingredients

- 4 garlic cloves
- 3/4 cup pine nuts (1/4 lb.)
- 2 cups grated Parmigiano-Reggiano
- 2 cups grated Pecorino Romano
- 3 cups packed Italian basil leaves
- 1 1/2 cups packed bush basil leaves
- 1 cup loosely packed fresh lemon basil leaves
- 2 cups packed flat-leaf parsley leaves
- 5 tbsps. olive oil

Direction

- Pulse garlic till finely chopped in a food processor. Add 1 tsp. of pepper, big handful of herbs, cheeses and nuts; process till chopped. One handful at a time, add leftover herbs, pulsing after every addition, till finely chopped. Add oil as motor runs; blend till incorporated.

Nutrition Information

- Calories: 672
- Total Carbohydrate: 9 g
- Cholesterol: 86 mg
- Total Fat: 55 g
- Fiber: 2 g
- Protein: 38 g
- Sodium: 1394 mg
- Saturated Fat: 19 g

333. Toasted-hazelnut Cake

Serving: Makes 8 servings | Prep: 40m

Ingredients

- 1 1/2 cups hazelnuts (8 oz.), toasted
- 1/4 cup matzo cake meal
- 1 cup sugar
- 4 large eggs, separated, at room temperature
- 1 tsp. finely grated fresh lemon zest
- 1/4 tsp. salt
- Warm Sweet Chocolate Glaze

Direction

- Preheat an oven to 350°F. Grease 9-in. springform pan.
- In a kitchen towel, rub hot toasted nuts to remove some skins; fully cool.
- Cake: Pulse 1/4 cup sugar, cake meal and nuts till nuts are chopped very finely without processing to a paste in a food processor.
- Use an electric mixer at high speed to beat 1/2 cup sugar and yolks till very thick and pale in a big bowl; mix in zest.
- Use cleaned beaters at high speed to beat salt and whites till soft peaks form in another bowl; beat in leftover 1/4 cup sugar slowly till whites just hold glossy, stiff peaks.
- Alternately fold whites and nut mixture into yolk mixture in 3 batches.
- Put batter in pan; smooth top.
- Bake cake for 35 minutes in center of oven till tester exits clean and golden; cool for 3 minutes in pan on rack. Use knife to loosen edge; remove pan's sides. Fully cool. Cake will slightly sink in middle.
- Glaze cake: On rack set above shallow baking pan, invert cake. Loosen bottom of pan carefully; remove. Put warm glaze on cake, letting it drip down sides; spread to evenly coat. Chill for 5 minutes till glaze is set.
- Cake keeps for 1 day, chilled, covered. Before serving, bring to room temperature.

334. Tofu Dream Pudding And Pie Filling

"You can change the flavor and use any nut. You can make this using graham crust pie shell."
Serving: 8 | Prep: 5m | Ready in: 5m

Ingredients

- 1 (12 oz.) package extra firm tofu, drained and cubed
- 1/4 cup brown sugar
- 1/2 cup walnuts
- 1/4 cup pure maple syrup
- 1 tbsp. lemon juice

Direction

- Process lemon juice, maple syrup, walnuts, brown sugar and tofu till smooth in a food processor. Cover; chill to thick as a pie filling or immediately serve as pudding.

Nutrition Information

- Calories: 133 calories;
- Total Carbohydrate: 15.3 g
- Cholesterol: 0 mg
- Total Fat: 6.9 g
- Protein: 4.6 g
- Sodium: 6 mg

335. Tomatillo-pepita Gazpacho

"A Mexican gazpacho with pepitas, or also known as pumpkin seeds."
Serving: Makes 8 servings

Ingredients

- 1/2 cup (generous) unsalted shelled pepitas (about 2 1/2 oz.)
- 2 lbs. tomatillos, husked, rinsed
- 1 large fresh poblano chile
- 1 garlic clove, pressed
- 1 cup vegetable broth
- 1/3 cup chopped green onion
- 1/4 cup chopped fresh cilantro
- 1/4 cup extra-virgin olive oil
- 1 small unpeeled English hothouse cucumber, diced
- 1 avocado, peeled, pitted, diced
- 1 12-oz. container cherry tomatoes, halved or quartered if large

Direction

- Set barbecue to medium-high heat. Add pepitas to the bowl of a food processor and finely grind; leave it in the processor. Grill poblano chile and tomatillos for 12 to 15 minutes, or until the chile is charred all over and the tomatillos are soft and slightly charred, turning occasionally. Transfer the tomatillos to the food processor. Peel the chile and remove the seeds, then coarsely chop and add to the food processor. Add garlic and process soup until it turns to coarse puree. Transfer to a large bowl and stir in vegetable broth. Add salt and pepper to season. Cover, and transfer to a refrigerator to chill for 3 hours, or until soup is cold.
- Mix in green onion and the rest of the ingredients. Split the soup among bowls.
- You can find pepitas in Latin markets, natural food stores, or supermarkets. Poblano chiles, also known as pasillas, and tomatillos can be found in Latin markets, specialty food stores, and the produce section of supermarkets.

Nutrition Information

- Calories: 205
- Total Carbohydrate: 14 g
- Total Fat: 16 g
- Fiber: 5 g
- Protein: 5 g
- Sodium: 13 mg
- Saturated Fat: 2 g

336. Tomato Chile Salsa

"This salsa is made with broiled onions and tomatoes."
Serving: Makes about 2 1/2 cups | Prep: 15m

Ingredients

- Olive oil for greasing
- 1 1/2 lb plum tomatoes (about 6 large)
- 1 medium onion, chopped
- 1 tbsp. chopped canned chipotle chiles in adobo plus 2 tsps. sauce from can
- 1 (2 1/2-inch) fresh jalapeño, seeded and remainder chopped (1 tbsp.)
- 1 tbsp. fresh lime juice
- 3/4 tsp. salt
- 1/4 tsp. black pepper
- 1/2 cup chopped fresh cilantro
- Accompaniment: tortilla chips

Direction

- Heat up the broiler.
- Oil a 9x13 inch non-glass roasting pan. Cut the tomatoes in half lengthwise and arrange them in the pan with the cut-side up. Sprinkle the onion over and around the tomatoes and broil them 4-5 inches from the heat until they start to brown, roughly 25-30 minutes.
- Cool for around 30 minutes to room temperature.
- Move the onions and tomatoes with their juices to a food processor along with salt, pepper, lime juice, jalapeno, and the chipotles with the sauce, then pulse until chopped finely.
- Move to a bowl and stir in the cilantro, then season with some salt.
- You can keep the salsa for up to 3 days, covered and chilled. Don't add the cilantro until ready to serve. Bring the salsa to room temperature before you serve.

Nutrition Information

- Calories: 56
- Total Carbohydrate: 8 g
- Total Fat: 3 g
- Fiber: 2 g
- Protein: 2 g
- Sodium: 398 mg
- Saturated Fat: 0 g

337. Tomato, Dill And White Cheddar Soup

"Omit cayenne pepper if you don't like spice."
Serving: Serves 6

Ingredients

- 2 tbsps. olive oil
- 3 cups chopped leeks (white and pale green parts only)
- 4 28-oz. cans diced tomatoes with juices
- 4 1/2 cups canned low-salt chicken broth
- 6 tbsps. (packed) chopped fresh dill or 2 tbsps. dried dillweed
- 1/4 tsp. cayenne pepper
- 1/2 cup light sour cream
- 4 oz. chilled sharp white cheddar cheese, sliced
- Fresh dill sprigs

Direction

- Heat oil on medium heat in a big heavy pot. Add leeks; sauté for 6 minutes till tender. Add cayenne, chopped dill, broth, tomatoes and their juices; boil. Lower the heat; simmer for 20 minutes till flavors blend and tomatoes are very soft, uncovered.
- Puree soup in batches till smooth in a processor; put back in the same pot. You can make it 1 day ahead, chilled, covered. Simmer on medium low heat; season using pepper and salt. Whisk in sour cream slowly; don't boil.
- Put soup into bowls; put cheese on top of each. Use dill sprigs to garnish.

Nutrition Information

- Calories: 285
- Total Carbohydrate: 29 g

- Cholesterol: 26 mg
- Total Fat: 16 g
- Fiber: 11 g
- Protein: 14 g
- Sodium: 255 mg
- Saturated Fat: 6 g

338. Torquato's Herb And Garlic Baked Tomatoes

"This recipe for stuffed baked tomatoes with good oil, basil or parsley, and garlic."
Serving: Serves 4 to 6

Ingredients

- 15 vine-ripened plum tomatoes
- 1/2 cup packed fresh basil or flat-leafed parsley leaves, washed well and spun dry
- 4 garlic cloves
- 1/4 cup extra-virgin olive oil
- fine sea salt to taste
- freshly ground black pepper to taste

Direction

- Set the oven to 400 degrees Fahrenheit.
- Cut the tomatoes in half lengthwise and use a small spoon to scoop out the seeds. Place the tomatoes in a single layer with the cut-side up onto a lightly oiled or nonstick jelly-roll pan.
- Blend pepper, salt, oil, garlic, and basil using a small food processor until it forms a paste and spread around 1/2 tsp. onto each of the tomato halves.
- Bake for 30-40 minutes, or until juicy and tender but still intact. Allow to slightly cool before you serve.

Nutrition Information

- Calories: 170
- Total Carbohydrate: 11 g
- Total Fat: 14 g
- Fiber: 3 g
- Protein: 3 g

- Sodium: 598 mg
- Saturated Fat: 2 g

339. Traditional Hummus

"A really amazing and creamy hummus recipe that you gotta try!"
Serving: 8 | Prep: 15m | Ready in: 15m

Ingredients

- 3 cloves garlic, peeled
- 2 (15 oz.) cans garbanzo beans, drained
- 1 cup olive oil
- 1 cup tahini
- 3 lemons, juiced
- salt to taste
- 1/4 cup olive oil

Direction

- Use a food processor to fully chop the garlic. Put in the garbanzo beans and process the mixture until it has pasty texture. Add in the lemon juice, 1 cup of olive oil, salt and tahini. Run the food processor until the mixture is creamy and smooth in consistency.
- Transfer the prepared hummus mixture to a bowl and drizzle it with 1/4 cup of olive oil on top.

Nutrition Information

- Calories: 560 calories;
- Total Carbohydrate: 22.5 g
- Cholesterol: 0 mg
- Total Fat: 50.5 g
- Protein: 8.6 g
- Sodium: 244 mg

340. Truly Coconutty Cream Pie

"A great coconut pie."
Serving: 8 | Prep: 45m | Ready in: 3h

Ingredients

- Crust:
- 1 cup all-purpose flour
- 3/8 tsp. salt
- 1/4 cup unsalted butter, chilled and cubed
- 2 tbsps. butter flavored shortening, chilled
- 1 1/2 tbsps. coconut water, or as needed
- 3/4 fluid oz. coconut-flavored rum
- Filling:
- 1 (18 oz.) can coconut milk
- 1 cup white sugar, divided
- 1 cup flaked sweetened coconut, toasted
- 1 vanilla bean, split and scraped
- 1/3 cup cornstarch
- 3/4 cup whole milk
- 2 eggs
- 1 egg yolk
- 2 tbsps. butter, room temperature
- Topping:
- 2 cups heavy whipping cream
- 1/4 cup confectioners' sugar
- 1/2 tsp. vanilla extract
- 1 tsp. lemon juice
- 2 tbsps. flaked sweetened coconut, toasted

Direction

- Crust: Pulse cold shortening, cold butter, salt and flour till shortening and butter are small pea-sized in a food processor's bowl. Put mixture into a bowl. 1 tbsp. at a time, add rum and coconut water, tossing to mix with a fork. Wrap in plastic wrap when it can get squeezed into ball; refrigerate for 30 minutes.
- Grease an 8-in. pie pan. Roll the dough out to a 12-in. circle on a lightly floured surface. Put the dough in pie pan carefully; trim the edges. Fold the dough under itself; crimp the crust. Loosely cover with plastic wrap; refrigerate for 30 minutes.
- Preheat the oven to 175°C/350°F.
- Use a fork to prick sides and bottom of the pie dough; line aluminum foil/parchment paper on dough. Weight it down using dried beans/pie weights. Bake for 15-20 minutes till bottom of the crust starts to color and crust's edges are golden. Take the crust from the oven; remove the beans and foil carefully. Put aside.
- Mix scraped vanilla bean seeds and the pod, 1 cup toasted coconut, 1/2 cup sugar and coconut milk in a saucepan on medium low heat; occasionally mix to melt the sugar. Boil; take off from the heat.
- Whisk leftover 1/2 cup sugar with cornstarch. Whisk egg yolk and eggs in a big heatproof bowl; whisk in cornstarch mixture and milk. Put hot coconut milk into the egg mixture slowly, constantly whisking. Put the custard mixture back in the saucepan.
- Cook custard on medium heat, constantly mixing with a wooden spoon/spatula. Boil; cook for 2 minutes, mixing. It'll thicken. Take off the pan from the heat; discard vanilla bean pod and whisk in butter. Put custard into the cooled pie crust; chill the pie for about 1 hour.
- To chill, put beaters and mixing bowl into the freezer for about 15 minutes. Whip the cream till it starts to thicken on high speed; add lemon juice, vanilla and confectioners' sugar slowly. Continue to beat till stiff. Spread/pipe cream onto the chilled pie; sprinkle with leftover toasted coconut.

Nutrition Information

- Calories: 723 calories;
- Total Carbohydrate: 58 g
- Cholesterol: 175 mg
- Total Fat: 53.1 g
- Protein: 7.1 g
- Sodium: 222 mg

341. Turkey Tonnato

"A fantastic dish for entertaining."
Serving: Makes 6 to 8 (main-course) servings | Prep: 30m

Ingredients

- 3 tbsps. black-olive tapenade
- 1 tbsp. finely grated fresh lemon zest
- 1 tbsp. finely chopped garlic
- 2 tsps. finely chopped fresh rosemary
- 1 (4- to 4 1/2-lb) boneless turkey breast half with skin
- 2 tsps. salt
- 1 tsp. black pepper
- 2 tbsps. extra-virgin olive oil
- 1 cup dry white wine
- 1 (6-oz) can chunk light tuna in olive oil (do not drain)
- 1/2 cup extra-virgin olive oil
- 2 tbsps. water
- 1 tbsp. fresh lemon juice
- 2 tsps. anchovy paste
- Accompaniments: lemon wedges; capers; chopped fresh flat-leaf parsley
- kitchen string; an instant-read thermometer

Direction

- Filling and roast: Place oven rack in center position. Preheat the oven to 350°F.
- In a small bowl, mix rosemary, garlic, zest and tapenade.
- On a work surface, put turkey with pointed, narrower end near you, skin side up. Choose which breast's long side is thickest. Starting from the thickest side, hold a knife parallel to work surface, horizontally cutting breast nearly in half, halting an inch from the other side. Open the breast up like a book. Season 1/2 tsp. pepper and 1 tsp. salt on breast. Evenly spread tapenade mixture on breast using a spoon's back. On all sides, leave an inch border. Beginning with side without the skin, roll turkey up sideways, finishing with the seam side down. The skin should be outside the rolled breast. At 1-in. intervals, use kitchen string to tie the turkey breast crosswise. Pat dry roast. Sprinkle leftover 1 tsp. salt and 1/2 tsp. pepper outside all over the roast.
- Cooking: In a 12-in. heavy skillet, heat 2 tbsp. olive oil till hot yet not smoking. Brown turkey, 8 minutes total, occasionally turning. Put into a 13x9-in. roasting pan. Put wine into pan. Roast turkey for 1 hour till an inserted thermometer diagonally 2-in. into the thickest part reads 160°F.
- On platter, put roast; cool. Keep pan juices. Completely cool roast. Chill, uncovered, wrapped tightly in plastic wrap for 2 hours.
- Sauce: In a blender, puree 4 tbsp. reserved pan juices, anchovy paste, lemon juice, water, 1/2 cup olive oil and tuna and its oil in a blender. Stop to scrape down sides if needed till very smooth. Put into a bowl. Season with pepper and salt. Use a plastic wrap to cover bowl. Chill for 1 hour till cold.
- Turkey tonnato assembly: Slice chilled turkey roast to 1/4-in. thick slices. Throw strings. Put chilled sauce on top. Bring sauce and turkey to room temperature for an hour. Serve with parsley, capers and lemon wedges.
- You can make sauce and turkey roast chilled, separately, for up to 2 days.

Nutrition Information

- Calories: 742
- Total Carbohydrate: 2 g
- Cholesterol: 194 mg
- Total Fat: 46 g
- Fiber: 0 g
- Protein: 72 g
- Sodium: 959 mg
- Saturated Fat: 9 g

342. Turtle Swirl Cheesecake

Serving: Serves 12

Ingredients

- 1 9-oz. package chocolate wafer cookies

- 6 tbsps. (3/4 stick) unsalted butter, melted
- 4 8-oz. packages cream cheese, room temperature
- 1 1/4 cups sugar
- 5 large eggs
- 1 1/2 tsps. vanilla extract
- 3 tbsps. whipping cream
- 4 oz. semisweet chocolate, chopped
- 1 cup purchased butterscotch caramel fudge sauce
- 1/2 cup (about) whole toasted pecans

Direction

- Crust: preheat an oven to 350°F. In processor, finely grind cookies; blend in butter. On 1-in. up sides and on bottom of 9-in. diameter springform pan that has 2 3/4-in. high sides, press crumb mixture. Use foil to wrap springform pan's outside.
- Filling: Beat cream cheese using electric mixer till fluffy in a big bowl. Add sugar slowly; beat till smooth. One by one, beat in eggs; stir in vanilla extract.
- Simmer cream in small heavy saucepan; lower heat to low. Add the chocolate; mix till smooth and melted. Take off heat.
- Put 1/2 cream cheese mixture in crust; by tbsps., put 1/2 chocolate mixture, evenly spacing. Swirl chocolate mixture into the filling using knife's tip. Put leftover cream cheese mixture on top; by tbsps., put leftover chocolate mixture on top. Swirl into filling. Bake for 1 hour 5 minutes till center slightly moves when pan is shaken and sides are set; cake might crack. Cool it in pan on rack and chill overnight.
- To loosen cake, cut around pan sides using small knife; release pan sides. On top of cake, drizzle 1/4 cup of caramel sauce; use whole pecans to decorate. Pass leftover sauce separately.

Nutrition Information

- Calories: 675
- Total Carbohydrate: 56 g
- Cholesterol: 181 mg
- Total Fat: 48 g
- Fiber: 2 g
- Protein: 10 g
- Sodium: 445 mg
- Saturated Fat: 26 g

343. Tuscan Bean Soup With Prosciutto And Grated Parmigiano-reggiano

"A lovely soup recipe."
Serving: 4 servings

Ingredients

- 4 15-oz. cans creamy beans (such as giant white beans, borlotti beans, or cannellini beans), not drained (about 6 cups)
- 6 large garlic cloves, grated or minced (about 2 tbsps.)
- 3 tsps. kosher salt
- 2 tsps. fresh thyme leaves
- 4 large fresh basil leaves
- 2 cups shredded Napa cabbage (about 1/4 head)
- High-quality extra-virgin olive oil, for drizzling
- Parmigiano-Reggiano wedge, for grating
- 4 thin slices prosciutto (about 2 oz.)

Direction

- Boil 2 cups water, basil, thyme, salt, garlic and beans and their liquid in a big saucepan on high heat. Lower heat to low; simmer to meld flavors for 5 minutes. Remove 1 1/2 cups bean; put basil/garlic in saucepan. Puree leftover beans with an immersion blender till smooth in a pot.
- Or, slightly cool soup then put it into a food processor/blender; puree, holding down lid tightly so hot liquid won't splatter out. Mix in cabbage and reserved beans; if needed, thin soup using water. Cook soup on medium heat

for 5 minutes till cabbage is slightly tender and wilts.
- Evenly divide soup to 4 bowls/big soup plates, filling to right under the rim. Drizzle high-quality olive oil on each serving; grate thin parmesan cheese layer on them. Tear 1 prosciutto slice to few pieces; rumple pieces onto 1 soup bowl. Repeat using leftover prosciutto slices.

344. Tuscan Garlic-pepper Toasts

"This recipe goes great with salad or soup."
Serving: Makes 8 toasts

Ingredients

- 8 1/3-inch-thick 7-inch-long slices pain rustique or other wide flat country loaf
- 1 large garlic clove, peeled
- 1/4 cup extra-virgin olive oil
- 1/2 cup grated Parmesan cheese
- 3/4 tsp. coarsely ground black pepper
- Dried crushed red pepper

Direction

- Set the oven to 425 degrees Fahrenheit. Place the bread slices onto a baking sheet. Place the garlic into a mini processor. As the motor runs, pour in the oil gradually, then add the black pepper and cheese. Season the mixture with salt to taste. Spread the mixture onto the bread slices and sprinkle crushed red pepper over all. Bake until edges are crisp, around 10 minutes. Place the toasts onto a platter.

345. Two-potato Soup

"This low calorie soup dish combines sweet potatoes with russets."
Serving: Serves 4

Ingredients

- 3 1/2 cups canned unsalted chicken broth
- 12 oz. (about 3 small) russet potatoes, peeled, chopped
- 1 10-oz. (about 1 large) orange-fleshed sweet potato (yam), peeled, chopped
- 3 large garlic cloves
- 1/2 tsp. minced fresh rosemary

Direction

- In a big heavy saucepan, combine the first 4 ingredients and simmer while covered on medium-low heat for 20 minutes until the potatoes are soft. Transfer the mixture into a processor or blender, then puree until smoothened and return to the saucepan. Stir in the rosemary and allow to simmer. Season with pepper and salt to taste. You can make this 2 days before, keeping refrigerated, then simmer before serving.

346. Vanilla Chiffon Cake With Chocolate Sorbet

"Puree sugar with some berries to create colorful sauce, if desired."
Serving: Makes 8 Servings

Ingredients

- 1 1/2 cups sugar
- 1/2 cup matzo cake meal
- 1/2 cup potato starch
- 1 1/2 vanilla beans, chopped
- 1/2 tsp. coarse salt
- 7 large eggs, separated
- 2 tbsps. vegetable oil
- 2 tbsps. brandy
- Chocolate Sorbet

Direction

- Preheat an oven to 350°F. Blend salt, vanilla beans, potato starch, matzo cake meal and 1/2 cup sugar till beans are chopped finely in processor. Into small bowl, sift mixture; in sieve, discard beans.

- Beat egg whites using electric mixer till medium-firm peaks form in a big bowl. Add 3/4 cup sugar slowly; beat till stiff yet not dry. Beat 1/4 cup sugar and yolks using the same beaters for 5 minutes till thick in another bowl. Beat in oil slowly then brandy; beat in the matzo mixture. In 3 additions, fold in whites.
- Put batter in 10-in. diameter ungreased tube pan that has removable bottom; bake for 37 minutes till inserted tester near middle exits clean. Invert center tube pan on narrow-neck bottle immediately; fully cool. You can make it 1 day ahead; in pan, cover cake.
- To loosen cake, cut around pan sides. Cut to wedges and serve with sorbet.

347. Vanilla Panna Cotta With Pear Jam

"Start this recipe 1 day before serving; panna cotta and pear jam are best chilled overnight."
Serving: Makes 8 to 10 servings

Ingredients

- 2 lbs. ripe Bartlett pears, peeled, cored, and cut into 1/4-inch-thick slices
- 1 cup sugar
- 4 tsps. unflavored powdered gelatin from 2 (1/4-oz.) envelopes
- 2 cups heavy cream
- 2 cups whole milk
- 1/2 cup sugar
- 2 vanilla beans, split lengthwise

Direction

- Pear jam: toss sugar and pears in a big bowl; cover. Refrigerate for a minimum of 8 hours – overnight.
- Panna cotta: Sprinkle gelatin on cream in small bowl; stand for 1 minute till gelatin softens.
- Meanwhile, whisk sugar and milk in medium saucepan on medium heat. From vanilla beans, scrape in seeds; add beans. Heat for 2 minutes till sugar is dissolved, occasionally whisking; take off heat. Whisk in cream mixture. Through fine-mesh sieve, strain; discard vanilla beans. Put mixture into 8 4-oz. ramekins; cover. Refrigerate for a minimum of 8 hours – overnight.
- Complete pear jam: Simmer pear mixture and 1/2 cup water in medium heavy saucepan on medium heat for 20 minutes till pears are tender, uncovered. Put mixture in food processor; puree till smooth. Put jam in medium bowl; tightly cover. Refrigerate for 1 hour till cool; jam keeps for a maximum of 1 week in fridge with cover.
- Unmold then serve: Around each ramekin's inside edge, run thin sharp knife to loosen. In bowl with very warm water, dip bottom of 1 ramekin for 6 seconds. On ramekin, put plate; invert panna cotta on plate, lifting off ramekin gently. Repeat to unmold leftover panna cottas. Put 1/4 cup pear jam on each; serve.

Nutrition Information

- Calories: 466
- Total Carbohydrate: 59 g
- Cholesterol: 88 mg
- Total Fat: 24 g
- Fiber: 4 g
- Protein: 4 g
- Sodium: 52 mg
- Saturated Fat: 15 g

348. Vegan Broccoli-hazelnut Spread

"A healthy, vegan spread that you can use as a side to potatoes or on top of the pasta."
Serving: 4 | Prep: 15m | Ready in: 35m

Ingredients

- 3 tbsps. olive oil, divided, or more as needed
- 1 shallot, minced
- 3/4 cup chopped hazelnuts
- 2 3/4 cups broccoli florets
- 1 tbsp. finely chopped fresh parsley

- 1 tsp. chopped fresh dill
- 1 pinch salt and freshly ground black pepper to taste
- 1 pinch ground nutmeg

Direction

- In a frying pan, heat 1 tbsp. of olive oil and cook the shallot for about 5 minutes, until it turns translucent and tender. Add the hazelnuts and let it cook for around 2 minutes, until it becomes toasted. Take it out of the heat and allow it to cool for 10 minutes.
- In the meantime, boil a pot of lightly salted water and cook the broccoli for approximately 3 minutes, until it becomes tender. Drain and wash under cold water, then drain well.
- In the bowl of a food processor, mix together the dill, parsley, broccoli and shallot-hazelnut mixture, then pulse until combined. While the processor is still running, gradually pour in 2 tbsp. of olive oil, until the spread becomes smooth. If necessary, add more olive oil. Sprinkle nutmeg, pepper and salt to season.

Nutrition Information

- Calories: 281 calories;
- Total Carbohydrate: 10.7 g
- Cholesterol: 0 mg
- Total Fat: 25.8 g
- Protein: 5.9 g
- Sodium: 62 mg

349. Vegan Gingerbread Scones

"I succeeded in making a festive version of my usual scones and several permutations later! You will love these scones."
Serving: 16 | Prep: 20m | Ready in: 50m

Ingredients

- 1 orange
- 2 tbsps. water, or as needed
- 2 tbsps. chia seeds
- 1 tbsp. blackstrap molasses
- 2 cups all-purpose flour
- 1/2 cup white sugar
- 1 tbsp. ground cinnamon
- 1 tbsp. ground ginger
- 2 tsps. cream of tartar
- 1 tsp. baking soda
- 1 tsp. ground nutmeg
- 1 tsp. ground allspice
- 3/4 tsp. salt
- 1/2 cup coconut oil, chilled
- 1/2 finely chopped pecans

Direction

- Preheat the oven to 150 degrees C (300 degrees F). Line parchment paper onto a baking sheet.
- Into a measuring cup, juice the orange and then pour plenty of water to reach 8 oz.. Mix in molasses and chia seeds. Reserve the wet mixture for about 10 minutes until gelled.
- In the bowl of a food processor, put nutmeg, flour, sugar, salt, allspice, cinnamon, ginger, baking soda and cream of tartar. Pulse for about 30 seconds until combined. Chop the chilled coconut oil into eight pieces, add to the flour mixture and then pulse for about 30 seconds until the mixture looks like wet sand.
- Into the food processor, pour the wet mixture and then pulse briefly for about 1 minute until the dough begins to come together. Scrape the dough into a large bowl. Pour in pecans and then distribute them in the dough by kneading about 5 or 6 turns.
- Onto a lightly floured surface, place the dough and then chop into two equal portions. Roll or pat each portion to form a 1-inch thick round. Chop into eight wedge-shape pieces and transfer into the baking sheet prepared.
- Bake for about 20 minutes in the preheated oven until the edges of scones look dry and the tops are firm.

Nutrition Information

- Calories: 152 calories;
- Total Carbohydrate: 20.3 g
- Cholesterol: 0 mg
- Total Fat: 7.4 g
- Protein: 1.8 g

- Sodium: 189 mg

350. Vegan Homemade Plain Cream Cheese

"This is a dairy-free, vegan cream cheese made from cashews."
Serving: 32 | Prep: 10m | Ready in: 9h10m

Ingredients

- 2 cups unsalted raw cashews
- 1/2 tsp. Himalayan pink salt
- 3 tbsps. plain non-dairy yogurt

Direction

- In a bowl of water, soak the cashews for 8 hours up to overnight.
- Drain the cashews and throw away the water. In a food processor bowl, combine salt and cashews, then pulse until creamy and smooth, 10-15 minutes. Stir in the yogurt, mixing well to combine. Allow to sit at room temperature for an hour before placing in the refrigerator.

Nutrition Information

- Calories: 48 calories;
- Total Carbohydrate: 2.7 g
- Cholesterol: 0 mg
- Total Fat: 3.8 g
- Protein: 1.5 g
- Sodium: 37 mg

351. Vegan Keto Lemon Fat Bombs

"Prepare these delicious vegan bombs that are made of coconut and lemon zest. You can make in advance for keto and raw diets and also for a quick energy snack!"
Serving: 16 | Prep: 20m | Ready in: 50m

Ingredients

- 1 cup dry unsweetened shredded coconut
- 1/4 cup coconut oil, at room temperature
- 3 tbsps. powdered erythritol sweetener (such as Swerve®)
- 2 tbsps. lemon zest
- 1 pinch sea salt

Direction

- In a food processor, blend the shredded coconut for about 15 minutes until the resulting mixture is creamy. Add sea salt, lemon zest, coconut oil, and erythritol and then blend until mixed well. Pour the mixture into the mini muffin cups and refrigerate for about 30 minutes until set.

Nutrition Information

- Calories: 68 calories;
- Total Carbohydrate: 3.4 g
- Cholesterol: 0 mg
- Total Fat: 7.2 g
- Protein: 0.4 g
- Sodium: 22 mg

352. Viennese Linzertorte Cake

"A fun cake recipe!"
Serving: Serves 14 to 16

Ingredients

- 1 cup hazelnuts, toasted
- 2 cups unbleached all purpose flour
- 1 tbsp. baking powder
- 1 1/2 tsps. Chinese five-spice powder*
- 1/2 tsp. ground nutmeg
- 1/2 tsp. salt
- 3/4 cup (1 1/2 sticks) unsalted butter, room temperature
- 1 1/2 cups sugar
- 3 large egg yolks
- 2 tsps. vanilla extract
- 1 tsp. almond extract
- 1 1/4 cups whole milk
- 5 large egg whites, room temperature

- 6 oz. good-quality white chocolate (such as Lindt or Baker's)
- 3 8-oz. packages cream cheese, room temperature
- 9 tbsps. unsalted butter, room temperature
- 1 1/2 cups powdered sugar
- 2 1/4 tsps. vanilla extract
- 1/2 tsp. almond extract
- 1 cup raspberry preserves, stirred to loosen
- 1 1/2 cups finely chopped toasted hazelnuts
- *A blend of ground anise, cinnamon, star anise, cloves and ginger available in the spice section of most supermarkets.

Direction

- Preheat an oven to 350°F. Butter then flour 15x10x1-in. jellyroll pan. In processor, finely ground flour and nuts; put into medium bowl. Stir in salt, spices and baking powder. Beat sugar and butter till well blended with an electric mixer in a big bowl; beat in extracts and yolks. Alternately with milk, add dry ingredients using low speed, beating till thick and just combined. Beat whites using dry clean beaters till stiff peaks form in another big bowl. Fold 1/3 whites into the batter to lighten; fold in leftover whites.
- Spread batter in prepped pan; smooth top. Bake for 25 minutes till inserted tester in middle exits clean. Cool cake for 20 minutes on rack. To loosen, run a sharp knife around the cake. Turn out cake on foil-lined rack and cool.
- Frosting: Mix white chocolate till melted on top of double boiler above barely simmering water; cool to barely lukewarm. Beat butter and cream cheese using electric mixer till smooth in big bowl; beat in white chocolate and then extracts and sugar. Chill till firm enough to spread if frosting is very soft.
- Crosswise cut cake to 3 5x10-in. rectangles using serrated knife. On platter, put 1 cake rectangle; spread with 3/4 cup frosting. Drizzle with 1/4 cup preserves; spread on frosting. Put 2nd cake over; spread with 3/4 cup frosting. Drizzle with 1/4 cup preserves; spread on frosting. Put 3rd cake over. Put 1 1/4 cups frosting in pastry bag with 1/4-in. star tip. Spread leftover frosting on sides and top of cake. Drizzle leftover preserves on cake's top; evenly spread to cover top. Refrigerate the cake for 20 minutes till frosting starts to firm.
- In 7 diagonal lines, pipe frosting on cake, spacing apart. In opposing direction, repeat, piping 6 lines and making lattice. On cake's sides, press chopped nuts. Pipe frosting line around cake's top edge where preserves and nuts meet. You can make it 2 days ahead. Use dome of foil to cover; chill. Stand before serving for 2 hours in room temperature.

Nutrition Information

- Calories: 838
- Total Carbohydrate: 79 g
- Cholesterol: 143 mg
- Total Fat: 54 g
- Fiber: 3 g
- Protein: 12 g
- Sodium: 391 mg
- Saturated Fat: 25 g

353. Vietnamese Chicken Sandwich (banh Mi)

"Despite the unusual name of this sandwich, the ingredients are all available at any supermarket. The traditional pork-pâté filling is called Liverwurst — the meatiness match nicely with the strong-flavored fresh cilantro and vegetables."

Serving: Makes 4 individual sandwiches | Prep: 30m

Ingredients

- 1/2 lb. daikon, peeled
- 1 carrot, peeled
- 1/2 cup rice vinegar (not seasoned)
- 1 tbsp. sugar
- 1 (24-inch) soft baguette
- 2 tbsps. vegetable oil
- 1 tbsp. Asian fish sauce

- 1/2 tsp. soy sauce
- 1/4 lb. liverwurst
- 2 fresh jalapeños, thinly sliced
- 1/2 sweet onion, cut into 1/4-inch rings
- 3/4 cup packed cilantro sprigs
- 2 cooked chicken breasts from a rotisserie chicken, thinly sliced
- Lettuce leaves
- 2 tbsps. mayonnaise

Direction

- Set the oven for preheating to 350°F placing the oven rack in middle.
- Shred carrot and daikon in a food processor with medium shredding disk fitted. Combine 1/2 tsp. salt, vinegar and sugar and toss with shredded vegetables together. Allow the slaw sit for 15 minutes while stirring from time to time.
- Meanwhile, place the baguette in the oven until crusty and heat for about 5 minutes. Cut off and remove round ends, divide the baguette.
- Combine together soy sauce, oil and fish sauce; brush over cut sides of the bread. On the bottom layer of bread, spread the liverwurst; top it off with cilantro, onion and chiles.
- Strain slaw in a colander.
- Arrange slaw, chicken and lettuce over cilantro. Fill and spread top layer of bread with the mayonnaise and slice the sandwich crosswise into quarters.

Nutrition Information

- Calories: 411
- Total Carbohydrate: 50 g
- Cholesterol: 25 mg
- Total Fat: 16 g
- Fiber: 4 g
- Protein: 17 g
- Sodium: 931 mg
- Saturated Fat: 2 g

354. Walnut Cheesecakes With Tokay Syrup

"Scrumptious cheesecake recipe."
Serving: Makes 6 servings | Prep: 30m

Ingredients

- 1/3 cup Grape Nuts cereal
- 3 tbsps. chopped walnuts, toasted
- 2 pitted dates
- 1/2 tsp. finely grated fresh lemon zest
- 1/8 tsp. cinnamon
- 1 cup 1% cottage cheese
- 4 oz reduced-fat cream cheese
- 2 tbsps. sugar
- 1 large egg white
- 1 tbsp. cornstarch
- 1 tsp. finely grated fresh lemon zest
- 1/2 tsp. vanilla
- 3 tbsps. sugar
- 1/3 cup water
- 2 tbsps. Tokay or Sauternes

Direction

- Preheat the oven to 300 degrees F.
- Prepare crust. In a food processor, combine crust ingredients until moist and crumbly.
- Grease six 1/3-cup muffin tins and place wax or parchment papers at the bottom. Split crust mixture between muffin tins and push firmly to even it out on the base.
- Prepare the filling and cake. In a food processor, cream cottage cheese until smooth; scuff down the sides of the bowl regularly. Blend in the remaining filling ingredients until smooth. Scoop mixture on muffin cups then place in a hot water bath. Bake in the middle of the oven for 20-25mins until firm. Take it out of the pan and let the pan cool down on a rack. Refrigerate while covered for two hours.
- Meanwhile, boil water and sugar in a small pot on high heat, mix until the sugar dissolves and the liquid reduces to a quarter cup. Mix in Tokay and move on a bowl; cover. Refrigerate.

- Using a small and wet knife, run it around the edges of the cake and flip onto baking sheet. Serve cakes with a drizzle of syrup.

355. Walnut-herb Pesto

"Great on chicken or pasta."
Serving: Makes 1 1/2 cups

Ingredients

- 3 garlic cloves, peeled
- 1 cup chopped toasted walnuts
- 1 cup (packed) fresh Italian parsley leaves
- 1/2 cup walnut oil
- 2 tbsps. coarsely chopped fresh chives
- 2 tbsps. coarsely chopped fresh dill
- 2 tbsps. coarsely chopped fresh mint
- 2 1/2 tsps. finely grated lemon peel
- 1/2 cup freshly grated Parmesan cheese

Direction

- Drop garlic into processor as machine runs; finely chop. Add walnuts and following 6 ingredients; process with on/off turns till chunky puree forms, scraping down sides occasionally. Put into a bowl and mix in parmesan cheese; season with pepper and salt to taste. You can make the pesto 4 hours ahead, refrigerated, covered.

Nutrition Information

- Calories: 166
- Total Carbohydrate: 2 g
- Cholesterol: 3 mg
- Total Fat: 17 g
- Fiber: 1 g
- Protein: 3 g
- Sodium: 68 mg
- Saturated Fat: 2 g

356. White Bean Dip With Pine Nuts

"The ingredients amount I uses makes a cup, but you can easily double/triple the amounts."
Serving: 8 | Prep: 10m | Ready in: 2h10m

Ingredients

- 2 tbsps. pine nuts
- 2 tsps. chopped fresh basil
- 1 tsp. chopped fresh oregano
- 1 cup cooked Great Northern beans
- 2 cloves garlic, cut in half
- 1 tsp. lime juice
- 1 roma (plum) tomato, roughly chopped
- sea salt to taste
- black pepper to taste
- 1 tbsp. olive oil

Direction

- Process oregano, basil and pine nuts 2-3 times to ground the nuts finely in a food processor, covered. Add garlic and beans; process for 30-60 seconds till smooth. Put pepper, salt, tomato and lime juice in; pulse 2-3 times till mixture is spreadable and smooth. Drizzle oil into the dip as food processor runs. Add 1 tbsp. of water at a time in till dip is at the preferred consistency if the mixture is too thick.
- Refrigerate for at least 2 hours – overnight to blend flavors; serve.

Nutrition Information

- Calories: 56 calories;
- Total Carbohydrate: 5.7 g
- Cholesterol: 0 mg
- Total Fat: 2.9 g
- Protein: 2.5 g
- Sodium: 41 mg

357. White Bean Purée

"Great with chicken or roast lamb."
Serving: Makes 3 1/2 cups

Ingredients

- 1 tbsp. olive oil
- 1/4 cup chopped bacon
- 1/2 carrot, finely chopped
- 1/2 cup chopped onion
- 1 tbsp. chopped fresh rosemary or 2 tsps. dried
- 3 15-oz. cans cannellini (white kidney beans), rinsed, drained
- 1 cup canned low-salt chicken broth

Direction

- Heat oil on medium high heat in a big heavy saucepan. Add bacon; sauté for 3 minutes till brown. Lower heat to low. Add rosemary, onion and carrot; sauté for 5 minutes till veggies are tender. Put heat on high. Add broth and cannellini; boil. Lower heat to low and cook for 20 minutes till nearly all liquid is absorbed, mixing often. In processor, puree mixture; put in saucepan. Season with pepper and salt.

Nutrition Information

- Calories: 232
- Total Carbohydrate: 33 g
- Cholesterol: 3 mg
- Total Fat: 6 g
- Fiber: 10 g
- Protein: 13 g
- Sodium: 677 mg
- Saturated Fat: 1 g

358. White Bean, Garlic, And Tomato Salsa

Serving: Makes about 4 cups

Ingredients

- 1 head garlic
- a 16-oz. can small white beans such as navy
- 3 medium vine-ripened tomatoes (about 1 1/4 lbs.)
- 1 small sweet onion such as Vidalia
- 1/2 cup packed fresh basil leaves
- 2 tbsps. fresh lemon juice

Direction

- Preheat an oven to 400°F.
- Separate the garlic head to cloves; discard the loosely papery outer skin but keep the skin intact on the cloves. Wrap in foil; to tightly seal, crimp seams. Roast garlic till soft for 30 minutes in center of oven. Unwrap garlic; slightly cool. From each clove, peel skins; mash garlic pulp till smooth with fork in a bowl.
- Rinse then drain enough beans to get 1 cup; keep leftover for another time. Put into garlic. Cut 2 tomatoes to 1/4-in. dice; put into beans. Quarter leftover tomato; puree till smooth in a food processor or blender. Put puree in bean mixture. Chop basil and onion finely; put in bean mixture with the lemon juice, tossing to mix. Season salsa with pepper and salt. You can make salsa 1 hour ahead, covered, chilled.

359. White Chocolate And Raspberry Cheesecake

Serving: Serves 8

Ingredients

- 18 vanilla wafer cookies
- 1 cup almonds, toasted
- 4 1/2 tbsps. unsalted butter, melted

- 4 oz. imported white chocolate (such as Lindt), chopped
- 2 8-oz. packages cream cheese, room temperature
- 2/3 cup sugar
- 2 tsps. vanilla extract
- 3/4 tsp. grated lemon peel
- 2 large eggs
- 3/4 cup fresh raspberries or frozen unsweetened, thawed, drained
- 1 8-oz. container sour cream
- 3 tbsps. sugar
- 1/2 tsp. vanilla extract
- 2 1/2-pint baskets raspberries or one 1-pint basket strawberries
- 1/2 cup seedless raspberry jam

Direction

- Crust: Preheat an oven to 350°F. Put big foil piece on big heavy baking sheet. Put 8x2-in. bottomless and heart-shaped cake pan on foil. Use 8-in. springform pan and omit foil if unavailable. 1-in. up sides and outside of pan, wrap foil. Butter pan and foil. Grind almonds and cookies finely in processor. Add butter; blend till it makes very moist crumbs. Firmly press crust 2-in. up sides and on bottom of pan using plastic wrap for aid. Bake for 10 minutes till golden; cool. Maintain the oven temperature.
- Filling: Melt the white chocolate till smooth on top of double boiler above simmering water, mixing often; take from above water. Beat vanilla, peel, sugar and cream cheese using electric mixer till smooth in big bowl. One by one, add eggs; beat till just combined. Beat in the white chocolate.
- Put 1/2 batter in crust; put 3/4 cup berries over. Put leftover batter over; bake for 45 minutes till middle 3-in. still moves when you shake cake and cake's edges are set. Cool for 20 minutes. Maintain the oven temperature. Gently press down on cheesecake's edges to slightly flatten using fingertips.
- Topping: Whisk vanilla, sugar and sour cream in bowl; put on cake, spreading to pan's edge. Bake for 5 minutes. Put cake in pan onto rack. Around cake's sides, run small knife; fully cool. Chill cake overnight.
- Along pan's sides, fold down foil. Lift the cake pan off the cheesecake. Put cheesecake on platter; discard foil. Use berries to cover cake. Simmer jam in small saucepan, mixing often. Brush jam on berries gently. You can make it 3 hours ahead, chilled.

Nutrition Information

- Calories: 751
- Total Carbohydrate: 70 g
- Cholesterol: 144 mg
- Total Fat: 49 g
- Fiber: 6 g
- Protein: 12 g
- Sodium: 301 mg
- Saturated Fat: 23 g

360. White Clam Sauce Dip

Serving: Makes about 1 1/2 cups | Prep: 20m

Ingredients

- 3/4 cup chopped flat-leaf parsley
- 1 tbsp. fine dry bread crumbs
- 6 tbsps. extra-virgin olive oil, divided
- 1/3 cup finely chopped onion
- 5 garlic cloves, finely chopped
- 1/4 tsp. hot red pepper flakes
- 1/4 cup dry white wine
- 1/4 cup bottled clam juice
- 3 (6 1/2-oz.) cans chopped clams, drained
- 1 to 2 tsps. fresh lemon juice

Direction

- Puree 1/4 cup oil, breadcrumbs and parsley in a food processor.
- Cook red pepper flakes, garlic and onion in leftover 2 tbsp. oil on medium heat in a medium skillet for 5 minutes till pale golden, mixing. Add clam juice and wine; boil for 1-2

minutes till slightly reduced, mixing. Mix in clams; cook till heated through. Mix in parsley puree; take off heat. Season with salt and lemon juice.

Nutrition Information

- Calories: 545
- Total Carbohydrate: 17 g
- Cholesterol: 92 mg
- Total Fat: 30 g
- Fiber: 1 g
- Protein: 47 g
- Sodium: 360 mg
- Saturated Fat: 4 g

361. White Gazpacho

"Refreshing and delicious."
Serving: 6 | Ready in: 2h20m

Ingredients

- 2 English cucumbers, divided
- 2 cups green grapes, divided
- 2 slices country white bread, crust removed if desired, torn into pieces
- 2 cups "no-chicken" broth (see Tips) or reduced-sodium chicken broth
- 1 cup chopped honeydew melon
- ½ cup sliced blanched almonds, lightly toasted (see Tips), divided
- 1 small clove garlic, halved
- 2 tbsps. extra-virgin olive oil
- 2 tbsps. white-wine vinegar
- ¾ tsp. salt

Direction

- Dice unpeeled cucumber enough to get equal 1/2 cup; slice grapes enough to get equal 1/2 cup. Cover; refrigerate.
- Peel the leftover cucumbers; cut into chunks. Puree salt, vinegar, oil, garlic, 6 tbsp. almonds, melon, broth, bread, the leftover grapes and peeled cucumber in 2 batches till smooth in a blender. Put into a big bowl. Cover; refrigerate till chilled for a minimum of 2 hours to a maximum of 1 day.
- Serve garnished with the reserved grapes, cucumber and 2 tbsp. almonds.

Nutrition Information

- Calories: 210 calories;
- Total Carbohydrate: 23 g
- Cholesterol: 0 mg
- Total Fat: 12 g
- Fiber: 3 g
- Protein: 5 g
- Sodium: 541 mg
- Sugar: 13 g
- Saturated Fat: 1 g

362. Yam Soup With Coriander

"Roasted yams lend this soup a rich flavor."
Serving: Serves 4

Ingredients

- 1/4 cup plain nonfat yogurt
- 2 tbsps. (packed) chopped fresh cilantro
- 1/2 small garlic clove, minced
- Nonstick vegetable oil spray
- 1 1/2 lbs. yams (red-skinned sweet potatoes), peeled, cut into 1-inch-thick slices
- 3 3/4 cups (or more) low-fat (1%) milk
- 1 1/2 tsps. ground coriander

Direction

- In a small bowl, combine garlic, cilantro and yogurt. Put a cover and chill.
- Preheat an oven to 400 °F. With vegetable oil spray, coat a big baking sheet, desirably nonstick. On prepped baking sheet, place yams in 1 layer. Roast for 20 minutes till base sides of slices of yam turn brown. Flip yams over and roast for 15 minutes more till soft.
- In the meantime, in medium heavy saucepan, mix coriander and 2 cups of milk. Simmer.

- Lower heat to lowest; place cover and allow to cook for 10 minutes. Take off heat.
- In a processor, mix milk mixture and yams. Puree till velvety. Put back to the same saucepan. Mix in leftover 1 3/4 cups of milk and simmer, thin with additional milk, if wished. Season with pepper and salt to taste. Soup and yogurt mixture may be made a day in advance. Cover individually and chill. Reheat soup over moderate heat prior to proceeding.
- Into bowls, scoop the soup. Into every serving, swirl a tablespoonful yogurt mixture.

Nutrition Information

- Calories: 402
- Total Carbohydrate: 60 g
- Cholesterol: 23 mg
- Total Fat: 14 g
- Fiber: 7 g
- Protein: 11 g
- Sodium: 126 mg
- Saturated Fat: 5 g

363. Zucchini Cucumber Gazpacho

""There is nothing perfect rather than enjoying this cool and healthy soup in the summer.""
Serving: 4 | Prep: 15m | Ready in: 45m

Ingredients

- 2 cucumbers - peeled, seeded, and cubed
- 2 zucchini, cubed
- 3 tbsps. lemon juice
- 8 basil leaves
- salt and ground black pepper to taste
- 1/4 cup yogurt

Direction

- In the food processor, combine pepper, salt, basil leaves, lemon juice, zucchini and cucumbers together; whisk until smooth. Transfer into a bowl; mix in yogurt.
- Keep it in a refrigerator for at least 30 minutes. Serve.

Nutrition Information

- Calories: 37 calories;
- Total Carbohydrate: 7.7 g
- Cholesterol: < 1 mg
- Total Fat: 0.5 g
- Protein: 2.2 g
- Sodium: 58 mg

364. Zucchini Ginger Cupcakes

"Moist and delicate."
Serving: Makes 12 cupcakes | Prep: 15m

Ingredients

- 1/3 cup crystallized ginger (1 3/4 oz), coarsely chopped
- 2 cups all-purpose flour
- 1 tsp. ground ginger
- 1 tsp. ground cinnamon
- 1 tsp. finely grated fresh orange zest
- 1 tsp. salt
- 1 tsp. baking soda
- 1/2 tsp. baking powder
- 2 cups coarsely grated zucchini (2 medium)
- 3/4 cup mild olive oil
- 3/4 cup mild honey
- 2 large eggs, lightly beaten
- 1 tsp. vanilla
- 8 oz cream cheese, softened
- 2 tbsps. unsalted butter, softened
- 1/2 cup confectioners sugar
- 1 tsp. vanilla
- 1/2 tsp. ground ginger
- 1/2 tsp. ground cinnamon
- 1/2 tsp. finely grated fresh orange zest
- a muffin pan with 12 (1/2-cup) cups; 12 paper liners

Direction

- Bake cupcakes: In the middle position, put oven rack; preheat the oven to 350°F. Line liners on muffin cups.
- Pulse crystallized ginger till finely ground in a food processor. Add baking powder, baking soda, salt, zest, cinnamon, ground ginger and flour; pulse till combined.
- Whisk vanilla, eggs, honey, oil and zucchini in medium bowl. Mix in flour mixture just till combined.
- Divide batter to muffin cups; bake for 20-24 minutes till inserted skewer/wooden pick in the middle of cupcake exits clean and cupcakes are golden.
- Cool for 10 minutes in pan on a rack. Take cupcakes out of the pan; fully cool for 1 hour.
- Frosting: Use an electric mixer on high speed to beat frosting ingredients for 3-5 minutes till fluffy and well combined.
- Frost cooled cupcake's tops.

Nutrition Information

- Calories: 393
- Total Carbohydrate: 44 g
- Cholesterol: 57 mg
- Total Fat: 23 g
- Fiber: 1 g
- Protein: 5 g
- Sodium: 272 mg
- Saturated Fat: 7 g

365. Zucchini Poppers With Sour Cream Dip

"The trick to make this recipe is to get the liquid out from the grated zucchini as much as you can. It can help make the batter lighter and firmer, making it easier to roll."
Serving: Makes 40 poppers and 2 cups dip

Ingredients

- 2 cups sour cream
- ¼ cup fresh flat-leaf parsley, coarsely chopped
- 1 tsp. sugar
- 2 tbsps. freshly squeezed lime juice (from 1 lime)
- ½ tsp. kosher salt
- 1/4 tsp. freshly ground black pepper
- 3 medium zucchini
- 1 large egg plus 1 large egg yolk, lightly whisked
- 2/3 cup all-purpose flour
- 2 oz. Parmesan cheese, finely grated (about ½ cup)
- 20 fresh large sage leaves, finely chopped
- 1 clove garlic, finely chopped
- About 1 1/4 cups vegetable oil

Direction

- To make the dip: In a small bowl, stir pepper, salt, lime juice, sugar, parsley, and sour cream together. You can make this up to 24 hours ahead, keep refrigerated while covered.
- To make the poppers: Use a triple layer of paper towels or a clean kitchen towel to line a colander.
- Grate the zucchini coarsely using a food processor to make around 3 cups. Move to the prepared colander. Wrap the towel around the zucchini and squeeze out as much of its liquid as you can. Move to a medium-size bowl and stir in garlic, sage, Parmesan, flour, egg yolk, and egg. Use your hands to roll the mixture into 3/4-inch balls.
- Use a big heavy skillet over moderately high heat to heat up 1/4 inch of oil until it is hot but not smoking. Working in batches of 5, drop them into the oil, using a slotted spatula to flatten each into a 1 inch round.
- Fry the poppers, turning them over once, until they become golden brown, 2-2 1/2 minutes for each side, then move to paper towels for them to drain. Serve this warm or at room temperature along with the sour cream dip. It is best to serve them after frying, but you can make them ahead and keep them at room temperature for up to 2 hours. If you want, you can rewarm them in the oven at 350

degrees Fahrenheit, turning over once, for around 10 minutes.

Nutrition Information

- Calories: 1057
- Total Carbohydrate: 31 g
- Cholesterol: 162 mg
- Total Fat: 100 g
- Fiber: 5 g
- Protein: 14 g
- Sodium: 519 mg
- Saturated Fat: 22 g

Index

A

Allspice, 17–18, 51, 110–111, 146–147, 204

Almond, 3–4, 6–7, 11–15, 17–20, 39, 44, 47–48, 50, 52–53, 55–56, 64–67, 73, 85, 87, 107, 115, 127, 130–131, 143, 155–156, 158–159, 167–168, 177, 181–182, 205–206, 209–211

Almond extract, 11–14, 17, 20, 64, 73, 130–131, 143, 205–206

Amaretti, 15

Anchovies, 54, 98, 168

Anise, 187, 206

Apple, 3–4, 6–7, 16–19, 23–24, 52–53, 85, 107, 133, 154–156, 173, 183, 189, 192

Apricot, 3–5, 13–14, 19–21, 63–64, 96, 119, 131

Arborio rice, 30

Artichoke, 3–4, 6–7, 21–23, 58, 61–62, 163, 175

Asparagus, 3–5, 23, 35, 60, 93, 118

Avocado, 3–4, 11, 23–26, 57, 69, 73, 119–120, 136, 160, 196

B

Bacon, 4, 6, 51–52, 58, 135–136, 179, 181, 209

Bagel, 82, 133

Baguette, 52, 63, 76, 79, 116, 166, 193, 206–207

Baking, 11–15, 17–20, 22, 24, 26, 32, 37–38, 42–43, 45–46, 50, 56–58, 60, 62–65, 68–69, 72, 74, 76, 78–80, 86, 94–96, 103–105, 108–109, 113–116, 118, 122, 124–125, 127–128, 131–132, 134–135, 137, 140–141, 143–145, 147, 149, 152–153, 155–159, 161, 165–167, 174–175, 177–181, 183, 185, 191, 193, 195, 202, 204–206, 208, 210–213

Baking powder, 14, 17–18, 20, 26, 42, 57, 104, 114–115, 122, 124–125, 135, 141, 147, 149, 159, 180, 205–206, 212–213

Balsamic vinegar, 27, 29, 61, 78–79, 90, 97, 99, 108

Banana, 3–4, 23, 27–29, 39, 82, 114, 141

Basil, 3–7, 21, 24–25, 27, 29–30, 33, 61, 63, 78–79, 87, 101, 106, 117, 129, 146, 150, 153–154, 167, 175–176, 187–188, 190–191, 194–195, 198, 201, 208–209, 212

Basmati rice, 162, 186

Bay leaf, 77, 170

Beans, 4, 29, 33–36, 40–41, 55, 66, 68, 83, 87, 90, 95–96, 103, 108, 116, 122–124, 126, 136, 153–154, 160–161, 179, 184, 187, 191–192, 198–199, 201–203, 208–209

Beef, 3, 31–32, 63, 181, 187

Berry, 12, 27, 36–37, 43, 48, 92–93, 95, 110–111, 115, 132, 159, 163, 188–189, 202, 210

Biscuits, 40

Black beans, 33–35, 87, 108, 123, 179

Black pepper, 21, 23–25, 27, 29–30, 33–34, 36, 51, 54–55, 58, 60, 69, 77–79, 83, 89–90, 92–93, 98, 105–106, 108–111, 114, 116, 122, 134–135, 142, 146, 148–149, 164–166, 168, 170–171, 175, 181, 186–187, 190, 193, 197–198, 200, 202, 204, 208, 212–213

215

Black sesame seeds, 186

Blackberry, 4–5, 73, 92, 104, 132

Blood orange, 4, 70, 118

Blueberry, 3, 36–38

Borlotti beans, 201

Bouquet garni, 23

Bran, 24

Brandy, 72, 125, 130, 140, 202–203

Brazil nut, 80–81

Bread, 3–4, 20, 28, 32, 35, 41–42, 44–46, 53–54, 58, 63, 74, 76, 79–80, 82, 90–91, 100,

108–110, 118, 146, 151, 154–155, 173, 175, 185, 202, 207, 210–211

Breadcrumbs, 46, 109, 144–146, 173, 181, 210

Breadsticks, 5, 103–104

Brie, 6, 165–166

Broccoli, 3, 7, 40, 92, 111, 126, 203–204

Broth, 33–34, 44, 52–53, 55, 57–58, 60–63, 77, 93, 150, 161–162, 172, 185, 196–197, 202,

209, 211

Brown sugar, 16–19, 24, 36–39, 47, 62–64, 68, 85, 94–96, 102, 112, 120–121, 127, 131,

139, 141–142, 147–148, 159, 180, 183, 193–194, 196

Brussels sprouts, 167

Buns, 35

Burger, 3–4, 6, 35, 88–89, 146, 153, 168

Butter, 3, 5–7, 11–14, 16–22, 24–28, 30–31, 35–39, 41–50, 53–54, 56–57, 63–68, 71–77, 80,

82–86, 89–90, 94, 96–97, 99, 101, 103–104, 106–107, 110–121, 124–128, 130–142, 144–150,

152–159, 161–162, 165, 169, 171, 175, 177–178, 180, 183, 186, 191–192, 199, 201,

205–206, 209–210, 212

Buttermilk, 3, 7, 17, 20, 36, 42–43, 75, 93–94, 135, 188

Butternut squash, 3, 24, 43–44, 142

C

Cabbage, 133, 201–202

Cake, 3, 5–7, 14–17, 19–20, 46–48, 94–95, 114–115, 121, 141, 145, 147, 159–160, 177,

179–180, 195, 201–203, 205–208, 210

Calvados, 17

Capers, 33, 54, 76, 79, 98, 102, 110, 129, 165, 200

Caramel, 3–4, 6, 13, 17, 28, 45–49, 65–66, 138–139, 142, 157, 201

Caraway seeds, 50

Cardamom, 4, 7, 62, 80, 127, 131–132, 145, 191

Carob, 5, 127

Carrot, 4–7, 24, 33–34, 55, 61, 77, 81, 89, 92, 95, 126, 133, 149–150, 154, 164, 166–167,

172, 182, 187, 206–207, 209

Cashew, 3–4, 49–50, 56, 68, 74–75, 88, 127, 205

Cauliflower, 4, 7, 50–52, 55, 126, 181–182

Caviar, 4, 52

Cayenne pepper, 21, 34, 56, 58, 85, 154, 184–186, 197

Celeriac, 53

Celery, 4, 44–45, 51–53, 70, 72, 89, 102, 110–111, 133, 154, 164, 166, 170, 187

Celery seeds, 70, 133, 164

Champagne, 138

Chantilly cream, 4, 53

Cheddar, 4, 7, 32–33, 55–56, 82, 97, 123, 144, 197

Cheese, 3–7, 18, 22, 30–33, 36, 38, 41, 52–56, 58, 64–65, 67, 73, 75, 78–82, 86–90, 96–97,

  106–107, 109, 113–114, 117, 120, 123–124, 129, 135–137, 139, 143–145, 151–154, 163,

  166–169, 173, 176, 181–182, 184, 186, 189–190, 193, 195, 197, 201–202, 205–208, 210,

  212–213

Cherry, 4, 6, 57, 92, 96, 124, 130, 150, 154–156, 189, 196

Cherry tomatoes, 92, 150, 196

Chicken, 4–7, 30, 33–34, 44, 52–53, 55, 57–62, 82–83, 95, 98–100, 109, 117, 119, 133, 150,

  161–162, 168, 172, 176, 183–185, 197, 202, 206–209, 211

Chicken breast, 5, 58–59, 61, 99–100, 207

Chicken liver, 82–83, 133

Chicken soup, 4, 60

Chicken stock, 30, 95, 176

Chickpea, 3–5, 21, 23, 26, 29, 33, 62, 88, 108, 111, 122

Chickpea flour, 88

Chipotle, 7, 91, 179, 183, 197

Chips, 23, 25–26, 28, 33, 57, 59, 63–66, 108, 119, 127, 141, 143, 153–156, 159, 169, 180,

  184–185, 197

Chives, 16, 36, 52, 70, 170, 178, 208

Chocolate, 3–7, 11, 15, 26, 28–29, 39, 47–49, 56, 63–67, 72, 82–83, 92–93, 95–96, 119,

  130, 136, 142–143, 145, 159, 161–162, 169, 179–180, 195, 200–202, 206, 209–210

Chocolate cake, 5, 95

Chocolate truffle, 4, 11, 72

Chorizo, 123

Chutney, 3–4, 44, 59, 102, 111

Ciabatta, 41

Cider, 7, 19, 23, 85, 107, 127, 133, 156, 166, 189, 192

Cinnamon, 3–4, 14, 16–19, 24, 28, 31, 36–37, 43, 48, 51, 57, 68–69, 80, 83, 85–86, 94,

  104, 110–112, 117, 121, 125, 127, 138, 140–141, 145–147, 156–157, 159, 180, 183, 204,

  206–207, 212–213

Clams, 210–211

Clarified butter, 113, 171

Cloves, 19, 21, 24, 26, 31–32, 34, 43, 51, 54–55, 61, 67, 71, 77–78, 80, 88–95, 98, 102, 105,

  108, 110, 114, 116–117, 122–123, 126–127, 129, 136, 140, 143–144, 146, 148, 153–154,

  161–162, 164–166, 168, 170, 176, 181–183, 185–187, 190–191, 195, 198, 201–202, 206,

  208–210

Cocktail, 58, 82, 113, 133, 137

Cocoa powder, 27–28, 64–65, 82–83, 95–96, 112, 136

Coconut, 4, 6, 27–28, 31, 44, 56, 65, 68, 74–75, 80, 127, 136, 143, 194, 199, 204–205

Coconut milk, 27–28, 31, 65, 194, 199

Coconut oil, 56, 65, 68, 74–75, 136, 204–205

Coffee, 4, 46, 56, 64, 68, 83–84, 112, 189

Coffee beans, 83

Cognac, 83, 118, 174

Coleslaw, 6, 133

Condensed milk, 28–29, 40, 180

Coriander, 3, 8, 32, 44, 55, 108, 123–124, 172, 192, 211

Coriander seeds, 172

Corn syrup, 28, 38–39, 68–69, 139, 142, 169

Cottage cheese, 207

Crab, 4, 70

Crackers, 29, 38, 66, 79–82, 86, 102, 110–111, 133, 153, 192

Cranberry, 4–5, 7, 47–48, 70–73, 86, 124–125, 173

Cranberry sauce, 72

Cream, 3–5, 7–8, 11–15, 17–19, 21–22, 27–29, 35, 38–39, 45, 47–49, 52–54, 57–58, 62–69,

71–74, 77–78, 85–87, 92–97, 106–107, 112, 114–116, 120–121, 124–125, 130–131, 134–136,

138–142, 145, 149, 152, 155–157, 159, 163, 170, 173, 176, 178–180, 183, 185, 188–189,

191, 193–194, 197, 199, 201, 203–207, 210, 212–213

Cream cheese, 4, 7, 18, 38, 64–65, 73, 86, 96–97, 139, 145, 173, 189, 201, 205–207,

210, 212

Cream of tartar, 47, 204

Crème fraîche, 17, 62, 124, 170, 178, 188

Crostini, 4–6, 76, 110, 116, 165

Crumble, 3–4, 6, 36, 64, 85–86, 89, 99, 116, 139, 158, 184

Cucumber, 5–6, 8, 72, 89–90, 92, 100, 108–109, 133, 159–160, 176, 196, 211–212

Cumin, 23, 25–26, 33–35, 40–41, 51, 55, 57, 62, 88, 95, 108, 122–123, 126, 145, 160–162,

166, 171–172, 179, 182–183, 186, 192, 194

Curd, 6, 138

Currants, 47, 145, 189

Curry, 7, 21, 194

Curry paste, 194

Curry powder, 21

Custard, 5–6, 12, 39, 43, 115, 157–158, 199

D

Daikon, 206–207

Dal, 6, 162

Dandelion, 4, 78

Date, 56, 65, 68, 83, 85, 207

Dijon mustard, 35, 44–45, 69, 81, 90, 102, 129, 148

Dill, 7, 55, 81–82, 178–179, 197, 204, 208

Dried apricots, 20, 63

Dried fruit, 4, 85, 125

Dulce de leche, 4, 86–87

E

Egg, 4, 6, 11–15, 17–18, 20–22, 24, 28, 32, 35, 38–39, 42–43, 45–47, 51, 54, 57, 60, 64–65,

67–68, 71, 77, 81–82, 86, 92, 94, 96–97, 104, 109, 114–115, 118, 122, 124–125, 127–128,

130–131, 133–136, 138–141, 143, 145, 147, 149, 151–152, 155, 157–161, 177–181, 194–195,

   199, 201–203, 205, 207, 210, 212–213

Egg wash, 21–22

Egg white, 12–13, 21, 43, 45–46, 64–65, 67–68, 81, 143, 149, 203, 205, 207

Egg yolk, 11, 21, 35, 39, 46–47, 57, 71, 77, 92, 96, 104, 115, 118, 124–125, 130, 135–136,

   138–140, 149, 155, 199, 205, 213

Evaporated milk, 95, 121

F

Falafel, 5, 108–109

Fat, 4, 7, 11–21, 23–46, 48–54, 56–59, 61, 63–88, 90–102, 104–129, 131–154, 156–160, 162,

   164–190, 192–201, 203–214

Fennel, 4, 60, 172, 187

Fennel seeds, 60, 172

Feta, 6–7, 41, 97, 136–137, 184

Fig, 6–7, 83, 85, 141, 174

Fish, 5, 60, 92, 101, 105, 119, 168, 172, 174, 178–179, 206–207

Fish sauce, 206

Five-spice powder, 205

Flank, 5, 91

Fleur de sel, 62, 86–87

Flour, 14–15, 17–18, 20–22, 24, 26, 36–43, 46–48, 51, 56–57, 63–66, 68, 71, 74, 77, 80, 82,

   84–85, 88–91, 94–97, 99, 103–104, 106–107, 111–112, 114–117, 119, 122–125, 127–128,

130–132, 135, 137–141, 143, 145, 147, 149, 152–159, 174, 177–178, 180, 183, 187, 191,

   199, 204–206, 212–213

Flour tortilla, 177

Frangipane, 6, 130–131

French bread, 46, 151

Fresh coriander, 32, 123

Fruit, 4, 6, 16, 20, 44, 73, 83–85, 107, 119–120, 125, 132, 146, 154–156, 163, 173, 194

Fruit juice, 20

Fudge, 3, 6, 28, 39–40, 50, 142, 201

G

Garlic, 3–7, 21, 23–26, 29–34, 36, 40–41, 49, 51–52, 54–55, 58–63, 67, 75, 77–81, 83,

   87–95, 97–102, 105–106, 108, 110, 114, 116–117, 122–124, 126, 129, 136, 141, 143–146,

   148, 153–154, 160–172, 175–176, 181–183, 185–187, 190–191, 193–196, 198, 200–202,

   208–211, 213

Ghee, 171, 186

Giblets, 109

Ginger, 5, 7–8, 16, 31, 43, 70, 80, 94–95, 110, 119, 125, 127–128, 131–132, 139, 162, 171,

   176, 186, 192, 194, 204, 206, 212–213

Gingerbread, 7, 204

Grain, 44, 53–54, 91, 109, 113

Grapes, 165–166, 173, 211

Grapeseed oil, 52

Gravy, 6, 161–162

Green beans, 4, 55, 126, 187

Green cabbage, 133

Ground ginger, 43, 70, 94, 127, 131, 162, 204, 212–213

Gruyère, 134–135

Guacamole, 3, 5, 23, 26, 119

H

Halibut, 5, 101

Ham, 3, 5, 44–45, 102, 193

Harissa, 4, 55, 108–109

Hazelnut, 5, 7, 57, 103–106, 134, 152, 195, 203–206

Hazelnut oil, 105

Heart, 21–23, 58, 161, 163, 210

Herbs, 92, 133, 195

Hollandaise sauce, 3, 35

Hominy, 4, 57–58

Honey, 4–7, 48–49, 62, 65–66, 69, 74–75, 80, 82, 86, 90, 106–107, 119, 128, 136, 156,

161–162, 180, 212–213

Horseradish, 129, 164, 178–179

Hummus, 3–7, 21, 23, 26, 29, 34, 41, 59, 80, 87, 90, 153, 184, 191–192, 198

I

Ice cream, 3, 7, 11–12, 27–29, 39, 66, 68–69, 86, 114, 130–131, 155–156, 183, 189, 191,

194

Icing, 20, 71, 141

J

Jam, 5–7, 71, 73, 104–105, 128, 158–159, 188, 203, 210

Japanese pumpkin, 5, 111

Jelly, 4–5, 17–18, 47, 56, 107, 132, 198

K

Kale, 4–5, 88, 114

Ketchup, 110, 133

Kidney, 160, 209

Kidney beans, 160, 209

L

Lamb, 6, 145, 209

Leek, 6, 52–53, 61, 148, 152, 170, 197

Lemon, 4–5, 7, 11, 13–14, 16, 18, 20–22, 24–25, 28–29, 35–41, 45–46, 52–55, 59, 62–63,

69, 71, 74, 77–81, 84–85, 87, 90, 92–98, 100–101, 104, 106–108, 110–111, 113–116, 118,

124, 128–130, 138–139, 154–155, 160, 163–164, 167–170, 172–175, 177–178, 184–185, 189,

191–192, 194–196, 198–200, 205, 207–212

Lemon curd, 138

Lemon juice, 11, 13–14, 16, 18, 20–22, 24–25, 28–29, 35–37, 39–41, 45, 52–53, 55, 59,

62–63, 69, 74, 78–81, 84–85, 87, 90, 92–95, 98, 100–101, 106, 108, 110–111, 113–116, 118,

128–129, 138–139, 155, 163–164, 167–169, 172, 175, 177–178, 184–185, 189, 191–192, 196,

198–200, 209–212

220

Lemongrass, 31, 194

Lentils, 162

Lettuce, 35, 44–45, 69, 110, 129, 207

Lime, 4–6, 16, 23, 25–26, 31–32, 34–35, 67, 74–75, 79–81, 89, 98, 105, 108, 110–111, 113,

   119–120, 123–124, 132–133, 141, 157, 159–160, 166, 176, 185, 193–194, 197, 208, 213

Lime juice, 16, 23, 25, 31–32, 34–35, 67, 74–75, 79–81, 89, 98, 108, 110–111, 113,

   119–120, 123–124, 132–133, 141, 157, 160, 166, 176, 185, 193–194, 197, 208, 213

Lime leaves, 31

Lingonberry, 163

Linguine, 5, 117, 182

Liqueur, 11, 15, 47, 72, 112, 130

M

Macadamia, 3, 5, 45, 80, 118

Macaroon, 3–4, 6, 12–13, 67, 143

Mango, 5–6, 102, 108–109, 119–120, 141, 148

Mango chutney, 102

Maple syrup, 27–28, 43, 139, 196

Margarine, 117

Marjoram, 181

Marmalade, 127–128, 140

Marzipan, 130

Mascarpone, 5, 64, 106–107, 120–121

Mashed potato, 54

Matzo, 4, 60–61, 149, 195, 202–203

Mayonnaise, 3, 6, 11, 29–30, 35–36, 44–45, 58, 75, 81, 97, 102, 129, 133, 168, 207

Meat, 25, 34, 49, 57, 79, 87, 148, 162, 181

Melon, 45, 53, 72, 163, 177, 211

Meringue, 3, 12–13

Milk, 4–5, 11–12, 20, 24, 26–29, 31–32, 38, 40, 43, 50, 54, 58, 64–65, 72, 74–75, 82, 84,

   89–90, 95–96, 103–104, 106, 111, 113, 119, 121, 140, 144, 148, 151–152, 154, 163, 171,

   176, 178–180, 189, 194, 199, 203, 205–206, 211–212

Milk chocolate, 72

Milkshake, 4, 82

Millet, 4, 77

Mince, 6, 55, 101, 140, 175

Mincemeat, 5, 125

Mint, 4, 6, 20, 32, 43–44, 53–54, 59, 61, 69, 80, 92–93, 115–116, 126, 159, 172, 188, 208

Molasses, 4–5, 68–69, 94, 122, 127–128, 204

Mozzarella, 58, 89–91, 113, 144

Muffins, 118

Mushroom, 5–6, 60–61, 88, 129, 146, 152, 171, 194

Mussels, 5, 129

Mustard, 6, 11, 35, 44–45, 55, 69–70, 81, 90, 102, 129, 135, 148, 171, 182

Mustard powder, 11, 55

Mustard seeds, 70, 182

N

Nectarine, 4, 6, 84, 130–133, 146–147

Nut, 3–7, 20, 30, 39, 45–46, 48–50, 57, 59, 66–67, 78–82, 87–88, 97–98, 100, 104–105,

114–115, 117–118, 120, 127, 134, 136, 142–143, 145, 152, 155–156, 158, 168–169, 176,

183, 186, 190, 195–196, 206–208

Nutmeg, 17–18, 21–22, 24, 43, 48, 51, 57, 74–75, 80, 104, 110–112, 121, 126, 135–136,

141, 147, 154, 163, 183, 186, 204–205

O

Oats, 24, 127

Octopus, 16

Oil, 4, 11, 13–15, 20–21, 23, 25–26, 29–35, 40–41, 44–46, 49, 51–57, 59–65, 67–69, 74–82,

86–91, 93–96, 98–101, 103–106, 108–110, 114, 116–117, 122–124, 126–127, 129, 133–136,

141, 143, 146, 148–154, 160–163, 165–170, 172–176, 178, 181–183, 185–187, 190–192,

194–198, 200–213

Olive, 3–7, 11, 20–21, 23, 25–26, 29–34, 40–41, 51–55, 57, 59–63, 67, 69, 76–81, 87–91, 93,

95–96, 98–101, 103, 105–106, 108, 110, 114, 116–117, 122–124, 126–127, 129, 134, 136,

143, 146, 148, 150–152, 154, 160–161, 163, 165–170, 172–173, 176, 178, 181–183,

185–187, 190–192, 195–198, 200–204, 208–212

Olive oil, 11, 20–21, 23, 25–26, 29–31, 33–34, 40–41, 51–55, 57, 59–63, 67, 69, 76–81,

87–91, 93, 95, 98–101, 103, 105–106, 108, 110, 114, 116–117, 122–123, 126–127, 129, 134,

136, 143, 146, 148, 150–152, 154, 160–161, 163, 165–170, 172–173, 176, 178, 181–183,

185–187, 190–192, 195–198, 200–204, 208–212

Onion, 5–6, 16, 21–23, 25–26, 32–34, 44–45, 49, 51–52, 55, 57, 59, 62, 69, 74, 77, 79, 83,

89–90, 92–93, 95, 97, 102, 108–110, 119–120, 122–124, 133–136, 141–142, 148–150,

152–154, 160, 162, 164, 166, 170–172, 179, 181, 183, 185–187, 193–194, 196–197, 207,

209–210

Orange, 3–4, 7, 19, 43–44, 47, 49, 53, 62, 67, 69–70, 72–73, 80, 85, 102, 104, 108, 118,

120, 125, 140, 161–162, 173, 176, 190, 202, 204, 212

Orange juice, 19, 44, 62, 69, 73, 80, 102, 108, 118, 125, 161–162, 190

Orange liqueur, 47, 72

Oregano, 33–35, 41, 61, 70, 76, 90–91, 97, 146, 160, 166, 175, 179, 190, 208

P

Palm sugar, 31

Pancakes, 149

Paneer, 7, 186

Paprika, 21, 25, 32, 34, 41, 57, 90, 126, 146, 183, 191–192

Parfait, 5, 92–93

Parmesan, 30–31, 41, 50–51, 53–54, 67, 78–81, 87–88, 97–98, 109, 114, 117, 129,

136–137, 144, 146, 153–154, 166–169, 176, 181, 186–187, 190, 202, 208, 213

Parsley, 6, 21–22, 33, 36, 51, 54, 59, 61, 79, 91–92, 98, 100–101, 105, 108–110, 136, 150,

163, 167, 173–174, 181–182, 184, 190, 195, 198,

200, 203–204, 208, 210–211, 213

Parsnip, 6, 126, 149–150, 166–167

Pasta, 5–6, 22, 89–90, 98, 117, 143–144, 146, 160, 168, 181–182, 203, 208

Pastry, 3, 6, 12–13, 19, 42–43, 46–47, 49, 64, 66, 77–78, 84–85, 96, 103, 115–116, 130, 132,

  137, 153, 157, 206

Pasty, 174, 198

Pâté, 206

Peach, 4–7, 62–63, 73, 99, 106–107, 130, 137–138, 146–147, 191

Peanut butter, 3, 5–6, 26–28, 106, 138–139, 154

Peanut oil, 106, 123

Peanuts, 40, 82, 106, 127, 139

Pear, 3, 5–7, 16, 121, 131, 139–141, 145, 177, 203

Peas, 103, 126, 143, 193–194

Pecan, 6–7, 48, 63–64, 94, 97, 120, 141–142, 166–167, 173, 179–180, 187, 201, 204

Pecorino, 4, 51–52, 106, 182, 195

Pectin, 107, 128

Peel, 13, 19, 37, 39, 46–47, 50, 53, 55, 67, 70–71, 73, 81, 96–97, 101, 104, 106–107,

  114–115, 124–125, 132, 135, 151, 167, 170, 173, 177–178, 185, 190–192, 196, 208–211

Penne, 6, 89, 142–143

Pepper, 4–7, 16, 21–27, 29–36, 49, 51–63, 67, 69–70, 72–79, 81, 83, 85, 88–93, 95, 98–102,

  105–111, 114, 116–120, 122–124, 126, 129, 133–136, 141–146, 148–151, 154, 160–175,

  178–179, 181–182, 184–187, 190, 192–198, 200, 202, 204, 208–210, 212–213

Peppercorn, 70, 154, 170

Pesto, 3–7, 29–31, 53, 59–60, 67, 78, 80, 87–88, 98, 100, 105–106, 114, 117, 123, 129,

  136–137, 143, 167–168, 172–173, 176, 186–187, 190, 195, 208

Pickle, 44–45, 102, 108

Pie, 3–7, 15, 36–39, 41, 43, 66, 68–69, 73–74, 84, 96, 99, 111–113, 115–116, 119, 125,

  130–131, 134–137, 140, 142, 152–153, 157–158, 183, 191, 196, 199

Pine nut, 7, 30, 67, 78–79, 87–88, 97–98, 100, 114, 117, 136, 143, 168–169, 176, 186, 190,

  195, 208

Pineapple, 6, 96, 111, 148

Pistachio, 3–4, 6, 20, 50, 59, 83, 144–145, 172

Pizza, 5–6, 91, 123–124, 136–137

Plantain, 4, 6, 75, 146

Plum, 3, 6, 14–15, 21, 34, 41, 77–78, 108, 132–133, 141, 146–147, 160–162, 193, 197–198,

  208

Pomegranate, 122–123, 145, 163

Pomegranate juice, 145, 163

Pomegranate molasses, 122

Poppy seeds, 80

Pork, 5–6, 98, 110–111, 119, 123, 148, 169, 206

Pork chop, 5–6, 110–111, 148

Port, 165–166

Potato, 4, 6–7, 50, 54, 76, 95, 148–150, 152, 154, 176, 185, 192, 202

Praline, 3, 13–14

Preserves, 57, 64, 71, 96–97, 107, 130–131, 206

Prosciutto, 7, 201–202

Prune, 77–78

Puff pastry, 6, 19, 103, 153

Pulse, 14, 17–20, 22, 24–25, 27–30, 32–33, 35–36, 40–42, 45, 48, 53, 55, 67, 70, 72, 74–75,

   77, 79, 81, 84–85, 87–89, 91–93, 96–97, 99, 101, 108, 110–111, 114, 117–119, 121, 123,

   125, 130–131, 135, 141, 147, 152–155, 157–158, 165–166, 169–171, 173, 175–177, 179,

   182, 184, 188, 192, 194–195, 197, 199, 204–205, 208, 213

Pumpkin, 3, 5–6, 15, 111, 123, 151–152, 196

Pumpkin seed, 123, 196

Q

Quince, 5–6, 120, 154–157

R

Rack of lamb, 6, 145

Radish, 4–5, 59, 89, 92, 100

Raisins, 24, 85, 139–140

Raspberry, 3–7, 11–12, 71, 84, 114, 120, 157–159, 163, 173, 188–189, 206, 209–210

Raspberry jam, 6, 158–159, 210

Red lentil, 6, 162

Red onion, 26, 44, 59, 62, 108, 110, 193–194

Red wine, 29, 69, 85, 91

Red wine vinegar, 29, 69, 91

Rhubarb, 7, 193–194

Rice, 5, 30–31, 33, 49, 53, 59, 95–96, 103, 109, 113, 119, 130, 157–158, 162, 174, 186, 189,

   194, 206

Rice flour, 95–96, 174

Rice vinegar, 119, 189, 206

Rice wine, 119

Ricotta, 5–6, 64–65, 106, 113, 163, 167, 184

Risotto, 3–4, 30–31, 53

Roast beef, 187

Roast chicken, 57

Roast lamb, 209

Roast turkey, 200

Roasted vegetables, 6, 166

Root vegetable, 5

Rosemary, 62, 76, 116, 122, 160, 165–166, 187, 200, 202, 209

Rum, 6, 46, 111, 132–133, 169, 174, 199

Rye bread, 44–45

S

Saffron, 21, 30

Sage, 6, 103–104, 142, 213

Salad, 3–7, 44–45, 58, 69, 81, 90–91, 100, 102, 110, 129, 150, 168, 173, 186, 202

Salmon, 6–7, 170, 177–178

Salsa, 4, 6–7, 32, 35, 54, 72–73, 79, 92, 141, 160–161, 166, 170, 193–194, 197, 209

Salt, 11–14, 16–18, 20–26, 29–32, 34, 36–44, 46–66, 68–70, 72–85, 88–112, 114–119,

121–127, 129–137, 140–175, 177–179, 181–187, 189–202, 204–209, 211–213

Sausage, 6, 123–124, 160–161

Savory, 42, 56, 103, 165, 192

Scallop, 3–4, 16, 30–31, 52

Sea bass, 7, 173–174

Sea salt, 14, 31, 49, 62, 70, 80, 91, 106, 119, 160, 168, 192, 198, 205, 208

Seafood, 164

Seasoning, 25, 44–45, 55, 60, 122, 148, 164, 170

Seeds, 21, 31, 37, 44–45, 50, 60, 63, 67, 70, 78–82, 99, 122–124, 133, 147, 152, 155, 160,

  164, 171–172, 174–175, 182, 186, 196, 198–199, 203–204

Semolina, 117

Sesame oil, 11, 34–35

Sesame seeds, 174–175, 182, 186

Shallot, 5, 30–31, 61, 74, 100–101, 129, 165, 194, 203–204

Sherry, 126–127, 150, 168

Sherry vinegar, 126–127, 168

Shiitake mushroom, 60, 146

Shortbread, 3, 38, 45, 73, 144–145, 188

Sirloin, 4, 31, 54

Smoked salmon, 7, 177–178

Smoked trout, 7, 178

Soda, 17–18, 20, 42, 68–69, 94–96, 108, 127, 135, 141, 174, 180, 188, 204, 212–213

Sorbet, 3, 5, 7, 28, 114, 190, 194, 202–203

Soup, 3–8, 34, 44, 50–53, 55, 57–58, 60, 62–63, 93, 95, 146, 149–150, 154, 159, 175–176,

  194, 196–197, 201–202, 211–212

Sourdough bread, 100

Soy sauce, 29–32, 88, 110, 207

Spaghetti, 7, 160, 167, 181–182

Spaghetti squash, 160

Spices, 4, 70, 87, 182, 206

Spinach, 4, 7, 30, 58, 74, 146, 171, 176, 185–186, 190

Squash, 3, 5, 24, 43–44, 111–112, 142–143, 151–152, 160

Steak, 5, 54, 91, 101

Stew, 60, 194

Stock, 30–31, 49, 95, 161–162, 176

Strawberry, 3, 5, 7, 27, 39, 83, 92, 94–95, 130, 188–190, 210

Stuffing, 163

Sugar, 6, 11–14, 16–20, 24, 26–27, 31–32, 36–43, 45–48, 50, 53–54, 57, 62–74, 77–86,

  89–97, 99, 102, 104–107, 110–117, 119–121, 123–125, 127–128, 130–136, 138–143,

  145–148, 150–152, 154–160, 163, 169, 171, 173–174, 177, 180, 183, 186, 188–191,

  193–196, 199, 201–207, 210–213

Summer fruit, 6

Sweet potato, 6–7, 152, 154, 176, 185, 192

Swordfish, 5, 101

Syrup, 6–7, 14, 27–28, 38–39, 43, 45, 53, 68–69, 113, 120, 130, 132–133, 139, 142, 147,

154–156, 169, 177, 188, 190, 196, 207–208

T

Tabasco, 35, 83, 129, 164, 175

Taco, 5, 92, 122, 160–161

Tahini, 3, 23, 26, 34, 62, 90–91, 108–109, 111, 191–192, 198

Tapenade, 3–5, 7, 33, 61, 76, 79, 98–99, 173–174, 200

Tapioca, 84

Taro, 174

Tarragon, 4–5, 59, 99–100, 178

Tea, 40, 189–190

Terrine, 3, 6, 11–12, 151

Thyme, 33, 60, 83, 110, 133–135, 150–152, 165–166, 172, 201

Toffee, 15

Tofu, 4, 7, 40, 66, 111–112, 176, 186, 196

Tomatillo, 7, 49, 79, 123–124, 196

Tomato, 3–7, 16, 21–23, 26, 33–34, 41, 49, 57–58, 63, 76–77, 90, 92, 99–100, 108–110,

117, 122, 141, 150, 153–154, 160–162, 164, 166, 170–171, 181, 191, 193–194, 196–198,

208–209

Tomato purée, 162

Trout, 7, 178–179

Truffle, 3–4, 11–12, 51–52, 72

Truffle oil, 4, 51–52

Turkey, 6–7, 33–34, 161–162, 200

Turkey breast, 200

Turmeric, 16, 31, 162, 194

Turnip, 108–109, 126, 167

V

Vanilla extract, 12–14, 16–17, 20, 24, 38, 43, 47–48, 56–57, 63, 65–66, 68, 71, 73, 86,

92–94, 107, 111–113, 115, 121, 136, 138–143, 145, 152, 177, 199, 201, 205–206, 210

Vanilla pod, 155

Vegan, 3–4, 7, 26, 49, 65, 95, 160, 176, 203–205

Vegetable oil, 14–15, 32, 35, 44, 49, 51–52, 61, 64, 76, 81, 86, 108–110, 117, 127, 133,

141, 149, 160, 162, 183, 186, 194, 202, 206, 211, 213

Vegetable shortening, 43, 68, 84, 115, 135, 157

Vegetable stock, 176

Vegetables, 5–7, 23, 33–34, 52, 55, 59–60, 89, 108, 126, 164, 166–167, 185, 187, 206–207

Vegetarian, 35, 49, 89, 152, 171

Vermouth, 133

Vinegar, 7, 23, 27, 29–30, 61, 69, 78–79, 81, 90–91, 95–97, 99–100, 107–108, 119, 121,

126–129, 133, 150, 156–157, 164, 166, 168, 188–189, 206–207, 211

Vodka, 113

W

Walnut, 3–4, 6–7, 17–18, 38–39, 46, 48, 50, 59–60, 65–66, 74, 117, 120, 139, 147, 163,

183, 196, 207–208

Walnut oil, 208

Watermelon, 4, 69

Whipping cream, 11, 27, 39, 48, 52–53, 65, 67, 73, 86, 92–93, 107, 112, 114, 120, 130,

   135, 138–139, 142, 152, 191, 199, 201

White bread, 58, 74, 173, 211

White chocolate, 3, 7, 39, 47–49, 92, 145, 206, 209–210

White pepper, 31, 52, 75, 118, 163, 192

White sugar, 26, 37–38, 40, 72, 79, 90, 99, 107, 110–111, 113, 128, 133, 138, 143, 150,

   171, 173, 199, 204

White wine, 20, 30, 62, 77, 81, 121, 129, 163, 165, 170, 181, 189, 200, 210

White wine vinegar, 81, 129, 189

Wild rice, 33

Wine, 20, 29–31, 62, 69, 77–78, 81, 85, 91, 119, 121, 129, 132–133, 150, 163, 165, 168, 170,

   177, 181, 189, 200, 210–211

Worcestershire sauce, 23, 36, 111, 129, 164, 175

Y

Yam, 8, 202, 211–212

Yeast, 51, 82, 88, 91, 103–104, 123

Z

Zest, 13–14, 25, 29, 36–38, 44, 62, 74–75, 77–78, 80, 98, 102, 113, 118, 120, 124–125, 130,

   154–155, 157, 173, 176, 192, 195, 200, 205, 207, 212–213

Conclusion

Thank you again for downloading this book!

I hope you enjoyed reading about my book!

If you enjoyed this book, please take the time to share your thoughts and post a review on Amazon. It'd be greatly appreciated!

Write me an honest review about the book – I truly value your opinion and thoughts and I will incorporate them into my next book, which is already underway.

Thank you!

If you have any questions, **feel free to contact at:** mseveryday@mrandmscooking.com

Ms. Everyday

www.MrandMsCooking.com

Printed in Great Britain
by Amazon